W9-BOE-856

SEX IN HISTORY

Food in History
Flesh and Blood: A History of the Cannibal Complex

SEX IN HISTORY

REAY TANNAHILL

i suppose the human race
is doing the best it can
but hells bells thats
only an explanation
its not an excuse.

DON MARQUIS
Archy says

STEIN AND DAY/*Publishers*/New York

First published in 1980
Copyright © 1980 by Reay Tannahill
All rights reserved
Designed by David Miller
Printed in the United States of America
Stein and Day/*Publishers*/Scarborough House
Briarcliff Manor, N.Y. 10510

Library of Congress Cataloging in Publication Data

Tannahill, Reay.
   Sex in history.
   Bibliography: p. 427
   Includes index.
   1. Sex customs—History. I. Title.
HQ12.T27   301.41'79   79-15053
ISBN 0-8128-2580-2

For

PATRICIA DAY *and* SOL STEIN
*in the hope that they will accept the dedication in
the spirit in which it is offered*

Contents

[10] *Contents*

Preface

The purpose of this book is to place the human sex drive and its social and moral consequences in their widest historical perspective, taking in the whole panorama of sexual attitudes, customs, and practices in all the world's major civilizations from earliest times until the present day. In effect, it is at once a history of sex, a history of relationships between the sexes, and a history of how sex and sexuality have influenced the whole course of human development.

This being so, it seems unnecessary to issue the customary disclaimers. The sympathetic reader will recognize, without having to be told, that a few hundred pages do not allow much deviation from the main highway, and will, I hope, consider the inclusion of Taoist sex manuals, Turkish eunuchs, ancient Greek dildoes, and Panamanian sodomites as adequate recompense for the omission of a certain amount of local and legal detail.

I should, perhaps, make two minor points. Despite the energetic attempts of modern language reformers to eliminate male-oriented words in contexts where the female is also implied, it seems to me that it places an unnecessary burden on readers to have to interpret artificial or clumsy adaptations. And is "the siblinghood of humans" any real improvement on "the brotherhood of man"? I have tried, on the whole to use "humanity" in preference to "mankind," but such substitutions have not always been possible. In the case of words directly related to sexuality, I have been confronted with the unsatisfactory choice of clinical jargon, vulgar colloquialism, or Victorian periphrasis. Since many people are offended by words that, until recently, were never uttered in public (and frequently not even in private), I have preferred to use clinical terminology as being less emotive.

The second point is that authors often fail to state their prejudices, but in a book where the history of sex is paralleled by a history of the changing role of women I ought, in fairness, to state mine. Essentially, I agree with the French psychoanalyst Jacques Lacan when he says that "woman with a capital W does not exist." In other words, woman is a person whose mental and physical shape differ somewhat from those of man; by the same token, man is a person whose mental and physical shape differ somewhat from those of woman. *Sex in History* is neither feminist nor antifeminist. On every aspect of the subjects with which it deals, it is as straightforward and objective as I have been able to make it.

As with my earlier book, *Food in History,* I find myself unable to list all the people who have answered my questions on anthropology, archeology, biochemistry, genetics, physiology, psychoanalysis and, of course, sexology, over the last six, almost seven, years. I hope I thanked them adequately at the time. However, I must express special gratitude to a few people who have given me continuing help and encouragement in the completion of a project that threatened, at times, to assume impossible dimensions. In strictly alphabetical order, then, sincere thanks to Janet Balshaw, Patricia Day, Michael Edwardes, John Parker, Christopher Sinclair-Stevenson, and Sol Stein. And, finally, to the consistently helpful and courteous staff of that unique and invaluable institution, the London Library.

PART ONE

The Prehistoric World

There is very little unequivocal evidence about relationships between the sexes before 3000 B.C., the beginning of recorded history. It seems probable that humanity was at first promiscuous, but that when cave living became common about a quarter of a million years ago closer "family" ties began to develop. Even so, there is nothing to suggest that man was even remotely aware of his own physical role in the production of children. That knowledge seems not to have come until the early days of farming, some time after 10,000 B.C., and it had a tonic effect on his ego. It also crystallized his sense of possessiveness, for the concept of "my son" required the child's mother to be tied to one man only. During the neolithic revolution, too, largely because of a series of coincidences, man's mind was directed along the path of technological advance and discovery, while woman's remained linked to immediate realities. Because of this, genetic adjustments took place that emphasized the intellectual divergence between them. Before the neolithic revolution, man and woman seem to have been more or less equal in status. During it, man experienced an enormous surge of self-assurance, became certain of his own superiority. After it, by the time humanity emerged into the light of recorded history, there was no question but that man was the master.

1.
In the
beginning

In the year 4004 B.C., at precisely nine o'clock on the morning of October 23, "God created man in his own image, in the image of God created he him; male and female created he them."

The year, the day, and the hour of the Creation, unspecified in the Bible itself, were calculated by two seventeenth-century scholars after a painstaking chronological study of the Old Testament,[1] and most of their contemporaries, accustomed to regarding the Bible as the literal truth, welcomed the information. To be able to put a date to the Creation gave it a comforting actuality.

Another 200 years were to pass before the new science of the Victorians began to chip away at the edges of the scriptural illusion. Then, in 1859, Charles Darwin's *The Origin of Species by Means of Natural Selection* was published. A synthesis of ideas long discussed within the scientific community but almost unknown to the general public, it was concerned with plants and animals, not man. But its logic was inescapable. There had been no single act of creation. Man, like others of the world's species, had developed from some lower form of life. *The Descent of Man*, in 1871, identified this lower form of life as a hairy quadrumanous animal belonging to the great anthropoid group. An ape, in fact.

The wife of the bishop of Worcester is said to have exclaimed: "Let us hope it is not true, but if it is, let us pray that it does not become generally known." History does not record whether it occurred to her to ask: "What kind of ape?"

The creation of Eve
from Adam's rib

Does it matter? Perhaps surprisingly, the answer is that in the history of relationships between the sexes the question of whether humanity's direct ancestor, *Ramapithecus*, more closely resembled the gibbon, the chimpanzee, or the gorilla, is by no means irrelevant.

Darwin himself could not have answered it. His work on evolution was hampered by the fact that, although the distinction between "nature and nurture"—heredity and environment—was already being made, the existence and roles of genes and hormones were not to be substantiated until the early 1900s, more than twenty years after his death. Nor was there as yet any fossil record of early man, or any reliable analytical study of animal behavior.

In the century since *The Descent of Man* was published, generations of biologists, zoologists, and anthropologists have filled gaps of which Darwin was scarcely even aware, but the story of human origins remains vague, and much of what is "known" is still highly speculative.

Broadly, the current view of the transition from ape to man is that, between twenty million and fourteen million years ago, the descendants of a true ape diverged along three different branches of the family tree. One group evolved into the ancestors of gorillas, chimpanzees, and orangutangs; another into a large ground ape, not unlike the baboon, that roamed Asia for an indeterminate period before becoming extinct; and the third into man's direct ancestor, *Ramapithecus*.[2]

Over the course of another few million years, *Ramapithecus* gave up life in the trees for life on the ground and began to eat meat as well as fruit and vegetables. This supplied him with extra protein which, if human history may be adduced as evidence, probably speeded up his evolution quite considerably; the last five thousand years have shown that peoples with a high protein intake are usually more dynamic than vegetarians.[3] And *Ramapithecus* needed to be dynamic, for he was now competing for his food, the only thing that really mattered to him, with the great sleek hunting cats that ruled the grasslands. Ultimately, he discovered that two feet and two hands—one of which could be used for hurling missiles at his enemies—were a good deal more useful than just four feet, and the result was a changeover to what is inelegantly known as bipedal locomotion.

In evolutionary terms, this proved a catalyst rather than a conclusion, but among its direct, if longterm, results were the Venus de Milo, the *Kamasutra*, Miss World, and *The Joy of Sex*. What a vertical posture did for humanity was force it to reconsider the traditional mating position of the primates and, later, to assess beauty from a different viewpoint.[4]

BEAUTY   AND   THE   MATING   POSTURE

In the usual primate position, the female presents her rear to the male and intercourse is brief, crude, and purposeful. The physiological reasons for this, however, do not apply when partners meet face to face. When that happens, muscles, nerve ends, sensitized tissues, and angle of penetration all contribute to a sensual experience that is impossible for the nonhuman primate. Or for the female, at least. The theory has been advanced that female orgasm, which other primates do not experience, emerged in response to the new position for intercourse.[5] Whatever the case, sex now became actively pleasurable as well as instinctively purposeful, and pursuit of the pleasure and fulfilment of the purpose have had their influence—sometimes obvious, sometimes subtle—on the whole subsequent course of human development.

There were a number of associated changes. By the time the frontal position was generally adopted, early humans had probably shed most of the body fur of their ancestors, but they found it necessary to grow some again so as to reduce friction during intercourse. Structurally, too, the new posture produced what the British geneticist C.D. Darlington describes as "the great anatomical variation of genitalia between human races and individuals today." The classic case is that of the Bushman of the Kalahari. The female Bushman has an unusually large *mons pubis,* so that the male needs an almost horizontal penis in order to bypass it—a perennial subject for humor among neighbouring tribes and no doubt a contributory factor in the Bushman's dislike of them.

On another level, it is said that frontal sex made the human female susceptible to something that is physiologically impossible for other primates—rape. In the living world, only one species of spider appears to share with humanity the ability to conclude a mating against the will of the female.[6]

Darwin did not think of natural selection as being one and indivisible. There must also, he believed, be some kind of sexual selection that operated continuously in favor of the qualities that had most appeal for humanity. The most attractive personalities would be the ones most likely to mate, to mate early, and to produce the greatest number of children, and the scales would therefore always be tipped toward an inheritance of increasing beauty and charm. Though a glance around today's world does not immediately confirm this as a proposition whose truth is self-evident, some kind of selection has certainly been responsible for man's beard and woman's hairlessness, as well as for man's greater height and woman's shapeliness.

For as long as humanity clung to the old primate mating posture, man had only a back view of his sexual partner, and he appears to have found esthetic satisfaction in opulent, rounded buttocks. Woman had no view at all. To her perhaps, should go the credit for the philosophy of "handsome is as handsome does." But when the changeover came, man's enthusiasm for buttocks gave way—except in one or two notable cases, such as that of the

Hottentots—to a liking for resilient breasts and stomachs. The face, too, began to assume importance for both sexes, and even today, looking back through civilization's five-thousand-year gallery of human portraiture, it is sometimes possible to catch an evanescent glimpse—beyond the hairstyles, the clothes, the cosmetic aids—of particular types of face that belong unmistakably to particular periods of history, products not of their own but of preceding generations' ideals of beauty.

No one knows when *Ramapithecus's* successors first began to change to the new mating posture. No one, in fact, even knows when they first appeared on the scene, and there are doubts about whether they should be classified as *australopithecus*, more ape than man, or *homo habilis* ("handyman"), more man than ape. But hunting and toolmaking, occupations that require not only manual dexterity but brainpower, led to a gradual conversion into the prehuman *homo erectus* (who knew how to use fire and was proficient enough at hunting to bring down elephant and rhinoceros, tiger and buffalo) and then—two hundred thousand years ago—into the protohuman *homo sapiens*, who very nearly qualified as the father of modern man.

MONOGAMY OR POLYGAMY?

The early world of *homo sapiens* remains only marginally less obscure than that of his predecessors, for until the appearance of written records in about 3000 B.C. most of what is known is based on an amalgamation of limited archeological facts with a projection back from the thought patterns of primitive peoples who have survived into modern times.

Archeological facts are all too often subject to a number of interpretations and primitive tribes, like statistics, can be used to prove almost anything. For at least the first one hundred and fifty thousand years of *homo sapiens'* existence, the only footholds in the shifting sands of academic speculation are those based on tools, bones, and the accumulated debris of man's living quarters. About his personal life, virtually all that is known is that he had evolved some kind of religious or humanitarian beliefs that led him to care for the sick and aged and to bury his dead. His sex life remains a mystery.

But all history is a sequence. Everything that happens is in some way related to what has gone before; so the sex and family life of early *homo sapiens*—like that of *homo sapiens* today—was a product, however remotely, of sex and family life five hundred thousand, five million, fifteen million years ago. This is why it is both interesting and instructive to look at the problem of which of the apes man's ancestors most closely resembled, even if there is no firm answer. For some of the emotive questions that exercise people's minds today—about whether early society was dominated by the man or woman, whether descent was traced through the father's or the mother's line, and whether fertility goddesses or male chauvinist gods were more deeply venerated—might (arguably) be answered if it were known whether *homo habilis* most closely resembled the monogamous gibbon, in which case the makings of patriarchy existed from the start, or the promiscuous chimpanzee, when only matriarchy would be possible.

At some time in man's prehuman state he found his tongue. Hunting and toolmaking were social skills that made it imperative for him to communicate on a more complex level than the primates. Even the gibbon, one of the more voluble of the apes, still has only a very limited number of sounds and sound sequences. Each of them, however, does have a specific meaning, and one of them has particular relevance to the early human condition. The message it conveys is: "Stay away from my wife!" [7]

Of the apes, only the gibbon would need to use such an expression, for only the gibbon *has* a wife. Other nonhuman primates live in mixed-sex groups, in which one sex often predominates and where there is no "pair bonding." The female chimpanzee, for example, mates with several males in swift succession and has no particular ties with any of them.

The gibbon's monogamous habit is usually attributed to the fact that the female—like the human female but unlike other primates—is not subject to an estrous cycle, the reproductive cycle that insures sexual receptivity only during the day or two of maximum fertility, at ovulation. The theory is that since the gibbon is receptive *all* the time, the male can satisfy his sexual urge as often as he chooses with only one partner, and one partner is therefore all he needs. It might be truer to suppose that one partner is all he wants. Monogamy must be restful in comparison with the situation of the chimpanzee, the gorilla, and the baboon, perpetually on call to satisfy the demands of every female in the troop who happens to be in heat.

It was Ernest Haeckel, scientific popularizer and contemporary of Darwin, who first publicized the idea that the gibbon was man's closest relative, and it was an idea that appealed to Western historians. It made early human development relatively easy to reconstruct as the gibbon's family life bears a convenient resemblance to that of modern Western man. Husband, wife, and children live together as a group, and when the children grow up they leave home (or are thrown out) and set up on their own. If this was how humanity started off, and how it has ended up, then the millennia between can be filled in comprehensibly, even sympathetically, with a homely picture of a daily round in which the man goes hunting, the woman keeps house (or cave), and there is an occasional break in the form of a get-together with neighbors over the hill. Unfortunately for this comfortable reconstruction, polygamy has been far more widespread than monogamy during most of the five thousand years of recorded history.

The promiscuous chimpanzee appears at first sight to be a more recalcitrant candidate for the role of humanity's closest relative, but chromosome counts and blood protein studies are only part of a substantial body of recent research that comes down strongly in his favor. The chimpanzee's intelligence is a major factor. Whereas the gibbon is intellectually the least well endowed of all the apes today, the chimpanzee, after evolving along his own branch of the family tree for the last fourteen million years or so, is able to use simple tools—sponges of crumpled leaves to soak up water from crevices, stalks to pry ants from their nests, sticks as levers—and to defend himself by throwing branches, rocks, and other missiles at marauders. He has learned to catch, kill, and eat young antelopes and monkeys; to stand and occasionally walk upright; and to communicate extensively, though still by means of gestures and grunts. The chimpanzee today, in fact, behaves very much as man's ancestor, *Ramapithecus,* must have behaved when he first set out on the road that was to lead to the evolution of the human race.[8]

If, in the very early days, humanity bore a strong family resemblance to the chimpanzee, at least one major biological change must subsequently have taken place, though there is no way of knowing when it began or when it was completed. The human female's menstrual cycle must gradually have replaced the estrous cycle of the primates, a modification with long-term results in the case of the female's own sexuality, and long-term repercussions on the relationship between men and women. But whether such a changeover would necessarily bring about a general preference for monogamy is a matter for debate. Though anthropologists equate monogamy with lack of an estrous cycle (an opinion that appears to be based more on hindsight than historical data), geneticists take a different view.

Darwin said that the central struggle of life was the struggle to survive and reproduce, and his spiritual heirs, the sociobiologists of today, claim that the participants in this struggle are not people but genes. These infinitesimal shreds of chromosome—which have replaced poets as the unacknowledged legislators of the world—are motivated by a drive for survival that would make the rising young corporate executive look diffident by comparison. Many of man's hitherto inexplicable acts and attitudes, say the sociobiologists, are a product of his genes' determination to propagate themselves. According to this theory, when conditions were harsh (as they often were) during paleolithic times, the cooperation of both parents was necessary to insure the survival not so much of their young as of the parental genes invested in them—producing a monogamous situation, regardless of what ancestral custom may have been. In more favorable conditions, however, when children could survive under their mother's care alone, men would tend to be promiscuous because it would be in their genes' interests for them to be spread around; in effect, the Stone Age Casanova was motivated not by the desire in his loins but by the DNA in his chromosomes. The female of the species had no such biological *carte blanche*. Her genes could be propagated only in the children born of her own body; the result, regardless of climatic conditions, was a powerful genetic urge toward protectiveness.[9] *

There is no reason to suppose that either monogamy or polygamy was "the rule" in the paleolithic era. The human female's lack of an estrous cycle may have made monogamy possible, but that is not the same as saying it made it probable. Equally, hu-

---

* None of this should be taken to imply that the human participants in the drama were aware of how procreation worked. Almost certainly they were not. But the genes knew about it, and that was good enough.

manity's genetic drive may sometimes have favored monogamy, sometimes polygamy, but genes were not the only forces at work. On balance, perhaps the most reasonable hypothesis is that the human race originally resembled its chimpanzee relatives in being promiscuous, but that as "human nature"—that ineluctable compound of hereditary and environmental factors—began to develop, so the style of living began to change. Throughout most of recorded history, it has been "human nature" for individuals to cling to other individuals when life has been uncertain, and to become more extrovert when the atmosphere improves. As living conditions fluctuated from good to indifferent to bad during the long ice-scarred millennia of man's early history, there may have been a slow pendulum swing from near-promiscuity to near-monogamy, and back again. And it may have been the women, not the men, who were promiscuous—for it was they who were in the minority (see page 30).

SEX   AND   THE   SOCIAL   ROLE

Whatever the marital status of *homo habilis* and his successors, the conditions under which they not only survived but, astonishingly, progressed, must at first have favored some kind of commune living.

Early man seems to have had a mobile habit of life, from necessity as much as from choice. Though he may have inherited the territorial instincts of his forebears, it seems that his brain must have begun to override them. As game grew scarcer and vegetation scantier during periods of climatic change, he would find that he had stripped his own section of the landscape so that it was necessary to move on. Sometimes he might have to dispute a new district with its current inhabitants, and there would be war, the vanquished being driven out or, if they were few, incorporated into the tribe of the victors.

Not until 350,000 years ago did he begin to settle down, and the reason for it appears to have been a deterioration in the world's climate. For much of the era known as the Pleistocene—geologically, the last two million years—there have been slow fluctuations from pleasant warmth to biting, vicious cold. During the worst of the cold spells, glaciers normally confined to high mountain ranges expanded and merged so that sometimes an ice sheet hundreds of feet thick advanced as far south as present-day New York, London, and Kiev. At such times, the half-million people who formed the total of the world's early human population [10] congregated in a few temperate regions around the Mediterranean, for example, where there was still something that might have been described as summer, and in areas like the Sahara, where—strange as it may seem today—heavy rainfall supported a thriving flora and fauna. But one branch of the *homo erectus* family, in the shape of Peking Man, discovered that it was possible to survive almost on the edge of the ice sheets by taking refuge in caves and utilizing something that the emerging human race had never conquered before: fire. It was to be another quarter of a million years before cave living became general in Europe, but the new mode of life, with warmth, light, and protection in place of the chill and menacing dark, must have had a revolutionary effect on the humanizing process.

Where abundant vegetation with its promise of plentiful game had been enough to attract man the wanderer, man the cave dweller had more specific requirements. Caves were scarcer than good pastures, and when he found a combination of the two that suited him, he stayed.

Cave living imposed its own logic. Caves as large as the famous painted one at Altamira on the northern coast of Spain, which stretches back through solid limestone for a distance of three hundred yards, were the exception rather than the rule. More commonly, they might be the size of the main rotunda at Lascaux in France, which—inhabited and splendidly decorated with paintings of animals more than fifteen thousand years ago—measures only thirty yards long by ten wide, not much more than a modern house built on a spacious ground plan. More commonly still, the immigrant human community would find itself having to fit into a honeycomb of smaller caves.

From open countryside to the physical and psychological constriction of stone walls must have resulted in some social upheaval, even if the campfire hierarchy dictated who should have the finest and who the least desirable lodging. Splintering and regrouping were inevitable, and it may have been at this stage that the idea of "the family" began to take on reality.

The prehistoric family was centered on the woman like cytoplasm around a nucleus, for the maternal relationship was the only one that was distinctively different from other tribal relationships.

It has to be remembered that it was probably very late indeed in terms of human evolution before *man's* role in procreation was discovered. It is not obvious. Over the last hundred years anthropologists have been consistently taken aback to discover primitive tribes still ignorant of the relationship between coitus and conception, and it seems likely that such ignorance was general until about as late as 9000 B.C. (see page 41ff.).

For much of the paleolithic era man lived on I-thou terms with the world around him. Where the modern city dweller views the rest of the world as "it," primitive man saw the river and the sea, the birds and the fish, earth, trees, animals, and plants as "thou," different from him in appearance but not in essence. Even while his toolmaking was developing, his style of living changing, his thought processes expanding, there remained many ways in which he scarcely diverged from the other animals that inhabited his landscape. He was still evolving *from* his primate ancestors; not until almost the end of the paleolithic era did he begin to evolve *toward* his space-age successors. There was much in his inheritance that he probably never questioned—because it was "natural," had always been so, and it is what appears natural that is usually the last to be explored. It was "natural" for the human female, like the wild mare or the reindeer cow, to be either pregnant or nursing for much of her adult life, just as it was "natural" for man and woman, stag and hind, ram and ewe, to indulge in the sexual act without seeing anything in it other than physical fulfilment. Sex and morality converged only at a relatively late stage of civilization.

Paternity has two levels, however—social and biological—and the first can exist without knowledge of the second. In a wholly promiscuous society, neither level is recognizable, and responsibility and kinship both rest with the female. But where there is a continuing relationship between one male and one female, or between one male and several females, social paternity is automatic. If modern primitive tribes can be taken as an example, paleolithic man may have been ready enough to shoulder the social duties of fatherhood, to act as guide, adviser, and provider to the children of the woman (or women) to whom he was sexually attached. Nevertheless, the male role was—if the word is permissible in the context of the Stone Age—psychologically a subsidiary one. In the Darwinian struggle to reproduce, man was no more than an auxiliary.

He made up for it, however—often with a fine panache—in the survival struggle. Without food to sustain life, woman's ability to create it became irrelevant. At the peak of the ice ages it was man who kept the human race alive, and his social status at such times must have soared to gratifying heights, even if it often slipped back when the climate improved and woman's contribution to the food supply rivaled his own.

There were two main kinds of community in the paleolithic world. In some areas the tribal economy was based on a single animal. In parts of France it was the reindeer; long afterward the people of the American grasslands were to depend on the bison in the same way. The migrations of such primary food animals shaped the lifestyle of the tribes that depended on them; where the reindeer or the bison went, the hunters followed. And where hunting was the mainstay of the tribe, it was the hunters—the men—who dominated the community.

Probably more common, at least toward the end of the period, was the hunting-gathering community which utilized whatever the countryside could provide: animals, fish, shellfish, birds, and plants. Such groups made their permanent homes in caves or rock shelters but often moved in summer to regular camps in the hills, following the smaller game animals like deer, sheep, and goats on their annual trek from low-lying ground to fresh upland pastures.

There is, of course, no firm evidence about the division of labor in paleolithic times, but the consensus of opinion is that man was the hunter and woman the gatherer; and in broad outline this was almost certainly true, although it is sometimes argued that women may have been just as proficient at hunting as men. In principle, there is no reason why a young and healthy woman should not hunt as well as a young and healthy man. Even pregnancy, in the primitive state, is by no means as incapacitating as it has become in advanced societies. The Ainu women of Japan still exercise strenuously when they are pregnant because they believe it encourages swift labor, and those of the Mbuti pygmies are so unconcerned by childbirth that they are often back on the trail within two or three hours of the event. Breast-feeding is no real problem when there are several women who can take turns in acting as wet nurse so that other mothers can go back to work in the fields. But working in the fields is very different from tracking deer or hunting woolly mammoth, activities which require the hunter to be in peak athletic condition—especially when the climate is harsh and game scarce. This is precisely when a pregnant woman is least likely to be of use, for it is she who is most vulnerable to cold and malnutrition. In the twentieth century, it is not unknown for parents to refuse to give an extended education to a girl who will "waste it by getting married," and paleolithic parents may have felt much the same about the prolonged hunting apprenticeship.

Genetic research suggests that man's expertise at hunting may have begun as much as a million years ago. Today, the male averages a higher score than the female in tests of spatial ability (the ability to see, hold, and adapt images in the mind), and two American scientists have recently succeeded in establishing an association between this ability and certain of the basic skills of hunting, including judgment of distance and accuracy in throwing. It is an ability that is genetically sex-linked in a way that implies that it must have conferred an advantage that worked primarily through the male.[11] Women's contribution to the food supply—gathering plants, collecting snails and river crabs, freshwater mussels and small turtles, acorns and pistachio nuts—did not depend on distance assessment or marksmanship. However, it has been established that women are able to see better than men in dim light and also have sharper hearing,[12] faculties that almost certainly were of use when it came to tracking small game hidden in the undergrowth, or crabs tucked into some crevice in a shaded pool.

Hunters or gatherers? The question is not just academic. For the whole life of hunting tribes was geared to the animals on whom they preyed, and because of that to the requirements of those who did the hunting. If game was there for the killing, all the energies of the tribe were directed toward aiding and preparing the hunters for their task. The life and survival of the tribe revolved around them, and even when the world changed and game no longer mattered the old attitudes survived. Man remained supreme.

In the hunting-gathering communities it was different. Under temperate conditions women gathered as much food as men, and some sort of equilibrium between the sexes was maintained. But ultimately man-the-hunter became man-the-herdsman, and woman-the-gatherer was transformed into woman-the-farmer. And that was to be a change that had almost incalculable effects on the future of man-woman relationships.

THE FIRST TABOO

Just as the new style of cave living influenced the internal structure of the tribe, so the stability the caves offered led to the development of wider institutions of a kind that any student of the modern aid mission would instantly recognize.

The cold conditions under which cave living developed were congenial to the larger, hardier game animals, the woolly mammoth, the musk ox, and the bison among them. This size of beast was not to be hunted and slaughtered by two or three five-foot men, with or without the aid of pregnant women and knee-high children. Cooperative enterprise was necessary, especially as it would have been bad survival business for any tribe to insist on territorial integrity when the only herd for miles around might choose to graze on the wrong side of the border.

Historians are generally agreed that this was the stage at which diplomatic negotiations were opened between neighboring tribes and hunting alliances formed. As a natural sequel, social gatherings would begin to take place, and eventually the smaller tribal units would begin to coalesce, however loosely, into clans. Though each tribe would maintain a degree of independence, all would tend to develop similar habits of mind, similar standards, and similar customs, and the federation would hold joint ceremonials such as the puberty rite, that combination of initiation ritual and personal ordeal that has persisted through the ages to find its present-day expression in sex education classes in schools.

One result of the increasing contact between tribes must have been a widening of amorous horizons; "love at first sight" is possible only between strangers. Historians, with the example of later royal houses in mind, believe that tribal intermarriage was encouraged as a means of cementing political alliances, and this is per-

An erotic engraving from the Stone Age

fectly possible, even if "marriage" is hardly the right word in the context. But—parsimoniously intent on killing the maximum number of birds with one stone—they often go on to suggest that such marriages were encouraged by banning any other kind and that it was this stratagem that (coincidentally) put an end to the incestuous relationships that had sustained humanity throughout the millions of years of its early development.

Incest is the extreme version of what is known as inbreeding, marrying always within a strictly delineated social group, and therefore within some degree of consanguinity. Consistent inbreeding of such a kind produces a uniform race, perfectly adapted to the milieu in which it lives, but it means that the only genetic choice is between precisely similar alternatives. Natural selection therefore cannot operate; so there is no mechanism by which a highly inbred society can change to meet changing external conditions. When the options are to change or go under, the inbred society goes under. Outbred societies, in contrast, provide the materials that allow natural selection to function, and are therefore genetically equipped to produce the adaptability essential to progress.[13]

In human society before intertribal contacts began to develop, inbreeding was almost inevitable. There were long periods of history when groups of no more than forty or fifty people might live out their lives together without ever seeing another human being. Even so, the human race could not have survived all the vicissitudes of the Pleistocene climate if there had been no scope in its make-up for some thread of mutant DNA that would enable it to confront each situation as it arose. Some avoidance of extreme inbreeding, of incest, must have been customary or there would have been no capacity to vary.

The universality of the incest tabu suggests that it may have been built into the human mechanism from the very beginning, and it was a taboo so widely recognized as "natural" to humanity that rulers in later times—from Egypt to Peru—chose to emphasize their superhuman, their divine status by deliberately breaking it.

It used to be held that animals, unable to recognize their kindred, were unable to avoid incest, but a recent study of African baboons has shown they have a breeding system that virtually rules out the possibility of it. Over a period of seven years, fifteen of the twenty males in the three groups studied transferred to another troop before they became established breeders; the remaining five either died or disappeared—which, from the incest point of view, was just as effective.[14] Other apes and monkeys also appear to have a built-in incest taboo, though on a lesser scale. Macaque monkey mothers avoid mating with their sons, and the same is believed to be true of chimpanzees.[15] But not of gibbons; a gibbon father deprived of his wife will mate with his daughter, and a widowed mother with her son.

Whatever the truth, it was incest—not cannibalism, as so many people believe—that was the world's first taboo. As soon as there was enough contact between tribes to make outbreeding possible, outbreeding seems to have become the general practice, and the accelerating speed of human development during the 50,000 years immediately preceding the neolithic revolution was at least partly due to the intellectual and physical adaptability that resulted from it.

THE POPULATION PROBLEM

The fact that it was "natural" for paleolithic woman to spend most of her life either pregnant or nursing did not mean that she progressed through that life with a graduated scale of infants clinging to her deerskin skirts. Not very many children were delivered, and of those that were, not very many survived.

In parts of Africa today, a high proportion of women (as high as 20 to 40 percent in areas of Gabon, Sudan, Cameroon, and Zaire) never have a live-born child, while in some districts of Zaire an infant mortality rate of 45 percent is not uncommon.[16] The situation can never have been as disastrous as this in paleolithic times (except in isolated pockets, perhaps), for if it had been the human race could scarcely have survived.

Estimated population figures give some indication of the number of children who were born and lived to maturity. A million years ago, the human population of the world is believed to have numbered about half a million. By 10,000 B.C., the eve of the neolithic revolution, it had increased to three million.[17] This suggests that for much of the time there can have been no more than zero population growth, with only enough people being born to replace those who died. In theory, if every couple (assuming monogamy) had succeeded in rearing three children instead of just the two needed to replace themselves, the human race would have multiplied by six in only four generations, or less than a hundred years. But it took a million years. These, of course, are rule-of-thumb figures, no more than a starting-off point and subject to a multitude of variations.

Women, for example, appear to have been in a clear minority. Skeletal evidence suggests that early man outnumbered woman by almost three to two and that a man could expect to outlive a woman by roughly eight years.[18] If that were so then it might have been necessary for each woman to raise as many as four children simply to maintain zero growth.

Further, a woman's childbearing years were comparatively few. In Neanderthal times (about 70,000 years ago), only two out of every ten people who survived childhood and adolescence could expect to go on living to the age of 30. There was a brief improvement 30,000 years ago, and 12 people out of 100 might hope to see 40, but the situation deteriorated again until it was worse even than in Neanderthal times, with 86 people out of 100 dying before 30 and only five of the survivors living beyond 40.[19] The average woman probably had only 15 or 16 childbearing years between puberty and death.

Even so, population development was slower than it might have been. There were a number of contributory reasons, some of them outside human control. Disease was probably a major factor though modern medical anthropologists, with only bones to work from, cannot do much to identify paleolithic diseases of the flesh. But the gonorrhea and filariasis that are held largely responsible for infertility south of the Sahara today undoubtedly had their prehistoric equivalents, even if the scattered nature of the population helped to keep contagion within bounds. Since hygiene is a modern concept, less specific infections may have been rife, both during pregnancy and at parturition.

Important, too, were the effects of malnutrition, a seasonal hazard throughout much of history and possibly a year-round hazard at the height of the ice ages. Malnutrition depresses fertility in several ways, delaying the onset of maturity in girls and leading to miscarriages and stillbirths. It is also responsible for mothers dying in childbirth and for a high percentage of infant mortality. Among the Bantu of Africa in the 1940s, a woman had to suffer 12 pregnancies for two children to survive; [20] in India even in the early 1970s, nine children in a hundred were likely to die of malnutrition before they reached the age of five.[21] It has also been suggested that inadequate diet during the first two years of life has a lasting effect on brain development,[22] and since malnutrition in the paleolithic era was something that affected not individuals but whole communities, this might have delayed the intellectual as well as the physical development of the human race.

Long lactation is something else that helps to depress fertility. As far back as the days of Peking Man, half a million years ago, the human child had become dependent on its mother for a good deal longer than other primates; fossil relics show that the infants who lived on Dragon Bone Hill had more milk teeth than apes at the same stage of growth. Even today, it is perfectly common in tribal societies for mothers to breastfeed their children until the age of two or three.

There were few ways in which the early human race could respond to such restraints on its expansion, and it may not even have tried. Bred into man's bones was the knowledge of what happened when there was not enough food to go round, and later history suggests that even as early as the paleolithic era this knowledge may have expressed itself in practices instinctively—sociobiologists would say genetically—designed to insure that population density never outstripped the available resources.

The simplest and most obvious method of keeping the population down was infanticide, which was to remain as commonplace in Europe, India, and China until the nineteenth century as abortion has become in the West today. Often it may not have been as positive as murder—a matter of leaving a newborn infant exposed to the elements or allowing an ailing one simply to drift away. Often, it may have been more positive. In comparatively recent times some Polynesian tribes are reported to have put two-thirds of their children to death, while the Jagas, warrior nomads of Angola, are said to have killed them all so that the women should not be encumbered on the march; when necessary, they adopted adolescents by force from other tribes. In nineteenth-century Western Australia, there was even a tribe that ate every tenth baby born so as to keep the population down to what the territory would stand.[23]

In most cases of infanticide, it was probably the female child who was the victim, not for male chauvinist reasons, but because she was herself a child-producer of the future, a threat not only in her person but in her progeny to the food supply. There was also a greater likelihood of boys dying in the normal course of events, in childish fights or intertribal feuds.

Another method of population control that may—just possibly—have been used during the latter part of the paleolithic era was contraception, not such a modern invention as many people believe. Long before farming began, women were intimately acquainted with the properties of most of the plants that grew near their settlements, and primitive peoples who have survived into the modern world have been using contraceptive plant drugs since long before the Pill was ever heard of. The efficacy of some of them has been attested. In the central forests of Paraguay, the plant used is *Stevia rebaudiana*, which is dried, powdered, and then boiled in water. A woman who wishes to avoid conceiving drinks a cup of the infusion every day. The Navajo use, or used, a tea of ragleaf bahia; the Shoshoni of Nevada an infusion of stoneseed roots; and the Hopis a powder made from the dried root of the jack-in-the-pulpit. Though scientists are supercilious about folk medicine, laboratory experiments with animals have suggested that the Paraguayan and Shoshoni drugs do, in fact, have contraceptive properties.[24] While the male role in procreation remained unrecognized, a drug affecting woman would be the only form of contraception likely to suggest itself.

Finally, there were purely social ways of attempting to control population growth, most of them necessarily directed at women. Certainly, some menstruation taboos (see page 43) make very little sense regarded in any other light. To take a single example, the nineteenth-century Carrier Indians of British Columbia used to dispatch girls who had just begun menstruating to spend three or four years in total seclusion in the wilderness; they were regarded as a threat to anyone who saw them, and even their footsteps were believed to defile any path they had trodden.[25] Stripped of the mystical accretions and the prognostications of doom designed to reinforce the system, this taboo was no more than a way of keeping the girls in an isolation that the Carriers knew to result in infertility.

Although from the vantage point of the twentieth century it may be difficult to believe that the real-life Flintstones of tens of thousands of years ago were even remotely aware of the dangers of population explosions and the desirability of population control, modern scholars have found correlations between static populations and bad conditions, between growing populations and favorable ones, that strongly imply some such awareness. Improvements in nutrition alone are not quite enough to explain the spectacular increase that occurred when the neolithic revolution took place and man at last discovered that he could control his food supply.

THE PALEOLITHIC SEX SYMBOL

The people of the paleolithic era are shadowy figures. Something is known about how and where they lived, but how they thought and how they looked remain a mystery. Were they as serious-minded as serious-minded historians make them appear? Or did they have a sense of humor? Was the "Venus figurine" over whom so much ink has been spilled an early fertility goddess? Or was she the Fat Lady in some paleolithic fairground?

Technology, a tangible asset, leaves direct traces for later generations to find, but some of those traces are not easy to decipher. A prehistoric fish hook is a prehistoric fish hook, and only the most passionate piscatologist would take the time to analyze its artistic quality, philosophical background, and spiritual implications. But the Venus figurines are a different matter.

More than sixty of these statuettes have been found, most of them in eastern Central Europe but a few in France and a few in the Ukraine and Siberia. Made more than twenty thousand years ago from mammoth ivory, soft stone, or clay mixed with ash and then baked, they are usually small—no more than four or five inches high—and, with two exceptions which are in any case incomplete, there is no attempt to portray the face. All the emphasis is on the luxuriant contours of the torso. As one historian writing fifty years ago austerely put it, the Venuses are "sculptures of feminine form, with the maternal parts grossly exaggerated." [26]

Current opinion has it that:

a. The emphasis in these figures is "undeniably sexual" (Grahame Clark).

b. "Never did sexuality play such a small part in the representation of the female figure" (René Nougier).

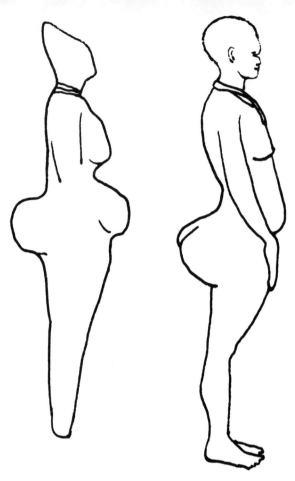

The thirty-thousand-year-old
Venus of Menton, compared
with a modern Bushman woman

    c. The Venus figure is "a magical invocation of fertility"
(Walter Torbrügge).
    d. It is "no fertility symbol, but a matron deformed by child-
bearing" (Richard Lewinsohn).
    e. The figurines must be viewed in the symbolic context of
cave art, which is fundamentally religious (school of André Leroi-
Gourhan).
    f. "It is safe to reject any belief that they have religious signifi-
cance" (Charles Seltman).[27]
    Partly because the linguistic convention that refers to the art-
ist as "he" carries its own sexual implications, there is a general
reluctance to consider that the paleolithic craftsman, already expert at producing two-dimensional pictures of wild animals, may
simply have been trying his hand at representation in the round,
using a model who could be persuaded to stand still while he

worked. The usual argument against accepting the figurines as pictures of real people seems to have its roots in an instinctive revulsion against the physical type they represent. As Richard Lewinsohn remarks: "Sex life in the paleolithic must have been quite unerotic, for this Venus [from Willendorf, in Austria] was no more than a lump of fat." Yet even the modern eye, conditioned by Western culture and corsets ought to be able to recognize a family resemblance between the pendulous breasts and stomachs of the Venus statuettes and those of women in tribal societies today. The Venuses may be more generously upholstered, but they were created at a period when—because of the genetic time lag—the human figure had probably not yet adapted to the milder conditions resulting from the retreat of the ice sheets. Recorded history shows that people who live in a cold climate often build up a layer of flesh as insulation against it, sometimes by the short-term practice of eating fatty foods, sometimes by a protracted process of inheritance. To say that no one— or no one desirable to the male—could look like the Venuses is modern Western arrogance. There is nothing to rule out the possibility that they were the paleolithic prototypes of the Playgirl of the Month.

All the accent is on the female sexual features of ample breasts and *mons pubis* and on the less exclusively female features of bulging stomach and buttocks. The artist may have chosen to exaggerate these lines very much as a caricaturist does today, though not necessarily for the same reasons, perhaps even for the sheer tactile pleasure and esthetic satisfaction of handling the smooth, globular shapes. This could account for the undeniably sketchy treatment of arms and lower legs and even for the fact that the faces of all the surviving, complete statuettes are blank and featureless.

Facelessness does not rule out portraiture. Realism was an essential element of the cave paintings, which were designed (it is believed) to exert magical control over the animals shown in them; and it is not difficult to envisage a stage in intellectual development that equated recognizability of an image with danger to its original. While a woman might consent to having a portrait made of her body, she might still recoil from allowing her face—so uniquely hers—to be carved in stone or modeled in clay. There are parallels for this in much later times; during the early centuries of

Islam, for example, on the authority of the *Hadīth,* portraiture was actively discouraged.

What the Venus figurines unequivocally suggest is that the paleolithic woman of Central Europe was chubby, well-developed, and suffered from relaxed breast and abdominal muscles, perhaps as a result of frequent pregnancies.

Authorities on prehistory, of course, read more into them than this. There are two main theories, one of which—currently somewhat discredited—is that they represent motherhood, a half abstract concept in which maternity and the role of protectress are cosily combined. Some of the figures could undoubtedly be of pregnant women, though as one medical historian points out of a figure from Laugerie Basse in France, while she "may indeed be expecting a happy event, it is idle to pretend that she could not equally well be suffering from an ovarian cyst." [28] Unfortunately for that breath of welcome, if gruesome, realism in the stuffy atmosphere of paleolithic studies, what matters is not what the artist *was* representing, but what he *thought* he was representing. The main argument against the mother-protectress idea is that no mother-and-child figures have ever been found, although something of that kind would have been a much more telling illustration of the theme.

The other theory combines the highly nubile appearance of the figurines with what is known of early humanity's tentative steps towards a formalized religion. Here the Venus becomes, if not a fully-fledged fertility goddess, at least a fertility cult figure. The trouble is that humanity, at this period, seems to have had very little enthusiasm for human fertility. Too many children posed more of a problem than too few. And if the idea of fertility existed at all, it must have embraced not only conception but the avoidance of miscarriages and stillbirths, the conquest of infant mortality, and the ability to rear a child safely to adolescence. It would have been an ambitious sculptor who attempted to crystallize all that into a four-inch statuette. If paleolithic man was interested in fertility at all, it was in the fertility of his food animals; a pregnant cow or a pregnant deer would have been a good deal more relevant than a pregnant woman. In fact, nearly all the fertility cults found in the earliest period of recorded history are directly related not to humans or animals, but to the soil, and the likelihood is that it was only when man became a farmer, some time after 9000 B.C. that he became obsessed by the subject.

Whether or not the Venuses had some magical importance, most of them can at least be taken to bear some resemblance, however distorted, to paleolithic women. But in the case of men, art has almost nothing to say. There are a few matchstick men in hunting scenes, and a number of figures impenetrably disguised in animal masks and skins, a costume used when stalking game and believed sometimes to have been worn by early shamans, or medicine men, for ceremonial purposes. But in all forms of paleolithic art, man seems to have been represented predominantly by phallic symbols, which is interesting if, in the present context, not very informative.*

Assuming that the biological role of the father was not yet recognized, these symbols reinforce the argument against seeing the Venuses as fertility figurines. For if the phallic symbols expressed anything at all, they could only express the idea of the male as male, and probably as sexual athlete. If that was so, then the Venus figurine can reasonably be seen as a matching representation of the female as female, and as sexual partner.

---

* Except, sometimes, about the minds of the experts who identify them. Dedicated seekers can recognize phallic intent even in designs and objects which were originally (*pace* Freud) unimpeachably innocent.

2.

Man into

master

Although by 12,000 years ago men and women had developed typically human—even modern—skills, they were still essentially no more than successful predators with as little influence on the world around them as the lion, wolf, or jackal. They had minds and had begun to use them. They knew how to make tools and clothes; how to build shelters. They were artists, sculptors, and good plain cooks. But none of these talents had freed them from dependence on their environment. The whole edifice of their life was built, as it had always been, on the food supply, and this was something they had not yet learned how to control. The revolution, however, was at hand. When it came, the discovery of how to grow crops and rear livestock changed not only the pattern of human existence, but the whole face of the earth and the life of everything upon it.

The neolithic, the New Stone Age, was not a revolution in the modern sense—a series of specific events to which specific dates can be assigned—but a stage in social development occurring at different times in different parts of the world. In southeast Asia it may have begun as early as 9750 B.C.; in the Near East, archeologically the ancient world's best documented zone, about 8000 B.C.; in Mexico, nearer 7000 B.C.; not much before 5000 B.C. in the northern parts of mainland Europe; and as late as 4000 B.C. in the British Isles.

During the neolithic, men and women became farmers. Botanists know what kind of grains they grew. Herdsmen; and zoologists can demonstrate the stages in their domestication of animals. Potters; archeologists have dug up relics of dishes and platters with their painted designs still intact. There are statues of the gods and kings to whom they subjected themselves. And, ultimately, incised clay tablets showing that they had learned to write, and calculate, and chart the calendar of their year; that there were laws to be obeyed, seasonal rituals to be observed, and taxes to be paid. But there is still a whole dimension missing from the seven thousand astonishing years that pitchforked humanity from an existence that has been described as "nasty, brutish, and short" into one of full civilization. The dimension of discovery.

THE NEOLITHIC REVOLUTION

It was a matter of timing, of harmony between attitudes of mind and aberrations of climate. On several occasions before, during the course of human development, the ice sheets had retreated and the climate become milder; but never before had the right people been in the right place at precisely the right time.

Somewhere around 11,000 B.C. the ice sheets began to retreat to the north for the last time (so far), and in the Near East cool moist winters and hot dry summers were the result, a situation that encouraged fast-maturing wild grasses at the expense of the kind of vegetation that took longer to grow. On open land, natural fields of wild wheat and barley sprang up; but wild grains do not hold their seed for long, and this rich harvest of free food was available only to people who were there to gather it during the two or three weeks when the ripe seeds still clung to the stalks. There was enough to feed a whole tribe for a year—several tribes, if the plain was wide—but the wheel had not yet been invented, and man had no draft animals. Logic and logistics both suggested moving the family to the fields instead of the produce of those fields to the family.

This, it is now believed, was the stage at which villages began to grow around the fields; and one of the results must have been that the wild grain, regularly harvested, began to thin out, a situation that could be remedied only by deliberate human intervention. Gradually, the age-old system of gathering what nature provided gave way to primitive but purposeful cereal farming.

If anyone deserved the credit for one of the few historical developments that can truthfully be described as epoch-making, it must have been woman, for hers was the knowledge on which agricultural development was based. It seems certain that she had known for several thousand years that new plants grew from seed, but to translate that knowledge into rippling fields of corn was a feat beyond the paleolithic imagination—until it happened by accident, the result of a trick of climate.

This was the starting point of almost all subsequent development, and of the work, routine, and responsibility that would have been meaningless in the context of paleolithic life. The human mind, with far-reaching effect, became subject to new and stringent disciplines.

More immediately, humanity's increasing control over one of its staple foods offered scope for new enterprise. Although the dog (the small Asiatic wolf) had been tamed toward the end of the paleolithic era, the risks entailed in trying to domesticate food animals whose own diet overlapped with man's had been too great to seem worthwhile. A single sheep can eat a hundredweight of greenstuff in a week, as much as a dozen people. But the new agriculture made livestock farming almost inevitable. The fields that had attracted humans also attracted some of the smaller game animals that had begun to multiply in the open shade around the margins of the new woods and forests, and it must have seemed easier to pen the marauders than protect the fields. Surplus grain could be rationed out, and after the harvest the beasts could be loosed to graze on the stubble. Sheep and goats, gregarious by nature and not too difficult to tame, were among them, and by 9000 B.C. the first stages of domestication had begun in both Iraq and Romania.

For hundreds of thousands of years, man had been the student of animals, woman the expert on plants. Common sense and genetics both favored an extension of existing roles. Woman converted the digging stick that had once pried roots from the soil and crabs from crevices into a hoe, and then a plough. Man devoted himself to domestic animals instead of wild ones and discovered that they could be made to supply the tribe not only with meat, fleece, hides, and tallow, but, for the first time, with milk, soured milk, and cheese, valuable new additions to the diet. Also, because he had more leisure than ever before—no intensive planning sessions, no keep-fit classes, no long days on the trail, none of the physical and mental strains of the hunt—he found himself with time to sit and think.

It does not, perhaps, sound like very much. But most of the institutions and many of the inventions that were to emerge between the beginning of the neolithic revolution and the beginning of recorded history seven thousand years later were to be unmistakably male in origin. Male historians—those whose nerves are still strong enough—sometimes attribute this to a natural masculine superiority. Feminist writers argue either that there was a female contribution that has been deliberately suppressed, or that neolithic woman was kept in such subjection that her ideas and opinions went for nothing. Modern emotions and prejudices aside, part of the explanation may well have been that woman was too busy for speculative thought. She had farming and fuel-collecting and housekeeping to attend to; child-bearing and child-rearing, and the endless, muscle-straining task of husking the grain. It was man, peaceably tending his flock, who had the time and opportunity for constructive thought, the time to dream up new ideas, to make connections, to wonder, to produce the materials that would, in the end, mesh together to make civilization.

But that can only have been part of the explanation. Time and opportunity would have meant little if they had not been accompanied by an outburst of the kind of self-confidence that reduces mountains to the size of molehills.

REPRODUCTION THEORIES

It is not altogether easy to accept that *homo sapiens*, after more than 100,000 years of fully-fledged existence, may still have been unaware of the biological facts of life when the neolithic revolution began.

Even in the twentieth century, however, there have been tribal peoples whose ignorance remains profound. The Bellonese of the Solomon Islands, until they were enlightened by Christian missionaries at the end of the 1930s thought that children were sent by their social father's ancestral deities and that the only function of sexual intercourse was to provide pleasure. In the 1960s, the Tully River Blacks of north Queensland believed that a woman became pregnant because she had been sitting over a fire on which she had roasted a fish given to her by the prospective father. Another Australian tribe believed that women conceived by eating human flesh. The Trobriand islanders, though perfectly realistic about the function of coitus between animals, apparently drew no human parallels from it. In Papua-New Guinea, the Hua tribe still think a *man* can become pregnant (by eating possum) and may die in childbirth.* And a woman of one Australian aboriginal tribe, when the Western facts of life and fatherhood were explained to her, flatly denied it. "Him nothing!" she said scornfully.[1] Even people who know of the biological role of the father are sometimes shaky on detail. In twentieth-century India, one distinguished headman of the Sema tribe told a European visitor that it was "ridiculous to suppose that pregnancy would result from coition on one occasion only." [2] And Darwin himself might have said the same. He never knew that fertilization was accomplished by a single sperm.

Some anthropologists regard most of these cases as pure fiction, a succession of wilful misunderstandings, or a gigantic legpull on the part of tribal peoples testing the extent of Western naivety. In the dying decades of the twentieth century, they argue, sex is an open book.

But is it? In modern, media-saturated England in 1977, a girl who had borne a child to a black lover wrote to the agony column of a leading women's magazine. She was about to be married to a white man; would the Negro blood still inside her mean that she would continue to have black babies? Another correspondent asked whether the Pill would save her from becoming pregnant by her lover as well as by her husband. And men, it appears, take the Pill as their wives and girl friends do, "just to be on the safe side." [3]

In paleolithic times it was natural for a woman to be pregnant, and there was no particular reason to wonder how it came about. Human females and animal females were very much alike in that respect. In one way, however, they differed, and this difference may have been the starting point from which all man's subsequent speculation developed. Animals in the northern hemisphere, where the human race grew to cognitive maturity, were

---

* The swollen stomach and subsequent death responsible for this belief are in fact attributable to the disease of kwashiorkor.

unlike women (and, indeed, unlike some animals in the southern hemisphere) in that they were not subject to the mysterious, periodic bleeding that the modern world calls menstruation.

T H E   S E C O N D   T A B O O

In the prehistoric world—as, much later, in the Book of Deuteronomy—the blood was the life. From almost the first moment when man (or woman) formulated the question "why?", the question that marked humanity's final, irrevocable divergence from the apes, he (or she) had begun to grope after ideas about the association between life and death, flesh, blood, and spirit. It is easy enough to understand how such early essays in coherent thought should have led to the conclusion not only that blood was essential to life, but that it was the essence of life itself. There was blood at the moment of birth, and blood, very often, at the moment of death. To early man it seemed to have a positive, intrinsic power, and because it was thought of as a vitalizing (and revitalizing) agent, it was used in many magical rituals, most cults of the dead, and most dealings with the gods and spirits.[4]

The mystical significance of *all* blood has to be remembered when the subject of menstruation crops up, as it increasingly does today in discussions on the relative status of the sexes, past and present. As with so many other sources of discord, it seems only too likely that menstrual taboos had their origin not in deliberate malice but in ignorance on the one side and lethargy on the other.

The biological function of menstruation was, of course, unrecognized until very recent times. All that was clear in prehistory was that although menstrual blood was indeed blood, and therefore magical, it also contravened the dimly recognized rules. Losing it did not bring death, or even pain or weakness. It flowed for no apparent reason, and instead of sealing itself off after an hour or two it persisted for days. And it was characteristic not of men, not boys, not children, but only of women—and usually only the youngest ones. In many ways it was inexplicable, and the inexplicable carries its own burden of fear. Not surprisingly, menstrual blood came to be seen as having a special power that was to commend it to every practitioner of magic, witchcraft, and alchemy until well into the seventeenth century; in some parts of the world (Tibet, for example), almost until the present day.

In time, of course, it became clear that the onset of menstruation was a sign of physical maturity. It showed that a woman was able to bear children, and its cessation during pregnancy suggested that it was directly related to the creation of new life. If modern primitive tribes may be taken as an analogy, paleolithic man may have responded to these discoveries in two ways. He may have felt simple envy for something that represented a sharp dividing line between youth and maturity. The adolescent boy slipped across the threshold of manhood by stages, none of them definitive, and some psychologists believe that the male puberty or initiation ceremonies that are such an important feature of tribal life were initially designed less as an introduction to adult responsibilities (the generally held view) than as an attempt to match first menstruation with an equally unequivocal male statement of maturity.[5]

But if that was so, imitation stopped there. What no puberty rite could do was endow the emergent man with the ability to bear children, to create life. For a while, he may have thought that blood could achieve it. Most puberty rites are bloody in one way or another, but few as suggestively so as one practiced among some of the tribes of twentieth-century central Australia and New Guinea. These use a type of mutilation called subincision, which entails slitting the underside of the penis from the point nearest the scrotum, sometimes for as little as an inch, sometimes for almost its whole length. The blood that flows is referred to as "men's menstruation," which might be taken merely as some kind of tribal joke if it were not for the fact that all the taboos imposed on women during their periods also apply to men while the bleeding persists.[6]

There is no way of knowing how long early man continued to try to draw from his own sexual organs the special kind of blood that was related to the production of children. The pages of history are littered with long-disproved myths that still succeed in renewing themselves, generation after generation. But the attempt itself could have been enough to stimulate serious questioning about why women could bear children while man, however hard he tried, could not. And frustration in a search for understanding very often produces resentment.

Blood magic and simple bafflement could have been enough to make man wary of woman during her periods. Isolating her may have appeared as sensible insurance against the unknown. And woman herself may not have objected.

It is debatable whether the view of the menstruating-woman-as-witch could have become so deeply ingrained in the human *id* if it had been constructed out of the prejudice of one sex alone. Woman must, at the very least, have acquiesced in the early taboos. Perhaps they seemed not worth arguing about. Perhaps she welcomed a few days' release from the routine of family life. Perhaps she herself found menstruation unnerving, for despite miscarriages, stillbirths, and all the other hazards of paleolithic motherhood, most women spent a good deal of their adult lives either pregnant or lactating, so that menstruation was an irregular experience. (As a rider, it should perhaps be pointed out that although there have been a number of extreme, sometimes cruel manifestations of the taboo throughout history, the recurring theme is one of uncleanness, which need not be taken only in the magical or religious sense. Regular washing is an activity in which a large part of the human race has only recently begun to indulge.)

But however the taboos began, they did not develop to woman's advantage. Some anthropologists argue that prehistoric man experienced a sense of wonder at the miracle of procreation—an emotion that better fits Snow White cooing over the baby animals in her Disney wonderland than cave dwellers shivering on the margins of the Pleistocene ice sheets—and deduce that the menstrual taboos that grew and fossilized as the human race developed were actually a reflection of woman's exalted state as the propagator of man, and that ritual seclusion during menstruation was an honor rather than a banishment.[7] This view might be more convincing if menstruation were an indication of pregnancy rather than the opposite; it also ignores the fact that childbirth was originally no more than one of the bodily functions inherited from humanity's primate forebears. There was no reason to exalt woman for doing what came naturally. Modern feminists may come nearer the truth in believing that the taboos, once established, were deliberately transformed into a weapon against woman's self-assertion.[8] For at some stage during the neolithic era, man took over the dominant role and learned to use every available means to sustain it.

No one knows when or how man discovered that women could not produce children unaided, but it seems probable that this occurred during the early part of the neolithic era and that the discovery hardened his attitude toward menstruation. If his semen was the mystical catalyst of the process that ended in childbirth, then menstruation, which demonstrated woman's failure to conceive, must have appeared as an insult and a rejection, a blood-letting that brutally denied his new role as child-maker.

THE   FATHER   FIGURE

Man's role in procreation was not one that could be easily deduced from the pattern of everyday paleolithic life, when intercourse was frequent and pregnancy a commonplace, when the only calendar was the moon, and nine months in relation to life expectancy almost as long as two years today. It was something that, in theory, could have been recognized at any time after man achieved the status of *homo sapiens*, perhaps even before, but there is nothing in all the long millennia of the paleolithic era to prove that he knew about it.

Three factors suggest that the moment of truth may have come in the early part of the neolithic era. In the first place, until that time neither sex seems to have been dominant. Secondly, if the discovery was prompted by some external stimulus, animal herding was the most obvious and the most likely. Livestock domestication began either with goats or, more probably, sheep, and the first farmers soon learned that segregated ewes produced neither lambs nor milk. Introducing one or two rams to the flock, however, brought spectacular results. For the first time, man was watching the same individual animals every day, all the year round, and he could scarcely fail to note the relatively constant length of the interval that elapsed between a ram servicing a ewe and the ewe dropping her lambs. What must have been traumatic in the full psychoanalytical sense was not only the discovery of the male contribution to procreation, but its potential scale. A single ram could impregnate more than fifty ewes. With power comparable to this, what could man not achieve?

The third factor—the most problematical, yet in many ways the most convincing—is that, quite simply, *something* happened during the mysterious seven thousand years of the neolithic in the Near East to change man from a more or less equal partner in human society into an acknowledged despot. His control over food and draft animals had something to do with it; so had his leisure to think; so, also, his role as warrior and protector. But if these had been the only bricks that went into the building, the edifice of male supremacy that was raised during the neolithic revolution could never have presented such a smooth and monolithic face. The men who emerged from the neolithic into the period of recorded history had the kind of assurance, arrogance, and authority that spring not from useful toil, not from knowledge of a good job well done, but from the kind of blinding revelation—beyond argument, beyond questioning—that was later to be experienced by the prophets of the Old Testament and the saints of the New. Was it that, discovering their own crucial role in an area where man's potency had always been denied, they had (very humanly) overreacted?

On a more specific level, it was now possible for a man to look at a child and call him "*my* son"; to feel the need to call a woman "*my* wife." Whatever the marital custom before that time—monogamy, polygyny, polyandry—after it, woman's sexual freedom began to be seriously curtailed. A man might have a harem if he chose, and if he could defend it, but the concept of "my" son required the woman to be monogamous.

Extramarital chastity, of course, could be imposed on a woman only if her desire for it matched the man's, or if she was indifferent, or if he was prepared to use force either of person or of personality. And to a certain extent the type of society in which they lived dictated the way in which the relationship between men and women developed.

During the neolithic revolution two kinds of society began to emerge, the agricultural and the strictly pastoral. Agriculture immobilized the communities that depended on it, tying them to their cultivated land and, later, to the waters that irrigated it. Their primary foodstuff was the product of their fields; livestock were secondary. In this kind of society, man's work role was important but not at first more important than woman's. In time, however, the balance began to shift. When cattle were domesticated, somewhere around 6000 B.C., man learned to castrate the bull and use it as a draft animal—humanity's first power tool, as revolutionary in its way as the first steam locomotive. It was man, the expert on animals, who was the one to handle it when it was yoked to the hoe or plough. From warrior, thinker, child-maker, stockbreeder, he was transformed for the first time into a cultivator, taking over one of the most important of woman's tasks and doing it demonstrably better than she had. It may have been this that laid the foundations of man's increasing tendency to experiment so that he soon added to his already powerful combination of roles those of inventor and technician. Essentially, his contribution to society remained little greater than woman's, but (intentionally or not) it was more ostentatiously demonstrated. His work, like justice, had not only to be done but to be seen to be done. Even so, in agricultural society, woman retained ancestral memories of her own importance and succeeded, if only partially, in maintaining some sense of self-assurance.

It was otherwise in pastoral societies. The pastoralists were highly mobile, shifting from season to season round the wide plains of Central Asia and the narrower but richer grazing lands of northern Europe. Some historians believe that these early nomads were direct descendants of paleolithic hunting communities, others that they were unsuccessful cultivators or surplus population driven out from agricultural land; but whichever was the case, they were wholly dependent on their flocks and on the men who reared and tended them. In the pastoral society, man was dominant, and woman as much his chattel as the beasts he herded. It is no coincidence that the male-oriented society of the West today should be in a direct line of moral and philosophical descent from a few tribes of Hebrew nomads, or that of modern India from the Indo-European pastoralists of the *Rig-Veda*.

THE   POPULATION   EXPLOSION

In 10,000 B.C., the world population is estimated to have numbered around three million; 7000 years later, it had expanded to a hundred million.[9] In the Zagros mountains of southwestern Iran, paleolithic people had averaged out (in 40,000 B.C.) at one person to every 31 square miles, or 50 square kilometers; by 5500 B.C., instead of one person there were 500.[10]

This explosive population increase was not, disappointingly, the direct result of man putting his new paternity theories to the test (though he may have done so), but of a substantial improvement in nutrition. The improved food supply that inaugurated and later shaped the neolithic revolution not only reduced the need for population control but made an enlarged population actively desirable. More children meant more field hands, more crops, and better crops. Better nutrition meant improved fertility, more live births, a lower infant mortality rate, and, on average, a slight increase in life expectancy.

In Morocco just before the neolithic, that statistical myth "the average man" died at just over 33 years of age, the woman at around 28. By 6000 b.c. at Çatal Hüyük in Anatolia, a man who survived beyond 18 could expect to go on living to a little over 34 and a woman to almost 30. On Cyprus a few hundred years later, the proportionate increase was maintained; a man's life expectancy was 35, a woman's over 33.[11] Clearly, it was woman who benefited more from improved nutrition; pregnancy became less of a drain on her physical resources. And every extension of a woman's life span also increased the number of her childbearing years. At Çatal Hüyük women appear to have had an average of four children each.

The changing climate, with its favorable agricultural conditions and apparently guaranteed food supply, also encouraged a kind of migration that had rarely been possible before, a generalized and voluntary mobility that had little or nothing in common with the grim pursuit of game that had in the past led bands of Asian hunters over the Bering Strait to the Americas. The neolithic population shifted, settled, drifted, moving from less to more favored areas, and then out of the favored areas as they became overcrowded to try the new agricultural techniques in new landscapes.

Excavations at Çatal Hüyük show that the resident population consisted of three different types: Eurafricans, proto-Mediterraneans, and Alpines [12]—a catholic assortment for such an early period. There was increasing trade, too, so that even settled peoples included among their numbers some who had seen "foreign" lands and perhaps even brought home "foreign" wives. The traders of southern Greece sailed to the island of Melos, seventy-five miles away, for obsidian—a dark, glassy volcanic rock used for knife blades—and obsidian, this time from east Turkey, was, with shells from the Persian Gulf and turquoise from the northeast, one of the materials imported to villages in the plains of southwest Iran.[13]

What migration and trade did for the people of the neolithic era was encourage a kind of extensive and consistent outbreeding that was entirely new in world history. By the end of the period, the resulting genetic diversity, combined with improved nutrition and humanity's new self-assurance, had produced a population that was not only vastly greater in number than at the beginning, but also of more dynamic quality.

THE   NOT-SO-GREAT   GODDESS

The divine status of a god very often depends on the secular status of his worshippers—a fact that must have become painfully clear as the tribes of the neolithic began to congregate in villages, towns, and eventually cities. The high gods of the most powerful tribes took over the supreme positions, while those of middle strength achieved a *modus vivendi* by the tactful allocation of specific roles and familial relationships. Moon gods, gods of wisdom, water gods; goddesses of summer, of birth, and of the fruits of the earth; brothers, sisters, cousins, wives—all of them were soon fitted neatly and often logically into the pantheon.

The fact that this kind of political legerdemain proved necessary during the restructuring of society that took place toward the end of the neolithic era has successfully obscured the origins of the early gods so that very little indeed is known about religion before the days of the civilized, literate Sumerians, the first people in history able to speak in their own words to later generations. Even so, many of the clay tablets that have survived five thousand years in the sands of Mesopotamia are broken, and some vital installments in the serial story of the gods are missing altogether.

When the early divinities materialize on the historical scene, they have names, occupations, and personalities that are distinctive, sometimes even eccentric. Before that, however, they are as unreal as symbolic fragments in some grand design, and as tantalizingly anonymous as the people who created them. There were certainly divinities who personified the sky and the sea, the sun and the moon, the rain and the earth, and no doubt these were common to most neolithic tribes even if their images differed. There are indications, for example, of some kind of fertility cult at Çatal Hüyük in Anatolia in about 6000 B.C., represented in one shrine by three bulls' heads in full relief, one above the other, with over them a female figure, arms and legs extended, giving birth to a bull calf.[14] This may have been a perfectly conventional neolithic way of illustrating human fertility—or it may not.

What emerge more clearly than the gods themselves are the myths in which they participated. Woven tightly into the fabric of early religion are a number of narratives that have obviously been carried on from previous times. Some are chronicles of actual events such as wars and floods, others a product of man's attempts to explain the inexplicable—the functioning of the universe. Two of these stand out in sharp relief in many of the world's religions—the creation myth and the resurrection myth.

It is impossible to say which is of greater antiquity, but in later times it was usually the creation myth (a magical explanation of the making of earth and heaven, of man, beast, bird, and fish) that preoccupied hunting peoples and pastoralists, and the resurrection myth (explaining the annual death and rebirth of the soil) that concerned agriculturalists as they waited in suspense for the bare winter earth to haze over with living green again.

During the first 3,000 years of recorded history, the agriculturalists of Mesopotamia, Egypt, and northwest India suffered a number of sometimes peaceable, sometimes warlike invasions by nomad pastoralists, male-dominated tribes with male-dominated religions, more dynamic than settled peoples because of the higher level of protein in their diet, more alert because of the mental and bodily demands of the nomadic life style. As they in turn settled, their myths and beliefs found a place in the existing structure, sometimes being superimposed on it, always leading to changes within it, and always increasing the masculine emphasis.

Their influence was not always obvious or direct. In, for example, the earliest known creation myth—that of Sumer, which survives only in a fragmentary state—the goddess Nammu, "the sea," is said to have been responsible for creating the universe by giving birth, apparently unaided, to heaven and earth. Three sets of pastoralist invaders later, many elements of the myth remained intact, but the role of Nammu (now known as Tiamat, "the salt-water ocean") had been considerably reduced. With the aid this time of Apsu, "the sweet-water ocean" she had given birth to the gods, but also to a horde of demons, scorpion men and centaurs. Ultimately, the hero god Marduk slew her with the aid of lightning, hurricane, and flame, split her down the middle "like a shell-

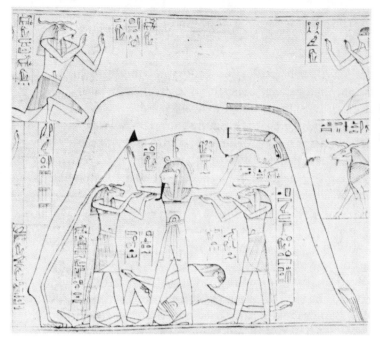

The sky goddess Nut arched over the earth god Geb. An Egyptian view of the structure of the cosmos

fish" and set up half her body to make the sky. In this revised version, a male god has taken over the responsibility for creation from the original goddess, not only because the social emphasis in the land now known as Babylon had become more masculine as a result of pastoralist incursions, but because Marduk was the god of Babylon itself, a third-rank deity who had to be upgraded if the city was to achieve the supremacy that its new (nomad) king—the great Hammurabi—desired for it.

In fact, most of the early myths went through a number of revised and enlarged editions during the centuries of their currency, for reasons that were frequently political. The high gods and goddesses often exchanged roles and even relationships, not because they themselves became more or less popular with their worshippers but because the cities they represented were temporarily dominant or submissive.

Yet though a number of powerful cities had presiding goddesses, they were never assigned supreme place in any pantheon. Of the creation myths that survive, many, indeed, feature a primordial marriage between earth god and sky goddess, a compromise perhaps between pastoral and farming beliefs. But more often a god or primordial man is solely responsible. In Egypt, where religious belief was fluid, cosmic creation assumed many forms, resulting sometimes from coitus, sometimes from divine *fiat*, sometimes from masturbation (the new-found power of the seed). In India, the early chronicles of the nomad Indo-Europeans tell how the universe was created from the sacrificed body of *purusa*, the primeval man. In the Near East, in the land of Canaan, the texts of the monotheistic Hebrews credit Jehovah with creating the world out of chaos by the power of speech alone. No creation myth, except possibly the first incomplete Sumerian one quoted above, makes any real concession to the female.

It is possible that in India, before the advent of the nomadic Indo-Europeans, there may have been a Mother Goddess. The south, to which the earlier peoples are believed to have fled after the invasion, has certainly always had a place for goddesses and female spirits.

The resurrection myths are a little more ambivalent, hinting still at the days when woman was sole child-maker and sole cultivator of the soil. Her continuing influence on productivity supplied the fertility goddess with at least some weapons in her fight against the predatory gods of the nomads, but she lost the most important battle, the last one. In the earliest form of the Sumerian resurrection myth, the goddess Inanna departs from the earth for a temporary sojourn in the underworld. Until she returns the soil remains barren. But with this single exception all the fertility deities who figure in the surviving literature are male. Nowhere in the mythology of the Near East—Sumerian, Babylonian, Egyptian, Ugaritic, Hittite, or Hebrew—is there any goddess whose power is supreme. The various pantheons certainly include female figures whose role is important, among them the shrewish Ishtar of Babylon (a version of the earlier Inanna), bloodthirsty Anath in Canaan, and patient Isis in Egypt. But all are subsidiary to husbands or brothers—Dumuzi/Tammuz, Baal, or Osiris—the dominant fertility gods whose disappearance to the nether regions is a signal for famine to strike the land and whose resurrection brings back fertility to the earth. Only the Chinese come near the concept of a pre-eminent goddess, with their view of early woman as the Great Mother, nourishing her mate through the sex act and replenishing his limited life force from her own inexhaustible supply.

There is a common misapprehension that, in Classical times at least, there were goddesses who reigned supreme, a theory based on the shaky foundation of Minoan Crete, whose art indicates the existence of a mother goddess of great significance, but about whose religious structure very little is really known. Later there was Demeter, the Earth Mother, though she rated no higher than Corn Goddess, Adonis being the true fertility deity. In imperial Rome, too, Cybele and Isis attracted enormous followings. But the general concept of the Great Goddess owes as much to the Victorian imagination as to historical truth. The men of the nineteenth century, rewriting early history with the new disciplines of anthropology and archeology as guides and a highly flattering view of women and motherhood always in their minds, adjusted their image of polytheistic religions to suit their own intellectual needs. In fact, the goddesses in question seem to have had a good deal in common with the ladies of Victorian times, rejoicing in just as much glory and just as little power.

By the Roman period, certainly, the idea of a Great Goddess had become socially irrelevant. Religion had developed into a branch of government on the one hand, and on the other into an outlet for personal desires and frustrations, cynically catered to by cults and priests who were as ready to supply the customers with what they wanted as any strip club owner today. When the cult divinity was feminine, the floor show was not very different.

By the time civilization found its feet, in fact, "pure" religion and instinctive worship were largely things of the past. It was not gods and goddesses who reigned supreme, but legislators and priests. In societies prepared to tolerate many gods—which meant virtually all early societies other than those of the Hebrews and the Zoroastrians of Iran—the varying status of gods and goddesses had more to do with politics and sales promotion than with religious feeling. And when the situation was reversed, so that religion took precedence over politics and both came under the auspices of a single divinity, there was no question of that divinity being anything but male.

If, indeed, there ever was an all-powerful female divinity, it must have been far back in the neolithic era, before woman the child-maker, woman the cultivator, abdicated her special role. Before man first discovered his sexual self-respect.[15]

PART TWO

The Near East, Egypt, and Europe, 3000 B.C.–A.D. 1100

Man's view of himself as superior in all ways to women was soon enshrined in the law and custom of the world's earliest civilizations, those of the Near East. Woman became a chattel first of her father, then of her husband, then of her son. But the situation was not yet irrevocable, for civil legislation trod a tortuous path between political aims on the one hand and polytheistic religious beliefs on the other. In Greece, partial heir to the Near Eastern tradition, the hetairai, the educated courtesans, were still able to chalk up a feminine triumph over the pederasts, and in Rome superficially respectable matrons grasped a freedom that helped to destroy the empire. But it was the monotheistic strand of Near Eastern culture that won in the end, that of the Hebrews, who had no need to compromise between religious and secular law. The Pentateuch was a mixture of Near Eastern customs and ordinances handed down from Sinai, but both had the authority of Yahweh and were thus mandatory. So the attitudes born of the neolithic era were preserved, and when the Christian Church, solidly based on Hebrew foundations, took over the Western world as successor to Rome, social and sexual relationships became fossilized in the amber of ancient Hebrew custom. To Near Eastern prejudices, the Church Fathers added their own. Sex was transformed into a sin and homosexuality into a danger to the state.

3.

*The First
Civilizations*

Recently, scholars working on the first comprehensive dictionary of the Sumerian language were disconcerted to find that, even after weeks of analysis and re-analysis, one phrase persisted in coming out as, "He put a hot fish in her navel." [1]

Mistranslation? Perhaps. But lovers throughout history have used the human navel as repository for a wide range of erotically stimulating objects, and, on balance, a hot fish seems no more improbable than the ice cubes fashionable in some circles today. On the other hand, "hot fish" may well have been ancient Sumerian slang for the penis, an organ that has attracted a fair number of picturesque colloquialisms in its time. To the late Victorians, for example, it was a goose's neck, or a live rabbit, a sausage or a hot pudding.

But though the Sumerian language may still seem ambiguous about intimate relations between the sexes, it was more explicit about public ones. Even its structure implied that man took precedence. There were words for mother, father, sister, brother, but a god was *dingir* and a goddess *dingir.ama*—literally "god mother"—while a son was *dumu* and a daughter *dumu.mi*, "son woman." The words for god and son may, in fact, have been abbreviations. "God father" may once have been opposed to "god mother" and "son man" to "son woman." The world's first written language had to be incised on small, heavy, half-dry clay tablets, and from the scribes' point of view brevity must have appeared to be the soul of commonsense. Even so, it is indicative that it was only the female specific that was retained.

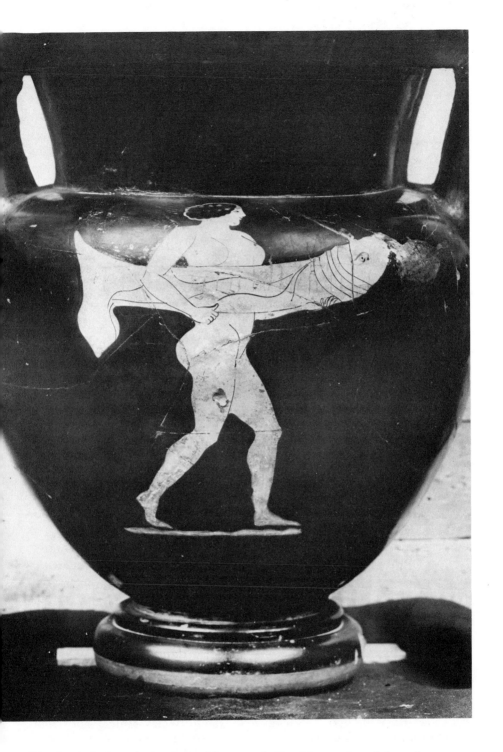

The Greeks had no doubt that a fish was a phallic object, and carried outsize images of it in Dionysiac processions.

In the case of the Sumerians' neighbors, the people of Akkad, there is no room for doubt. Akkadian was an inflected language where the general concept of a word was implied by its root syllable and given more precise definition by the insertion of additional letters. A son was *mar-u* and a daughter *mar-t-u;* a brother *ah-u* and a sister *ah-at-u.* Even a root syllable expressing an unequivocally female concept had to have the feminine "t" inserted so that the word for woman was *sinnish-t-u.* The entire Akkadian vocabulary, like modern French, was divided into two genders, the masculine, which required no separate distinguishing letter, and the feminine, which did.[2]

Language, however, is no more than an indicator of what exists, or formerly existed, in custom and law, and it is shaped by the same people who shape society. In Sumer, as in Egypt and later among the Hebrews, it was man who shaped society.

Though humanity's passion for classifying has led to many advances in civilization, particularly in the fields of science and technology, it has also done irreparable damage in terms of human relations, permitting people to be grouped by race, color, and sex, and encouraging politically convenient generalizations that take no account of them as individuals who live and die, love and hate, dominate and submit, on an entirely personal level. But the legislator cannot govern according to the multifarious individual preferences of the governed, and the social historian has no way of evaluating the emotional interaction of two anonymous cogs in the wheel of history. To say that the male sex has been dominant in the great majority of societies ever since written records began is to ignore any personal vibrations between the sexes. But there is no way of estimating the effect of those vibrations except in the rare cases where biographical or autobiographical details survive.

In the days of the early civilizations it cannot have been great. By cultivating a way of life that legally and socially favored the male sex, the people of the ancient Near East also created a climate in which it was easy for the man to dominate. When all social forces conspired to anchor a woman to her home, to limit her acquaintance to her family, to forbid her to appear before strangers, the result was to imprison her mind as effectively as her body. As in later times, there may well have been strong-minded women who focussed all their energies, their ambitions, their intensity of purpose on their husbands and children. With uncomfortable results for all. But if some men paid for public dominance with their own private peace, it can only be conjectured.

No more than a handful of women made any mark on early history. There was a First Dynasty queen of Egypt, Meryet-nit, around 3000 B.C., sovereign in her own right, who is believed to have been important in the precarious political situation that followed the unification of northern and southern Egypt. Fifteen hundred years later came Queen Hatshepsut, a widow who reigned from 1505 until 1483 B.C. and did much to expand Egypt's trading activities; for political reasons, Eighteenth-Dynasty artists usually represented her in masculine costumes and poses, even wearing the symbolic royal beard.[3] Other names in the records of ancient Egypt include Tiy, Nefretiti, Arsinoe, Berenike, and Cleopatra, while in Assyria history speaks of Naqi'a, wife of Sennacherib, and Sammuramat (Semiramis), libeled by Herodotus as "the most beautiful, most cruel, most powerful and most lustful of Oriental queens." The Hebrews, still unrepentant pastoralists as far as their womenfolk were concerned, had no queens—only wives, mothers, and daughters of kings. It took real force of personality to win such women as Jezebel, Tamar, Abigail, and the heroic Deborah a place in the scriptures.[4]

According to Egyptian law, men and women were virtually equal, but although this allowed women a freedom to come and go that was to scandalize the Greeks, it was a meaningless equality for most. Then, as now, only money brought independence, and only inheritance was likely to provide it. There were very few ways in which a woman could earn a living. The only self-supporting professions seem to have been those of dancer and musician, which, more often than not, required a talent for prostitution as well as music. Otherwise, woman was either a wife or a slave, and it depended on the man of her house whether her life was easy or hard. Skeletal evidence suggests that lower-class women submitted to a good deal of heavy physical drudgery and that wife-beating may not have been uncommon; a high incidence of women's arm fractures studied by medical anthropologists show them to have been of the type that usually results from guarding the head against a blow.[5] And when a woman's husband was convicted of a crime, Egyptian penal law punished her and her children as well, usually by making them slaves. (The Maya of Central America, in late medieval times, had the same custom.)

In Babylon, although the legal position of women was inferior, their scope for employment was wider. There were women scribes as early as the third millennium B.C., the world's first stenographers; diviners, too, and necromancers, "wise women" and free-lance maids-of-all-work, employable by the day. Hairdressers, shopkeepers, singers, specialty cooks, brewers, wet nurses, water carriers, spinners, weavers, lamp tenders—women held down all these positions, few of them challenging, some of them menial, but all offering an escape from the tyranny of hearth and home. Some women devoted themselves to the service of the gods, and in exchange for their vows of chastity received freedom of the mind. *Naditu* priestesses engaged in commerce on equal, perhaps more than equal, terms with men. They bought, sold, and hired out; lent money and grain; invested, imported, exported, dealt in slaves, managed land and people, played from their cloisters an essential and important part in the expanding economy of the country.

Hebrew women had less latitude than the Babylonians, fractionally more than the Egyptians. They could own property, but rarely seem to have done so. On their own account they could be servants, perfumers, cooks, bakers, and—in the early days—prostitutes. And that was all. But on their husbands' account they were expected to be a great deal more.[6]

THE MARRIED STATE

"A good wife who can find?" asked the Book of Proverbs (31, 10ff.), and the list of qualifications that followed amply justified the question. A good wife had to seek wool and flax and food, rise before dawn to care for her family and instruct her servants, buy fields and plant vineyards, keep accounts, work late into the night. She had to use the distaff and spindle, help the needy, clothe her household in scarlet and herself in linen and purple, make and sell linen garments, look on the future with optimism, be wise, kind, a conscientious housekeeper, never idle. Charm and beauty were not required—the first being deceitful and the second vain—but fruitfulness was essential. "Like arrows in the hand of a warrior are the sons of one's youth. Happy is the man who has his quiver full of them!" (Psalm 127, 4–5).

In return, the Hebrew wife was granted the right to share her husband's favor with one or more secondary wives and concubines, to be divorced out of hand if she offended him, and stoned to death if she strayed from the path of marital fidelity. She was, perhaps, slightly worse off here than her contemporaries in Babylon and Egypt, for in Babylon a husband had the choice of pardoning his wife's adultery and allowing her to live, while in Egypt (provided she had not actually been caught in the act) her own oath of innocence was enough to clear her.

In Egypt, too, it was possible for a woman to divorce her husband, a dispensation not granted to the women of Babylon or the early Israelites (or, indeed, to most Europeans until the nineteenth century). The most common ground for divorce was the wife's barrenness, but a Babylonian husband could divorce his wife for being a spendthrift or, if he preferred, reduce her to the status of slave.[7]

Somewhere around 2350 B.C., the Sumerian monarch Urukagina claimed the credit for having put an end to the custom of polyandry, although there is no evidence that it had ever been generally practiced in Sumer. Certainly, by the Babylonian period there was no question of a woman having more than one husband (at a time) anywhere in the Near East. Polygyny, however, was quite another matter, and it was the Hebrews who were most deeply dedicated to it. Even as late as the first century A.D., the Jewish historian Josephus recorded, "It is our ancient custom to have many wives at the same time." [8] Solomon, who ruled from c. 955 to 935 B.C., was reputed to have had 700 of them, as well as 300 concubines, and when the Assyrians sent an army against Jerusalem in 700 B.C., Ezekiah bought it off with 30 talents of gold, 800 of silver, and "all kinds of treasures, as well as his daughters, his harem, his male and female musicians." [9]

In Egypt, polygyny was common during the third millennium B.C. but appears gradually to have given way to monogamy, partly for economic reasons, except among the pharaohs themselves. It was a monogamy, however, that made full allowance for supplementary concubines and slaves, and the same was true in Babylon. There, a man was not allowed more than one fully accredited wife at a time, but secondary wives and concubines were a matter for his purse and his conscience. Domestic harmony may have imposed limits. The term for secondary wife was *ashshetu* or *esirtu*, meaning "rival." (That the Hebrews had the same problem is clear from the name given by the rabbis to secondary wives—*sarot*, or "jealous associates.") There was one unusual provision in Babylonian law; if a man's legal wife was barren, it was incumbent on her to provide her husband with a substitute child bearer.[10]

In general, whether she was Egyptian, Babylonian or Jewish, the "free" woman—as distinct from the slave, whose lot appears to have been very little worse—was the property of her father during childhood and of her husband from adolescence on. Unless by some fortunate chance love intervened, she was to her husband essentially a mother for his children and a housekeeper, a kind of upper servant to be treated well unless she failed in her duties, in which case she could be dismissed or pensioned off according to inclination. Although she might remain in possession of her dowry, might even inherit from her husband, the financial provisions made for her had a grudging note. Money and property were for the anxiously desired sons, not for women. As the *Maxims* of the Egyptian scribe Ani put it, "Marry a wife when you are young, she will bring your son into the world. Let her give birth for you while you are young. It is wise to make children; happy the man whose family is numerous." [11]

This overall pattern of relationships, established in the Near East well over 3,000 years ago, was to persist not only in Europe but in Asia, Africa, and the Americas, with minor variations according to time and place, until the middle years of the nineteenth century.

MALADIES D'AMOUR

The fact that so many people in the ancient world took Ani's advice about marrying young was almost certainly responsible for a number of the "diseases of women" mentioned in medical treatises. In Mesopotamia and among the Hebrews, marriages appear to have been consummated when the girl was 11 or 12 years old; in Egypt, according to one authority, sometimes as early as six.[12]

Egyptian physicians, unfortunately, were not strong on diagnosis, and the Kahun Papyrus, the earliest surviving medical work (which dates from about 1900 B.C.), makes it clear that they had not yet learned to distinguish the symptom from the disease. When one modern German scholar made an intensive study of the gynecological and obstetrical material in the early papyri, he found it possible to identify only a handful of ailments. Undoubtedly Egyptian women suffered from digestive problems—"the urge to vomit" and "a swelling of matter that runs in the body" were among the diseases listed—and irritation of the genital organs seems not to have been uncommon, the "lips of the vagina" being described as "ill" or possibly ulcerated. Prolapse of the uterus was also known and, for once, adequately described. "In the case of a woman with backache and a dragging-down feeling between her thighs," said the Kahun Papyrus, "tell her it is a dropped womb." [13]

The papyri were rather better informed about men's sexual problems, including that hardy perennial, impotence. Doctors noted cases where the patient was "incapable of doing his duty" (the ancient world was no less prone to euphemism than the modern), and soothsayers sometimes threatened a man with having his "virility melt away before his partner." The protohistoric lover was also liable to "copulation sickness," which was not an acute form of postcoital melancholy but a general term for venereal infections such as gonorrhea and abscesses on the testicles. It is not clear whether the Egyptians knew how venereal diseases were transmitted, but the Akkadians did. "These white pimples . . . he has caught them from being in bed with a woman." [14] One early source also describes something very close to infectious hepatitis, which researchers now suspect of being an infection to which homosexuals are particularly vulnerable.[15]

The Near Eastern preoccupation with sons meant that the problems of conception merited special study. Pregnancy testing was as commonplace 4,000 years ago as it is today, even if the results may not always have been as reliable. It was recommended to the Egyptian doctor that he put wheat and barley seeds into separate cloth purses and then tell the woman to "pass her water on it every day . . . If both sprout she will give birth . . . If they do not sprout, she will not give birth at all." Assuming the test was positive, would the child be a boy or a girl? If the wheat sprouted first, it would be a boy, if the barley, a girl. (Wheat was a more valued grain than barley.) Mesopotamian medical men argued, less persuasively, that "if the forehead of the mother-to-be is heavily freckled, the child she is carrying is a boy." But they did have a sure test for permanent sterility. "To know a woman who will bear from a woman who will not bear: Water-melon, pounded and bottled with the milk of a woman who has borne a male child; make it into a dose. To be swallowed by the woman. If she vomits, she will bear. If she belches, she will never bear." [16]

For 30 days after giving birth the Babylonian woman was ritually unclean, as she was during her monthly period. For the regulation six days during which she wore a sanitary towel (in Sumerian *tùg.nig.dára.úsh.a,* or "blood bandage"), she contaminated everything she touched, whether the bread she made or the man who "approached" her.* She was forbidden by royal edict to go anywhere near the king at such a time. After her period, she was instructed to purify herself either by taking a bath or washing her hands, which casts some doubt on the Egyptians' reputed enthusiasm for daily hygiene. (So does the fact that the pharaoh Rameses II was noted not only for the number of his children—he fathered upwards of 170—but for the number of his blackheads.[17])

The Hebrews, too, favored ritual hygiene more than the sanitary kind. They bathed neither more nor less frequently than their neighbors, but the information had been handed down from Sinai that if a man touched the bed, chair, or clothes of a menstruating woman he would be unclean for the remainder of the day, and that if he himself had bodily discharges or emissions of semen he was to be regarded as unclean for seven days thereafter. It almost seems as if the people of the Near East might have been groping toward some recognition of the idea of quarantine.[18]

THE SIGN OF THE COVENANT

Modern scholars sometimes argue that circumcision—the minor surgical operation of cutting away the retractable envelope of skin that sheathes the tip of the penis—was originally carried out for reasons of hygiene,** because when clothing was loose and scanty,

---

* Nineteenth-century European doctors still believed that the touch of a menstruating woman would turn a ham rancid (see page 352).

** There is more than a touch of hindsight about this view. The benefits of circumcision (as a preventive of penile carcinoma) were so widely recommended in the United States in the mid-twentieth century that a substantial majority of American boys were routinely circumcised in the hospital after birth. In 1966 the sex researchers Masters and Johnson reported that, out of 300 male volunteers for sexual observation, they could find only 35 uncircumcised.

grit could find its way under the foreskin and cause irritation and sometimes damage. Minor changes in loincloth design, it might be thought, would have been a simpler way of dealing with this problem. Furthermore, the operation was most common in Egypt and Africa, and was not performed until just before adolescence—rather late in the day if hygiene was the object. Everything, in fact, points to a puberty rite: the age of the patient, the triumphant exposure of the masculine glans, and the removal of the flaccid folds of skin that to the envious primitive male may have had something of a feminine look about them.

No one knows how widespread the practice of circumcision was in dynastic Egypt. Archeological and literary sources, mummified remains, paintings and statues of nude figures, offer conflicting evidence, but it does not appear to have been universal, nor to have had class connotations. Priests might be circumcised, and so might shepherds, but pharaohs sometimes were and sometimes not.[19]

According to the first-century B.C. Greek geographer Strabo, the Egyptians, as well as circumcising the males, "excised" the

A circumcision operation in Egypt, c. 2300 B.C.

females. They still do. What is often (inaccurately) called female circumcision has had a variety of meanings throughout history. Sometimes it has entailed no more than breaking the virginal hymen, a ritual defloration; sometimes it has meant complete excision of the clitoris and all or part of the labia of the vagina, the sensitive external sexual tissues. In its extreme form it is painful and dangerous, both physically and psychologically. The purpose appears to have been to discourage promiscuity by depriving the woman of the areas most susceptible to pleasurable stimulus. In a recent survey conducted by the Cairo Family Planning Association, 90 percent of the young women interviewed had had some part of the clitoris and labia removed.[20]

Though circumcision may have been perfectly commonplace in Egypt—as it was later to be among the Maya, the Aztecs, the Incas, and in some parts of Polynesia—it was not practiced in Mesopotamia until the Hebrews made it an article of faith. Possibly they brought the idea back from Egypt at the time of the exodus. Israel's lawgivers, however, transferred it from adolescence to infancy, made it mandatory, and represented it as an eternal symbol of God's covenant with the Jewish people, thus turning a pagan rite into an index of grace. It is occasionally argued that, to begin with, circumcision was used as a mark of the tribe, a sign that would distinguish the children of Israel from their polytheistic neighbors; if so, it was a singularly inconvenient one in a fully clothed society where "indecent exposure" was a cardinal sin. Nor did it permit evasion or denial of race when the circumcised fell into the hands of enemies. Something like the *tikka* mark of the Hindus, the sprig of herb stuck in a Highlander's bonnet, or the characteristic handshake of the Masonic order, would have been a more satisfactory recognition symbol.

The probability is that circumcision was precisely what it claimed to be, the symbol of a blood covenant. God said to Abraham, "This is my covenant, which you shall keep, between me and you and your descendants after you: Every male among you shall be circumcised. You shall be circumcised in the flesh of your foreskins, and it shall be a sign of the covenant between me and you" (Genesis 17, 9-11). When a blood covenant was made between men, the blood was usually drawn from whichever limb happened to be most convenient. But God's covenant was with Abraham's descendants as well as with Abraham himself. For it to take on full meaning, the blood had to come from Abraham's reproductive organs.

Psychoanalysts today believe that Jewish circumcision, performed when a boy is in a state of utter dependence, appears to the child as a continuing reminder of that dependence—at once the mark and the cause of it—and leads him as he grows up to fear an extension of it, inducing castration anxiety in a mild or acute form. It is a neat theory, even if it does not account for the castration anxiety from which, according to Freud, the uncircumcised also suffer.[21] In Biblical times, it should perhaps be added that there were enough eunuchs around the Near East to produce a thriving crop of castration complexes without benefit of circumcision (see page 247).

A MATTER OF PRODUCTIVITY

Whatever the truth of the castration complex theory, there is no doubt that the early Hebrews were deeply preoccupied by their testicles.* In the only verses in the whole of the Old Testament that forbid a woman to help her husband, the Book of Deuteronomy says, "When men fight with one another, and the wife of the one draws near to rescue her husband from the hand of him who is beating him, and puts out her hand and seizes him by the private parts, then you shall cut off her hand" (25, 11-12). It seems that other Near Eastern women were also prone to reach for a man's testicles in a brawl, for the Assyrians, too, legislated against it. "If a woman has crushed a man's testicle in an affray, one of her fingers shall be cut off; and if although a physician has bound it up, the second testicle is affected with it and becomes inflamed or if she has crushed the second testicle in the affray, both of her [breasts or nipples] shall be torn off." [22]

The law also exacted a penalty for injury to a pregnant woman. "When men strive together," said the Book of Exodus, "and hurt a woman with child, so that there is a miscarriage, and yet no harm follows, the one who hurt her shall be fined . . . If any harm follows, then you shall give life for life, eye for eye, tooth for

---

* In Israel today, men with injured genitals are barred from marrying born Jewesses; they may, however, marry converts to Judaism or bastards.

tooth ...." (21, 22-24). In Assyria, any man who struck a wellborn lady and "caused her to cast the fruit of her womb" was liable to a heavy fine, a beating, and a month's forced labor; if the lady was not wellborn, the only penalty was a fine. The Hittites were coolly businesslike. Ten shekels of silver if she was near full term, only five if she had not yet passed the sixth moon month.[23]

Abortion was a criminal offense. For an Assyrian woman, the penalty was "to be impaled and not to be given burial." If she died of the abortion, the same punishment was meted out to her corpse. But no one was much interested in infanticide, presumably because it was a fate usually reserved for girl children, while miscarriage or abortion might prevent a boy from being brought into the world. Only the Hebrews ruled against it by forbidding children to be given to Molech—not a demon, as was once thought, but a technical term for child sacrifice—which amounted to much the same thing.[24]

As such laws show, the people of the early civilizations were concerned about productivity, particularly the Hebrews. Only parental fertility and adequate child care could strengthen and multiply the chosen people, the children of Israel, and the breeding rules that were imposed and the sexual practices that were banned were both designed to attain that end.

The first-century Jewish historian Josephus said, "The Law recognizes no sexual connections, except the natural union of husband and wife, and that only for the procreation of children," and there were various provisions, positive and negative, to enforce this principle. It was ordained, for example, that a newly married man should be free of military and business obligations for a year "to be happy with his wife whom he has taken." The object was to insure that the newlyweds started their family right away, although one unintended side effect may have been to encourage an annual increase in the number of rich men's new wives.

The other side of the coin was thunderous denunciation of all types of nonproductive sex. While Babylon was prepared to recognize whole corporations of homosexual prostitutes, the Lord had said to the people of Israel, "If a man lies with a male as with a woman, both of them have committed an abomination; they shall be put to death, their blood is upon them." And, without any perceptible change of tone, "If a man lies with a beast, he shall be put to death; and you shall kill the beast. If a woman approaches any beast and lies with it, you shall kill the woman and the beast." Zoophilia—sexual intercourse with cattle or any of the (larger) domesticated animals—was not uncommon in pastoral societies but, when the nomads began to settle down, came to be seen as a custom belonging to the bad old days. Even the tolerant Hittites imposed the death penalty for it—in an attempt, perhaps, to break people of the habit.[25]

CONTRACEPTION

In the course of time, the command to "be fruitful and multiply" lost some of its force. Nonproductive sex in the forms in which it had been denounced from Sinai remained anathema, but when the Jews were compelled to scatter into new lands large families became a liability and the idea of birth limitation seemed increasingly attractive. By this time, 300 years before the Christian era, contraceptive techniques had a long and erratic history.

Not until the end of the seventeenth century A.D. were scientists to discover that seminal fluid was not just a liquid but a suspension medium for millions of individual sperm, and it was more than another 200 years before they learned that a single one of these was all that was needed to accomplish fertilization (see pages 341–46). Until then, those who advocated or practiced contraception had not been aware of the scale of the challenge.

Basically, however, even the early Egyptians had the right ideas. Their object was to prevent the seminal fluid from entering the womb either by mopping it up before it reached there (by trapping it in a spongy or absorbent fabric inserted in the vagina) or by blocking off the cervical opening that connects the vagina with the womb (uterus). In the prescriptions that survive from dynastic times, it is not always clear which method is intended, some of the ingredients still not having been identified. The Kahun Papyrus, which includes the first such recipes, suggests mixing crocodile dung with a paste of *auyt* (unidentified) and inserting the result in the vagina, rather like a tampon. Other ideas were to use a glutinous compound of honey and natron (sodium carbonate), or a preparation of *auyt*-gum.

Initial revulsion apart—and, in fact, the contraceptive recipes are quite fragrant in comparison with most of the Egyptian pharmacopoeia—did they work? No one is very sure, especially since early chemistry (like early cookery) never troubled to list quantities so that it is difficult to judge the finished texture. The crocodile-dung prescription may, for example, have had an absorbent texture, in which case it would be used in the vagina to soak up seminal fluid; more compacted, it would do as a cervical plug, perhaps even having enough resilience to expand and contract with the vaginal and uterine muscles, which would give it increased effectiveness.

Three hundred years after the Kahun Papyrus, the Papyrus Ebers suggested soaking a pad of lint in a mixture of acacia tips and honey and using it to block the opening into the uterus. It may be noted that none of the surviving recommendations for barrier devices, either at this time or later, explains how they are to be maneuvered into position. It was not something that could be achieved with the fingers, which are far too short. The physician, or the woman herself, must have used some kind of applicator, or the plug may have been quite large, filling the whole rear projection of the vagina as well as the part round the opening into the uterus. In this case, a lint base would certainly be preferable to one of degradable crocodile dung, for ease of removal as well as insertion.

Contraception appeared essentially as a mechanical challenge, but Egypt was the home of chemical ingenuity, and Egyptian physicians may well have recognized—though without knowing why—that certain chemical influences improved the effect of mechanical contraceptives. Scientists today, well informed not only about the existence of sperm, but about their mobility and sensitivity to various substances, are aware that oily or gluey media reduce the sperm's mobility, that acidity helps to discourage fertilization, that lactic acid will stop a sperm dead in its tracks, and that salt is also an excellent spermicide. In the Egyptian recipes, the honey and *auyt*-gum must certainly have slowed the sperm down. More interestingly, acacia tips, by a natural process, produce lactic acid, which is the active ingredient still favored in most spermicidal creams and jellies today. Modern authorities, however, suspect that the Egyptians would have done better to use elephant rather than crocodile dung, the latter being alkaline and therefore favorable to sperm survival. Elephant dung is mildly acid; it was still being recommended for contraceptives in the Islamic world as late as the thirteenth century.[26]

There were, of course, other prescriptions that savored more of optimism than scientific conviction. One papyrus mentioned "fumigating" the vagina before intercourse with the drug *mimi*; on the following four mornings the patient had to swallow a decoction of "grease, *m'atet* herb, sweet ale" boiled together, which sounds laxative rather than contraceptive.

All these methods foreshadowed the modern cervical cap and diaphragm, but the ancient Egyptians and many generations of their successors were also busily engaged on research aimed at discovering the ultimate contraceptive, the Pill. An astonishing variety of leaves, herbs, and roots, as well as other less prepossessing substances, have been pulverized, liquefied, and swallowed during the course of history with the object of reducing fertility. They are generally dismissed by medical historians as magical nonsense, but they can be more fairly described as unsuccessful experiments. There was usually some logic in the ingredients used, even if it was the logic of religious faith rather than laboratory knowledge.

The early world had nothing to learn as far as general approaches to family limitation were concerned. As well as mechanical and chemical methods of contraception, they practiced abortion, infanticide, abstinence, and nonproductive sex—homosexuality, zoophilia, and probably heterosexual anal intercourse—tried to depress fertility through prolonged breast-feeding, and used anaphrodisiacs to immobilize the semen at its source by killing the urge. There is no way of estimating the relative popularity of the various methods, but all later history suggests that infanticide was not the last, but the first resort.

Where people were prepared to make a serious attempt at contraception, they seem usually to have used *coitus interruptus* (withdrawal), a cost-free and uncomplicated system that has probably been more widespread than any other since the days when semen was first discovered to be essential to conception. The disadvantage of it—apart from its unreliability—was that it depended on the man, and it was very often the woman who was more anxious to avoid conceiving. Indeed, one reason why experiments continued to be made with contraceptive potions, even when they proved ineffective, was that no other means offered woman the possibility of controlling her fertility for herself; it seems unlikely that linen pads or crocodile-dung diaphragms would have escaped a husband's notice.

For the Hebrews, *coitus interruptus* had another disadvantage. The *Torah*, the first five books of the Old Testament, on which all Jewish law rested, enjoined *men* to be fruitful and multiply. If family size was to be controlled this meant that it was up to the woman to take precautions. The sponge appears to have been acceptable. Indeed, some authorities declared its use to be compulsory for girls of between 11 and 12, pregnant women—because it was believed that a second fertilization was possible and that this would damage the fetus that was already developing—and for nursing mothers. Alternatively, a wife could do what prostitutes did after intercourse and jump up and down in the hope of expelling the semen; or she could swallow "the cup of roots." Raban Yohanan explained how to prepare the third-century version of this multipurpose brew. Alexandrian gum, liquid alum, and garden crocus, "each in the weight of a denar," had to be mixed together to form the foundation. If this was mixed with three cups of wine it was useless as a contraceptive but good for gonorrhea; on the other hand, if mixed with two cups of beer it would not only sterilize the consumer but cure jaundice as well. Only women were permitted to drink "the cup of roots."

One Biblical personality who practiced *coitus interruptus* in defiance of the *Torah* was Onan—and he was struck dead on the spot. Onan's was a case that gave rise to a number of misinterpretations in later times, and a good deal of confusion as to what his sin actually was. It was the ancient custom among Jews that when a woman married she married not only her husband but his family. She had been bought and paid for, and if her husband died she became a liability; more, if she had not yet borne him children, his death cut him off as conclusively as if he had never lived. Levirate marriage was the solution. If an elder brother died without leaving an heir, it was the younger brother's responsibility to take the widow to wife and to rear their firstborn son as the legitimate child of the dead man.* Onan, however, rebelled.

According to the Book of Genesis (38, 8–10), the eldest son of Judah died without issue, and "Judah said to Onan, Go in unto thy brother's wife, and marry her, and raise up seed to thy brother. And Onan knew that the seed should not be his; and it came to

---

* A very similar system operated in India until the beginning of the Christian era, and the Incas of Peru also encouraged it in the fifteenth century.

pass, when he went in unto his brother's wife, that he spilled it on the ground, lest he should give seed to his brother. And the thing which he did displeased the Lord: wherefore he slew him . . ."

What precisely was it that displeased the Lord? *Coitus inter-ruptus?* Masturbation? Or refusal to obey the law of levirate? Catholic theologians in later times, determined to outlaw all forms of contraception other than abstention, were to come out strongly in favor of the first. A Lausanne physician, S.A. Tissot, in 1760 decided on the second and wrote a book entitled *On Onanism, or a physical dissertation on the ills produced by masturbation,* with the result that later generations blamed Onan for originating the horrible sin of "self-abuse." * The rabbis, however, decreed that this downfall was a result of wilful disobedience to the levirate law—a necessary conclusion, for disobedience to the law was not desirable, whereas *coitus interruptus* sometimes was. While a wife was still breast-feeding a previous child, it was, said one rabbi, the husband's duty "to thresh inside and winnow outside." [27]

Long after the days of Onan and the woman he refused to inseminate, the law of Halizah was evolved to settle problems of this kind. Levirate marriage could thereafter be abjured, provided it was done in a public court and with appropriate ceremony. But it remains an odd fact that, in a society totally antipathetic to incest, the emotionally incestuous practice of brother/sister-in-law marriage should have been not only acceptable but required.

THE   OEDIPUS   COMPLEX

On other levels, the Hebrews rigorously observed the taboos handed down from Sinai, couched though they were in language of uncharacteristic gentility. "You shall not uncover the nakedness of your sister . . . You shall not uncover the nakedness of your son's daughter or your daughter's daughter . . . You shall not uncover the nakedness of a woman and of her daughter, and you shall not take her son's daughter or her daughter's daughter to

---

* In 1976 the Vatican, leaving Onan out of it, still condemned masturbation (in language of majestic obscurity) in its *Declaration on Certain Questions concerning Sexual Ethics* because "the deliberate use of the sexual faculty outside normal conjugal relations essentially contradicts the finality of the faculty."

Portrait study of Akhenaten

uncover her nakedness. . . ." (Leviticus 18, 7-18). By the time the
rabbis had finished with them, the incest laws also forbade un-
covering the nakedness of one's "maternal grandmother's paternal
brother's wife." [28]

Since it was always the man who was assumed to take the
initiative, such laws were addressed primarily to him. Kinship with
his in-laws took effect not just from the moment of marriage, but
from the moment of betrothal, and any contravention of the incest taboo brought penalties ranging from flagellation to stoning
or burning to death.

How much of the Hebrew's attitude to incest dated back to
prehistoric custom, how much was attributable to the influence of

their Assyrian and Hittite neighbors (who also held it to be an abomination), and how much was a reaction against their memories of Egypt, where they lived at a time when the hated pharaohs regarded it almost as a royal requirement, is difficult to say. It may even be possible that the Jews, obsessed by a need for sons to strengthen the race, remembered however distantly that the incestuous marriages of the pharaohs had been productive only of daughters.

For long stretches of Egyptian history, royal blood ran more purely in the veins of women than of men, and it was possible for a woman to reign in her own right. But such a situation was not popular and usually led to dynastic trouble. Sometimes, a pharaoh's primary marriage would produce only daughters, but he might have a son by a secondary wife, whose claim to the succession, legitimate but weak, was best reinforced by marriage to someone with a more immediate claim, such as one of his half sisters. According to modern geneticists, this kind of alliance would again tend to produce only daughters, so that the whole situation would repeat itself in the next generation, beginning one of those occasional sequences of incestuous marriages for which the pharaohs became notorious particularly during the second millennium B.C. and again in the days of the Greco-Egyptian Ptolemies.

Though the complexities of pharaonic relationships make accurate analysis difficult (not to say contentious), the British biologist C.D. Darlington has produced a tentative genealogical map of the Eighteenth Dynasty (1570–1320 B.C.). The most interesting part of it relates to Amenophis IV, who renamed himself Akhenaten—the "mystic pharaoh" who made a dramatic but unsuccessful attempt to destroy the political, social, and religious power of the priests of Amon at Thebes.

Akhenaten started off with certain disadvantages. From statues and portraits medical historians have diagnosed tuberculosis, hyperpituaritism, hypogonadism, and acromegaly (or possibly a chromophobe adenoma).[29] Nor was his emotional life any healthier. His first wife appears to have been his mother, Tiy, a strong-minded lady from Nubia; they had one daughter. Then he married his maternal cousin, Nefretiti, and fathered three more daughters. His third and fourth wives were not blood relatives, and there was one son of each marriage, the second of whom was to rule as the boy pharaoh Tutankhamon. Akhenaten's fifth and last marriage was to the third of his own daughters by Nefretiti; they had one daughter who died young. Although none of Akhenaten's own marriages was necessary to reinforce his claim to the throne, both his sons found it necessary to marry their half sisters. In the first case there were no children of the marriage; in the second there were two, both of them stillborn.[30]

Historically, Akhenaten's only real success was as patron of a new and refreshing, though short-lived, style in art and architecture. Yet he was to achieve immortality not only as one of the interesting but irrelevant eccentrics who litter the pages of the past, but as the prototype of Oedipus, central character of Boeotian myth, great tragic figure of Sophoclean drama, and symbol of the particular type of parent-fixation neurosis that was to be a cornerstone of psychoanalytic theory for the first 30 years of the twentieth century.

Akhenaten, unlike Oedipus, did not kill his father; instead, he obliterated all traces of his rule. But in the hidden childhood, the encounters with the sphinx-oracle, predictions of death, the marriage to his mother, the deposition by his son, and his own exile, there are strong parallels. It seems unlikely that Akhenaten suffered from the guilt in which Sophocles (and Freud) enshrouded him, but there appears to be little doubt that it was, indeed, his own curious tale that was carried across the Mediterranean almost 3,000 years ago to become enshrined in Western literature and tradition.[31]

THE SECOND-OLDEST PROFESSION

If the word "profession" is taken to imply specialization on a more or less full-time basis, then the shaman, or witch doctor, was probably ahead of the prostitute by thousands, or even tens of thousands, of years. But when the shaman donned the garb of priest in the very earliest days of civilization, the prostitute also found—in the temple—a comfortable niche that she was to inhabit for a very long time to come.

Much historical material on sex is tangential rather than direct, coming from the law, medicine, and literature. But the law is more concerned with what is inadmissible than what is admissible;

medicine with what is abnormal rather than normal; and literature, where it is not making deliberate concessions to romance,
caricature, dogma, or the dramatic unities, with the extraordinary
rather than the ordinary.

Fortunately, an occasional breath of earthy realism creeps in,
however unintentionally. The *Epic of Gilgamesh,* for example, is
perhaps one of the most striking epic tales of the ancient world
and one which encapsulates the whole philosophy of Sumer and
its neighboring states 4,000 years ago. The hero, Gilgamesh, is two-
thirds god and one-third man, and the tale of his adventures begins with the people of his city, Uruk, muttering complaints
against him. "His lust leaves no virgin to her lover, neither the
warrior's daughter nor the wife of the nobleman." To take his
mind off such undiplomatic activities, the goddess Aruru creates
Enkidu, a huge, brutish, hairy creature who lives on the steppe
lands among the beasts, a symbol of the pastoral nomads and a
menace to Gilgamesh's subjects. Gilgamesh, nobody's fool, de-
cides force is not the answer to this threat and sends instead "a
harlot from the temple of love, a child of pleasure" to find and
tame him.

The harlot, duly encountering Enkidu, "made herself naked
and welcomed his eagerness; she incited the savage to love and
taught him the woman's art. For six days and seven nights they lay
together," and afterward "Enkidu was grown weak." When he
recovered, the harlot described to him the wonders of civilization
and "led him like a mother" away from the steppes and down to
the plains.

The profession of harlot carried no stigma in Sumerian times,
or in Babylonian. In the days of Hammurabi (c. 1750 B.C.), temples were staffed by priests, servants, and artisans, and by a number of highly respectable priestesses and nuns, often from the best
families, as well as sacred prostitutes who acted as congenial intermediaries between worshipper and deity. The exact purpose of
sacred prostitution is obscure; it may well have had its origin in
fertility rituals. But by historical times, the sacred prostitutes'
earnings accounted for a substantial part of the temples' income.

A thousand years after Hammurabi, the Greek historian Herodotus was confused by the sheer number of temple prostitutes.
"Every woman who is a native of the country," he reported, "must
once in her life go and sit in the temple and there give herself to a

strange man. . . . She is not allowed to go home until a man has thrown a silver coin into her lap and taken her outside to lie with him. . . . The woman has no privilege of choice—she must go with the first man who throws her the money. When she has lain with him, her duty to the goddess is discharged and she may go home." Characteristically unable to resist improving on a good story, he added, "Tall, handsome women soon manage to get home again, but the ugly ones stay a long time before they can fulfil the condition which the law demands, some of them, indeed, as much as three or four years." [32] Despite this touch of verisimilitude, Babylonian prostitution does not appear to have been a game for amateurs, and there is nothing to suggest that either the law or the husbands of Babylon were any more tolerant of extramarital activity on the part of wives than the laws or husbands of any other country.

Sacred prostitutes were classified into groups, though the specialities associated with some of the classifications remain obscure. The *harimtu* (the word is related to "harem") seems to have been a semisecular prostitute, the *qadishtu* a sacred one, and the *ishtaritu* specifically a servant of the goddess Ishtar. One Babylonian father advised his son, "Never take a *harimtu* to wife, her husbands are beyond counting; nor an *ishtaritu*, she is reserved for the gods."

It was often a girl's parents who set her to the trade, probably because it cost less than seeing her safely married, but some *harimtu* were married women who had chosen or been forced to leave their husbands. Sacred courtesans were not permitted to have a job *and* a husband, so marriage meant retirement; and although some girls never married, a number of them resigned in order to look after the children they had acquired in the course of their professional life. Some, however, never retired. One Babylonian proverb refers to an elderly prostitute's objection to being regarded as "obsolete" when the tools of her trade are still in perfect working order.[33]

The higher-rank prostitutes appear to have been accommodated in a special part of the temple, but others lived out and picked up clients by parading the "streets, crossroads, and public places." Their center of operations was not the temple but the tavern, usually one situated near the quay, the busiest part of town. The tavern keepers had a special ritual designed to please

Babylonian prostitute soliciting
from an upper window

Ishtar, the goddess of love, and encourage her to send plenty of customers to "this tavern, her cherished abode." The sacredness of the tavern courtesan, in effect, appears to have been strictly nominal, her dedication to Ishtar neither more nor less meaningful than that of the modern motorist to the St. Christopher whose medal gleams from his dashboard.[34] No one in the least objected to her soliciting in the streets, and the Assyrians (like many other peoples) virtually forced her to advertise. "A common harlot shall not veil herself [as other women do]; her head shall be uncovered. Anyone who sees a common harlot veiled shall arrest her. . . . They shall beat her fifty strokes with rods, and they shall pour pitch on her head." [35]

As far as it is possible to discover, "concubines of the gods" in Egypt had no sexual role but were responsible for escorting whichever queen or princess bore the title of "Divine Consort" on ceremonial occasions. Herodotus said, "It was the Egyptians who first made it a matter of religious observance not to have intercourse with women in temples," [36] but whether or not this was true there seems to have been little need for organized prostitution in Egypt. From a very early period, rich households were adequately supplied with foreign slave girls, while the poor (particularly the artisans) often lived communal lives, free of the ties of marriage. Of five women cited in one judicial document, four were "living together," as the document put it, with one workman or another, and only the fifth was legally married.[37] Casual sex may well have been supplied by traveling troupes of "dancers and musicians" who regarded it as a secondary trade.

The Jews, whose religion had no place for a goddess,* fought hard against the imported foreign cults that countenanced the harlotry, sacred or profane, of both sexes. But the fight was more apparent than real. Even in Judah, just after the time of Solomon, there were "male cult prostitutes in the land" who "did according to all the abominations of the nations which the Lord drove out before the people of Israel" (I Kings 14, 24). Moralistic objections regularly had to be raised against consorting with the women who traded their bodies in the red light districts which, in Palestine, were usually located against the city walls. "One who keeps company with harlots squanders his substance . . ." (Proverbs 29, 3). And despite the prohibition against Jewish men and women prostituting themselves, Jewish women undoubtedly did become harlots, mainly, it seems, those who had no other way of staying alive; foremost among them were childless widows and women who had been repudiated by their husbands. They always found customers, for only a minority of the male population could afford to satisfy their desire for variety by investing in extra wives or concubines.

There is no obvious reason why the compilers of the Old Testament should have hated prostitutes, but at best their language was intemperate and at worst bordering on the obscene. The Book of Ezekiel, politically motivated and using harlotry as a synonym for the sins of Jerusalem, was typical. "She did not give up her harlotry which she had practiced since her days in Egypt; for in her youth men had lain with her and handled her virgin bosom and poured out their lust upon her. . . ." She "doted upon her paramours," men "whose members [penises] were like those of asses, and whose issue [ejaculation] was like that of horses. . . . 'I will deliver you,' said the Lord, 'into the hands of those you hate . . . and they shall deal with you in hatred, and take away all the fruit of your labor, and leave you naked and bare, and the nakedness of your harlotry shall be uncovered . . .'" (Ezekiel 23, 8; 28-9).

It was not without irony that such vulgarities should have been

---

* Although Protestants today, equally tied to the Old Testament, are making serious attempts to androgynize Jehovah. In June 1974, at a World Council of Churches consultation in West Berlin, an American theologian, Professor Nelle Morton, helpfully pointed out that Elohim, the early Hebrew name for God, was a combination of Eloh, the name of a female goddess, and Im, the Hebrew masculine-plural suffix, while Yahweh (the pure form of Jehovah) owes its derivation to the name of an earlier Samarian goddess.[38] As Mrs. Pankhurst is reported to have said to a troubled suffragette: "Pray to God, dear. She will help you."

directed against the city of Jerusalem, the glorious capital of Solomon, one of whose 700 marriages is said to have been the occasion on which the tender, exquisite poetry of the *Song of Songs* was composed.

"My beloved is unto me as a cluster of samphire in the vineyards of Engedi. Behold, thou art fair, my love; behold, thou art fair. . . . My beloved speaks and says to me: 'Arise, my love, my fair one, and come away; for lo, the winter is past, the rain is over and gone. The flowers appear on the earth, the time of singing has come, and the voice of the turtle dove is heard in our land. . . .' " 39

4.

Greece

Classical Greece, chaste and irreproachable as a newly-laundered dollar bill. Pure intellect. Pure beauty.

Just as the centuries have washed the paint off the Parthenon frieze, so generations of scholars have bleached all that was physical out of the Athenian image. Yet the Greeks were not wholly obsessed by philosophy and the Golden Mean. If they had been, twentieth-century dictionaries would not include such words as androgyny, aphrodisiac, eroticism, hermaphroditism, homosexuality, narcissism, nymphomania, pederasty, satyriasis, and zoophilia—all of them Greek in derivation and most of them relating to activities that can be found in the pages of Homer.

Homer, Hesiod, Plutarch, Pausanias—the professional myth-preservers and myth-improvers—created a vivid, adventurous, amoral world in which gods and heroes spent as much of their time bedding and brawling as they did in performing deeds of valor, and in which the commonplace and the esoteric were inextricably mixed. These were the authors who served as reading primers for the children of the Classical world, and the children learned not only their letters from them, but tolerance and a realistic callousness as well. Aphrodite, for example, goddess of sexual intercourse,* was born from the foam, but not the foam that so innocently caps a Botticelli wave. According to Hesiod's *Theogony*, Cronos, son of earth and heaven, castrated his father with a

---

* Eros, her son, was god of the emotional state of "love."

billhook and hurled his testicles into the sea. They drifted away in the foam of their own semen, and it was from this that Aphrodite was born. Later, she herself was to give birth (from her union with Hermes) to the androgynous god Hermaphroditos, equipped with the physical characteristics of both sexes, and from a union with Dionysus to Priapus, whose physical characteristics were unarguably male and in a permanent state of erection.

The heroes were as lusty as the gods. Heracles, admired by all the peoples of Greece for his strength, courage, and tenacity, was said to have ravished fifty virgins in a single night; bisexual, he also had an affair with his nephew Iolaus and fell in love with "sweet Hylas, he of the curling locks." Theseus, the Athenians' particular hero, seduced almost as many maidens as he slaughtered monsters during the long and intricate saga of his life.[1]

Heroes and gods were expected to be full-blooded and very much larger than life, and the average Greek did not expect to rival their achievements. But he did try to cultivate some of their virtues. It was characteristic of the legends that all heroes were not only noble in spirit but handsome in body—a convention that was to persist in the Western world in literature, drama, and ultimately in the cinema until the arrival of the antihero in the 1950s. To the Greeks, however, these two aspects of beauty were integrally related. One could not exist without the other and, conversely, the existence of one implied the existence of the other. The handsome body *had* to contain a fine-drawn soul. The origins of this curious and frequently disproved belief have never been satisfactorily explained, but it was probably an extension of the Greeks' conviction that there was symmetry in all things, moral, material, metaphysical. Whatever the case, beauty and symmetry were fundamental to the Greek view of the world; fundamental, too, to the unique social institution of pederasty.

MAN AND BOY

Nowadays, the word pederasty is generally used to describe the sexual attraction of an adult to an immature child, but to the Greeks it signified the love of a man for a boy who had passed the age of puberty but not yet reached maturity. "The bloom of a twelve-year-old boy," said Straton, "is desirable, but at thirteen he is much more delightful. Sweeter still is the flower of love that blossoms at fourteen, and its charm increases at fifteen. Sixteen is the divine age." [2] Homosexuality in the modern sense, between two adults of the same age group, is seldom attested to in ancient Athens, and intercourse with a boy under puberty was as illegal there as in most other civilizations.

Throughout the two centuries (from the early sixth to the early fourth B.C.) during which pederasty flourished, the Greeks staunchly maintained that it was a branch of higher education. In theory, what happened was that when a boy finished his orthodox schooling he was taken under the wing of an older man, usually someone in his thirties, who made himself responsible for the boy's moral and intellectual development, treating him with kindness and understanding and warming him with that pure love whose only aim, according to Socrates, was the cultivation of moral perfection in the beloved.*

Classical scholars are unable to agree about the origins of pederasty in ancient Athens, though the majority consensus is that it was imported from the neighboring state of Sparta, where military organization and segregation of the sexes had made it something of a commonplace. In fact, it would have been necessary to import no more than the germ of the idea—if that—for the political and social structure of Athens was such as to favor the rapid spread of any new fashion among the upper classes. It is easy to forget that the civilization that was to have such a deep and abiding influence on all subsequent Western culture was created and perpetuated by a population smaller than that of Newport, Rhode Island, or the cathedral city of Canterbury today. Athens had its foreign residents and its slaves, but it was the 30,000 accredited citizens who shaped the development of the state. Until the fourth century B.C., when a kind of political lethargy set in, every male citizen who could spare the time exercised his right to attend the Assembly and speak on matters of moment. Every year, a working committee of 500 was elected by ballot. When justice had to be

---

* The Greek tradition of pederasty was to be reincarnated in the tenth century A.D. by Buddhist monks in Japan, who favored very much the same master-disciple relationship, with an elder monk acting as teacher and guardian, and the younger responding with love and devotion. The warrior class, too, echoed it in slightly later times, sealing the relationship with an oath of faithfulness for life. By the seventeenth century, however, the classical form of pederasty had given way to adult homosexuality, which became extremely common in the all-male Japanese theater.

done, there was a jury (numbering from 101 to 1,001, depending on the importance of the case) to do it. The Athenian's duty to take part in the affairs of the *polis* was very dear to his heart, and he was prepared to forego many of the luxuries he might have earned in order to have the leisure to fulfill that duty. And not only for his own satisfaction, but because he attached great importance to other men's views of his conduct. As one historian said, he was both ambitious and ambitiously imitative.[3] In such a small, competitive society, where everyone of consequence was known, at least by sight, to everyone else, it would be enough for one or two leading citizens to be seen always in company with a young and handsome disciple for the custom to gain currency. And it was an arrangement that could be advantageous to both parties. The more beautiful the disciple, the nobler his mind, and the greater the implied compliment to the man he chose to acknowledge as teacher. Equally, the more distinguished the man, the greater the implied compliment to the boy he was prepared to accept as disciple. Vanity was a factor on both sides.

Scholarly disagreement also extends to the question of whether Greek pederasty involved love of the mind only, or of the body. Those who take a Biblical view of homosexuality prefer to believe that it was of the mind, and that the philosophers' earthier statements were designed to be understood on a metaphorical level. This is an argument not always easy to sustain. There was, for example, the occasion on which Socrates' young disciple, Alcibiades, arrived at a dinner party to find the master comfortably sharing a couch with his host.

"Oh, yes!" the young man said crossly. "You would move heaven and earth to sit next to the best-looking person in the room!"

Socrates, irritated, turned to his host. "My love for that fellow is always landing me in trouble," he said. "Ever since I fell for him, I have not been allowed even to glance at a good-looking boy, far less talk to one. He gets jealous straight away. . . . I'm afraid that one of these days he'll go for me in earnest." [4]

This piece of naturalistic dialogue permits (just) a metaphorical interpretation, and even the sequel leaves the master himself untarnished by carnality. For Alcibiades declares that when he tried climbing into bed with Socrates and putting his arms around him, "the most cunning of my efforts merely increased his triumph. . . . He disdained the 'flower' of my beauty, scoffed at it, and insulted it." [5] If Socrates was making an intellectual point, he was obviously prepared to go to some lengths to do it.

In fact, the real interest of this story lies in the casual sexuality of the conversation and the frankness with which Alcibiades describes his attempt to seduce the master. There was clearly no stigma attached to what many people today would regard as near enough physical pederasty to fall within the scope of the definition. Socrates' friends placidly regarded it as a normal subject for conversation.

Socrates, however, was an oral teacher who wrote nothing. All that is known of him has been filtered through the minds of other authors, and much of it comes from *symposia* by such writers as Xenophon, Plato, and Athenaeus, books of table talk that enshrine at least as much gossip as truth. Some of the stories are undoubtedly suspect, and the intellectual-love school of thought argues that publicly Socrates condemned carnal love, that Plato never preached any other love than that of the mind, and that Aristotle believed pederasty to be depraved.

The opposition, less prone to apply Judeo-Christian moral standards to a society that had never heard of them, considers such a complete intellectualization of sex as, at best, improbable. Athenian society was by no means immune to the physical, and physical responses must have been encouraged by the general habit of treating as meeting places the gymnasia where the boys of Athens engaged in wrestling, running, jumping, and throwing the discus or javelin, naked except for the oil on their bodies and fine strings that tied the foreskin protectively (and suggestively) over the tip of the penis. The boys themselves may have been receptive enough. Adolescent homosexuality is a common phenomenon, even in societies where there are plenty of girl slaves and prostitutes to stand in for the heavily guarded daughters of respectable citizens. Most civilizations have tried to ignore or repress it; only the Greeks and the Maya of fifteenth-century Yucatan (see page 292) successfully institutionalized it.

It seems probable that Greek pederasty, like the medieval fantasy of courtly love (see pages 259–69), was one of those sentimental ideals that are pure in theory but a good deal less so in practice. Even Plato conceded that there was a certain amount of steamy emotion involved, and wrote of the prayers and entreaties with which lovers supported their suits, of "the oaths they swear, the nights they spend on the doorstep of the beloved one, and the slavery they endure for his sake." [6] Aristophanes made a joke of it. In the *Birds*, one of his characters complains to another, "Well, this is a fine state of affairs, you damned desperado! You meet my son just as he comes out of the gymnasium, all fresh from the bath, and you don't kiss him, you don't say a word to him, you don't hug him, you don't feel his balls! And yet you're supposed to be a friend of ours!" [7] And Sophocles, mysteriously, chose to have Oedipus condemned to his gloomy fate because a curse had been placed on his father for falling in love with a handsome boy. Yet no one knew better than Sophocles that pederasty was not a crime, nor tragedy its inevitable concomitant; in his own life, farce would have been nearer the mark.[8]

Perhaps the main difficulty in estimating what pederasty was all about lies in the impossibility of distinguishing genuine teacher-disciple relationships from the counterfeit. The true philosopher may have had the kind of involvement with his pupil that has characterized a number of schools of idealized love throughout history, notably (on a secular level) among the Arabs of the medieval period (see pages 236–37), but more often among religious revivalist groups. The physical sublimated into the spiritual. The evidence of Greek vase painting, however, suggests that many Athenians took a more cynical view.

In vase painting, homosexual relationships are shown with a very few exceptions in one of two ways. There are a number of examples of anal intercourse, in which the participants are members of the same age group; a Greek physician explained that some men enjoyed this because sexual enjoyment depended on friction of that part of the body in which seminal fluid was secreted, and owing to a natural defect theirs happened to be secreted in the rectum.[9] But more often what is shown is interfemoral connection, the placing of one partner's penis between the other's thighs. The elder partner is usually shown as making the advance, standing with bowed head and shoulders, and conveying the impression that he is both cringing and begging. The younger partner, in contrast, stands straight and upright, and sometimes appears to be repelling the older man.[10] There is no suggestion of distinguished teacher and admiring pupil here, and unless all the vases were commissioned by arrogant youths, the only other explanation

In this vase painting there is some ambiguity.

must be that the vase painters considered the upper-class sport of pederasty in very much the same light as later generations viewed elderly men who pursued lovers (of either sex) many years younger than themselves.

But although the average Athenian may have looked on pederasts without any great enthusiasm, he often admired them from a safe distance in the political or military arena. There was a spate of assassinations in Classical times; Archelaus of Macedonia, Alexander of Phelae, Periander of Ambracia, and Hipparchus of Athens were all murdered by beautiful boys who had either had—or in the last case refused to have—pederastic relations with them. The motives may not have been disinterested, but because it was tyrants who died, pederasty acquired a gloss of political enterprise, a reputation for love of liberty, that did it no harm in Athenian eyes. In the matter of valor, too, it was held admirable. In Sparta, on the Greek island of Euboea, and in the Boeotian city of Thebes, it was directly associated with success in war. As Plato said (though he was prejudiced), "A handful of lovers and loved ones, fighting shoulder to shoulder, could rout a whole army. For a lover to be seen by his beloved forsaking the ranks or throwing away his weapons would be unbearable. He would a thousand times rather die than be so humiliated. . . . The worst of cowards would be inspired by the god of love on such occasions to prove himself the equal of any man naturally brave." [11] The famous Sacred Battalion of Thebes was entirely composed of pairs of lovers. After 33 glorious years, it was finally annihilated at the battle of Chaeronea, but it took the combined power of Philip and Alexander of Macedon to achieve it. During the battle, all 300 of its members fell dead or mortally wounded.*

These were the acceptable levels of pederasty, the levels on which even those who did not practice it could understand and sometimes approve. But there were less respectable kinds.

His literary friends might look indulgently on Agathon, the tragic poet, when he greeted them dressed like a woman in long robe, saffron-colored tunic and cape, with a bust-bodice, a hair net, and tight-fitting buskins, but when boy prostitutes did the same, parading the streets in effeminate dress and make-up—so that an Athenian proverb said it was "easier to hide five elephants in one's armpit" than one of these boys—it was regarded as shameful. The boys could be hired by the hour, or on a contract basis. There was

In this one, none at all.

a case that came before the courts of a boy named Theodotus, one of whose lovers accused another of intentional violation of the young man's body, an offense that was punishable at this time (the beginning of the fourth century B.C.) by banishment and confiscation of property.[12] It was a kind of jealousy that may not have been unusual among the patrons of boy brothels.

There was a wide range of legislation on man-boy relationships. At the beginning of the sixth century B.C., Solon the lawgiver, himself a pederast, had imposed the death penalty for any adult male found, without authorization, on the premises of a school (where the boys would be below the age of puberty); it was a punishment that suggests that pederasty in the modern sense was not unknown. Solon also declared it illegal for a slave to have connection with a free-born boy, an unlikely eventuality in the case of genuine educational pederasty, but an indication that the noneducational kind may have been on the increase. Further, any man who incited a free boy to offer his charms professionally was liable to be deprived of his civic rights for life.[13] On the whole, however, the general impression conveyed by Athenian sources is that most pederastic offenses, like towaway-zone parking today, were recognized as illegal only by those who were unfortunate enough to be caught.

The two centuries during which pederasty was in fashion were also the finest period of Classical achievement, but the association (if any) is obscure. If homosexuality had been kept underground, it might be argued that the magnificence of Athenian art and architecture was a sublimation. But this was not the case. Nor would it be true to speculate that the homosexual, free to live an open life, gave expression to the allied freedom of his spirit by pouring out his creative talent in superb painting, sculpture, and building. The Parthenon, for example, was built by thousands of separate contractors—little men, hardworking craftsmen who knew nothing of the intellectual circles where pederasty was fashionable, and many of them foreigners. One citizen, aided by one slave, had a contract to bring ten cartloads of marble from Pentelicus. Another, with two Athenian employees and three slaves, was responsible for the fluting of one column. Not much is known about the personal life of the men who were responsible for the grand design—Phidias, Ictinus, and Callicrates—but if their social class can be adduced as evidence, fashionable pederasty can have meant little to them. And Praxiteles, the last and greatest artist of the period, was unequivocally heterosexual, lover of the most famous courtesan of her day, Phyrne, who was the model for his Aphrodite of Cnidos.

What can be said, however, is that the Athenian cast of mind at this period, deeply influenced by educational pederasty, must have been much more sympathetic to cultural enterprise than if muscle-bound disciplinarianism had been the rule. And in the realm of philosophy Western civilization would have been the poorer if pederasty had never been in fashion. As the Spanish humanist José Ortega y Gasset observed, "It is impossible to say how deeply Platonic thought has penetrated the basic layers of modern Western civilization. The most ordinary people in the West constantly make use of expressions and ideas which go back to Plato." Robert Flacelière, the French scholar and no supporter of pederasty, remarks, "But Plato's theory of love would retain precisely the same value for us if he had founded his argument on heterosexuality instead of its opposite." [14] This, however, is an evasion of the issue. Plato, who never married but had many "passionate friendships" during his 80 years of life, might never have evolved his theory of love at all if it had not been for the pederastic climate of his times.

BY NO MEANS INFERIOR

"Women are by no means inferior to men," Socrates remarked kindly—then spoiled the effect by adding, "All they need is a little more physical strength and energy of mind." [15] He was, however, being generous, for the Greeks had no very high opinion of women, and during the period when pederasty was in vogue the feeling was reciprocated.

What the relationship was between pederasty and the Athenian attitude to women remains a matter of debate. Some scholars consider the whole question of pederasty irrelevant—a shortsighted view that ignores the fact that any widely-held attitude inevitably colors adjoining areas of the mind. Others hold that women were treated with disdain long before pederasty was ever heard of; others, still, that Greek women were never treated with disdain at all.

The women's quarters of a middle-class Greek house in the fifth century B.C.

Most of the literary evidence, however, does suggest an inferior position for women, and the theory is that this resulted from the invasions of the uncouth Dorians, who began to flood into Greece at the end of the second millennium B.C.. It is not a very convincing argument, since women were more considerately treated in the Dorian-settled states than in Athens, but it is generally felt necessary to provide the Athenians with some excuse for being discourteous to the ladies.

In Athens, women had no more political or legal rights than slaves; throughout their lives they were subject to the absolute authority of their male next-of-kin. They received no formal education, were condemned to spend most of their time in the women's quarters of their home, and were subject to arranged marriages. A wife seldom dined with her husband—and never if he had guests—and on the rare occasions that she went out of doors, was invariably chaperoned; it was illegal for her to take with her more than three articles of clothing, an obol's worth of food and drink (in today's terms, a sandwich and a glass of milk), and if she went out after dark she had to go in a carriage with a lighted lantern.[16]

For her to make the acquaintance of any man other than her husband or male relatives was unusual. Plutarch reported the story of the ruler Hiero, who was taunted by an opponent with having bad breath; he went home in a rage, demanding to know why his wife had not told him. "I thought all men smelled like that," she replied naively.[17] A husband could repudiate his wife without cause and was legally bound to if, by some miracle of ingenuity, she succeeded in committing adultery. A wife, however, could obtain a divorce only on grounds of extreme provocation, which did not include either pederasty or adultery.*

The opposing school of thought argues that things were not really as bad as they looked and that although admittedly there were legal disabilities, women were nevertheless permitted to go to the theater, to visit sculptors' studios, and even to take a few days off to attend the all-women festival of Thesmophoria, which their menfolk were convinced was the occasion for a great many undefined but lascivious goings-on. Euripides—described by Sophocles as a woman-hater in his tragedies, but very fond of them in bed [18]—complained that they were always having other women "coming into the house gossiping," and they appear to have been no less vocal in the presence of the male members of the family. As the prosecutor reminded the jury in a court case involving a prostitute, "If you acquit this woman, what will you say to your wives and daughters when you go home? . . . You will tell them all the details of the case, and you will tell them how carefully and completely the case was proved. When you have finished, they will say, 'And what did you do?' And you will reply, 'We acquitted her.' And *then* the fat will be in the fire!" [19]

What the evidence on both sides makes clear, in fact, is that women in Athens were on very much the same legal and social footing as their contemporaries among the Babylonians, the Egyptians, and the Hebrews. In politics, philosophy, and art the Greeks were creating a new orchestration for the music of the spheres, but on a more mundane level they were still stuck in terrestrial mud. As everywhere else in the first millennium B.C., women were chattels, even if some of them were independent-minded ones. To the Greeks, a woman (regardless of age or marital status) was *gyne*, whose linguistic meaning is "bearer of children."

They do, however, appear to have added one new element to the equation. Although in Babylon and Egypt there was a fairly frequent disgruntled note in references to the female sex, and although the Hebrews actively detested adventuresses (unfaithful wives) and harlots, until the third century B.C. the Greeks condemned *all* women as irrational, oversexed, and morally defective. It may be deduced that they were irrational because they were

---

* The view that it is permissible for a man, but not a woman, to commit adultery has persisted almost to the present day. It was 1923 before Englishwomen, for example, won the right to divorce their husbands for it.

denied education, oversexed because they complained that their
husbands rarely slept with them, and morally defective because
they criticized them for wasting so much time philosophizing in
the Assembly when they ought to be out earning their living.
Domestic harmony was not a feature of Greek life.

Many of the figures in Greek tragedy were women. Clytem-
nestra, who slaughtered her husband. Medea, who chopped her
brother in pieces and later murdered her children. Phaedra, who
followed perjury with suicide. And Electra, accomplice in ma-
tricide. Even their heroines were flawed. The goddess Aphrodite
was beautiful, charming, and a bitch. So was Helen of Troy. The
faithful Penelope, by the time she welcomed her rather less faithful husband Odysseus back from his wanderings, had 20 such
tough-minded years behind her that no sensible Greek would have
given a fig for their chances of conjugal bliss. And the self-sacrificing Alcestis was clearly a doormat.

The Athenian male recognized all this. He would have been
intolerably bored by Alcestis—except as a wife. But if he found a
wife with such qualities he counted himself fortunate. Hesiod, the
peasant poet who lived in the latter part of the eighth century B.C.
and whom the Greeks revered only slightly less than Homer, explained why it was necessary to marry at all. "He who evades, by
refusing marriage, the miseries that women bring upon us, will
have no support [children] in the wretchedness of his old age. . . .
On the other hand, he whose fate it is to marry may perhaps find a
good and sensible wife. But even then he will see evil outweigh
good all his life." The best ages were 30 for the man and 16 for the
girl, and on the whole it was better to "buy the woman, don't
marry her. Then you can make her follow the plough if necessary."[20]

Other husbands were equally unromantic. As Ischomachus
blightingly pointed out to his new 14-year-old wife, "We could
easily have found someone else to share my bed, and I'm sure you
realize that perfectly well. But after thinking it over, I in my interests and your parents in yours, and after reviewing all possible
candidates for household management and the care of children, I
selected you, and your parents myself—no doubt from a good
many others."

The Athenian's view of a good wife was an almost exact echo
of the Hebrew's. She was to be chaste and sober-minded, compe-

tent at spinning, weaving, and tailoring, able to allocate suitable tasks to the servants, to be economical with her husband's money and property, to bear children, and to govern the household wisely and virtuously. If it was necessary to beget an heir in a hurry, she was expected to have intercourse with her husband "at least three times a month" until the matter was put right.[21]

Anachronisms apart, the Greek male would wholeheartedly have agreed with Rudyard Kipling more than 2,000 years later when he said that "a woman is only a woman, but a good cigar is a smoke," [22] and his generalized resistance both to women and marriage helped to produce—probably for the first time in history—a surplus of unmarried women. The situation would have been exacerbated by the high male mortality rate in the wars that scarred Greek history if it had not been for the custom of female infanticide, which helped to correct the imbalance. In Sparta, male infanticide was also practiced, however, for the Spartans were interested in controlling quality as well as quantity. Theirs was the first society other than the Jewish to be preoccupied with eugenics, and all children, boys and girls, were officially examined when they were a few days old, so that the weak, feeble, or deformed could be exposed to die on the slopes of Mount Taygetus.

From the mid-tenth until the end of the seventh century B.C., Athens in particular had been overpopulated because of the number of refugees who had flooded in as a result of the Dorian invasions. A surge of overseas colonization beginning in about 750 B.C. helped to reduce the numbers, but it is possible that both pederasty and men's suspicion of women gained momentum as the result of some kind of half-conscious attempt to bring population figures down to an acceptable level. Aristotle was later to make the point that, in Crete, pederasty was regulated by the state as a means of controlling population.[23] He himself advocated a legal limit on family size, and recommended olive oil blended with cedar oil, lead ointment, or frankincense, as a contraceptive; it was to be applied to "that part of the womb in which the seed falls." More than 2,000 years later, Marie Stopes claimed a zero-failure rate in controlled tests using olive oil.[24]

Athenian wives seem scarcely to have needed advice about either abortion or contraception, for their relationships with their husbands were infrequent and often sterile. In some ways they may have helped to perpetuate this situation by directing all their emotional drive towards their sons (if any), sometimes idolizing, sometimes reviling them, in a way that an adult might have understood but a child could not.[25] As a result, generation after generation of boys grew up in the conviction that women were wholly unpredictable and best avoided whenever possible.

Plutarch laughed at the Spartans, whose idea of marriage was for the husband to live with his men friends, slipping away only on rare and secret occasions to visit his wife.* Sometimes "a husband had children without ever having seen his wife by daylight." [27] But the same may well have been true of Athenians. In Sparta and Athens alike, large families were almost unknown except perhaps among the poorer classes whose lives have gone unrecorded. It was, in the end, the problem of too few citizens, not too many, that brought the great days of Greek civilization to a close.

SELF-SATISFACTION

Neglected wives did not always repine. Some of them, despite the difficulties, succeeded in finding consolation elsewhere with the aid of one of the professional procuresses who infested the city, but more of them seem to have resorted to the less dangerous expedients of masturbation or homosexuality (which is, of course, derived not from the Latin *homo*, "man," but from the Greek *homos*, meaning "the same").

Masturbation, to the Greeks, was not a vice but a safety valve, and there are numerous literary references to it, especially in Attic comedy. But authors before the third century B.C. wrote little and knew less about the private lives of women, and most of the references concern men. However, if women did not also practice it, then the salesmen of Miletus were falling down on their job.

Miletus, a wealthy commercial city on the coast of Asia Minor, was the manufacturing and exporting center of what the Greeks called the *olisbos*, and later generations, less euphoniously, the dildo. One modern dictionary cagily defines it as "an imagic substitute for the *membrum virile*." This imitation penis appears in

---

* Until the beginning of the twentieth century, the Nayar peoples of Kerala, on the Malabar coast of India, also favored the custom of husbands visiting their wives only at night.[26]

Greek times to have been made either of wood or padded leather and had to be liberally anointed with olive oil before use. Among the literary relics of the third century B.C., there is a short play consisting of a dialogue between two young women, Metro and Coritto, which begins with Metro trying to borrow Coritto's dildo. Coritto, unfortunately, has lent it to someone else, who has in turn lent it to another friend. Metro, disappointed, asks where she can buy one, and Coritto recommends her to a cobbler called Cerdon. "Dear me!" Metro says; she knows two master workmen of that name, but would not "care to entrust such work" to either of them. Coritto's raptures over the beautiful workmanship of hers, however, convince Metro, and off she goes to order one for herself.[28]

The dildo was used not only for solitary satisfaction but by women homosexuals, whom the Greeks (when they mentioned them at all) called tribads. Tribadism was believed by the Athenians to be more common in Sparta than in Athens and Plutarch recorded that "at Sparta love was held in such honor that even the most respectable women became infatuated with girls." [29] He did not draw the obvious parallel with the pederasts of Athens. The island of Leucas was suspect, too, partly because the first illustrated book on tribadic postures was reputed to have been written by a Leucadian woman, Philaenis. But it was Lesbos that was regarded as the heartland—that isle of Greece "where burning Sappho loved and sung."

Very little is known about Sappho, or indeed about her poetry, which was written in the Lesbian dialect and imperfectly understood by Hellenistic and Roman copyists and commentators. She is said to have been the distinguished principal of an academy for young ladies (Lesbos being presumably more advanced than Athens in the matter of women's education) and a poetess of such stature that her contemporaries called her "The Tenth Muse." Byron's adjective, "burning," seems to have been appropriate. Such fragments of her poetry as remain—most of them addressed to one or other of her pupils—quiver with a far from intellectual passion. They are almost impossible to translate. In metrical renderings they sound like bad Tennyson; in prose, very little better. "Return, I implore thee, clad in thy milk-white tunic. Ah, what intense desire attends thy beauteous form. No woman could not but tremble at its seduction."

Some modern scholars believe that the love and poetry of The Tenth Muse were purely spiritual, but those who were able to read her complete works had no doubt about their erotic character. Apuleius, who knew what he was talking about, called them "sensual" and "wanton," and Ovid described them as a complete course of instruction in female homosexuality. But whether or not Sappho was a tribad, as time passed her name and that of the island on which she lived began to take on special meaning, and it was not long before the Greeks gave up using the word tribadism and talked of "Lesbian love" instead.

SERVANTS OF APHRODITE

"We have hetairai for our pleasure, concubines for our daily needs, and wives to give us legitimate children and look after the housekeeping." [30]

During the latter part of the fourth century B.C. and, with more conviction, in the third, Athenian men began to rediscover an interest in women, though not in wives; they still had no ambition to become family men. The less resistant attitude toward women was partly a result of the widening of horizons brought about by the overseas conquests of Alexander the Great and partly the effect of reduced political activity and increased wealth, which meant that men had both time and money to spare. It showed itself in art. Formerly, male statuary had usually been nude, female clothed; now the veils began to drop from the female form. It showed itself on stage, too. The Old Comedy had been predominantly political; in the New, romantic love between man and woman became acceptable although female roles were still played by boys, clad for nude scenes in body-socks with breasts and pubic apron carefully painted in. But above all it showed itself in the profits of prostitution. The servants of Aphrodite were kept so busy that one of the best-known of them, whose name was Metiche, earned the nickname of Clepsydra because she used her water clock *(klepsudra)* as a stopwatch for timing the length of her clients' visits.[31]

The top-level courtesans of the day were the hetairai, beautiful, talented, witty, often as knowledgeable about classical literature as they were about profit-and-loss accounting. The true courtesan's appeal has never depended entirely on physical attraction; the classic example from later history is Madame de Pompadour, who was mistress of Louis XV of France for only five years but a formidable political influence for fifteen more. What Athenian men liked about the hetairai was that they excelled at all the things those same men prevented their wives from learning, which must have been extremely galling for the wives. They were not allowed, as the hetairai were, to join men at the supper table where they might have picked up enough about culture and public affairs to allow them to sustain an intelligent conversation. They were reared on *Kinder, Küche und Kirche,* whereas the lowborn hetairai had been trained almost from childhood in the social arts. And the vast majority of wives knew no more about love than they had been taught by husbands less concerned with worker satisfaction than the manufacturer's end product, sons. They could not hope to compete. As throughout most of history, courtesans had a better time than wives.

The hetairai were successful women in a man's world, sometimes very successful. Thargelia, an Ionian who flourished as early as the sixth century B.C., was said to have acted as secret agent for Cyrus the Great of Persia, working so persuasively on the minds as well as the bodies of her distinguished lovers that they offered to deliver Ionia peacefully up to Persian domination.* Another, Thaïs of Athens, was mistress of Alexander the Great, and appears to have been responsible for the burning of Persepolis; she later married Ptolemy I and became queen of Egypt. One of the greatest of them all, Aspasia, had a literary and political salon in Athens and was visited by the most powerful men of the time. For her, Pericles repudiated his wife and children, and it was she who was believed to have been directly responsible for Athens' declaration of war on Samos.[32]

When the hetairai became too influential, Athenians raised an outcry about women in politics, but for most of the time criticism was directed mainly at their habit of money-grubbing. Lucian's *Dialogues of Courtesans* (14) includes an exchange between a recently impoverished sailor and his former mistress, who has ex-

---

* Between Thargelia and the Mata Haris and Christine Keelers of the twentieth century there is a long historical roster of courtesans involved marginally or deeply in the business of intelligence-gathering. In the early nineteenth century, particularly, Fouché in France and Metternich in Austria deliberately organized prostitutes into police-informer networks.

changed his protection for that of a rich Bithynian merchant. "Everything was all right," says the sailor, "when I could give you fine presents," and Myrtale, with spurious sympathy, agrees to a reckoning.

Dorion: First, Sicyonian shoes—two drachmae. Put down two drachmae.

Myrtale: But for that you had two nights with me.

Dorion: Then when I came back from Syria I brought an alabaster scent bottle for you, which again—ye gods!—cost two drachmae.

Myrtale: But before you put out to sea I gave you the most beautiful shirt.... The one the second mate left here after he spent the night with me.

Dorion: That's true enough ... Then I brought you onions from Cyprus, five herrings, and four perch. *And* eight ship's biscuits in little wicker baskets, and sandals with gold thread, you ungrateful woman. Oh! And a large cheese!

Myrtale: About five drachmae altogether, maybe....

Dorion: But your Bithynian has never bought even a head of garlic for your mother! I'd very much like to know what you've had from him!

Hetaira with client

Hetaira with client

Unfortunately for Dorion, Myrtale has had the rent paid, as well as pearls, earrings, a carpet, and a useful sum of money. She is on her way up in the world and knows the value of material possessions. The hetairai were well aware that their attractions would not last forever and that money in the bank was the thing to aim for. As Philumena, a courtesan who may have been fact or fiction, briskly said in a letter to a lover, "Why do you bother writing long letters? I want fifty gold pieces, not letters. If you love me, pay up; if you love your money more, then don't bother me any more. Goodbye!" [33]

Some, in their heyday, made enough to allow them to indulge in good works. Lamia of Athens rebuilt a ruined picture gallery for the people of Sicyon, near Corinth, and Rhodopis, a Thracian who practiced in Egypt, was reputed to have constructed a whole pyramid at her own expense.[34]

Below the hetairai on the social scale were the concubines, of whom very little is known. By Classical times, the habit of keeping concubines as secondary wives seems to have faded in the face of stiff competition from beautiful boys, clever hetairai, and cheap and willing brothel girls. The concubine's situation was not, in any case, a happy one; she had neither the independence of the hetaira nor the notional legal protection afforded to a wife, and if her master tired of her there was nothing to prevent him from selling her off—to a brothel, if he wished.[35]

With a poor sense of timing, Solon had established and stocked the first Athenian brothels at the beginning of the sixth century B.C. Trade appears to have been slow to begin with, but by the fourth century B.C. it had begun to pick up. The girls were now lined up outside the premises, "with bared breasts and thin gauze dresses. . . . Any man can pick out the one that pleases him—thin, fat, plump, lanky, crooked, young, old, middle-sized, ripe. . . . They drag you into the house willy-nilly, calling you 'daddy' if you are an old man or 'little brother' or 'little lad.' And you can have any of them for a small sum, without any risk." [36] The fee covered an honorarium for the girls, varying from an obol to a stater (proportionately, from half a cent to a dollar, or a halfpenny to a pound), depending on the class of house and the services required. The brothel keepers paid an annual state tax.

There were streetwalkers, too, with a novel soliciting technique that worked very well on unpaved surfaces. One streetwalker's sandal has survived the centuries. Studded in reverse on the sole is a message that would print itself on the roadway for the next passerby to read. The message, of course, is, "Follow me."

Prostitution flourished particularly in towns where there was a good deal of transit traffic. Corinth, for example, with its two harbors and thriving maritime trade, swarmed with brothel-girls and streetwalkers ready to serve sailors ashore. Its temple of Aphrodite was also said to have more than a thousand hetairai dedicated to the service of the goddess (and her worshippers).

Such dedications were made not by the girls themselves but by people attempting to barter with the gods. The "pious athlete" Xenophon of Corinth vowed that if he won the footrace and the pentathlon at Olympia he would dedicate a contingent of prostitutes to Aphrodite. He won, and the goddess benefited to the tune of a hundred new handmaidens. They had a religious as well as an amorous role to play. When Greece was threatened by the power of Xerxes, it was the temple hetairai of Corinth who offered up the prayers and sacrifices of the nation. There is undoubtedly a moral somewhere in the fact that Xerxes was defeated.

No one, least of all the hetairai themselves, would ever have claimed that the secular members of the sisterhood had any other mission in life than to make maximum profit out of their assets.

But they were, in fact, pioneers—the first group of women in recorded history to achieve détente with men. The *naditu* priestesses of Babylon had been accepted because of the quality of their minds; prostitutes in all countries for their bodies. But the hetairai used both and were admired for both.

Ironically, their success was to encourage wives—not courtesans—in Greek-influenced Rome to hurry on the process of their own emancipation. Roman women, however, faced with much the same generalized dislike on the part of their menfolk as the hetairai had overcome in Athens, were not prepared to use the same ingratiating means to achieve their end. They chose instead to wage war, and it was a war that was to have an indirect but unfortunate effect on the whole future of the Roman empire.

5.
Rome

Chastity, said the poet Juvenal at the beginning of the second century A.D., was a virtue that had scarcely been seen in Rome since the Golden Age—by which, Stoic that he was, he meant that stern and simple era of the long ago when one cold cavern sufficed to house the "acorn-belching" early Roman, his gods, his flocks, his "gigantic children," and his "rough highland wife." [1]

Every man to his idyll. Certainly, by the time Juvenal turned his jaundiced eye on the women of imperial Rome, chastity was not one of their more striking attributes, but until at least the fifth century B.C. the great majority of them had lived out their lives in a state of unblemished rectitude.

Initially, the Romans had been a race of pastoralists, influenced by the Etruscans and, through them, by the civilizations of Greece and Carthage. They were not a frivolous people. When, later, they began to idealize the *mores maiorum*, "the manners of the ancestors," it was duty and service of which they spoke, firmness of purpose, discipline, industry, clemency, frugality, and responsibility. *Pietas* and *officium, constantia, virtus* and *gravitas*—a sonorous rollcall of objective morality. Dedication was an integral part of their being, as was its concomitant, the kind of blind possessiveness that embraced land and family without distinction. When the rhetoricians displayed the Roman matron of the early republic as a model of nobility and virtue, they ignored the fact that she had been motivated as much by self-preservation as by self-sacrifice. Until the end of the first century B.C., a husband was legally entitled to kill his wife on the spot if she were caught in the act of adultery.* In some circumstances, she could be condemned to death even if she were not caught in the act. If she drank more than a bare minimum of wine, it was taken to indicate moral and sexual laxity and she could be divorced for it. "Perverse and disgusting conduct" also provided grounds for divorce, and so did infertility.

As elsewhere in the ancient world, wives and children were the chattels of their menfolk, but there was one difference. In Rome, child-bearing and housekeeping were considered to be only part of a woman's duties. She was expected to play an active role in the wider business of the family. In some ways it was a continuation of the neolithic situation, a reflection, perhaps, of the speed with which Rome had changed from a scattered, family-based society in which the woman's contribution was economically essential, to that state of civilization which—more gradually achieved and more dependent on division of labor—would have relegated her to domestic duties only. One result was that her life was less secluded than that of her contemporaries in other countries; another, that she had sufficient awareness of her own value to give her self-assurance.

For many women, this was enough. There is no reason to doubt that, in Roman times as today, a great number of women—perhaps the majority—willingly abrogated their liberty in exchange for the comforts of intellectual and emotional dependence. The protection of the family cocoon, however harsh its texture, was to many of them more desirable than freedom. Despite this, even women who had no desire for emancipation were capable of recognizing that their lives could be easier. The apparently innocuous and legalistic changes that they helped bring about in the marriage laws led ultimately to a general self-indulgence that was to have far-reaching results.

Traditionally, there were three forms of marriage. The first, *confarreatio* was roughly the equivalent of a Catholic church wedding today, highly ceremonious and by no means easy to dissolve. Second was *coemptio*, a relic of bride purchase, which resembled a modern civil ceremony and appealed to those with no money to

---

* In effect, this permission was perpetuated in some European countries, notably France, until the twentieth century. *Crime passionnel* was not only a legally recognized defense, but one that juries were often prepared to accept even from women.

waste on glossy trappings. In both cases, the bride passed straight from her father's possession into that of her husband—*in manum*, "in[to] his hand," as the legal phrase had it—complete with her property (if any) and her dowry. Henceforward she belonged entirely to her husband's family, and if she committed some marital crime it was to *his* family council that she had to answer.

The third form of marriage was *usus*, which was legally binding only after a year's continuous association. In the early days, this form may not have been entirely respectable, a kind of trial marriage that was acceptable if it developed into something permanent but frowned on if it did not. Until the trial year was up, the Roman wife remained a member of her father's family; only afterward did she enter fully and legally into her husband's.

Marriage by *usus* contained a loophole large enough for independence to slip through. To the literal Roman mind, "continuous association" meant precisely that; if a woman absented herself from her common-law husband's house for three successive days and nights the qualifying period had to begin all over again. With careful timing and a little ingenuity, a woman could postpone almost indefinitely the moment when she became legally subject to her husband instead of her presumably more sympathetic father. Such a system had obvious appeal for a bride married off at the age of thirteen or fourteen to a man she scarcely knew. He might still slaughter her on the spot if he caught her *in flagrante delicto*, but for lesser crimes she could anticipate a lecture from her father rather than the stringent punishments her husband's family council had every right to prescribe.

If marriage by *usus* had found favor only with the bride, it would never have become popular. But it also conferred benefits on her father. Little is known about the period between the fifth and third centuries B.C. when the changeover occurred, but it appears that for as long as a man's daughter remained "in his hand" he also retained control over her assets and was able to reclaim a substantial portion of her dowry if the marriage failed. To the property-conscious Roman, as obsessed with holding his acres together as any landed gentleman in Georgian England, the prospect was irresistible.

It gradually became customary for a bride to remain under her father's aegis. The legal benefits offered reason enough, but others also emerged. Though a man's married daughter might be legally "in his hand," she was seldom under his eye, and the supervision exercised by most fathers must have been less than rigorous; indeed, when she attained the age of 25 (which was admittedly a ripe old age in the Roman period) it became little more than a formality.

By the end of the third century B.C., woman was more out of hand than "in hand," or so her male contemporaries complained. Unfortunately, there are no feminine literary sources to confirm or deny this, but the stage had certainly been reached when the women of Rome were prepared not only to contemplate but to indulge in action that would have horrified the noble and well-behaved matron of earlier times.

THE FIRST SUFFRAGETTES?

In 215 B.C., during a critical period in the war with Hannibal, there had been enacted the Oppian law (named after the tribune C. Oppius), which ruled that women were allowed to keep only half an ounce of gold, were forbidden to drive in carriages through the streets of Rome, and banned from wearing dyed clothes. Superficial though such a law may appear, it was the Roman world's equivalent of the clothes rationing imposed in Europe during the second world war. Gold, to a woman, meant bracelets and earrings; to the army it meant survival. Carriages cost money better spent on defense. The dyes for the blue, rose, scarlet, amethyst and violet collectively known as "purple" had to be imported at some expense from Tyre in the eastern Mediterranean. The Oppian law, like most sumptuary laws in later history, was an attempt to limit conspicuous consumption in the only way open to legislators and was aimed at women not so much because of the perennial male belief that only women are extravagant, but because men's extravagance took different and more diverse forms. They spent their money on wine and oil, amber and glass, linen, papyrus, statuary, terracottas, spices—goods which it would have been practicable to control only at point of sale. So it was the women who suffered from legislation that was probably designed as much for psychological effect as economic benefit.

Rome survived the crisis of 215 B.C., and 14 years later the war came to an end. But another six years passed before, in 195 B.C., there was any move to repeal the Oppian law. The die-hards were against it, and the debate raged for days. It looked as if the move were going to fail, and the women grew angrier and angrier. "Neither influence, nor modesty, nor their husbands' commands could keep the married women indoors. They beset all the streets in Rome and all the approaches to the forum. . . . Every day the crowds of women grew, for they even came into the city from the provinces." When they actually mobbed the offices of the two tribunes most strongly opposed to the repeal, it was too much.

"It made me blush," exploded Cato in the Senate, "to push my way through a positive regiment of women a few minutes ago in order to get here." If a woman had something to say, she should say it in private, to her husband; and even so, she had no business even to hold an opinion about something that was a political matter. If husbands kept their wives in order, there would be no such vulgar demonstrations as he had just witnessed. "Woman is a headstrong and uncontrolled animal, and you cannot give her the reins and expect her not to kick over the traces. . . . What [they] want is complete freedom—or, to put it bluntly, complete license." If they were allowed the opportunity to plot in secret, their husbands' lives would not be worth a moment's purchase.

No, Cato went on, they must not be permitted to force this issue through. "If you allow them one right after another, so that in the end they have complete equality with men, do you think you will find them bearable? Nonsense!" Rich women only wanted the law repealed so that they could strut about in gold and purple that their inferiors could not afford. "Do you want to inaugurate an era of competitiveness in dress? . . . When a woman's resources will stretch to something she will buy it; when she cannot, she will go to her husband for the money. Pity the poor husband, whether he gives in to her or not. For if *he* does not find the money, some other man will. . . ."

The tribune L. Valerius, however, did not subscribe to this hair-raising view of Roman marriage. Cato had said that if the law were repealed, men would find themselves unable to control their womenfolk. "Nothing of the sort," replied Valerius. "As long as her menfolk are alive, a woman never seeks to escape from her dependence. The independence which they acquire if they lose their parents or if they are left widows is a thing from which they pray to be spared." All that the ladies wanted was justice. After all, it was only the wives and daughters of Roman citizens who were forbidden to adorn themselves. The wives of Rome's allies, in contrast, were "a striking sight in their gold and purple; these women drive through Rome while [ours] have to walk, as if it were the allies and not Rome that ruled the empire. This is an experience which men would find distressing enough. What of women, whom even trifles can upset? Elegance, jewelry, and the cultivation of beauty—these are the distinctions that a woman prizes." [2]

Though the tone of Valerius's championship was rather more insulting to women than Cato's honest bigotry, the Oppian law was repealed. In the long run, however, it was Cato who was proved right. Two hundred years later, the historian Valerius Maximus remarked that the men who had repealed the law "had no conception of the extravagance to which women's inexorable passion for novelty in fashion would lead, or of the extremes to which their brazenness would go once it had succeeded in trampling on the laws." [3]

If fashion then had been like fashion today, with constant changes of style, length, and cut, perhaps the Roman empire would never have fallen. But what happened was that the shape of women's dress remained much the same; it was fabric and decoration that were the index of fashion. Luxurious Tyrian dyes, necklaces, brooches, rings, heavy gold bracelets, cottons from India, diadems, earrings encrusted with precious stones from the far reaches of Asia and valued at more than a landed estate, robes made from the finest silk from China which was literally, pound for pound, worth its weight in gold—these were what mattered.

As in Greece, the expansion of the known world at first brought to Rome a rush of money and luxury, but time passed and the flow was reversed. By the first century A.D., Pliny estimated that Roman trade with Asia was operating at a deficit of around $30 million, or £15 million a year in today's terms. Though this is very little by modern standards, it was a great deal in the ancient world—four or five times the annual value of the loot Rome had acquired during her conquests of the Mediterranean, Gaul, Spain, and western Asia in republican days.[4] Almost half the listed classifications of goods imported into the Roman world from Asia and the eastern coast of Africa consisted of spices, and the other four of Rome's five "essential luxuries" were silk from China, ivory from Africa, amber from Germany, and incense from Arabia.

Unfortunately, there was very little that other countries wanted from Rome in exchange. The caravans that traveled from Lo-yang in China to meet Roman traders or intermediaries at the famous Stone Tower in the wilds of central Asia, somewhere north of the Pamir, bartered exquisite silks and exotic spices for small quantities of Roman glass, pottery, asbestos cloth, coral beads, intaglio gems, and grape wine, and large quantities of gold and silver. For a while the balance worked out well enough; the Chinese preferred gold, the Romans silver. But there came a shortage of precious metals. The great silver mines of Greece gave out, and by A.D. 200 Rome's own sources had been so deeply worked that the engineers were having the greatest difficulty in clearing them of water. Gradually at first, and then swiftly, Roman coinage began to depreciate until at length the whole economy foundered.

Among the variety of political, social, military, and economic causes that contributed to the downfall of the Roman empire, no scholar has succeeded in pinning down one that was more important than all the rest. But there is no doubt that extravagance—and particularly the extravagance of Roman women—was an important ancillary factor.

ARTIFICIAL AIDS

The women of the upper classes were in the position of having a freedom rare in the ancient world, and yet useless to them. They were permitted to do a great deal—as long as they did nothing constructive. Legal disabilities and social pressures combined to draw round them a kind of intellectual *cordon sanitaire,* within which they could think and act almost as they liked. But they could not break it, in case they tried to influence others, to trespass on man's preserves, even—unthinkably—to shape the political and imperial policies of Rome itself. So they contented themselves with spending money, beautifying themselves (not for their husbands but for their lovers), taking to religion, or suing for divorce.

Seneca criticized certain of his contemporaries for having mastered the art of laboriously doing nothing.[5] It was certainly a fair description of how women passed their days. A man needed only to rise before daybreak, put on his sandals, pick up his toga—the only item of clothing he discarded when he went to bed—swallow a glass of water, and he was ready to face the world. Later, perhaps, he might go to the barber for a shave, and the afternoon would see him at the baths. His wife, by contrast, rose in her own

A Roman lady
at her toilet

time in her own room (only the vulgar shared a bedroom with
their husbands), drew on her slippers, donned her under-robe on
top of the loincloth, breast-band and tunic in which she had slept,
drank a glass of water, and was ready to face, not the world, but
her mirror, her maids, and her innumerable pots of cosmetics.

Women and men alike had been doing their best to improve
on nature throughout most of recorded history. As far back as
Sumerian times they had painted kohl round their eyes to enlarge
them and tinted their cheeks with red dyes. Athenian women, said
Aristophanes, used grease paint, antimony ore (mascara), red
paint, white lead (as face powder), seaweed paint (possibly as an
eye shadow), and beauty plasters (face packs). Many of these preparations were unfortunately not waterproof. "When you go out in
the summer," said the Greek poet Eubulus nastily, "two black
rivulets flow from your eyes, the sweat from your cheeks carries
trickles of rouge right down to your neck, and your hair turns gray
from the powder on your forehead!" [6]

The Greek *peplos* and *chiton* were clinging garments, belted,
and sometimes bloused at the waist, and the Greeks, as a result,

had made notable advances in corsetry. It was they who invented the half-cup brassiere, not quite as scientifically structured as the modern kind but satisfactory enough. They had girdles, too, usually worn by hetairai to conceal pregnancy. And for girls whose figures were underdeveloped, the hips could be "fitted with a quilt, so that people exclaim: 'There's a well-turned rump for you!' " 7

The Roman woman, however, wore a gown that was more voluminous and more concealing, unless she could afford the finer silks and was prepared to ignore the storm of criticism that invariably ensued. Since she was unable to show off her figure to best advantage, therefore, she spent a great deal of time and money on her face and hair. First thing in the morning she would wipe away such remnants of face cream and bread-paste face pack as a night in bed had left on her skin and then settle down to the long process of having her hair done. "Some treat it with lotions that make it shine like the midday sun, and some dye it reddish-yellow, considering the natural color ugly. [Red-blond hair had become fashionable as a result of Roman contact with the Germanic tribes.] If they happen to be satisfied with black hair, they spend their husbands' money on anointing it with all the perfumes of Arabia. Then there are iron implements heated over a gentle flame, which crimp the hair and twirl it into ringlets. What pains are taken to make it lie over the eyebrows; there is hardly any space left for the forehead!" 8 Graying hairs were ruthlessly

Hairstyle of the early first century A.D.
Octavia, sister of the emperor Augustus

Hairstyle of the later first century A.D.
Julia, daughter of the emperor Titus

plucked out, and in extremity a Roman woman could wear a wig made from hair imported from India. It was expensive, being subject to customs duty, but even so must have been preferable to the trichological prescriptions advocated in earlier times. For gray hair, Mesopotamian experts had recommended a mixture of opium with a dash each of the gall of a black ox, a scorpion, and a pig, brewed up with the head of a black raven and the head of a stork. The Egyptians preferred a blend of laudanum, oil, cat's womb, and raven's egg. For baldness, they said, it was best to rub into the scalp a salve made from the fat of a lion, a hippopotamus, a crocodile, a cat, a serpent, and an ibex.[9]

Once her mistress's hair had been dressed, the Roman *ornatrix* started work on her face, an equally protracted business. The foundation was derived from the grease of sheep's wool (a kind of lanolin), and there were other creams and lotions with ingredients like barley meal, ground antlers, honey, and froth of red niter. For eyes, cheeks, brows, and lips the Roman woman appears to have used much the same preparations as those mentioned by Aristophanes. When the work of art was complete (it would have to be done again later in the day, after the bath), all that remained was to select sufficient jewelry to adorn every part that was capable of being adorned, to put on an outer tunic, pick up the kerchief used as a cross between napkin and duster, the peacock-tail fan that doubled as a flywhisk, and a bright green sunshade if the weather seemed to require it. Then, with the final drapery of a cloak, the lady was ready to venture out for the real business of the day—visiting the dressmaker or jeweler, being carried around town in a litter, going to call on friends, to worship at the temple, to attend the theater, or the amphitheater for the vicarious and bloody excitement of some gladiatorial contest, and of course to visit the public baths, a favorite social center even for those who had private ones. Finally, she would return home to supervise the preparations for dinner, whether a private one or a banquet, the only part of her day's activities that might charitably be described as work.[10]

RELIGIOUS DIVERSIONS

Religion, then as now, offered different things to different people. But for Roman women it was an escape from boredom, an escape tinged sometimes with spiritual, sometimes with physical excitement.

Most of Rome's own gods were either forbidding symbols of abstract morality, or survivors of an era when the gods' role had been to protect humanity in exchange for favors received. One of the protective deities was Vesta, guardian of the hearth and household, and for many centuries the well-being of the state was thought to depend on the diligence with which the Vestal Virgins, her priestesses, tended the sacred fire. There were only six Vestals, chosen by lot from a short list of candidates culled from the noblest Roman families. It was an honor not always sought. Suetonius recorded that when a vacancy cropped up in Augustus's day "many citizens busily tried to keep their daughters' names off the list of candidates." [11] The fact that a Vestal Virgin's property passed to the state instead of to her family may have had something to do with it.

The Vestal was enrolled at the age of ten or less (when she could still be guaranteed Virginal) and was committed to religious chastity for the next 30 years; afterward, she could be released or remain a priestess, as she chose. Her morals were a matter of national importance. When Rome suffered disaster at Cannae in 216 B.C., the blame was placed not on military incompetence but on erring Vestals. Two were denounced and condemned. A century

"To the sisters." Signboard of a Roman brothel

later, all six were declared corrupt, and three were found guilty of having surrendered their virginity. The penalty was lingering death, immured in a small underground chamber with a bed, a lamp, and a few days' food. Plutarch, describing the procession that escorted guilty Vestals to their death chambers, said, "There is no spectacle in the world more terrifying, and in Rome no day of comparable horror." [12]

Early contacts with Greece, however, began to bring color and warmth into the Roman pantheon, to introduce gods who were sufficiently human to awaken a personal response in their worshipers. Venus, originally the agricultural goddess of the Romans (in the days before Ceres), coalesced with tempestuous Aphrodite to become mother of the nation, guardian of marriage, and, incongruously, patron of the harlots who frequented the Circus Maximus in search of clients whose blood had been stirred up by the Games, or the camp of the Praetorian Guard on the eastern outskirts of the city, or the evil-smelling brothels that were to be found in every town in the peninsula. There were annual festivals to Venus. Married women worshiped her on the first of April; harlots (male and female) on the twenty-third.

In the same way, the Roman god Liber, once patron of growth and fertility, took on some aspects of the Greek Priapus. He was generally represented by a phallic symbol, which stood not only for sex but for conquest, defiance, and protection against the evil eye—a kind of magical, multipurpose obscene gesture. The word phallus comes from Greek. The Latin was *fascinum,* which had the associated meaning of "magical spirit," and this is the derivation that most dictionaries prudishly give for the modern word "fascinate."

Most striking of all the early imports was Dionysus, god of the vineyards and the vintage, who became Bacchus, god of drink and drunkenness. His cult made its first appearance soon after the war with Hannibal and was regarded with tolerance—for a while.

Then, said Livy, came the revelation. The stepfather of a young man named Aebutius, soon to come of age, had been misappropriating his property and was now faced with the danger of exposure. His only options were to kill the boy or find some way of blackmailing him into silence. One day, therefore, the young man's mother asked him to please her by becoming an initiate of Bacchus, and innocently he agreed. Unfortunately for the conspirators, he mentioned the matter to his mistress, a kindhearted and experienced girl named Hispala. "The gods forbid!" she cried, horrified, and under pressure revealed what it was all about. Originally, the cult had been unexceptionable, a thrice-yearly festival for women administered by respectable matrons. Then, under pretext of divine revelation, all had been changed. Men were admitted, and the festivals began to be held under cover of darkness five times a month. All emotional and sexual restraints were thrown off, and the only law was that all the laws of ordinary life should be transgressed. Frenzied women, their hair flying in the wind, ran screaming down to the Tiber to plunge burning torches into the river and bring them out again, miraculously, still alight.* The men, raving, incoherent, scarcely in control of their limbs, devoted themselves to the initiates, young men under twenty whom they "forcibly debauched." In this highly charged, orgiastic atmosphere, murder was the natural sequel for any initiate who struggled against his fate.

---

* The torches were tipped with quicklime and sulphur, probably blended with inextinguishable naphtha; the sulphur was included to give volume and pungency to the fumes.

Hispala's revelations led to the arrest of 7,000 people (Roman historians were fond of round numbers), and many of them came from distinguished families. The men who were condemned to death were executed by the state, while the women were returned to their families who were responsible for seeing justice done. It was claimed, probably with truth, that the Bacchic rites, in which all participants were fellow conspirators, helped to encourage or cover up for other kinds of crime, such as murder, false witness, and the forgery of wills and similar documents.[13] Henceforth, public worship of Bacchus was forbidden except to groups consisting of no more than three women and two men and even then only with official permission. The matter was considered important enough for the Senate to circulate this decree (of 186 B.C.) to dependencies not subject to Roman law, conveying that cooperation would be diplomatically tactful.

Although it was the worship of Bacchus that first attracted attention from Rome's administrators, there were other foreign gods and goddesses now massing on the eastern frontiers, deities who already had a vanguard of worshipers among the foreign slaves in Rome, and others who had been brought back to Greece by the soldiers of Alexander the Great and had already been partly naturalized.

Cybele was the first to arrive in Rome, brought in under the most distinguished auspices a few years before Bacchus. During the war with Hannibal, there was a prophecy drawn from what the anthropologist J. G. Frazer called "that convenient farrago of nonsense, the Sibylline Books," which said that Rome would be saved if the Great Goddess, the Magna Mater, was brought to the city. Ceremoniously, her symbol was shipped from Phrygia to be housed in a special temple and cared for by her own eunuch priests. But once the requirements of the prophecy had been complied with, it did not seem necessary to go any further, and for many decades Cybele was known to the people of Rome mainly through her priests, who wore strange oriental clothes and paraded the streets to the music of cymbals and tambourines, flutes and horns, very much as the disciples of Hare Krishna wander the capitals of the Western world today. When the religions from beyond Rome's eastern borders began to attract followers in large numbers, the rites of Cybele became less innocuous, marked by blood, hysteria, and self-mutilation (see pages 251–52).

Bacchus and Cybele were followed by Mithras and the Baalim, by Isis, Serapis, and others. Mithras became the soldiers' god, and Isis one of the women's favorites so that misogynists inevitably attributed all the trappings of female sensuality to her worship. They had a field day in A.D. 19 when a gullible young matron, Paulina, believing that she had spent the night in holy intercourse with Isis's associated god Anubis, discovered that the god's part had been played by one of her own entirely mortal admirers. The outcome was crucifixion for the priests of Isis, and the deportation of a great number of worshipers to the mosquito-ridden island of Sardinia, where, as Tiberius said, "If the climate killed them they would not be missed." [14]

But despite occasional persecutions when the new religions appeared to threaten the moral and political standards of Rome, they made steady headway. They had much in common, for all belonged in the tradition of the resurrection myth that had been such a feature of the early agricultural communities. They had gods who suffered, died, were buried, and then rose again. They imposed ceremonial initiation and occasional soul-cleansing periods of asceticism. And all worshipped *one* god, even if they did not claim that theirs was the only god. This stress on single deities, in contrast with the numerous gods of the old Roman religion, helped to pave the way for Christian monotheism.

The new religions also stressed personal piety, a salvation to be achieved not by the mechanical observances of the old creeds, but by personal commitment and personal virtue. Even to women for whom conventional religion meant little, the color and music, the ecstasies, and the spiritual peace that followed on periods of self-denial had a strong appeal. The eastern religions were new and different. They appeared, however falsely, to give meaning to lives that were otherwise meaningless; pointed bored minds along roads that appeared, however falsely, to lead *some*where. Under-employed women have always been the least critical and most conscientious supporters of the Christian church. It was a habit that began, perhaps, with the Near Eastern religions that immediately preceded the assault of Christianity upon the Roman empire.

A characteristically acrimonious exchange between the sexes

GROUNDS FOR DIVORCE

Much was to happen before the women of Rome became apostles of the new Christian church. At the beginning of the second century A.D., many of them were rootless and restless. "Her score is mounting," remarked Juvenal sourly of the gay divorcee of his day. "She has had eight husbands in five winters. Write *that* on her tombstone!" [15]

Women divorced their husbands because they were bored, husbands their wives because their wrinkles were beginning to show or because they were immoral or vain or shrewish. As early as 131 B.C., one Roman official—discussing the need to improve the birth rate—had said, "If it were possible to live without wives, gentlemen, we should all save ourselves the trouble. But since Nature has decreed that we can neither live with them in peace, nor without them at all, we should act with future benefits rather than present comfort in mind." [16] A few decades later, Cicero, who had just divorced his wife Terentia, was asked whether he would marry again. Certainly not, he replied. He "could not cope with philosophy and a wife at the same time." [17] Almost at once, however, he was forced to retract. It had slipped his mind that he would have to repay Terentia's dowry, and the only way he could raise the money was by marrying someone else.

Roman women and Roman men must have been equally difficult to live with. The emancipated woman of early imperial Rome had much in common with the more competitive type of feminist today—a peremptory mind, a domineering manner, and a whole-hearted contempt for moderation. Socially, her husband was just as hard to take; selfish to a marked degree, intellectually finicky, prone to moralize, lacking in imagination, and with a sense of humor as subtle as a custard pie. Husbands and wives, in effect, were no more compatible than they had ever been, but because there were more women of positive character in Rome than anywhere else in the ancient world, the sound of mismatched personalities grating together was painfully audible.

In early republican times, proof of marriage had depended on ceremonies and consummation. By the third century B.C. the criterion was a state of "living together in mutual consent," a simple agreement that was equally simple to reverse. Formerly, it had been impossible for a wife to divorce her husband for any reason; now she could, for almost no reason. And did, with enthusiastic and increasing frequency.

Easy divorce, however, turned out to be something that cut both ways, especially for a woman whose emotional was greater than her financial independence. If she belonged to one of the bluer-blooded families who used marriage as an adhesive for political alliances, she was likely to find her marriage dissolved by her family, whether she herself wished it or not, as briskly as it had been set up. Livia, mother of Cato the Younger and grandmother of Brutus (two of Julius Caesar's most bitter enemies), was first married to a political associate of her brother's, then, when the two men quarreled, divorced and coolly married off to another. Caesar himself divorced Pompeia because through no fault of her own her morals had ceased to be "above suspicion"—which would not do at all, said Caesar, for the wife of a man who was not only political *praetor* of Rome, but also *pontifex maximus,* head of the college of priests.

Augustus, Caesar's great-nephew and adopted son, whose public pronouncements on morality were unimpeachably sanctimonious, did not hesitate to divorce his wife Scribonia for "moral perversity" (she had taken a dislike to one of his mistresses) when he fell in love with Livia Drusilla, seventeen years old and six months pregnant by her current husband. And Julia, his daughter by Scribonia, was also to suffer from the Roman habit of viewing matrimony as a coalition between parties rather than people, though it was generally held at the time that her husbands suffered more than she did. Two of them had to divorce their wives in order to marry her, one of them, Tiberius, with the greatest reluctance. It proved worthwhile in the end, however, for when Augustus died Tiberius succeeded him as emperor, even if, after ten years of marriage to the enterprising Julia, he turned out to be a somewhat antisocial one.

By early imperial times, many women were beginning to find their extramarital activities curtailed, not because their husbands complained (though some of them did), but because the Emperor Augustus instituted legislation which almost accidentally brought adultery into the public domain, introducing statutory penalties for an offense that had formerly been a matter for the family alone.

These penalties applied, of course, mainly to women. If a husband discovered his wife's adultery, he was forced to divorce her or run the risk of himself being prosecuted. She was banished, deprived of half her dowry and a third of any other property she possessed, and it was a criminal offense for any other man to marry her. Her seducer (if married) was also banished, though not to the same island as the lady. Any man, in fact, who could be regarded as conniving at a woman's adultery was liable to penalties, if he himself was married. Bachelors were apparently exempt. A husband with a mistress who was not a registered prostitute could be prosecuted for "unnatural vice," and when there was a sudden increase in applications to be put on the register of prostitutes, many of them from quite respectable women, the Senate had to take hurried action. It was not until the fourth century that adulterous husbands were made subject to the same penalty as adulterous wives, though this advance was offset by the ruthlessness of the penalty—which was death.

Roman history is full of the names of strong-minded women. There was Sempronia, who was said to be involved in the Catiline conspiracy of the first century B.C., and Fulvia who betrayed it. There was Cornelia, the high-minded wife of Pompey, and the rather less high-minded Praecia, who was thought to be all-powerful by reason of the influence she wielded over her lover, Cornelius Cethegus, the leading politician of the day. There was Brutus's remarkable mother, Servilia, and his decisive wife Porcia. In later times, Augustus's consort, Livia, helped to stabilize a new order which was promptly to be undermined by the activities of other imperial ladies, among them Julia and Julilla, Livilla, Drusilla, Poppaea, and Messalina.

It is sometimes difficult to distinguish between the women of the imperial house, not because they bore any particular resemblance to one another, but because of the similarity of their names and of the crimes that were attributed to them by the historians of the time. In early Rome, men had two names, sometimes three, but women customarily had only one, the family name. If there were several sisters they had to be distinguished by numbers, although when they married the addition of their husbands' names (in the possessive) helped with identification. Thus the three sisters of a man named Publius Clodius might have been known as Pius's Clodia, Agrippa's Clodia, and Octavian's Clodia. In imperial times, women began to take two names of their own, the family name first, followed by their father's second "given" name or mother's second name. Nevertheless, the possible permutations were very limited when two families intermarried as busily as the Julians and Claudians, which is why, to the modern reader, there appears to be a superabundance of Julias and Claudias among the women of the imperial house.

Confusion, of course, is worse confounded by the fact that so many of them were accused by their contemporaries of remarkably similar crimes. Were nymphomania, intemperance, and a free hand with the poison phial hereditary diseases in ancient Rome? It seems, on the whole, that many of the women involved were victims of the age-old tradition of imputing to nonconformists the nastiest habits that sprang to their critics' minds. From the second century B.C. until very recent times, accusations of sex orgies, blood drinking, and cannibalism were thrown with monotonous and improbable frequency at every heretic or heathen in the religious book—Jews, Carpocratians, Manichaeans, Montanists, Gnostics, Euchites, Catharists, Bogomils, Albigensians, and Waldensians, not to mention Henricians, Apostolici, Luciferans, Adamites, witches, gypsies, Aztecs, Incas (see pages 289–91), and a great many others.[18] The Romans were too logical and too irreligious to carry their denunciations of women to quite such lengths, but sex orgies and an arbitrary way with the opposition seemed reasonable charges to level at women who offended against the conventions. Sex orgies may well have been a feature of the mystery religions to which many of them subscribed, but until the nineteenth century it seems probable that most of the poisonings for which women were blamed were in reality the work of the salmonella bacterium.

Even so, many well-educated, intelligent, bored women undoubtedly did run wild, and the question is why, in a society that was essentially masculine, were they allowed to get away with so much for so long?

One reason, no doubt, was that sexual mischief kept them out of political mischief. Another, that the Roman husband did not greatly care what his wife did as long as she did not trouble him. But most important of all was that there were not enough women to go round. A man was attracted to marriage by the prospect of a son and heir, and the certainty of a useful transfusion of money in the form of the traditional dowry. No matter how he subsequently felt about his wife, if he wanted to keep the dowry the only sure way of doing so was by keeping her well. The competition, therefore, was stiff. There is no word in Latin that corresponds with the modern word "spinster."

POPULATION PROBLEMS

In the ranks of the freeborn, according to Cassius Dio, there were far fewer women than men at the time of the early empire, and some estimates make the difference as large as 17 per cent.[19] The major reason was probably that fathers looked upon girls as an expensive luxury—the going rate for dowries among the rich was said to be a million sesterces, roughly the equivalent of one-and-a-half hundredweights of gold bullion, which had to be paid in three annual instalments. When Cicero had to find a dowry for his daughter Tullia his financial situation when the third instalment fell due was so desperate that he wondered whether he ought not to arrange for her to be divorced instead.[20] Among the less well-off citizens, the sums were of course smaller, but often still heavy in proportion.

Rome's most ancient laws, the so-called "laws of Romulus," had enjoined parents to raise all male children and the first-born girl, and until well into the imperial period many Romans did just that. In the city there were places such as the foot of the Lactaria column that were specifically set aside for the abandonment of unwanted infants, girls usually, but sometimes boys who were illegitimate or deformed or whose birth had been accompanied by evil omens. A few might be picked up by strangers and adopted or brought up as slaves, but most were left to die in their baskets from exposure and starvation.[21] Not until the fourth century was infanticide in the form of exposure forbidden, and even then the equally ancient practice of simple neglect was often just as effective. An inevitable sequel to the destruction of baby girls was a shortage of potential mothers in subsequent generations, which had its own effect on population figures.

Although girl children were discriminated against, there was no countervailing enthusiasm for boys. None of the five classes of Roman society favored large families, and couples who were childless, whether by choice or chance, were by no means unusual. When contemporaries remarked on the situation of Sempronius Gracchus and his wife Cornelia, who had 12 children of whom only three survived infancy, it was not the high mortality rate but the high fertility rate that interested them.

The two upper classes of citizens consisted of the patricians— members of the great families—and the *equites* or "knights," whose title was a relic of the days when they had been landed gentry expected to supply their own horses in time of war, but who were now the business and mercantile barons of the empire. The fragmentation of estate or business that was bound to result if either class produced too many heirs was a recurring nightmare. Except in time of war, when the wastage rate was high, two sons appeared to be quite enough, one to inherit, and one in reserve in case something happened to the first.

The third class of citizens covered a wide range, from comfortably-off professional men, through intellectual and literary figures who were often impecunious (and correspondingly resentful), to the poor provincials who relied on state handouts for their daily bread. The first group took much the same economical view of families as the patricians and knights; the second included the most vocal critics of the institution of marriage; and the third could not afford it at all, since the *annona* (the bread dole) was for men only and would not stretch to feeding wives and children.

Slaves and freedmen formed the other two classes of the community; neither had citizenship. Slaves rarely married, since men far outnumbered women, and their owners in any case did not approve, although some encouraged concubinage as a means of increasing the work force at minimum cost. Freedmen, slaves who had bought or been granted a qualified freedom, seem to have been an interesting group, though, as writers like Petronius make clear, they were considered exceedingly vulgar, possibly because they often had a good deal of business acumen and some became very rich. If freedmen wanted to marry, they had little choice but to marry freedwomen, who were both few in number and independent of mind. Since it was unusual for slaves to be freed while still young, the odds against such marriages being productive of large families were high.

Social pressures, therefore, often operated against the production of children, and against marriage itself. But there were personal pressures, too. Rome had first had to begin legislating against celibacy as far back as 403 b.c., partly because of the unsettling effect of continuous war, but partly also, no doubt, because the people of Italy had learned more from the Greeks settled on the bay of Naples than just the principles of the alphabet and the names of the Homeric gods. In imperial times, Rome still had a number of distinguished pederasts in the Athenian tradition, and many others who were homosexual or heterosexual as opportunity offered, the poets Horace and Martial among them.

Romans who did choose to marry and set their sights on a family of two, or perhaps three, would have been psychologically incapable of leaving the matter in the lap of the gods. They were proud of their logical minds and took genuine pleasure in formulating neat and orderly laws, even if another and more intense pleasure lay in thinking of ways to circumvent them. They deplored leaving things to chance. Historians who believe that the Romans did not practice contraception point out that Ovid's *Ars Amatoria*, that discursive and rather limited handbook for ladies of easy virtue,* did not mention the subject (wisely, as his readers probably knew more about it than he did), and that neither, as a rule, did Roman poets, philosophers, or letter writers. No doubt they had different but equally valid reasons. Juvenal, of course, was the exception. He could always find a reason for mentioning

---

* It is, in fact, little more than a cynical summary of the art of flirtation, not love, and certainly not sex. The nearest it comes to explicitness is in a brief section on how women can show off their figures to best advantage in bed. "Whom the long hip-line graces, on the bed/Should kneel and slightly backward bend her head,/While youthful thighs and faultless breasts demand/That you lie slantwise and your lover stand. . . ."[22]

something that might be chalked up to the score of humanity's sins.

There was plenty of contraceptive information available for those who needed it, or thought they needed it, especially among the literate upper classes. However, in view of the general tenor of relationships between husbands and wives, it is possible that the most widely used form was the simplest and most reliable of all— abstention. The main alternative, particularly for men who liked to feel they were in control of the situation, would be *coitus interruptus*, while women, if they were sensible, relied on the olive oil recommended by Aristotle in the fourth century B.C. rather than the technique Lucretius attributed to harlots 300 years later. It was their custom, said Lucretius, to undulate their hips during intercourse, which gave their partners pleasure and at the same time directed the seminal fluid away from the danger zone.[23] In fact, the evidence of Greek vase painting makes it clear that the hetairai knew a better method. Unless their clients were strongly opposed to it, they usually insisted on anal intercourse.[24]

The indefatigable Pliny, a moral man, could not bring himself to approve contraception except for women who were overproductive. His solution was to try to diminish the desire for sexual intercourse, and his recipes must have been quite effective, even if not always for scientific reasons. "Mouse dung . . . applied in the form of a liniment" was one suggestion; another involved swallowing either snail excrement or pigeon droppings mixed with oil and wine; a third required the testicles and blood of a dunghill cock to be secreted under the bed. Further, he pointed out that if a woman's loins were "rubbed with blood taken from the ticks on a wild black bull" she would be inspired "with aversion to sexual intercourse." [25] First catch your bull. . . .

Pliny's contemporary, Dioscorides, whose works were still being consulted and relied on as late as the sixteenth century, had some equally interesting suggestions. After intercourse, he recommended inserting pepper (quantity unspecified) into the mouth of the uterus. It is not clear whether, like his predecessors Theophrastus and Hippocrates, he still attributed curative qualities to *piper nigrum*, or whether it occurred to him that, since sneezing was often recommended as a way of expelling semen, it would be a good idea to take the sneeze closer to source. One of his formulae, however, must have proved as near infallible as he could have wished, for it was guaranteed to prevent conception during the first five days after menstruation—in other words, the days when, according to the "safe period" or "Vatican roulette" theory, a woman is highly unlikely to conceive even without benefit of potions.[26]

A more reliable adviser was the early second-century gynecologist, Soranus of Ephesus, who had studied in the advanced and sophisticated Greco-Egyptian city of Alexandria before he began to practice in Rome. Unusually for the time, Soranus distinguished clearly between contraception and abortion and also regarded with the gravest suspicion all contraceptive and abortifacient prescriptions intended to be taken by mouth; apart from anything else, he said, they ruined the digestion. Nor did he think much of amulets, whose magical properties he described as delusive.* Soranus's main recommendations were for wool plugs for the uterus, impregnated with gummy substances (which would have the effect of rendering the sperm sluggish) or with astringent solutions designed to contract the opening to fit closely round the plug. No doubt the formulae varied in effectiveness, and some of the astringents may have worked for only a very short time. But the combination of mechanical and chemical inhibitors was as good as any the world was to devise for many centuries to come.

One of the most serious failures of Roman contraceptive techniques, as far as women were concerned, was that they rarely made allowance for unpremeditated intercourse. It cannot always have been easy to lay hands on cedar gum, opobalsam, and galbanum in the hectic interval between the first kiss and the final consummation, and this may have been why so many medical writers had so much to say about abortion (nauseous potions and physical jerks being the usual recommendations). Soranus, however, was equal to anything. In such a situation, he advised, "the woman ought, in the moment during coitus when the man ejaculates his seminal fluid, to hold her breath, draw her body back a little so that the semen cannot penetrate into the mouth of the uterus, then immediately get up and sit down with bent knees, and in this position provoke sneezes." Fortunately, he recommended following this performance with a thorough douche, which may have had some effect.[28]

There is a theory, based on one version of the legend of Minos

---

* Later generations showed a continuing willingness to be deluded. Aëtios of Amida, in the sixth century, said, "Wear part of the womb of a lioness in a tube of ivory. This is very effective." [27]

and Pasiphae, that the Romans may already have invented the condom, using goat bladders for the purpose.[29] There is no real reason why they should not have thought of it, but the fact that nothing more was heard of it until the sixteenth century (see page 336) makes it seem unlikely.

Altogether there was plenty of advice available for the literate minority, even if potions brewed up by the local witch would in many cases have been just as effective. For although the Romans probably used contraception, it is equally probable that they may not have needed it.

The Romans' failure to raise families had as much to do with involuntary as with voluntary factors. Mortality rates were high and child-bearing years correspondingly few. Despite the number of tough old gentlemen whose Latin was to tax the capacities of so many later generations of schoolboys, most Romans, like the people of the pre-neolithic era, could expect to die before they reached 30. Infant mortality ran at 20 percent. Ten percent of the population of Italy was crammed into Rome itself, helpless prey for any marauding virus.[30] In the middle of the second century A.D. soldiers brought smallpox back from Mesopotamia; the Italians had no immunity, and some towns and provinces lost almost one-third of their inhabitants. A hundred years later another pestilence struck, possibly measles, which is a killer for people exposed to it for the first time; deaths in the city of Rome totaled over 5,000 a day at the height of the epidemic.[31] As always, it was the weak who suffered most, the women and children of the poorer classes.

But women and children of all classes suffered as their predecessors had done from lack of adequate medical care—more, perhaps, for the urban attitudes, tensions, and stresses that take pregnancy out of the realm of "natural" phenomena in the West today must already have appeared in Rome, which, with three-quarters of a million inhabitants, was the world's first modern-scale city. Even when women did conceive, they frequently suffered miscarriage, or difficulties at parturition, or postnatal infections. Babies who were not stillborn were in danger not only for the first few days, but for the first four or five years of life.

Unspecified "feminine disorders" were responsible for many deaths, and recent medical research has suggested one possibility not previously explored. In teenage girls the membrane covering the cervix is immature and sensitive; it is believed to be irritated by contact with semen and does not become more resistant until the twenties. There is evidence to suggest that early sexual intercourse therefore not only increases the risk of cervical cancer but does so at an early age; in Britain since the Pill has come into use, there has been a perceptible increase in the number of girls under 20 who have died from cervical cancer, even though deaths in other age groups have dropped by between 11 and 15 per cent.[32] Despite slightly earlier maturity, it seems that Roman girls must have run the same risk, particularly those of the upper classes, who frequently married at the age of 13 or 14. The poor, for once, would be in less danger. Marriage for them usually came later because young men were often sent overseas with the legions or auxiliaries, and those who stayed at home could not afford to marry young.

These were all general factors, influencing the number of potential child-bearers and the number of their reproductive years. But there were almost certainly other, invisible hazards directly related to sterility and/or impotence which, ironically enough, affected precisely those of the upper classes who were most likely to be in the market for contraceptives, the free-living rich.

In 1966, American sociologist Seabury Colum Gilfillan convincingly showed that the Roman upper classes must have suffered from chronic lead poisoning, an illness capable of causing sterility in men and bringing about miscarriages and stillbirths among women.[33] Clinical and laboratory investigations in 1978 further indicated that lead poisoning even on an extremely low level is directly related to poor learning ability, inattentiveness, and misbehavior in children.[34] This would influence the personality development of Roman children, quite apart from any more extreme physical effects that might manifest themselves as their lead intake increased in later life.

The Romans absorbed lead from the water that ran through their lead pipes, from cups and cooking pots, from cosmetics such as the white lead women used for face powder, and from their wine. To improve the frequently rough Roman wine, a sweet grape syrup was often added that had been boiled down in lead-lined pots until it reached the right consistency; during the process it also became strongly contaminated with lead.

It was not, however, only the lead content of their water and wine that contributed to nonproductiveness in the Roman male. As Shakespeare said in *Macbeth*, alcohol may increase sexual desire but is inclined to detract from performance, and scientists today believe that alcohol also has a direct toxic effect on the testes, bringing about a substantial decline in secretion of the male sex hormone, testosterone. An American study of 14,000 male alcoholics over a 37-year period showed that almost one in ten suffered from total impotence.[35]

The Romans' intake of alcohol was far from negligible, even if their orgies may not have been all they were later cracked up to be. There were the exhibitionists, of course—Novellius Torquatus was said to have swallowed ten liters at one draft—but on a more everyday level other men began drinking at the baths in the late afternoon and did not stop until dawn was in the sky. The poet Martial, wondering what had possessed him to invite someone he disliked to dinner, decided that the five pints of wine he had drunk had been responsible. The alcohol content of Roman wine was about 17 percent (roughly two-fifths of the strength of a modern 80 percent U.S. or 70 percent British proof spirit), so Martial's five pints of wine must have had the total potency of around one and a half bottles of whiskey or gin. Even if he drank it watered, as so many Romans did, it was not negligible. In fact, if Martial and his contemporaries regularly drank at anything approaching this rate, they must have come close enough to alcoholism to suffer from the toxic effects, if not quite total impotence. Half a bottle of bourbon a day over five to ten years is estimated to be the danger level.[36]

If the Romans escaped sterility from lead poisoning, therefore, they were in danger of reduced fertility or impotence from excessive drinking. But even this was not all. Every time a Roman went to the baths he further endangered his sex life. Most men went every day.

The first room a man entered after disrobing was the *tepidarium*, the warm room, where the temperature was controlled by hot-air ducts embedded in the floors and walls. Next he passed on to the *caldarium*, heated by the same ducts but to a higher temperature. This was the room with the bathing tank in it, which was so hot, said Seneca, that one would scarcely condemn an erring slave to be washed alive in it. Nowadays, he complained, people would have accused even a man like Scipio of being provincial "because he did not stew in full daylight and enjoy being cooked in his bath." [37] This was where the bathing hours were passed,

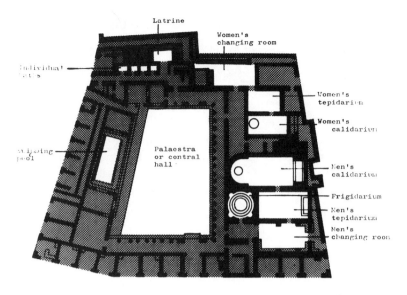

Ground plan of the Stabian baths at Pompeii, built in the second century B.C.

alternately soaking in water and sweating on the benches around it. Finally, by way of the milder *tepidarium*, the bather progressed to the *frigidarium* for a swift cold plunge, if he were strong-minded enough.

Unfortunately, hot baths appear to have the effect of reducing fertility by inhibiting sperm production. The normal temperature of the testicles is lower than that of the rest of the body, and recent experiments in Kansas have shown that if the temperature is raised even just to the normal body temperature (37°C or 98.4°F) it is enough to have an effect on fertility; the Roman *caldarium* appears to have maintained a temperature of something in the region of 43°C or 110°F. During the Kansas experiments, one man who had been infertile for two years succeeded in becoming a father after two weeks (or, more precisely, nine months after two weeks) of taking long cold baths instead of long hot ones, and two other men, following the same treatment, more than doubled the number of sperm they produced, while the sperm themselves were more active.[38]

Logical modern theories and small-scale experiments can only be measured tentatively against what happened in the past, but it is a mistake simply to dismiss them, as one authority does lead poisoning, for example, by remarking, "If this is true, there must have been remarkable differences between individuals in resistance to the disease. The community's water came through the same lead pipes; within any class of society, food was cooked in the same kind of pots."[39] But a man who drank little water, and a decent wine that did not need to be sweetened with grape syrup, was obviously less susceptible than most to lead poisoning, while a woman who powdered her nose several times a day would be more susceptible. An analysis of what is known about the personal habits of specific Roman couples could provide the answer. In the meantime, it is perhaps significant that in the case of Agrippa and Julia, who had five children, and Germanicus and Agrippina who had eight, both husbands spent much of their adult lives abroad away from Rome with its lead pipes and hot baths, and both appear to have been abstemious; Tacitus described Germanicus as being "modest in his pleasures," and Agrippa was a straitlaced Roman of the old school.[40]

The Romans were only too aware of the dangers of a falling birth rate, and from the second century B.C. had been obsessed by it. It was all very well for Cicero to claim that what was needed was "less lust and larger families," [41] but there was a limit to what legislation could achieve.

The Emperor Augustus did try. By laws of 18 B.C., supplemented by others in A.D. 9, he ruled that widows must remarry within two years and divorcees within 18 months.* Unmarried men were barred from accepting legacies, and childless couples within the productive age group were permitted to receive only half of anything bequeathed them. The ancient customs that had controlled intermarriage between classes were relaxed, and it became permissible for the freeborn (except for those of senatorial family) to marry freed slaves. There were rewards for couples who had three living children—"living" being taken to include any sons killed in war.** In the countryside, four children were needed to qualify, and beyond the peninsula five. Freedmen, like citizens, were encouraged to multiply. If they had one child, they had to bequeath half their property to their former owner; two children, and he was still entitled to one third; three, and he received nothing. Adultery became a matter for the public courts, not the

---

* The same general rules were still being applied in early nineteenth-century Poland, though the object was agricultural efficiency. A farmer's widow had to remarry within a year or have the farm sold over her head; a man with young children and no wife had only six months to remarry if he were not to lose his holding.[42]

** The "rights of three children" applied only in the city of Rome and soon degenerated into an all-purpose award for good behavior. The Emperor Domitian bestowed it on Martial, who had no children at all.

family. And all property bequeathed in contravention of the laws went to the Treasury—which was no doubt one of the reasons why the laws were retained even after they had been seen to fail.[43]

This legislation appears to have had some effect on the febrile atmosphere of upper-class life in the city itself, which was fortunate, as Augustus had indulged in a good deal of high-minded rhetoric about a return to ancient morality. But it had no effect on the birth rate. The Romans, in fact, were trying to bring social pressures to bear on a problem that was as much medical as social, and medical in a way that was as unique to Rome as Roman society itself.

Other early societies had also suffered from short life spans; from high mortality due to famine, epidemics, and wars; from "feminine disorders" stemming from precocious sexual experience; and from social tendencies (such as Athenian pederasty) that inhibited reproduction. Sometimes, as in Greece, population figures had taken a downward plunge. But not so fatally or so consistently.

There was something specific about Roman society that accounted for the population decline. Partly, it was the instinct of the luxurious rich, so often seen in later history, to limit childbearing both for their own convenience and that of the next generation. It was an instinct that worked in innumerable, often indefinable ways, and contraception was only one facet of it. Partly, too, it was a matter of the new and nervous stresses of city life. And partly it may have been a compound of the unrecognizable physiological side effects of what the Romans themselves saw as the agreeable perquisites of the good life, the life to which they—the men who had expanded all the boundaries of the known world—were entitled by right of conquest. Piped water, hot baths, and plentiful wine, however inconsiderable they may appear, may well have had a place among the great determinants of history.

For it was shortage of manpower that, in the last analysis, brought about the downfall of Rome. That, and a currency that had become almost worthless. Quite unable to police the frontiers of her empire, or to administer directly within those frontiers, Rome had to work through the "barbarians" who simultaneously hated and envied her. And it was the infiltration of those barbarians into the management of the empire that led to the final disintegration of what had once been the most elegant and logical structure yet created by mankind.

6.

The Christian
Church

The disintegration of the Roman empire was a gradual process, a matter of slow erosion and patchy subsidence. Although the year 410, when the city of Rome itself was sacked by Alaric the Goth, is sometimes taken as the turning point, the Roman era had in fact ended and the new one begun almost a century earlier when the Emperor Constantine allied himself, and by implication the state, with the Christian church.

Constantine's decision was as much political as religious. The army, on which his predecessors had relied to hold the empire together, was instead contributing to its ruin. Roman law, and the Roman monetary and trading systems, were likewise unequal to the task. It seemed that Christianity alone—a foreign religion transfigured by almost three centuries of proselytizing within the empire—held out some hope of unifying the vast and heterogeneous collection of peoples contained within Rome's wide frontiers, from the lowlands of Scotland in the far northwest to the Asian shores of the Black Sea in the east.

The Church, organized on the lines of the imperial administration, with its dioceses and provinces corresponding to Roman divisions, had the makings of a functional authority, and in the long run Constantine's judgment proved to be right. As the European empire crumbled away into independent and often ephemeral kingdoms, and as the territories ruled by his successors from the "new Rome" of Constantinople (Byzantium) shrank into a nimbus around the Bosphorus, the Church did succeed in standing firm and did succeed in holding together the heterogeneous peoples of the empire. But not for the benefit of Rome.

During the confused and still obscure centuries between A.D. 400 and 1000, populations shifted, rulers came and went, the whole face of Europe changed, and changed again. But the Christian church, its Galilean message grafted on to a heritage of Babylonian realism, Hebrew absolutism, Greek Platonism, and Roman materialism, survived and expanded as the one cohesive force in an unstable world. In almost every sense—even militarily, with the Crusades—the Christian church proved itself to be the true successor of imperial Rome.

In other political circumstances, Christian morality might never have gained the grip it did on all Western thought, a grip so paralyzing that it is only now beginning to relax. But there were two factors in the European situation during the centuries immediately following the collapse of Rome that made the result almost inevitable. These were the general absence of state-imposed law and order, and the disappearance of literacy from public and private life.

The collapse of the central power and the reversion to a barter economy in Europe had combined to turn society in upon itself. Life became highly localized, and secular law either unenforced or unenforceable. But the Church had a strong vested interest in social stability, which alone could produce the steady flow of income it needed, and parish priests stepped in to fill the secular gap with Christian precepts. The moral law they preached was backed with threats of hellfire (a more effective deterrent than any law-enforcement agency could have devised), and it was also universal, as valid in the village as in the town, in the next county as the next country. In this way, and over a period of several centuries, Christian morality was not only disseminated but infused with social as well as religious authority.

It was a morality drawn, basically, from only three sources—parts of the Old Testament, all of the New, and the commentaries and meditations of early Christian thinkers concerning areas of doubt in the fundamental texts.

The Church Fathers, outstanding though they were in their generation, were no more than human and their experience was limited. In a period of general literacy, their conclusions would have been contested, modified, and modified again. But literacy and learning were two of the most important victims in the collapse of the Classical world. During the so-called Dark Ages, reading and writing became the preserve of the monasteries, and what was read and what was written were virtually at the sole discretion of the Church. Monastic scribes were fully occupied in copying what was orthodox; what was unorthodox simply did not exist. Whether deliberate or not, censorship was very close to being complete.

As a result, the words and conclusions of the Church Fathers remained unassailed, and so, in time, became unassailable. Their deliberations—products often of a highly personal and highly prejudiced view of life and society—took on an aura of revealed truth, and their morality, almost entirely relative in its origins, achieved the status of the absolute. It is undoubtedly a tribute (if an ambiguous one) to such men as St. Jerome and St. Augustine that much of what the modern world still understands by "sin" stems not from the teachings of Jesus of Nazareth, or from the tablets handed down from Sinai, but from the early sexual vicissitudes of a handful of men who lived in the twilight days of imperial Rome.

THE CELIBATE VIEW OF SEX

"I should like," said St. Jerome in the fourth century, "every man to take a wife who cannot manage to sleep alone because he gets frightened at night." [1]

Jerome, one of the most redoubtable and (from a safe distance) stimulating of the Church Fathers, had the utmost contempt for matrimony, and in this he was not alone. It was not wholly a matter of personal preference. Missionary faiths rarely make the mistake of undervaluing what seems likely to bring in converts, and sexual continence was an important element in the asceticism that attracted the sated peoples of the Roman world to Christianity, as to other Near Eastern religions. Most of the other religions asked only temporary continence from their followers, but the Christians urged it as a permanent state.*

---

* Though not irretrievably permanent. When Origen of Alexandria settled the problem of his own continence once and for all by castrating himself (taking too literally the reference in *Matthew* 19, 12 to men who "made themselves eunuchs for the kingdom of heaven's sake"), he put an end not only to his sex life but, because of the orthodox Biblical attitude to men with injured genitals, to any possibility of subsequent canonization.

As early as the first century A.D., St. Paul had laid the foundations of the view that celibacy was superior to marriage. Forced to reprove the small Christian community at Corinth—one of the less inhibited cities of the ancient world—for its highly secular attitude toward sex, he had said, "Do you not know that your bodies are members of Christ? Shall I therefore take the members of Christ and make them members of a prostitute? Never! Do you not know that he who joins himself to a prostitute becomes one body with her? For, as it is written, 'The two shall become one flesh' " (I Corinthians 6, 15-16).

He was perhaps the first thinker in Western history to equate spirituality with sex, though it looked, to begin with, as if he had painted himself into a corner. If the spiritual implications made sex with harlots inadmissible, then sex with wives must be a desirable religious experience. Paul, however, solved the problem logically enough by declaring that, even so, celibacy was a more Christian condition, since it imposed no worldly obligations that might interfere with devotion to the Lord. Nevertheless, he recognized that it required a level of self-control that not all could achieve. To the hot-blooded he said, "It is better to marry than to burn [with desire]," and advised that "the husband should give to his wife her conjugal rights, and likewise the wife to her husband. . . . Do not refuse one another except perhaps by agreement for a season, that you may devote yourselves to prayer; but then come together again, lest Satan tempt you through lack of self-control" (I Cor. 7, 9 and 3-5).

St Paul, in fact, was not quite the reactionary that later interpretation of his words often made him appear. In essence, he was a man of his time who believed that marriage could be good but that celibacy was better—for those who could take it. Gradually, however, Church leaders allowed the modification to wither away, leaving only the gaunt skeleton of his conclusions. But the idea of marriage had been blessed by God and sanctified by Christ, and a certain amount of ingenuity was necessary when it came to justifying the proposition that celibacy was superior. If there were no intellectual challenges, however, there would be no theology, and the Church Fathers proved themselves entirely equal to the task. They were aided by other philosophies current at the time—by Gnosticism and Manichaeism, which held that what was of the flesh was inherently evil, and by the Severian argument that

"St. Jerome tempted by thoughts of maidens"—a medieval artist's view

woman as a whole and man from the waist down were creations of the devil.[2]

They were aided, too, by the wide currency of the folk legends contained in the New Testament Apocrypha, with their popular stories of early Christianity and the adventures of the apostles, not the shadowy figures of the Gospels, but outspoken personalities who said bluntly that sex was "an experiment of the serpent" and marriage "a foul and polluted way of life." [3]

Also influential were the very personal attitudes of some leading Christian thinkers, among them Tertullian, Jerome, and Augustine, the three men who, with St. Paul, were to leave the most lasting impression on all subsequent Christian sexual ideas. They were not bloodless natural ascetics, but men who had led full lives (and full sex lives) before being converted to celibacy, and they had reacted with sometimes morbid revulsion against the sins they now abjured. Jerome, for example, compulsively recalled the hideous torments he had undergone during his austerities in the desert of Chalcis—a popular, even slightly overcrowded resort for fourth-century hermits—when he had burned with remembered desire, his fevered imagination filling his cell with troupes of dancing girls. And Augustine admitted that he had prayed constantly to God, "Give me chastity—but not yet." [4]

It was Augustine who epitomized a general feeling among the Church Fathers that the act of intercourse was fundamentally disgusting. Arnobius called it filthy and degrading, Methodius unseemly, Jerome unclean, Tertullian shameful, Ambrose a defilement. In fact there was an unstated consensus that God ought to have invented a better way of dealing with the problem of procreation. Augustine, retrospectively offended by his own experiences, set his mind to the problem and concluded that the fault lay not with God but with Adam and Eve.

According to his reconstruction, the man and woman made by God were at first creatures of the mind, wholly in control of their bodies. "Perish the thought that there should have been any unregulated excitement, or any need to resist desire!" [5] Sex in the Garden of Eden, if it had ever taken place, would have been cool and rarefied, with no eroticism, no uncontrollable responses, certainly no ecstasy. A matter, simply, of utilizing the mechanical equipment designed by the Creator to fulfill, with deliberation and a kind of grave appreciation, the requirements of the reproductive process.

But when Adam and Eve fell into sin they became conscious of new and selfish impulses (which Augustine called concupiscence, or lust) over which they had no control. The immediate effect of their lapse from grace was that they became aware and

Expulsion from
the Garden of Eden
of an embarrassed
Adam and Eve

ashamed of their nakedness, and Augustine interpreted this as meaning that their own disobedience to the Creator was reflected in sudden and willful activity on the part of their genitals. It was their inability to govern this new phenomenon that led them to sew fig leaves together to make aprons, to conceal what were now to be called pudenda (from the Latin *pudere,* "to be ashamed").

Augustine believed that the guilt of the original transgression, transmitted by the inherited concupiscence of Adam and Eve's descendants, still persisted in humanity, and that this explained the perversity and independence of the sexual organs, the intractable nature of the carnal impulse, and the shame generally aroused by the act of coitus. Lust and sex were integral to the doctrine of Original Sin, and every act of coitus performed by humanity subsequent to the Fall was necessarily evil, just as every child born of it was born into sin. Though God had irradiated the first man and woman with a blameless physical instinct designed to provide for continuation of the species, lust had converted it into something shameful.[6]

One result of this ingenious piece of rationalization was a reemphasis on the purity of Jesus of Nazareth, whose conception had not been tainted by any carnal contact. But it also implied that humanity's best hope of redemption lay in rejecting coitus and, with it, the burden of guilt inherited from Adam and Eve. Only the celibate could hope to achieve the state of grace that had existed in the Garden of Eden.

It was incumbent on those too weak to be celibate to strive to recapture the original, blameless physical instinct of God's purpose, to use sex without passion to beget the next generation of

Christians.* The cold-blooded, purposeful intercourse preached by Augustine may appear today almost to merit the adjectives the Church Fathers used about sex in general—unseemly, degrading, shameful—but at the time nothing could have been better suited to the intellectual climate.

Augustine had set out to validate the Church Fathers' revulsion against sex, and had succeeded in providing a justification that satisfied both faith and intellect. The body was no more than a flawed vessel for the mind and spirit, and it was now up to the Church to propagate Christian morality in these terms. Augustine's meditations, as a result, were to have incalculable effect on the lives of future generations, not always in ways that could be neatly particularized but in more subtle matters of stress and emphasis. What was clear right from the start, however, was that if it was sinful to find enjoyment in sex, then the great majority of ordinary people were sinners.

HOLY MATRIMONY

Obviously, it was now necessary for the priesthood to become chaste. Celibacy was to be the badge of moral authority. But this was not easy to bring about, for at this time married men could be accepted for ordination although no man could marry *after* he had been ordained. Already in A.D. 386, Pope Siricius, in what is believed to have been the first authentic papal decree, had attempted to prohibit married presbyters and deacons from having intercourse with their wives.** This, apparently, had no effect, and neither did a later oath of self-denial administered prior to ordination. In fact, even if such attempts had achieved the desired results, they would have done little for the visible image of the clergy, however much they might have done for its soul.

The Church struggled unavailingly with the problem over a period of several centuries, for the central power was not quite

* The idea that sex without passion was "better" than sex with passion took a curious twist in Victorian times, leading some medical men to recommend sex with prostitutes as less harmful than sex with wives (see page 354).

** In England in 1978, the Archbishop of Canterbury decreed that over 200 married Anglican bishops attending the international Lambeth Conference should be segregated from their wives during the course of the three-week conference. The bishops were housed at the University of Kent and their wives more than a mile away.[7]

strong enough to risk taking a step that might be widely and publicly disobeyed, especially when its own record was·less than immaculate. (The papacy had its ups and downs, and one of its more spectacular downs came in the tenth century when two domineering and disreputable Italian noblewomen, Theodora and Marozia, became virtual dictators in matters of papal appointments.)

By the latter part of the eleventh century, however, the papacy was in a stronger position, and Gregory VII issued a prohibition on clerical marriage. There was violent reaction in some parts of the Christian world—the Germans announced that they would rather give up their lives than their wives—but the Church won in the end, and the principle of clerical celibacy was established. It was the nearest the Church was ever to come to establishing what it was really aiming at, not just celibacy, but chastity, which remained an unattainable ideal. The essential problem was that a great many clerics entered the Church because it was the only way of pursuing a professional career in law, administration, or scholarship. The fact that in thirteenth-century England one adult male in every twelve was a cleric [8] did not mean that one man in every twelve had a true religious vocation, or that he saw any need to suppress his sexual instincts. Fortunately, not all flouted the rules as energetically as one bishop of Liège who, by the time he was deposed in 1274, had fathered 65 illegitimate children.

It was in some ways curious that the prohibition on conventional marriage should have come so long after that on "spiritual marriage," or *syneisaktism,* which had been not only acceptable but approved until the fourth century, and was complete in everything except sexual intercourse. Some desert hermits had *syneisaktic* wives as housekeepers, for desert retreats were not quite as bare of creature comforts as they are generally supposed to have been. But a trace of doubt began to creep in, and Church conclaves from the fifth century onward issued continuing denunciations of *syneisaktism* and its associated custom of introducing "strange women" into clerical establishments as housekeepers or "companions." [9]

Until clerical celibacy was imposed, many priests appear to have opted for the best of both worlds by marrying young and then applying for ordination when domestic life began to pall. Others, however, did abstain from marriage, some from genuine conviction, but some because virtue was guaranteed to bring its own reward in the form of promotion within the Church. A career priest who hoped to become a bishop knew that preference depended on celibacy. But it seems unlikely that the majority of priests, celibate or not, succeeded in abjuring the sins of the flesh. In the ninth century, for example, the bishop of Verceil found it necessary to reprimand his subordinates in the bluntest terms. "Several among you," he wrote, "are such slaves to passion that you allow shameless courtesans to live in your dwellings, share your food, show themselves with you in public. Subjugated by their charms, you allow them to direct your households, make settlements on their bastards. . . . In order that these women may be well attired, the churches are despoiled and the poor made to suffer." [10] The task of imposing chastity on men who were not by nature ascetic proved, in the end, to be beyond the power of the Church.

SECULAR MATRIMONY

Modern churchmen sometimes speak of "the family" as if it were a Christian invention, but their predecessors were more inclined to blame it on the devil.

Marry if you must, said the Church Fathers grudgingly to the laity, and went on to describe the joys of matrimony in terms that any Greek or Roman would instantly have recognized. Children were "a most bitter pleasure," and wives by definition weak and frail, slow of understanding, emotionally unstable, light-minded, deceitful, and wholly untrustworthy as far as public affairs were concerned.[11] Marital sex was a grievous hazard, although John Chrysostom and Methodius conceded that, as long as a husband and wife rationed their embraces, wedded bliss need not be an insuperable obstacle to salvation. Clement of Alexandria was even prepared to admit that it might have positive value, since by offering greater temptations it also offered greater opportunities for self-discipline.[12]

On the whole, the Church saw marriage as a series of concessions to human weakness—to the need for companionship, sex, and children—and it did what it could to undermine all three. One marriage, it claimed, should supply enough companionship for any man; second marriages were adultery, third fornication, and fourth nothing short of "swinish."

More specifically, it refused to regard sex as an integral part of

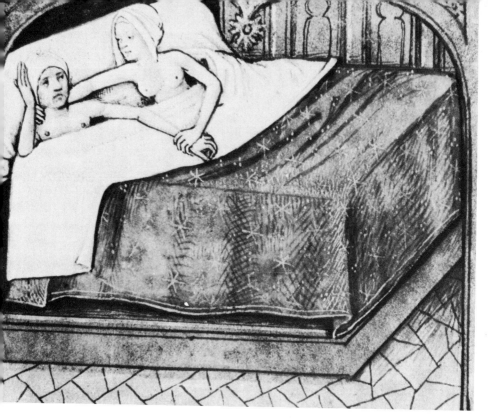

The virtuous husband rejects the advances of his wife

marriage. From the seventh until the twelfth century, there was a continuing discussion about what marriage actually was. Was it a moral contract authenticated by the ceremony itself, or did it have to be confirmed by sexual intercourse? The final judgment was that *nuptias non concubitus sed consensus facit*—"consent, not coitus, makes marriage." [13] What marriage did was confer the right (not the duty) to indulge in sexual intercourse, a right that existed only within marriage.

Though not very often. Some rigid theologians recommended abstention on Thursdays, in memory of Christ's arrest; Fridays, in memory of his death; Saturdays, in honor of the Virgin Mary; Sundays, in honor of the Resurrection; and Mondays, in commemoration of the departed. Tuesdays and Wednesdays were largely accounted for by a ban on intercourse during fasts and festivals— the forty days before Easter, Pentecost, and Christmas; the seven, five, or three days before Communion; and so on. [14]

Still, as Tertullian said with perfect sincerity, it was quite splendid how a priestly blessing could transform a sinful act into a sanctified one, even if it were sanctified only in moderation, and only if children might be born of it. In fact, the Church Fathers viewed even the production of children with some dubiety, for they were not sure that the Old Testament command to "be fruitful and multiply" was still valid. Its original purpose had been to establish a line from which the Messiah might arise; now that the Messiah *had* arisen, salvation no longer seemed to depend on procreation.[15] However, propagation of the faithful was a useful aid to propagation of the faith, and the Church resigned itself to having its flock regularly augmented by new lambs.

But it still hankered after an ideal of marital chastity, and one result was that, even before marriage was declared a sacrament in the twelfth or thirteenth century—which meant that it could not, under any circumstances, be dissolved—the Church was quite unable to consider childlessness as a ground for divorce, although it had been acceptable as such in every society since the beginning of recorded history. However unintentionally, this new dispensation gave unprecedented security of tenure to a large class of women who had previously been liable to rejection for something that was as likely to be their husband's fault as their own.

It is often suggested that Christianity brought about an instant improvement in the position of women, but in fact, with this single exception, their legal and social status scarcely changed. Where there was no doctrinal conflict, the early Christian church merely perpetuated what had been the civil and conventional law of Rome.

WOMAN   AND   THE   EARLY   CHURCH

Woman, St. Peter had said (sounding very much like Cato the Censor) should ornament herself not with braided hair and golden bracelets and fine clothing, but with "the imperishable jewel of a quiet and gentle spirit, which in God's sight is very precious." St. Paul, equally a man of his time, pointed out less poetically that she had been created for the benefit of man and must defer to him in all things; that she was not to teach in church*; must cultivate

---

* A view still maintained today. In 1977 the Vatican declared that the Roman Catholic Church did not "consider herself [sic] authorized to admit women to priestly ordination." Christ had decided not to call any woman, not even the Virgin Mary, as an apostle, and the Church had held to an unbroken tradition of male priests ever since. Priests must have a "natural resemblance" to Christ, and if a woman celebrated Mass "it would be difficult to see in the minister the image of Christ." [16]

silence and submit meekly to instruction as became the daughter of Eve who had beguiled Adam into transgression.[17]

It was almost as if the apostles had looked at the women of early imperial Rome and deliberately taken them as a reverse model of all that was desirable in Christian womanhood. Certainly, they were adamant that every good Christian woman should hide her charms, veil herself in church, and permanently abjure cosmetics—"these poultices of lust," Jerome called them, adding, "What can [a woman] expect from Heaven when, in supplication, she lifts up a face that its creator wouldn't recognize?" [18] It was not a matter of cleanliness being next to godliness; far from it. Every seductive woman was a threat to male salvation. "Even natural beauty," wrote Tertullian, "ought to be obliterated by concealment and neglect, since it is dangerous to those who look upon it." [19]

What Christianity did offer woman was spiritual equality, a gift of greater benefit to the giver than to the receiver. By treating her as an important convert, the Church was able to make public use of her in works of charity and evangelism, while keeping her (on the private level) firmly in her place. Even in the eastern Church where, because of female segregation, women's pastoral role was of considerable importance, and where widows, virgins, and deaconesses all had specific places in the hierarchy, they were still forbidden to perform oblations, to baptize, to teach or pray aloud in church, to approach the altar, or pronounce a blessing. Clement of Alexandria neatly, if unintentionally, summed up the attitude of the early Church when he said that woman was man's equal in everything, but that men were always better than women at everything.[20]

But not quite everything. Where women were as invaluable to the Church as they had always been to the state was in the matter of political marriages. The Church had no hesitation in sending well-born Christian ladies off into the wilds to marry and convert Frankish or Saxon leaders. In A.D. 496 Clotilda of Burgundy was dispatched north to convert Clovis, king of the Franks, and in due course their granddaughter, Bertha, sailed off to England to marry Ethelbert of Kent.

As the centuries passed, marriageable Christian princesses— some of them, especially among the Merovingians and Carolingians, women of powerful personality—had to go farther afield

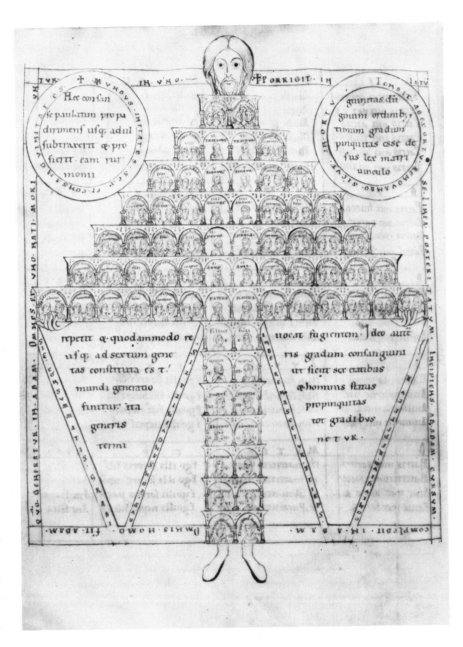

"The tree of consanguinity," a table of kindred and affinity devised by Isidore of Seville, c. 600 A.D. The closest prohibited relationships come at the center, where the trunk joins the formalized branches; they are mother, father, son, and daughter. The further out toward the perimeter, the more distant the degree of kinship.

for their husbands. It was not only because the number of the unconverted steadily diminished, but because the Emperor Justinian had decreed that marriage within five degrees of kinship was incest. Gregory VII, 500 years later, raised it to seven degrees. The ban on marrying anyone more closely related than a fifth or seventh cousin led to a web of royal marriages that stretched from Ireland to Jerusalem, from Castile to Novgorod.

SINS OF THE FLESH

In the limited, local world of the village, where every inhabitant was in some way related to every other, enforcement of such a ban would have been impossible, and it seems unlikely that parish priests even attempted it. Indeed, the probability is that this, like most Church edicts, was filtered through to the village on a highly selective basis. The semiliterate priest was expected, with the aid of his penitential, his do-it-yourself guide to sins and penances, to deal single-handed with a wide range of transgressions, referring only the most difficult or the most major to the bishop or the penitentiary-general, who toured the deaneries like some spiritual circuit judge. If the priest leaned rather too heavily on what he thought of as "general principles," it was not to be wondered at. And as far as sex was concerned, the general principle was that only marital sex was permissible, and only with children in mind.

It is, and always will be, impossible to judge how the Church's emphasis on sex for procreation influenced population figures in early medieval Europe. For one thing, scholars are still unable to chart overall fluctuations between the end of the third and the beginning of the seventh centuries. Wave after wave of plague (fifteen in all) struck the continent, starting in Byzantium in 541–44, where it claimed, according to the contemporary historian Evagrius, 300,000 victims (between one-third and one-half of the population), and gradually moving westward until it finally died out 200 years later. Around the year 570, too, there was a violent epidemic of smallpox that struck the whole of continental Europe. Modern estimates place the population of Europe, which in A.D. 200 had been about 36 million, at only 26 million in the year 600.[21] Christians, it may be noted, probably suffered more than Jews or Muslims, for hygiene was not part of their faith. As Jerome put it, the man who had bathed in Christ needed no other cleansing.[22] It seems unlikely that spiritual purity offered much defense against the fleas that transmitted the plague.

The ravages of the plague, which struck southern Europe, the heartland of the Christian church, much more seriously than the north, may have helped to crystallize the Church's attitude towards sex and procreation as well as its total opposition to any practice that seemed likely to interfere with fertility. But whether this had much effect on population figures remains debatable. When the figures did begin to rise again, steeply, they did so in the north, and the probability is that this was more in response to a breakthrough in agriculture and nutrition than to the admonitions of the clergy.[23] In effect, the Church's view of morality may well have brought an increase in the number of children conceived and raised by married couples, but for several centuries at least it was probably also responsible for a clear drop in the illegitimacy rate. Though its pronouncements today frequently go unheeded, it must be remembered that, particularly in the early medieval period, they were enormously influential, and able, in an uncomplicated society, to color most aspects of everyday life. There was little that escaped the priest in his small parish; little that escaped the penitentials, which laid down atonements for almost every variant of sex other than the heterosexual, conception-oriented, man-and-wife, man-superior position. And even that incurred a year's fast if practiced during Lent.*

The penitentials bore no Vatican imprimatur. They were not the product of some central scriptorium, but regional compilations by authors who appear to have had a wide, if presumably theoretical, knowledge of sexual eccentricity. The fact, however, that so many sins were covered in them did not mean that a priest came across them very often (or, indeed, at all) in the normal course of duty. He may have been very much in the position of the modern Customs official, who would be considerably surprised if a traveler, asked whether he had anything to declare, admitted to a Colorado beetle in his baggage.

One sin which most priests had to deal with regularly was semi-

---

* Theologians (celibates all?) recognized only one "natural" position for intercourse. The others were "unnatural" because they modeled man on the animal, because they inverted the nature of male and female, or because they were suspected of preventing conception and therefore contrary to the nature of marriage.

nal emission, which attracted only seven days' fasting if it was involuntary; 20 days if manually assisted. Even a monk who masturbated in church was liable to no more than a 30-day fast, and a bishop to 50. The fact that this was a solitary practice made all the difference. The Church's view of *coitus interruptus*, essentially a shared version, was a great deal more stringent.

The major sex sin was contraception. A modern American scholar who has studied 20 surviving penitentials dating from the sixth to the ninth centuries found that all but one considered it very grave indeed, especially if it involved "poisons creating sterility," anal intercourse, or oral intercourse (*seminem in ore*, "semen in the mouth"). These were almost as culpable as homicide and attracted penances ranging from three to 15 years. It appears that "a poor little woman" who "acted on account of the difficulty of feeding" extra mouths was likely to receive lesser penances, whereas one who "acted to conceal a crime of fornication" would rate the greater.[24] A similar distinction was presumably drawn in the case of *coitus interruptus*, which rated two to ten years. The long-term penances usually seem to have consisted of fasting in one form or another—abstaining from food and drink (with the exception of bread and water), or from sex, or from anything that could be interpreted as self-indulgence. An alternative that came in during the eleventh century was self-flagellation (for monks) or, for the laity, whipping by the parish priest, while there was another category that entailed the singing of penitential psalms. A man who, however involuntarily, experienced nocturnal emissions, was expected to rise at once and intone seven psalms, followed by another 30 in the morning.

Abortion within 40 days of conception (before the fetus had acquired its human soul) was fractionally less sinful than contraception, possibly because abortion so often carried its own pains and penalties. As St. Jerome pointed out with unsaintly venom, promiscuous women who took potions in order to bring about an abortion sometimes died as a result and went to hell as "threefold murderesses: as suicides, as adulteresses to their heavenly bridegroom Christ, and as murderesses of their still unborn child." [25]

One curious implication of the penitentials was that, although contraception was a major sin within marriage, it may have been less so outside it. "If a layman corrupts a virgin devoted to God and loses his [*sic*] reputation and if he has a child of her, let this man do penance for three years. . . . If, however, there is no child, but nevertheless he corrupts the virgin, he shall do penance for one year." [26] In fact, a man who indulged in rape or seduction was virtually recommended to practice some form of contraception (and to keep quiet about it in the confessional).[27]

In general, however, the Church's opposition to contraception had the undoubted effect not only of discouraging it within marriage, but of suppressing all knowledge of the protoscientific methods developed since the days of Aristotle. [With literacy the preserve of the monasteries, anything of which the Church did not approve was erased from the record.] As a result, a woman who in defiance of husband and priest decided to take the matter into her own hands had little choice but to fall back on traditional methods, old wives' tales, amulets, and brews supplied by the local "wise woman." It was a situation that was to last for hundreds of years. Not surprisingly, modern scholars have noted that when contraception reappeared on the later medieval scene the subject was as riddled with magic and superstitition as it had been in the very earliest days of recorded history.

THE SIN OF SODOM

While the heterosexual sinner might plead social mitigation even for a crime as major as contraception, the homosexual had no such recourse. His crime (for the Church rarely concerned itself with women homosexuals) was assessed according to a sliding scale of values. The minor felony of a kiss? Or full-scale sodomy, "a vice so abominable in the sight of God," said Pope Gregory III, "that the cities in which its practitioners dwelt were appointed for destruction by fire and brimstone"? [28]

The inhabitants of Sodom could have sued him for this.* All the Bible had actually said on the subject (Genesis 19, 4–11) was that God had sent down two angels to investigate the wickedness perpetrated there; that Lot had offered them hospitality for the night; but that all the men of the city had then surrounded the house and shouted to Lot, "Where are the men who came to you tonight? Bring them out to us that we may know them."

---

* As indeed, four leaders of Fuori, Italy's Turin-based gay liberation group, sued Pope Paul VI in 1976, claiming that their personal dignity had been harmed by the Pope's description of homosexuality as "shameful," "infamous," and "horrible." [29]

A view, from the earliest surviving illustrated Bible, of the saving of Lot and the destruction of Sodom

Did they mean, "Where are these mysterious strangers who arrived tonight? Bring them out so that we can have a look at them"? Or did they mean, "Bring them out so that we can rape them"? The laws of probability apart, the answer hinges on the use of the word *yādha'* for "know." According to the painstaking research of three modern scholars, this word occurs in the Old Testament 943 times, but is used in a sexual sense only 15 times. On every other occasion, with the exception of the doubtful Sodom story and a derivative passage in Judges (19, 22), it means simply "become acquainted with."[30]

To begin with, the name of Sodom was treated as a kind of portmanteau word for sins that the Jews were particularly familiar with, or that particularly offended them—pride, adultery, abuse of hospitality, and an irreligious spirit. But by the second century B.C. the free-living and promiscuous Greeks had attracted Jewish censure, and references to Sodom in such literature as the Palestinian Pseudepigrapha began for the first time to specify "fornication" and "uncleanness." Then, with homosexuality common in Rome and pederasty by no means unknown in the Hellenized cities around the Mediterranean, the matter was settled once and for all.

In the first century A.D., Philo of Alexandria expressly interpreted the story of Sodom in homosexual terms. He knew exactly what that wicked place had been like, and any resemblance to the Alexandria of his own day was no doubt purely coincidental. "The land of the Sodomites," he declared, "was brimful of innumerable iniquities, particularly such as arise from gluttony and lewdness. ... [The inhabitants] threw off from their necks the law of nature, and applied themselves to deep drinking of strong liquor and dainty feeding and forbidden forms of intercourse. Not only in their mad lust for women did they violate the marriages of their neighbors, but also men mounted males without respect for the sex nature which the active partner shares with the passive; and so when they tried to beget children they were discovered to be incapable of any but a sterile seed." His Parthian shot was a beauty. "As, little by little, they accustomed those who were by nature men to submit to play the part of women, they saddled them with the formidable curse of a female disease." [31]

Philo's interpretation was the one that was adopted by the Church Fathers; it seems probable that it had been in general circulation before he gave it such inventive form. Many centuries later, however, Western lawgivers—perhaps out of innocence, perhaps out of understandable confusion—again began to use the word "sodomy" in a less restricted sense, treating it as a compendium of all they understood by "unnatural vice." Today, in such states as Virginia, for example, the so-called sodomy statutes do not specifically ban homosexuality but anal and oral intercourse, regardless of the sex of the persons involved.

Until at least the third century A.D., despite some shadowy legislation that may have survived from republican times, imperial Rome took no legal measures against adult homosexuality. The emperors, in fact, were in a difficult position before Christianity became the state religion, since the army in the main favored Mithraism, another eastern religion but one with strongly homosexual undertones. To legislate against homosexuality would have meant alienating the very men who were responsible for making and breaking emperors. Even after Christianity was established, legislation was seldom if ever rigorously enforced.

In the "new Rome" of Constantinople, however, the Emperor Justinian combined Roman law with Christian morality and, for a brief time, succeeded in imposing both over a wide area of the old empire. Blasphemy and homosexuality, in his view, were equally

impious. "Because of such crimes," he believed, "there are famines, earthquakes, and pestilences; wherefore we admonish men to
abstain from the aforesaid unlawful acts, that they may not lose
their souls. . . . We order the most illustrious prefect of the capital
to arrest those who persist in the aforesaid lawless and impious
acts after they have been warned by us, and to inflict on them the
extreme punishments, so that the city and the state may not come
to harm by reason of such wicked deeds." [32] That was in A.D. 538.
One of the punishments, according to Procopius (who was himself
appointed prefect a few years later) was castration, followed by
public exhibition of the offender.[33]

   Justinian's words can scarcely even have been circulated when,
in A.D. 541, there began in Constantinople the great plague that
was to wipe out more than one-third of the city's inhabitants in
the course of the next three years. To the emperor and to the
Church alike it was a clear indication that Justinian's assessment
of the situation had been correct. When the plague died out,
another *novella* was issued. "Though we stand always in need of
the kindness and goodness of God, yet is this specially the case at
this time, when in various ways we have provoked him to anger on
account of the multitude of our sins. . . . We ought to abstain
from all base concerns and acts—and especially . . . the defilement
of males which some men sacrilegiously and impiously dare to
attempt, perpetrating vile acts with other men." The destruction
of Sodom and Gomorrah, described in the scriptures, was God's
way of saying that "by means of legislation we may avert such an
untoward fate." [34]

   Thus, by easy stages, an imprecise Bible story, colored by Jewish disapproval of Greek habits and then by Christian revulsion at
"sins against nature," had the ultimate effect of transforming the
homosexual into a danger to the state.

   In a different way, he was also a danger to the Church, a living
repudiation of Christian morality. At the beginning of the fourth
century, baptism was refused to him, and so even was instruction
in the faith until he had renounced his evil ways.[35] Despite this, as
the Church knew very well, there were homosexuals within its own
ranks, and as monastic life spread, canon law began to suffer an
occasional nervous tremor. In 567, the second Council of Tours
decided to endorse the Benedictine rule that monks should never
sleep two to a bed, and several centuries later a similar rule was

made for nuns. Furthermore, dormitory lamps had to be kept burning throughout the night.[36] In 693, the Council of Toledo, describing sodomy as being "prevalent" in Spain, enacted that "if any one of those males who commit this vile practice against nature with other males is a bishop, a priest, or a deacon, he shall be degraded from the dignity of his order, and shall remain in perpetual exile, struck down by damnation." A hundred lashes, a shaven head, and banishment were the penalties for guilt by association. To the Church punishment the king added the secular one of castration.[37]

Even so, there is little to suggest that monasteries were hotbeds of sodomy. The general tenor of ecclesiastical rules and regulations, in fact, implies that clerical heterosexuality was a good deal more of a problem than homosexuality.

As far as the laity was concerned, the Council of Ankara in A.D. 314 issued two canons whose wording was not entirely clear. Modern scholars believe that they were concerned only with zoophiliacs, "those who have committed fornication with animals," but in the early Western Church they were taken to refer also to homosexuals. As a result, penances designed for zoophiliacs were taken in the West as a basis for the treatment of homosexual offenders, while in the East the Church treated sodomy on the same basis as adultery. Punishment varied according to whether the offender was under or over the age of twenty, whether he was single or married, and whether the offense was habitual. A regular offender over 50 years old and married could expect to be refused Communion unless he was actually at the point of death.[38]

As the Church expanded its area of influence and found it necessary to tabulate Christian morality for easy reference in the parish, it became, not more lenient, but fractionally more rational. It would, if it could, have stamped out every kind of homosexual act or instinct, but it was capable of recognizing that homosexuality had as wide a range of expression as heterosexuality, that it could exist as a passive state of being, or show itself in heightened affection, or in a desire for physical contact, or for passionate intercourse. In view of its basic attitude, the Church should have made no distinction; if the homosexual state was in itself an absolute sin, there was no possibility of assessing different aspects of it on a relative basis.

What it chose to do, however, was gloss over doctrinal hesitancy with the theory of justice tempered by mercy. As a result, the penances prescribed became extraordinarily complex. All permutations had to be allowed for. The offender's age made a difference, and so did his occupation; a monk was more harshly treated than a layman. Whether he had played the active or the passive role also had to be taken into account, as had the frequency of the offense and its extent. Some variants were particularly heinous. Nuns who made use of a dildo were treated with extreme severity and so were brothers who had incestuous homosexual intercourse.

Not surprisingly, the penitentials showed some inconsistency in the penalties prescribed. In sixth-century Wales, a practicing homosexual rated three years' penance; in Burgundy in the early eighth century, ten years. For oral intercourse, depending on where he resided, a homosexual might find himself liable for anything from seven years to life.[39]

The seventh-century Cummean Penitential, Frankish in origin, was reasonably representative of the manuals used by priests in the confessional during the early medieval period. Homosexual sins were treated as follows:

KISSING *Offenders under 20 years of age:*
"Simple kissing." Six special fasts.
"Licentious kissing." Without emission, eight special fasts.
Kissing "with emission or embrace." Ten special fasts.

Offenders over twenty years of age:
There was no distinction made here. The penance was to live in continence, eat separately (on bread and water), and to be excluded from church; the length of it was presumably at the discretion of the confessor.

MUTUAL MASTURBATION *By men over twenty:*
Twenty or forty days' penance.
One hundred days for a second offense.
If habitual, "the persons concerned are to be separated and to do penance for a year."

INTERFEMORAL CONNECTION (insertion of the penis between the thighs of the passive partner):

A penance of two years.
Or 100 days for the first offense and one year for the
second. (The first penance may have been for over-twen-
ties and the the second for under-twenties; or the first
for clergy and the second for laymen.)

FELLATIO   (oral intercourse):
A penance of four years.
For habitual offenders, seven years.

SODOMY   (anal intercourse):
Seven years' penance.

From the sixth until the early eleventh century, homosexuals
were in fact treated no more harshly than couples who practised
contraception.[40] But then the climate began to change. The imposition of clerical celibacy may have aroused fears that homosexuality would increase among the clergy, who would contaminate
the laity. Peter Damiani in the eleventh century raised an outcry
against the practice of homosexual offenders making confession to
the very men with whom their sins had been committed.[41] But it
was not enough to increase the penances; indeed, the longer the
penance the more likely it was to be counterproductive. Instead,
the Church removed sins that particularly offended it from the
jurisdiction of the parish priest into that of the bishop or his
penitentiary-general. In France in 1300, all "sins against nature by
a man over twenty years of age" had to be referred to the bishop;
by "sins against nature" were meant interfemoral connection, fellatio, sodomy, and zoophilia. The penitentiaries dealt with the
same sins committed by men under 20, with female equivalents,
and with "manual pollution," which appears to have meant mutual masturbation. The parish priest was left with the rest—homosexual acts committed by boys under 14 and women under 25,*
and with solitary masturbation.[42]
   If any one man was responsible for the hardening of the
Church's attitude toward homosexuals, it was the great philoso-

---

* The age limit for woman may appear a trifle odd, coming a dozen years after puberty
and not much more than five years before the end of her expected life span, but it must
have been an echo of the Roman view that a woman came of age at 25 (see page 108).

pher and theologian of the thirteenth century, St. Thomas Aquinas. Just as Augustine had given a rationale to the Church Fathers' distaste for the heterosexual act and rendered it acceptable only in terms of procreation, so Thomas Aquinas consolidated traditional fears of homosexuality as the crime that had brought down fire and brimstone on Sodom and Gomorrah, by "proving" what every heterosexual male had always believed—that it was unnatural in the sight of God as of man. It was not difficult to prove, especially as he started from Augustine's proposition that the sexual organs had been designed by the Creator specifically for reproduction, and could only be legitimately used in ways that did not exclude the possibility of it. Homosexuality was thus, by definition, a deviation from the natural order laid down by God (as, of course, were heterosexual anal and oral intercourse, and, obviously, zoophilia), and a deviation that was not only unnatural but, by the same Augustinian token, lustful and heretical.*

Aquinas, fascinated by the harmony of a single moral pattern, was enormously influential in his time and for long after. But the disadvantage of a single moral pattern is that anything that does not find a place in it finds no place, either, in societies based upon it. From the fourteenth century on, homosexuals as a group were to find neither refuge nor tolerance anywhere in the Western Church or state.

THE CHRISTIAN ACHIEVEMENT

As far as the history of sex is concerned, the record of the early Christian church was a formidable one. Other Western societies had condemned, with varying degrees of severity, adultery (usually), contraception (rarely), abortion (sometimes), homosexuality

---

* The Catholic Church today still follows Thomas Aquinas, and so, more hesitantly, do the Protestant churches. In the 1976 *Declaration on Certain Questions Concerning Sexual Ethics*, the Vatican reiterated that there could be no justification for homosexual acts, which opposed the "moral sense" of Christians, the teachings of the Bible, and the "objective moral order." One Jesuit priest, himself of "homosexual orientation," optimistically responded that "once the church is aware of the destructive impact of its policies on hundreds of thousands of lives [after another 700 years?] it will have to change its policies." Meanwhile, the United Presbyterian Church of the United States, the Episcopal Church, and the Methodists continue to maintain that homosexual practice is "incompatible with Christian teaching" while the United Church of Christ and the Christian Church Disciples of Christ are prey to uncertainty.[43]

(sometimes), infanticide (rarely), zoophilia (sometimes), masturbation (never). The Church proscribed them all.

Other societies had ventured to suggest suitable frequencies for marital intercourse. "Three times a month," said Solon. "Every day for the unemployed," said the Jewish *Mishnah;* "twice a week for laborers, once a week for ass drivers." The Church said never, unless children were the object.

Other societies had regarded sex as pleasurable, in any position. To the Church, sexual pleasure was a sin * and only the man-superior position was acceptable.

There is no way of knowing how the new dispensations affected the lives of ordinary people. Almost the only literature that survives from the early medieval period consists of Christian theology, state documents, and estate inventories. But the increasingly tight grip of the priest on the minds of his flock undoubtedly helped to shape an attitude to life that spanned geographical frontiers, giving a kind of supranational unity to Christian society—a unity founded on a less than healthy combination of shame, fear, and spiritual uplift.

By the time the Western world emerged from the "dark ages," sin had come to play a more important, because more immediate, role in Christian morality even than redemption. And of all the sins encompassed by this morality, none had such wide application as the sins of sex. Because of this, even the notional chastity of the priest gave him moral authority. Consciously or not, men and women with normal sexual appetites became obsessed by guilt. Sex might be their only sin, but in the eyes of the Church it was the greatest.

What happened, almost inevitably, was that the Christian *sense* of sin, which might have been a force for good, was diverted from areas where it could have been more usefully employed. By some mysterious alchemy, sexual purity came to neutralize other sins, so that even the moral oppression and physical barbarity that became characteristic of the Christian church in later medieval and Renaissance times scarcely appeared as sins at all in comparison with the sins of sex and heresy.

It was, indeed, a remarkable achievement.

---

* "The husband who, transported by immoderate love, has intercourse with his wife so ardently in order to satisfy his passion that even had she not been his wife, he would have wished to have commerce with her, is committing a sin." [44]

PART THREE

Asia until the Middle Ages, and the Arab world

In Asia, as in the West, man was dominant. Here, too, he was concerned with fertility, but instead of merely discouraging any sexual practices that might interfere with it, he actively encouraged those that might promote it. Sex was part of the pattern of life, and in its perfected form a contribution to the expansion of the spirit. Taoism in China and Tantra in India both leaned heavily on sexual disciplines. Legally and socially, women were no less repressed than in the West, but in practice their life was often far less circumscribed. China and India were both polygamous, and so were the Arabs, whose harems were to form the stuff of fantasy in the monogamous West for well over a thousand years. Under the stimulus of their new Islamic faith, the Arabs in the early medieval period swept over the whole Mediterranean and conquered the great civilization of Persia. From unsophisticated nomads, they became the Western world's great cultural middlemen, passing on arts, inventions, and techniques from one end of the known world to the other. Among their legacies to Europe was their own, unique system of "pure love" that was to influence not only poets and troubadours of courtly love, but the whole image of woman in the West.

7.
China

While the Fathers of the early Christian church advocated sexual abstinence as the only sure route to heaven, other equally devout men in another part of the world took precisely the opposite view. "The more women with whom a man has intercourse, the greater will be the benefit he derives from the act," said one, and another added, "If in one night he can have intercourse with more than ten women it is best."[1] This was one of the doctrines of Tao, "the Way," "the Supreme Path of Nature," a philosophy that permeated the whole structure of Chinese thought and society for more than 2,000 years.

The ideas on which China built one of history's most refined civilizations were ideas that had been discarded by almost all other peoples somewhere on the long march from the paleolithic to the postneolithic era. Only the Chinese, refusing to contract out of the old I-thou relationship with nature (see page 24), began to develop a world view that owed nothing to gods created in the human image. To them, existence appeared as a dynamic movement of perpetual change, a space-time continuum of fluid energy in which man and beast, grass, trees, rocks, mountains, clouds, rain, wind, river, and sea were all indissolubly merged. Nothing *was* because everything was in the process of becoming. In effect, the reader who reads the end of this sentence is no longer the same being as the reader who began it.

For the non-abstract mind, perhaps the least unsatisfactory way of visualizing the Chinese concept of creation is as a kind of multidimensional weather map, with constantly varying channels of atmospheric pressure, air currents flowing, colliding, and recoiling, clouds teased out into wisps of cirrus, fluffed into slow-moving cumulus, or towering in thunderheads. And weaving an erratic vapor trail through them all, powered as if by a series of spectral gear wheels, the force known as *ch'i*—the vital essence, the breath of life—whose path is the Supreme Path, the Way, Tao.

The key feature of this Chinese perception of the world, as of the weather map, is movement, unevenness, undulation. All the elements are in a continuing state of advance or retreat. When one thrusts forward, another must fall back. When one contracts, another expands. There is no active without a corresponding passive, no positive without a compensating negative.

Until the middle of the first millennium B.C. these ideas remained vague, understood but unexpressed. Then the divination manual, the *I-ching* (the "Book of Changes"), named the passive force *yin* and the active *yang* and described how they meshed together to propel the *ch'i* along the Supreme Path. "The interaction of one *yin* and one *yang* is called Tao, and the resulting constant generative process is called 'change.' "[2]

The philosophy that grew around the concept of the Way was known as Taoism, and its adherents believed (and still believe) that long life and happiness, immortality even, would result if instead of being subjected to the artificiality of tightly structured societies man could learn to live in perfect harmony with nature. To achieve this, it was necessary for each individual to aim, in his or her own existence, at the same harmonious interaction of *yin* and *yang* as was responsible, in nature, for energizing the *ch'i*, the breath of life, and to learn how to strengthen both elements as, in nature, they were strengthened by contact with, and absorption of, each other.

The opposing yet complementary forces of *yin* and *yang* could be observed in many natural phenomena. The moon and winter were both *yin*, the sun and summer *yang*. When the sexual parallels came to be drawn, woman—despite a common misapprehension not only in the West but sometimes in China itself—was classified not as pure *yin* but as "lesser *yin*," and man, similarly, as "lesser *yang*." It was a recognition of the psychological truth that there is an element of active *yang* in even the most passive woman and of negative *yin* in even the most positive man. The associated belief that, in both sexes, the subsidiary element fed and strength-ened the principal one was to play a crucial role in the develop-ment of Taoist and indeed all Chinese views on sex.

Since it was the exercise of mind and will that had led human-ity astray from the natural Path, the disciplines that led back to it were necessarily disciplines of the body. One of the most impor-tant of these was, of course, sex, whose relevance was easy enough to explain without recourse to too much obscure symbolism. It took little effort of the imagination to recognize that sexual inter-course was the human equivalent of interaction between the cos-mic forces of *yin* and *yang*, even when the parallels were drawn not in the direct fleshly sense of vagina and penis, but more subtly as *yin* essence (the moisture lubricating a woman's sexual organs) and *yang* essence (man's semen).

The sexual disciplines of Taoism were easy to understand and, within limits, pleasurable to follow, but others required a more positive approach, a deliberate dedication. This was not because they were mysterious in themselves. Indeed, few modern doctors asked to prescribe a regimen for a long and healthy life would find much to argue with in the basic Taoist program—regular exercise, balanced diet, good breath control, sun therapy, and a full sex life—although for the final item on the list, the elixir of immor-tality, they would probably substitute its twentieth-century suc-cessor, the vitamin pill.* When the requirements of *yin-yang* harmony were grafted on to such a program, however, most of the disciplines ceased to be simple either to perform or to understand.

The whole philosophy of Tao, in fact, became at an early stage so abstruse, so inextricably linked with the mysteries of divination, that only the most committed student could hope to progress beyond first principles. The real problem was that although the basic concept could be perceived without very great difficulty by means of instinct or intuition, it was resistant to the constraint of language. Words, except for the true adept, only too often made nonsense of it. "Being is Non-Being and Non-Being is Being. . . . The Real is Empty and the Empty is Real. . . ." [3] Partly as a result, diagrams, calligraphy, painting and sculpture—whose meaning did not have to be filtered through the rational mind—became a char-

---

* Wisely. The early elixirs usually brought mortality rather than immortality. Large numbers of royal personages and high officials joined their ancestors prematurely after consuming potions that frequently included lead and arsenic.

A Sung landscape, with vulva-shaped hills exhaling a mist of *yin* power

acteristic philosophical-religious device. Whereas a Renaissance painting of the Virgin and Child, or the Last Supper, or the Crucifixion, illustrates only a fragmentary part of the whole of Christian belief, a thirteenth-century Sung landscape conveys the entire philosophic harmony of *yin* and *yang*. That this same harmony could also be conveyed by frankly erotic representations of sexual intercourse was a bonus for Taoists who were low on artistic sensibility.

The Tao Masters lived and thought on a level too rarefied for the common man, their dissertations as unrelated to the mind of the "average" Chinese as those of modern theologians to the once-a-month Western churchgoer. On the level of ordinary life, as a result, the convoluted, sophisticated philosophy of Taoism was transformed into a magical creed whose followers abandoned reason in favor of faith. But just as the Fathers of the early Christian church helped to shape the attitude to sex of the whole Western world, so the Taoist Masters helped to shape that of the Chinese. Just as the European of early medieval times knew, without quite understanding why, that sex was sinful but occasionally permissible, so his contemporary in China knew, without quite understanding why, that sex was a sacred duty and one that he must perform frequently and conscientiously if he was truly to achieve harmony with the Supreme Path, the Way, Tao.

THE   CLOUDS   AND   THE   RAIN

Since sexual intercourse was one of the main highways to heaven there was no reason to remain silent about it. Quite the opposite, even if normal Chinese reticence on personal matters often had the effect of excluding it from general conversation. This scarcely mattered, for it was the Chinese who produced the world's earliest known, most comprehensive, and most detailed sex manuals. Many Westerners even today would regard these as pornographic, but pornography is a matter of cultural conditioning. To the Chinese they were serious works, seriously designed to educate their readers in the manner of achieving *yin-yang*, woman-man, harmony. Since they were Taoist in conception and Taoism was a *yin* creed, calm, flexible, intuitive, they were intended as much for the woman as for the man, and indeed were frequently given to a bride before her wedding.

The official bibliography listing the most important books in circulation during the early Han dynasty (206 B.C.–A.D. 24) included eight such manuals, all but one of them running to 20 or more chapters. Although the texts of these no longer exist in their original form, scholars believe that they were rewritten, re-edited, reissued again and again over the centuries, so that the eight "new" Art of the Bedchamber books listed (together with thirteen "Taoist classics" on the subject) in the bibliography of the seventh-century Sui dynasty were not very different from their Han predecessors. Even the Sui books have vanished, but substantial fragments of them were preserved in a Japanese work compiled in the tenth century, the *I-shin-pō*. It was at about this time that Japan came under the spell of Chinese culture and began to build her own prosperous, worldly, tolerant civilization along very similar lines. The Japanese, in fact, were to preserve traditional Chinese appreciation of sexual activity long after it had been suppressed in China itself.

Most of the Chinese handbooks appear to have been divided into six sections. First, there were introductory remarks on the cosmic significance of the sexual encounter; then came recommendations about foreplay; then a description of the act of intercourse, including approved techniques and positions. The practical side having been dealt with, there followed sections on the therapeutic value of sex and on how to choose the right woman and how she should conduct herself during pregnancy. The final section contained useful recipes and prescriptions. Like all good instruction manuals, the sex handbooks were illustrated with pictures that were not purely decorative but designed for handy bedside reference.

> When the red flower shows its beauty
> And exhales its heady perfume,
> While she stays with you in the night
> And you play and take your pleasure with
>   her,
> Pointing at the pictures, you follow their
>   sequence,
> While she blushes and looks abashed
> And coyly protests. . . .[4]

Yin-yang harmony was the primary concern of all the handbooks, and intercourse the first stage in its achievement, intercourse that was a human reflection of the mating of earth and heaven, when clouds rose mistily from the land to meet the rain descending from the skies. "Clouds and rain" is still, today, the standard literary expression for the act of intercourse, an echo of nature beliefs far more primitive than those of Taoist times.

Not inappropriately, perhaps, woman's *yin* essence was believed to be inexhaustible, while man's *yang* essence, or semen, was limited in quantity and correspondingly precious. Its quality was of supreme importance. It could be (and, the experts insisted, should be) regularly fed and strengthened by the *yin* essence that was its natural supplement. This was a process that was achieved during intercourse.

The ideal, according to the handbooks, was for man to prolong intercourse for as long as possible; the longer he remained inside the woman, the more *yin* essence he would absorb. He must also, without fail, rouse her to orgasm, when her essence reached maximum potency. To the Chinese, uniquely, a woman's orgasm was no less important to the man than to herself.

But there was an important qualification. There was little purpose in strengthening the man's *yang* essence if he promptly squandered it by himself reaching a climax.

The basic way of avoiding this, said the Master Tung-hsüan (who is believed to have been a seventh-century physician), was as follows. At the last moment, "the man closes his eyes and concentrates his thoughts; he presses his tongue against the roof of his mouth, bends his back, and stretches his neck. He opens his nostrils wide and squares his shoulders, closes his mouth, and sucks in his breath. Then [he will not ejaculate and] the semen will ascend inward on its own account." [5] What the Master recommended, in effect, was a few moments' powerful self-discipline.*

---

* In 1976, the West caught up with the Master Tung-hsüan. Ten years earlier, the researchers Masters and Johnson had discovered that, in man, orgasm and ejaculation are two separate physiological processes and that it is possible to experience the pleasure of the first, several times, before it need be terminated by the second. In 1976, California sexologist Dr. Mina Robbins reported to the second International Conference of Sexology that a machine would soon be available to warn men when the moment of ejaculation approached, so that they could postpone it—by staying still and breathing slowly and regularly.[6]

As well as this method of *coitus reservatus,* the Chinese used *coitus obstructus.* It was described in *Important Matters of the Jade Chamber.* "When, during the sexual act, the man feels he is about to ejaculate, he should quickly and firmly, using the fore and middle fingers of the left hand, put pressure on the spot between scrotum and anus, simultaneously inhaling deeply and gnashing his teeth scores of times, without holding his breath. Then the semen will be activated but not yet emitted; it returns from the Jade Stalk* and enters the brain." [7] What this method achieved, in fact as distinct from theory, was diversion of the seminal fluid from the penis into the bladder, from which it would later be flushed away with the urine. It was a kind of internal *coitus interruptus* and had the same contraceptive effect; in fact, it was used for birth control purposes in later times by Turks, Armenians, the islanders of the Marquesas, and the sophisticated nineteenth-century commune founded by John Humphrey Noyes at Oneida, New York (see page 413).

The authors of the handbooks, well aware that *coitus reservatus* and *obstructus* were techniques that not all men could be expected to practice on a regular basis, also specified how much semen a man could afford to lose without damaging his system. As a general rule, said the *Principles of Nurturing Life,* "in spring man can allow himself to emit semen once every three days, in summer and autumn twice a month. During winter one should save it and not ejaculate at all." The loss of *yang* energy caused by one emission in winter was "a hundred times greater than one emission in spring." [8]

Readers of the *Secret Instructions concerning the Jade Chamber* were vouchsafed more detail. "Strongly-built men of 15 years can afford to emit semen twice a day; thin ones once a day, and the same applies to men of twenty. Strongly-built men of 30 may ejaculate once a day, weaker men once in two days." At the ages of 40, 50, and 60 there was a diminishing frequency, from once in three days to once in 20 days, and the sturdy 70-year-old might

---

* "Jade Stalk" was one of several Chinese synonyms for the penis, and the reference was not, of course, to green jade but to the more precious, creamy-colored "white" jade. Other synonyms were Red Bird, Coral Stem, Heavenly Dragon Pillar, and Swelling Mushroom. A woman's sexual organs might be The Open Peony Blossom, Golden Lotus, Receptive Vase, or The Cinnabar (or Vermilion) Gate.

still risk it once a month. But "weak ones should not ejaculate any more at that age." [9]

One of the great Taoist physicians, Sun Szû-mo, who lived in the seventh century, had a cautionary tale to tell about the dangers of ignoring this advice. Some years earlier, he reported, a peasant of over 70 had come to consult him. "He said, 'For several days my *yang* essence has been most exuberant, so much so that I want to have intercourse with my wife even during daytime, and reach a climax every time. Now I do not know whether this is bad or good at my advanced age?' I replied, 'It is most unfortunate! You know what happens with an oil lamp? Just before it goes out, its wick first burns low and then suddenly flares up. *Then* it goes out. . . . I greatly fear for you and can only advise you to take great care of yourself.' Six weeks later the man fell ill and died." Sun chose to put the case on record as "a warning to future generations." [10]

Taoist philosophy was fundamentally more interested in the cosmic than the human reproductive properties of a man's semen, but it recognized the desire to produce children as a fact of nature. In this, as in all else, there were *yin-yang* rules to be obeyed. For the child who would be conceived to be born sturdy and healthy, it was necessary for the father's *yang* essence to be at peak potency, which meant that it had to be built up over a number of sexual encounters without ejaculating until the final, crucial occasion. All the handbooks emphasized that the preliminary *yin* nourishment should come from a number of different women. "If a man continually changes the women with whom he has intercourse, the benefit will be great. If in one night he can have intercourse with more than ten women it is best." The reason for this was that "if he always couples with one and the same woman, her vital essence will gradually grow weaker, and in the end she will be in no fit condition to give the man benefit. Moreover, the woman herself will become emaciated." [11]

Some discrimination was required in the choice of preliminary partners. There was no need for the girls to be beautiful, but they should be pleasant, well brought up, small, plump, and shapely, and, for preference, just reaching maturity. The *yin* essence of a woman who had "disheveled hair and coarse face, a long neck and a protruding Adam's apple, irregular teeth and a manly voice" would be more likely to ruin the man's *yang* potency than strengthen it.[12]

Like the Greeks and many later generations in the West, the Chinese believed that a woman was most likely to conceive during the first few days after menstruation. Said the Master Tung-hsüan, "If [a man] mates with her on the first or third day thereafter, he will obtain a son. If on the fourth or fifth day, a girl will be conceived. All emissions of semen during intercourse after the fifth day are merely spilling one's seed without any purpose." [13]

It was not only purposeless but extremely foolish to spill one's seed when the heavens were unfriendly. Children conceived during the day or at midnight, when there was thunder, an eclipse of the sun, a rainbow, or a waxing or waning moon, were all liable to meet unpleasant fates. Even if the father had made the understandable mistake of drinking too much just before the momentous occasion, he condemned his child to a life of epilepsy, boils, and ulcers.[14]

There must have been times when even the most dedicated Taoist felt that celibacy would be easier. But it was a quite unacceptable escape route for the Chinese: improper, a betrayal of man's duty to his ancestors, and contrary to the rhythm of nature. Taoism held that a man's mind grew restive if he were deprived of sex and that his spirit suffered accordingly. However unwittingly, the physician Sun Szû-mo agreed with St. Paul that it would be excellent if the mind could be "always serene and entirely untroubled by thoughts of sex. . . . But among 10,000 men there is perhaps one who can achieve this." [15] This guarded view of celibacy was to prove a serious obstacle to the spread in China of Christianity and Hinayana Buddhism, both of which denounced the sexual impulse.

SECRETS OF THE JADE CHAMBER

When the handbooks progressed from general principles to practical details—all "debility" of body and spirit being attributable to "faulty exercise of the sexual act"—they worked conscientiously through everything the novice needed to know, although the Chinese literary custom of making lavish use of poetic imagery and expressions originating in magic, divination, and alchemy often makes them difficult to follow.*

All of them emphasized the importance of the man and woman both being in a receptive mood. "If the man moves and the woman does not respond, or if the woman is roused and the man does not comply, then the sexual act will not only injure the man but harm the woman." If both were in a suitably relaxed and agreeable frame of mind, the next stage was foreplay. This was heavily stressed by the manuals, not because of the sensual pleasure involved but because it stirred up woman's *yin* essence, to the benefit of both partners.

In his *Ars Amatoria,* a work that could scarcely have been more different from Ovid's insipid essay on the same topic, the Master Tung-hsüan was careful to differentiate between the techniques that should be used with a first-time partner and those adapted to a continuing liaison. It was a matter of tenderness, consideration, exploration; of soft caresses, reassuring words, and gentle kisses. Though later Western observers reported that the Chinese were offended by the mere idea of kissing and regarded it as a form of cannibalism, this was a misunderstanding; it was simply that kissing belonged by definition to the intimate world of the Jade Chamber and was never practiced anywhere else. A woman who kissed a man in public was acting like a cheap harlot.**

With the preliminary embraces "a thousand charms" were unfolded and "a hundred sorrows" forgotten. The woman began to fondle the Jade Stalk, and it stiffened, responded. She, in turn, feeling the strength of the man's *yang,* sensed her own impulses stirring and her Cinnabar Cleft became moistened as if by some hidden spring. "As soon as they have reached this stage, they are in a condition to unite with each other."

---

* Despite this, even as recently as 1961, Dr. Robert van Gulik (the first serious Western writer on the subject of sex in China) felt it necessary to translate more than half of his quotations from the practical parts of the handbooks into Latin rather than English. With sometimes piquant results. For example: "The Yellow Emperor said, '*Cum coitum perpetrate desideranti Caulis mihi jaspius surgere nolet, utrum sollicitare eum debeo an non?*' The Dark Girl said, 'Certainly not!' "

** It is an attitude that persists in some parts of the world today. In May 1974, the Criminal Court of Kuwait, following a case in which a boy and girl, both under 18, were charged with indecency for kissing in the street, ruled that it was a criminal offense to kiss in public.

But they were not recommended to do so immediately. The Master strongly advised "further dalliance before penetration." The Jade Stalk, he said, should hover lightly around the precious entrance of the Cinnabar Gate while its owner kissed the woman lovingly or allowed his eyes to linger over her body or look down upon her Golden Cleft. He should stroke her stomach and breasts and caress her Jewel Terrace. As her desire increased, he should begin to move his Positive Peak more decisively, back and forward, bringing it now into direct contact with the Golden Cleft and the Jade Veins, playing from side to side of the Examination Hall, and finally bringing it to rest at one side of the Jewel Terrace. Then, when the Cinnabar Cleft was in flood, it was time for the Vigorous Peak to thrust inward.*

"A slow thrust should resemble the movement of a carp caught on the hook; a quick thrust the flight of birds against the wind. Inserting and withdrawing, moving up and down and from left to right ... all these movements should be properly correlated." A man could "flail out to right and left in the way a brave general breaks up the enemy ranks," or "push on slowly, like a snake entering its hole to hibernate," or "first rise and then plunge low, like a big sail braving the gale." And each of these movements was to be applied at the proper time. A man should "not always stubbornly cling to just one style to serve his own convenience." [16]

The man regularly faced with ten or more sexual encounters in a single night obviously ran the risk of beginning to find it all (at the very least) something of a bore. The handbooks tried to counteract this by listing a variety of possible positions. The Master Tung-hsüan reported that there were really only 30 basic ones, and did not even trouble to define the first four—Close Union, Firm Attachment, Exposed Gills, and The Unicorn's Horn—on the assumption that everyone knew about them. The titles of the other positions were highly poetic, and the descriptions frequently acrobatic. There was the Winding Dragon position and the Mandarin Ducks; Bamboos by the Altar and the Cleaving Cicada; Phoenix sporting in the Cinnabar Cleft; and Gamboling Wild Horses. The

---

* Positive Peak and Vigorous Peak = erect penis. Jewel Terrace = clitoris. Golden Cleft and Jade Veins = front and back of the vulva. Examination Hall = *labia* or lips of the vulva.

"Hovering butterflies" position

Phoenix holding its Chicken was a mild joke, describing the participants themselves rather than the activity in which they were indulging; a tall plump woman and a very small man.[17] Some of the positions were guaranteed not only to provide sexual pleasure but to cure various infirmities ("the seven kinds of ache," for example), especially when magical numbers of thrusts were used. Nine was a particularly powerful *yang* number, and its square, 81, was often called "complete *yang*." [17]

Despite this inventiveness, the Chinese, like their contemporaries in Europe, regarded the recumbent, face-to-face, man-superior position as the "natural" and most important one. "Man and woman should move according to their cosmic orientation," said the Master. "The man should thrust from above and the woman receive below." And the *Ts'an-t'ung-ch'i*, the great second-century classic of alchemy (a subject rich in sexual symbolism) stressed that, "When one contemplates female and male united in sexual congress . . . this is not achieved by special skill, and it has not been taught to them. It must be compared with man being born face down, and woman on her back. And not only do men and women assume these positions when they are born, they are seen to assume them also when they are dead. [The Chinese believed that drowned men floated face down and women face up.] This was not taught to them. . . . It is rooted in [the basic position assumed during] intercourse, which fixes the original pattern." [18]

Noticeably missing from the handbooks that revealed the secrets of the bedchamber were any practices that could be described as sadistic or masochistic. Nor were these much of a feature even in less respectable literature until the repressed era of the Ch'ing, which began in the latter seventeenth century and had much the same attitude toward sex as the Puritans. Until almost that time, too, supplementary sexual activities were viewed rationally on their *yin-yang* merits. Anal intercourse and fellatio were quite permissible as long as no *yang* essence was lost by ejaculation, although they did not do much to strengthen a man's *yang*. Cunnilingus was actively approved, as preparing the woman and simultaneously procuring *yin* essence for the man. Masturbation, a matter of indifference where women were concerned, their supplies of *yin* being inexhaustible, was condemned in men for its wastefulness. Particularly worrying was emission during sleep. The Chinese believed that this often happened as a result of some succubus assuming the guise of a beautiful woman so as to steal a

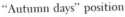

"Autumn days" position

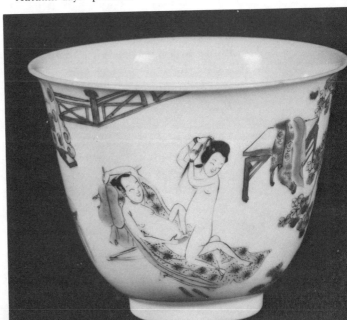

man's *yang* essence by having intercourse with him in his dreams.*
The Chinese seriously criticized some of their less respectable
emperors for having erotic murals painted on the walls of their
living halls. (Hsiao-ching, who introduced this practice in the second century B.C., was regarded as the "inventor" of erotic art.) Nor
were they any too sure of the mirrored screens surrounding the
bed in more than one seventh-century imperial Jade Chamber.
But they had no particular reservations about public ceremonial
mass sex, which made its first appearance toward the end of the
second century and appears to have been relatively common by
the fourth. Toward the end of the Han period, when Chinese
economy and society were in a state of crisis, the head of the
Taoist "church," a man named Chang Chüeh, decided to try to
overthrow the Han and set up a Taoist empire. He embarked on
this ambitious scheme with an army whose men wore yellow
scarves around their heads and practiced mass sexual disciplines on
nights of the new and full moons, their aim being *shih tsui*, "deliv-
erance from guilt." The revolt of the Yellow Turbans was bloodily
suppressed, but the same kind of mysticism was to flare up again
and again during the centuries, especially in Shantung province,
the traditional abode of mediums, magicians, and sorcerers. Even
in Communist China as late as 1950 there was a Taoist secret sect,
whose "shamelessly lustful leaders" (said the newspaper *Kuang-
ming-jih-pao*) induced its members to engage in promiscuous sexual intercourse as a route to immortality and freedom from
disease.[19] Whether the report was truth or fabrication scarcely
matters; what is interesting is the ready acceptance of the association between Taoism, mass sex, and immortality.

Homosexuality between consenting adults was sometimes fashionable, as in the Han period and again during the time of the
Sung (A.D. 960–1127), and rarely productive of strong reactions
because intimate contact between two *yang* elements, though not
as nourishing as between *yang* and *yin*, was certainly not destructive. Lesbianism was accepted, with a shrug, as a natural result of
herding a number of wives and concubines together in the women's quarters—what might be called the "harem effect." It was a

---

* Much the same idea was held in early medieval Europe (see page 272).

wasteful practice, but not dangerous except when dildoes were used to excess. All the handbooks warned against too much reliance on these in case they damaged the tissues, a particular hazard, perhaps, with the double kind, a ribbed stick made of wood or ivory. The "male" partner inserted one end of the dildo in her own Cinnabar Cleft, harnessed the central portion round her waist by means of silk ties, and used the other end as if it were a Jade Stalk. One medieval novel refers to something called a "Cantonese groin," which appears to have been a phallus-shaped sprouting plant that when soaked in hot water swelled and hardened into an excellent dildo.

Male homosexuality was commonly known as *lung-yang*, after a young man called Lung-yang-chün, favorite of a fourth-century B.C. Prince of Wei, or as *tuan-hsiu*, "the cut sleeve," because of a story relating to one of the Han emperors who cut off his sleeve rather than disturb his handsome young bedfellow who had fallen asleep with his weight resting on it. Several of the Han emperors were homosexual in the Greek pederastic sense: bisexual rather than strictly homosexual. In later times, the Chinese became suspicious of bisexuality. One writer of the Ming period (A.D. 1368–1644) was convinced that bisexual fathers frequently had hermaphrodite children. During the latter part of the third century, he said, when bisexuality was very common, there had been an unusually large number of hermaphrodites born.[20] And hermaphrodites, as everyone knew, were unnatural monsters, capable of the blackest, most dastardly crimes.

BALD CHICKENS AND TINKLING BALLS

The Chinese were by no means the first to use aphrodisiacs, but their need was undoubtedly greater than that of most other peoples and their approach to the problem of stimulating desire (and staving off exhaustion) was more consciously scientific. While the Greeks regarded onions, eggs, honey, mussels, crabs, and snails as among the most reliable stimulants,[21] the Chinese carefully blended such ingredients as *boschniakia glabra, schizandra sinensis, cuscuta japonica, polygala japonia, cridium japonicum*, and others into physics with colorful names like "the bald chicken drug." The story behind this was that a civil official who consumed it regularly not only sired three sons after the age of 70 but made so many demands on his wife that she finally became unable either to sit or lie down. Not before time, he threw it away—into the barnyard, where the cock swallowed it. The cock then mounted the nearest hen and passed the next few days in uninterrupted intercourse, all the while pecking at the hen's head until the unfortunate bird was completely bald. History, in the shape of Master Tung-hsüan, did not record any sequel to this lively tale, but the Master said that if the "bald chicken drug" were taken three times daily for 60 days, a man would easily be able to satisfy 40 women.

The "deer horn potion," which had powdered antler among the ingredients, was designed more to prevent impotence than to increase vigor (though it also cured tiredness and an aching back), and the Master further included formulae designed to deal with a problem seldom mentioned in Western works until very recent times, the mismatching of penis and vagina. If *boschniakia glabra* and sea grass were powdered, sieved, mixed with liver extract from a white dog killed during the first moon, and applied three times to the penis, finally being washed off with fresh, early-morning well water, this was guaranteed to lengthen the penis by three inches.* Parallel recipes were given for shrinking the vagina to make a neater fit, though the Master warned against using too much of the shrinking powder in case the Cinnabar Cleft closed up altogether.[22]

The ingredients used in most of the early aphrodisiacs appear to have been harmless; some of them, in fact, had a high protein content and may even have been beneficial to people whose normal diet consisted of rice and vegetables. Others were probably included because of their phallic symbolism; *boschniakia glabra*, for example, is a fungus not unlike an erect penis in appearance. By medieval times, however, more dangerous constituents were being used, such as the Telini fly, which can result in chronic urethral infection.**

---

* Even if only in the eyes of its owner. Medical science knows no way of enlarging the penis, flaccid or erect. The average length in Western Europe today is 9.51 cm or 3¾ inches. Statistics are not, unfortunately, available for seventh-century China.

** In the eighteenth century aphrodisiacs became fairly innocuous again, dog and goat wine being regarded as particularly beneficial (the meat was fermented with other ingre-

The majority of drugs used in the early Chinese aphrodisiacs are still available from Chinese and Japanese druggists today, while European sex shops stock modern versions of mechanical devices popular in China half a dozen, perhaps more, centuries ago. Both penis rings and "tinkling balls" (or "exertion bells") are mentioned in erotic novels dating from the Ming dynasty.

The penis ring was designed to ensure that the Jade Stalk, once erect, stayed that way. The ring, made appropriately of jade or sometimes ivory (though the poorer classes had to make do with a strip of fabric), was fitted round the base of the Stalk and held in place by a silk band passing between the legs and up round the waist. Some rings were exquisitely carved in bas-relief with, no doubt, the secondary purpose of stimulating the woman's Jewel Terrace during intercourse.

What are now known by the Japanese name of *rin-no-tama,* meaning "tinkling balls," are a variation of what the Chinese once called "Burmese bells," although they may have been no more Burmese than French letters are French. They were originally as common in southeast Asia as in China. The English traveler, Ralph Fitch, described them in the Shan States of Burma at the end of the sixteenth century. The men, he said, wore "bunches of little round balls in their privy members . . . They cut the skin and so put them in." The aristocracy had silver ones, "gilded and made with great cunning," which rang "like a little bell"; the lead ones used by poorer people rang "but little." The king "sometimes taketh his out and giveth them to his noblemen as a great gift." Less than a dozen years later, the Florentine merchant Francesco Carletti also reported on them, this time in Thailand. "The rattles," he said, were "as large as hazel nuts" and made in round or oval shape. When two or three were inserted under the skin of the penis, they had the result of "enlarging the member, as anyone can imagine." He added that according to Niccolò dei Conti, a

---

dients for a few days and then strained off). The mid-twentieth century reverted to exotica. When the late K.M. Panikkar ended his second term as Indian ambassador to China, he was entertained at a banquet by Chou En-lai. Afterward, he reported, some small drops of a clear liquid were added to the remains of his wine. He was told that they were the bile of a black monkey, newly killed, and a strong aphrodisiac.[23] (The combined Chinese and Indian senses of humor make this story slightly suspect.)

Venetian nobleman who visited Burma early in the fifteenth century, there had then been "certain old women who had no other
calling than that of selling these rattles." Carletti thought the
original idea of the bells had been to enlarge the penis to such an
extent as to "rule out and render impossible the practicing of
venery in illicit parts of the body even with men"—by which he
presumably meant anal intercourse—while Fitch, rather more ob-
scurely, claimed that they had been "invented because they
should not abuse the male sex, for in times past all those countries
were [so] given to that villainy that they were very scarce of people." He probably had homosexuality in mind. Both authors
added, however, that whatever the origins of the practice it was
perpetuated by the fact that women considered the effect highly
stimulating.[24]

Women themselves made use of the "Burmese Bell," at first
inserting one in the vagina before intercourse, but later using
them for solitary pleasure. In this case a pair of the little silver
globes was necessary, one containing a drop of mercury and the
other a tiny vibrating metal tongue; they gave a uniquely erotic
sensation even at the slightest movement of hips or legs. *Rin-no-
tama* bells for women became popular in the West in the eighteenth century and again in the late twentieth, though the modern set consists of three, not two, and the third is hollow.

Mechanical aids to sexual satisfaction began to be invented or
adopted in China only when society had become too prudish to
tolerate the sex manuals that had been so important for more
than a thousand years. And besides, the sex taught in the manuals
presupposed both money and leisure, which had both become
scarcer as the world changed. By about the year 1600, knowledge
of the manuals had faded to such an extent that other methods of
sex instruction became necessary.

In the "hall of the joyful Buddhas," said the Ming scholar
Shen Tê-fu, there were "pairs of Buddhas, richly adorned, who
embrace each other with their sexual organs linked together [one
of the Buddhas being female]. Some statues have movable genitalia, all plainly visible. . . . When a Prince marries, the couple is
first led into this hall. After they have knelt and worshiped, both
bride and groom must feel the genitals of the statues with their
fingers, in order thus to learn without words the method of sexual
union. . . . The reason is that it is feared that such august persons

may be ignorant of the various methods of sexual intercourse." [25]

It was the supreme irony. No sex-approving early Taoist Master, and certainly no sex-abjuring early Buddhist, could ever have foreseen the day when Chinese royal brides and grooms had to be taught the facts of life by reference to a working model—of a Buddha!

THE MYSTERIOUS ROOM

The prudish element in Chinese society that ultimately triumphed over the mild and indulgent philosophy of Taoism was based on the thought of Confucius. It had gained momentum during the last two centuries B.C. and represented all that Taoism was opposed to—rites and ceremonials, administrative controls, legalism, class distinctions, authoritarianism, all the "artificiality" of man-made social institutions. Though the destination of the Way might be shrouded in mist, its point of departure was the rational, unspiritual Confucian state. Yet Taoism and Confucianism were not altogether conflicting ideologies; indeed, it can fairly be argued that between them they kept the Chinese world in motion through their own *yin-yang* interaction—Taoism the *yin* creed, flexible and intuitive; Confucianism compelling, uncompromising, unmistakably *yang*. Until as late as the twelfth century, the Chinese people placidly subscribed to both, ruling their personal lives according to Taoism while recognizing Confucianism as a creed admirably suited to the needs of society and the state.

One of the essential elements in the Confucian state was the close-knit, well-ordered family, in which past, present and future coexisted just as they did in the Taoist view of creation. A man was but a link between his ancestors and his sons; "filial piety" was a duty not only to his own father but to endless past generations, on whose continued other-worldly wellbeing the whole of the future depended. Women were absolutely and unconditionally inferior, besides being "difficult to deal with. If you are friendly with them," Confucius said, "they get out of hand, and if you keep your distance, they resent it." [26] They were a mere biological necessity to the production of male children who could continue to minister to the needs of "the ancestors." One curious result (from the Western viewpoint) of the Confucian preoccupation with sons was that this extremely straitlaced school of philosophy was prepared to encourage sexual activity on the most munificent scale, confidently endorsing the handbooks' advice to maximize *yin* intake before ejaculation because that was the way to beget healthy sons.

However philosophic the sex manuals may have been in intent, their practical importance was considerable, for they were an essential thread in the intricate web of familial relations. They, the desire for sons, the polygamous system, and the sex and class ratio of the population were all interdependent.

Polygamy on the generous Chinese scale differed from polygamy in most other societies and, as a system, lasted much longer. Though Solomon, for example, had a great number of wives and concubines, the vast majority of his subjects probably considered themselves lucky to have one of each. As far as is known, this was equally true of the Chinese peasantry. But between peasantry and royalty in China there was an unusually substantial middle class, a class that was very much family-conscious. The ordinary middle-class householder had between three and a dozen wives and concubines, the lesser nobility thirty or more—which made the handbooks' insistence on intercourse with ten different women in one night not only practicable but strategically necessary.

The rights of every wife and concubine had to be respected, for it was the husband's absolute duty to provide for his women not only economically, but emotionally and sexually. The *Li-chi,* the Confucian "Book of Rites," stated categorically that "even if a concubine is growing older, as long as she has not yet reached 50, the husband shall have intercourse with her once every five days." [27]. Favoritism in the hothouse atmosphere of the women's quarters was calculated to result in the ruin of domestic peace, which in turn could damage a man's career. One who was unable to keep his own household in order was unlikely to be trusted in a position of official responsibility.

Marriages were customarily arranged through intermediaries, and acquiring a wife was not unlike buying a house in modern times. The intermediary checked that the description of the property was accurate—virginity intact, no undisclosed structural weaknesses, acceptable parents; that there were no legal or social restraints on the sale, particularly in the sense of bride and groom being related, however distantly (even the "incest" of having the same surname was enough to rule out any possibility of marriage), that there were no undesirable development plans for the area (i.e. that the omens were favorable), and that the price was right.

Once negotiations were complete, the groom went to visit the bride's parents, taking with him, for some inscrutable Chinese reason, a goose. When the visit ended the bride returned home with him, the wedding dinner being held the same day and consummation taking place the same night in the "mysterious room," the bridal-night chamber.

Usually, a marriage ceremony united a man not only with his principal wife but with her sisters and maids as well, whom she brought along as secondary wives for him. This saved the husband time and expense, and also eased the transition for the wife, who did not have to face her new world entirely alone. She had enough problems, for she now belonged utterly to her husband's family— an extended family in which parents, brothers, sisters, uncles, aunts, all had their own households gathered together in a family compound, a close-knit community to which she was not even introduced until the morning after the wedding. On the same day she was taken into the ancestral hall to be presented to the souls of "the ancestors," and two days later went home to bid farewell forever to her parents, whom she was not expected to see again. Three months were still to pass, however, before her probationary period was over and she was finally and solemnly established as First Lady. A husband did have the right to repudiate his principal wife, usually for sterility or incurable disease, but the practice appears to have been relatively uncommon, partly because it offended the wife's family and partly because a departing First Wife took most of the seraglio with her. Repudiating a wife meant repudiating the sisters and companions who had been married at the same time.

But however much marriage systems might differ between East and West, Chinese husbands would have found that they had a good deal in common with their Hebrew, Greek, or Roman contemporaries, especially over the view of what constituted a good wife. There was no need for her to be extraordinarily intelligent, or clever, or handsome, as long as she was "gentle and sedate, chaste and orderly," willing to "concentrate on spinning and weaving, to shun jest and laughter, to be neat in preparing food and wine for the guests. . . . She must not listen to lewd talk, nor look at unseemly things; inside the house she should not look slovenly, or outside the house be extravagantly made up; she should not mix with crowds, nor spy through windows. . . ." [28] The only real point of interest about this catalogue of wifely virtues was that it emanated not from a Hebrew Psalmist or Athenian misogynist, but from the wellbred and highly intelligent Lady Pan Chao, one of the first and greatest Chinese woman scholars, who was partly responsible for compiling the official history of the Han dynasty.

A scholar, a Confucianist, but not a feminist (or not in the modern sense of the word), the Lady Pan did believe that girls should be vouchsafed the same elementary education as boys. In her day (she died c. A.D. 116 at an advanced age) and for more than eight centuries after, respectable women were mostly illiterate unless they had the will and the opportunity to teach themselves, or unless they were courtesans who, like the Greek hetairai, considered reading and writing as among the tools of their trade. One result was that most poems bewailing the married woman's lot were the work of men.

Bitter indeed it is to be born a woman,
It is difficult to imagine anything so low!
. . . . No one sheds a tear when she is married off. . . .
Her husband's love is as aloof as the Milky Way,
Yet she must follow him like a sunflower the sun.
Their hearts are soon as far apart as fire and water,
She is blamed for all and everything that may go wrong. . . . [29]

Wives were essentially mothers and housekeepers, each having her own place in the hierarchy of the women's quarters and each her specific daily tasks. Many of the empty hours were filled before the mirror, attending to hairdressing and make-up; others were occupied with illicit love affairs, which appear to have been easy enough to pursue. The Roman woman would have felt suprisingly at home with her Chinese sister's routine.

Despite the injunctions of the manuals, the women's quarters were often a reservoir of frustrated feminity, and it was not unusual for adult sons to have affairs with their father's secondary wives or concubines. In general, women met their husbands only at meal times or in bed, and conversation was restricted to domestic subjects. Confucians abhorred women who tried to share their husbands' interests and, like the Romans, considered feminine participation in public affairs to be the root of all evil. "If women are entrusted with tasks involving contact with the outside world," the statesman Yang Chên said in the second century A.D., "they will cause disorder and confusion in the empire, bring shame on the Imperial Court. . . . Women should not be allowed to take part in government affairs." [30] Yang Chên, in fact, had some justification for his complaint, as the imperial court was at that time effectively ruled, or misruled, by an irresponsible seraglio clique, an unholy alliance of concubines and eunuchs, which succeeded in rattling the very foundations of the Han dynasty.

The Confucians also abhorred casual physical contact between husband and wife or concubine—essentially, it appears, because such contact could arouse desires that might interfere with the careful calendar of polygamous intercourse. "A man and a woman shall not give anything directly one to the other from hand to hand," said the *Li-chi*. "If a man gives something to a woman, she receives it on a bamboo tray." Nor should they go to the same well or bathing place, or hang their garments on the same clothes rack.[31] * It was, perhaps, carrying things to extremes, but extremes that were certainly no odder than some of the regulations framed by Christians to rule out any possibility of improper contact between the sexes. In A.D. 585, for example, the second Council of Mâcon ruled that no male corpse should be buried beside a female corpse until the latter had decomposed.[32]

Some people at first treated the Confucian separation rules with healthy derision. As the poet Szû-ma Hsiang-ju remarked, he himself was more virtuous than the most upright Confucian; scarcely a day passed when he did not face temptation and overcome it, whereas the Confucian simply ran away from any situa-

---

* Somewhere around 2,000 years after the *Li-chi*, the American Shakers had the same idea. Men and women ate apart, worshiped apart, were not even permitted to shake hands. They carried it further and forbade sex, too. The reason for this was that the sect's founder, "Mother Lee," had been transported in a vision back to the Garden of Eden where she had witnessed the act of intercourse between Adam and Eve that started all the trouble.

故曰翼翼矜矜福所以興靜恭自思榮顯所期

此之由

取尤冶容求好君于所沈結恩而絕寔

Confucian separation rules required avoidance of physical contact between man and woman.

tion in which it might conceivably arise.[33] It was a point that some disrespectful Christian might have made, with equal justification, about those of the Church Fathers who insisted that all good women should hide their charms because they endangered the souls of men. Yet however erratically observed and however unnatural the Confucian rules may appear to modern eyes, they eventually succeeded in establishing a code of domestic formality and courtesy that assured to even the least of a man's concubines a degree of human dignity that was rarely accorded to any but the highest-born women in the monogamous societies of the West.

The paternalism of the Confucian state did not, in fact, inhibit wives, concubines or widows—the latter known with doubtful accuracy as "persons waiting only for death" *—nearly as much as might have been expected. The third-century philosopher, Ko Hung, after summing up the separation rules, gloomily reported that women and girls paid them scant heed. Instead, they chose

---

* The modern Japanese word for wido, *bibōjin*, still has this meaning.

"to gad about in the market place. . . . They go out visiting, to see their relatives, and proceed there by starlight or carrying torches, night after night; they take a large suite with them, setting the street ablaze . . . maids, messengers, clerks and footmen. . . . These women also make pleasure trips to Buddhist temples, they go out to watch hunting and fishing, they organize picnics on hills and river banks. They even travel . . . in open carriages with the curtains raised, stopping in every hamlet and town they pass through, drinking toasts, singing, and making music on the way." This kind of disregard for the rules of propriety, said Ko Hung forbiddingly, argued nothing less than the decay of the family and the ruin of the state.[34]

A GIRL IN A GREEN BOWER

It might reasonably be thought that where polygamy flourished there would be no need for prostitution. But this was very far from the case. The conscientious Chinese husband, in fact, frequently went to prostitutes not for sexual intercourse but to escape from it. The privately operated "green bower" (so called because the woodwork was lacquered green, as in the mansions of the rich) was a refuge from the responsibilities and rivalries of home, offering calm and relaxation, good food and drink, music, dancing, and a night's hospitality if required. Until the nineteenth century, the sex-only brothel was a rarity except in districts where poverty and a concomitant monogamy prevailed.

Until about the second century B.C., princes and high officials had maintained troupes of dancing girls and musicians, who went the amorous rounds of master, retinue, and guests, sometimes being sold off or presented as gifts to visiting dignitaries. Whole companies of them might be dispatched from princely state to princely state as diplomatic *douceurs*, and there was one case in which a litigant hoping for a favorable verdict offered a troupe of such girls to the judge by way of bribe. In Han times, however, the first public brothels were opened, partly to cater for the new merchant class who either could not afford, or did not dare, to have their own private troupes, and the Han emperor Wu also began the institution of "camp followers" for the army—in which, historically, he was slightly ahead of his time.

As in all other societies, there were several classes of prostitute, ranging from girls who had nothing but physical attraction to recommend them to the level of the great courtesans, who were skilled in music, dancing, and literature, rated a private bedroom and salon, and were in a position to select or reject suitors as the fancy took them. The girls' backgrounds were varied; some of the brothel owners purchased from poor families, some they kidnapped, and some were the repudiated concubines of respectable men who had drifted into the business because they had nowhere else to go. There was usually a contractual relationship between the brothel owners and the girls. The owners belonged to trade associations, paid taxes to the government, and in return were granted the same official protection as other commercial enterprises over such matters as breach of contract. It was possible for the girls, if they were registered professionals, to denounce cruel owners. Neither side approved the intrusion of non-union labor.

Once the girls entered the brothel compound, their abilities were assessed and they were trained accordingly. They learned willingly, for it was the ambition of every prostitute to be bought out by a distinguished customer who would take her for a wife or concubine. The ordinary girl was unlikely to achieve more than middle-class concubinage, but a top-class courtesan, though expensive to buy, was a good investment for an ambitious young man. Her knowledge of official and business gossip was often considerable, and it was not uncommon for a former regular client to maintain a fatherly interest in her and to extend that interest to her husband.

Like the Greek *hetairai,* the courtesans of China were quick and anxious to learn about matters of which husbands never talked to their wives, but which they would discuss willingly with an intelligent courtesan. Literature, philosophy, business, politics—all the subjects that were conspicuously absent from the education of the well-brought-up young woman until the end of the first millennium. The girls very often learned from the young scholars who came to study and take examinations in Ch'ang-an, one of the twin capitals of China, and gravitated in the time-honored way of students to the least formal part of the city, the bohemian "northern quarter" where most of the brothels were situated.

By the time their training was completed, the brothel girls were very presentable indeed, and perhaps for that reason their activities were circumscribed. Customarily, they were permitted to leave the brothel compound only for religious festivals or to take part in marriage ceremonies (when it was their task to conduct the new bride to the "mysterious room") or to entertain guests at banquets. In fact, the Chinese cuisine helped to sustain Chinese prostitution throughout most of its history, for not even the most expert domestic kitchen could be expected to contend with the vast number of dishes required at a banquet designed to impress a man's professional or social acquaintances. From early times it had been usual to eat out on such occasions, and the resemblance to the modern business convention ultimately became quite striking. Lavish food and drink, no wives or concubines, professional entertainment, and high-class escort agency services provided by one of the better brothels.

There appear to have been three ranks of brothel in Hangchow, the Sung capital that fell to Kublai Khan in 1276. At the bottom was the *wa-shê*, a kind of cheap government establishment designed to meet the needs of common soldiers and sailors, and also to cater for the poorer classes. The girls here might be prisoners of war, or sometimes the wives of condemned criminals, penalized, as in other societies, for their husbands' misdemeanors.

In the middle rank were the "wine houses," some controlled by the Board of Revenue and intended for government personnel only, others under private management, but all of them charming places with cheerful, handsome, well-dressed girls, excellent wine served in silver cups, a splendid selection of hot and cold snacks to tempt the customer, and an atmosphere that was "full of music and laughter from evening till dawn." In some of them, the customer could expect the girls only to keep him company while he ate and drank. Others had "secretly installed beds" on an upper floor. "Such special wine houses have bamboo lamps of red [silk] suspended on their front doors; they are displayed both in dry and rainy weather, being protected by covers of plaited bamboo leaves; for it is by those lamps that such special wine houses can be recognized." [35] The first red light district, in fact.*

* The expression "red light district" is generally held to have late nineteenth-century American origins, but the derivation may well have been Chinese. The Chinese who flocked to California in Gold Rush times and after seldom brought "respectable" women with them; it was a situation tailor-made for the enterprising brothel owner.

The downstairs room in a brothel of the Ming period

The top-class brothel, patronized by high officials, wealthy merchants, writers, and artists, was variously known as a "house of singing girls," a "sing-song house," or a "tea house," and was very expensive indeed. The guest paid out several thousand cash (small pierced coins strung together for convenience) the moment he stepped through the door, ostensibly for his "teacup of checking flowers." He was led upstairs and relieved of several more strings of cash for a cup of wine. Then the girls appeared and he was able to choose his companion. Through the food, wine, singing, and entertainment that followed, every stage had its ritual and its price. But houses like these supplied the best of everything, not only accomplished women and quality food and wine, but stylish decor, antique furniture, rooms heated by braziers in winter, cooled by bowls of ice in summer. The guest could hire almost anything he needed; one source quotes a mildly eccentric list of drinking cups, headgear, quilts, robes, all clean and new.

Only a small part of the brothel's income was accounted for by the fees paid for going to bed with the girls, and in fact neither management nor girls were very enthusiastic about the sexual side of the business. General entertainment and escort-agency work offered fewer risks and considerably more profit. But not all customers saw it in quite the same way, since none of the ordinary *yin-yang* restrictions applied to intercourse with a prostitute whose *yin* essence was so powerful because of her numerous liaisons that she easily gave back to a man far more than he could possibly lose by ejaculation. To the harassed husband, this offered a welcome relaxation from the control required in the domestic bedchamber.

It was only in the seventh or eighth century A.D. that physicians, trailing far behind the Egyptians, began to realize that some diseases (including a form of gonorrhea) were transmitted by sexual intercourse. Possibly the Chinese emphasis on frequent and multipartner sex obscured the relationship between cause and effect that was more readily visible in a frugal society; otherwise it is difficult to explain why Chinese medicine, in most ways far more sophisticated than that of the contemporary West, should have lagged behind in this matter. Indeed, it was not until the beginning of the sixteenth century, when syphilis was identified, that physicians seriously began to warn men against sexual contact with prostitutes.

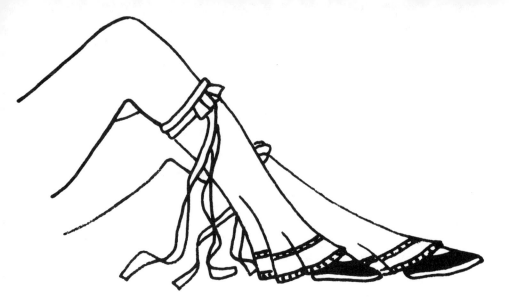

In about A.D. 1000—no one knows why—tiny feet became a criterion of beauty and the symbol of sex incarnate. Footbinding became mandatory among the upper classes. Artists might draw the most explicit nudes, but the feet were never shown uncovered. A woman's leggings were far more erotic than the Victorian garter, the exposed foot and ankle absolutely indecent.

Even in the class-conscious world of Confucianism, prostitutes had considerable social mobility. Most of them came from poor households; many of them were accepted into middle- or upper-class ones. If this had not been the case, Chinese polygamy could scarcely have survived. Except for very brief, usually postwar periods, no society has ever had enough surplus women to allow a small but substantial segment of the male population to arrogate to themselves anything from three to 30 women per head. Chinese population figures are not always easy to interpret, though the subject is more adequately documented there than in most other countries, but they are nevertheless suggestive. In A.D. 754, there were roughly 52 million inhabitants. Eight years of civil war followed, and then three-quarters of a century of peace; but the population was still at a 30-million low. Again, in about 1125 the population had reached a hundred million; the Mongol wars broke out, and in 1290 the figure was back down at under 60 million.[36] It may be assumed that in both cases a high casualty rate among male peasants was an important, perhaps a key element. Because of this, and because the surviving poor had only one wife (if any), there were probably more women than men over the whole spectrum of the population.

It was usual for a man's principal wife to belong to the same social class as himself, and the same applied to the secondary wives she brought with her. But when he decided to increase his household he was bound by no particular rules and could ignore class in favor of attractiveness. The unattached women he was most likely to meet were prostitutes, and they, by the very nature of their calling, represented the most attractive members of the poorer classes. It was an economical and, on the whole, satisfactory system for all concerned. With more women than men among the lower classes, filtering the prettiest out into prostitution and then into middle- or upper-class concubinage meant that the less pretty had much less competiton to face in the lower-class matrimonial stakes. And perhaps they were fortunate in more ways than one. They did not have to confront the serried and unsympathetic ranks of their new husband's First, Second, and Third Ladies when they entered the married state—or the marriage bed.

The Chinese gentleman, practical in all things, took care not to cause emotional crises in the women's quarters when he introduced a new concubine. There was a "correct" way to do this, as everything else. In about 1550, a wealthy landowner or merchant (whose identity is unknown) left to his sons a piece of sound advice on how to deal with the situation. "The right method," he said, "is for the man to control his desire, and for the time being not to approach the newcomer, but to concentrate his attention on the others. Every time he has sexual intercourse with his other women, he should make the newcomer stand at attention by the side of the ivory couch. Then, after four or five nights of this, he may have intercourse with the newcomer, but only with his principal wife and the other concubines present. This is the fundamental principle of harmony and happiness in one's women's quarters." [37]

THE CHINESE PENITENTIAL

It makes an interesting *envoi* to consider the Chinese "penitential" in relation to that of the early Christian church. Not for the fasts and penances involved, but for the relative values of different sins. The Chinese version, in fact, was very much like the modern glossy-magazine quiz, which allows the reader to assess, on a points system, his or her responses in a variety of social or emotional situations.

In the early days of Mongol ascendancy (during the last years of the thirteenth century), the Chinese became sensitive about the safety of their womenfolk—which was not surprising when they had Mongol soldiery billeted in their homes. A new prudishness began to develop, and one of its expressions was the Table of Merits and Demerits, listing good deeds versus sins and evaluating each on a moral basis. Murdering someone rated a thousand demerits, saving a life five hundred merits. By consulting such a list the conscientious Chinese could work out for himself whether his morality was on the debit or credit side of the ledger.

The first and most detailed of these moral calorie counts was the *Shih-chieh-kung-kuo-lu*, which was divided into ten sections.[38] The third dealt with debauchery, and only demerits were listed.

RAPE: Of a married woman, 500 demerits; if the woman was the wife of a servant, only 200 demerits.
Of a widow or virgin, 1000 demerits; if she were a servant's widow, or a maid, only 500.
Of a nun, demerits too numerous to count.
Of a prostitute, 50 demerits.

SPUR-OF-THE-MOMENT PASSION: 200 demerits in the case of a married woman; only 100 if she was a servant's wife.
500 for a widow or virgin; if she were a servant's widow, or a housemaid, only 200.
1000 for a nun.
100 for a prostitute.

PREMEDITATED ILLICIT INTERCOURSE: With a married woman, 100 demerits; half for a servant's wife.
With a widow or virgin, twice as much in each case.
With a nun, 500.
With a prostitute, 20.

BOASTING ABOUT THESE SINS: 50 demerits if the partner was a married woman, 100 if a widow or virgin, 200 if a nun, 5 if a prostitute.

BOASTING UNTRUTHFULLY ABOUT THESE SINS: 50 demerits in the case of a married woman; 200 in the case of widows, virgins, and nuns; 10 in the case of a prostitute.

The distinctions are interesting, particularly in the case of married women and widows. Where most other societies would have assessed crimes against a wife as rather more serious than crimes against a widow (even if only because they cast doubt on the legitimacy of any children born), to the Chinese it was far more reprehensible to insult the relict of an "ancestor." Equally, but less easily explainable, the cold-blooded rape of a prostitute was held less culpable than rape in hot blood. And it seems peculiarly unjust that the demerits for blackening the name of another man's wife should have been the same, irrespective of whether it was true or not.

There were a great many other items on the list, all of them illuminating.

	Demerits
Keeping an indecently large number of wives and concubines	50
Showing favoritism to one woman	10
If it encourages her to be rude to the others	20
Comparing the charms of one's womenfolk	1
Gloating over them	1
Lewd dreams	1
If they result in lewd actions	5
Singing frivolous songs	2
Studying such songs	20
Keeping erotic pictures on the shelves	Per picture 10
Touching the hands of one's womenfolk by accident	1
With lustful intent	10
Unless when helping them in an emergency	None
But if such help arouses lust	10
Having lewd thoughts about a woman in the street	10
Associating with friends who go whoring and gambling	50

Going to the theater	1
Taking part in a play	50
Praising the virtue of one's women	None
Praising their wisdom and generosity	5
Telling one's women dirty stories	20
Unless they are told to excite the women's sense of shame, in which case	None

In the last analysis, the Chinese seem to have had a more interesting and varied list of sins and, however eccentric, a better sense of balance than their contemporaries in the agonized Christian West. It was only when neo-Confucianism, a composite philosophy incorporating the theories of the sage with fragments of Taoism and shreds of Buddhism, began to take a vicelike hold on Chinese society in mid-medieval times that what had been one of the most sophisticated and civilized cultures in the world began its long slide into moral Victorianism.

8.
India

Whose idea was it? Who thought of it first? Who—if anybody—passed on the message from culture to culture, civilization to civilization?

The problem of the transmission of ideas, arts, and inventions throughout the ancient world remains one of the most mysterious in the historical process, an irresistible field for speculation, an area where facts are scarce and it is necessary to hold possibility in the most delicate balance against probability. As one modern English historian says, "Who was talking about gear wheels in first-century B.C. Bactria? Did the Roman-Syrian merchant Ch'in Lun, who visited China in A.D. 226, happen to take an active interest in cartography? Could a copy of a tractate of al-Haitham's on optics have reached Canton or Hangchow during his lifetime?" [1] In the present context, two other equally unanswerable questions might be added. "Did some Roman sea captain, sailing home with his cargo of ivory, cotton and spices from western India, leave his copy of Ovid's *Ars Amatoria* behind in Barygaza?" And, "Might the Chinese traveler, Fa-hsien, who traversed most of the subcontinent at the end of the fourth century, have carried the latest edition of *Master Jung-ch'eng's Principles of Sex* in his baggage roll?"

There is no real reason to doubt that the great Indian handbooks of sex were anything other than Indian in origin and execution. But the germ of the idea may well have come from elsewhere. The Chinese sex manuals had been in circulation since at least the second century B.C., Ovid's *Ars Amatoria* since the end of the first, and India had long had trading relations with both countries. What was probably the first and is certainly the most famous of the Indian sex manuals, the *Kamasutra* (attributed to the sage Vatsyayana), seems not to have been compiled until some time between the third and fifth centuries A.D., and it bears certain resemblances to its predecessors, classifying sexual techniques as coolly and clinically as any Taoist Master (though without resort to poetic euphemism) and treating the art of flirtation as cynically as Ovid (though without the gloss of elegiac couplets).

There was, however, a great deal more to the *Kamasutra* than this, for it was as much a product of the India of its time as the *Ars Amatoria* was of Augustan Rome. Its special qualities—its passion for classifying, its tolerance, its occasional tenderness, its elitism, its arbitrary mixture of sentimentality and ruthlessness—were all characteristic of Indian society and the type of mind that had been shaped by it.

By the time of the *Kamasutra*, India was saturated with the ideas of Hinduism, a class-conscious, color-conscious religion whose essential beliefs influenced every facet of life. It was based on the sacred authority of the Vedas—the Bible of the light-skinned Aryan invaders who, in the second millennium B.C., had driven their dark-skinned predecessors down to the south of the peninsula—and it divided society into four unequal classes. Brahmins were superior to kshatriyas, kshatriyas to vaisyas, and vaisyas to sudras. And all were superior to the conquered peoples, who had no status at all.

The socio-religious class system of the Vedas was reinforced by the doctrine of *karma*, or transmigration of souls, which held that when a living thing died—man, beast or insect—if it had lived its life "correctly" its soul would be reincarnated at a higher level, if "incorrectly" at a lower one. Even the least of men might, by virtuous living during a number of incarnations, so improve his *karma* that he could rise to the highest level and finally achieve the paradise of release from the cycle of rebirth. For this reason, "correct behavior" was of the utmost importance, especially for brahmins who had reached the very edge of release and so had most to lose from slipping back.

There were Four Aims in life, integrally bound up with the concept of correct behavior. Success in the fourth of these, release from the cycle of rebirth, was a natural sequel to conscientious observance of the first three, and so was not directly controllable. Religious and secular leaders therefore tended to concentrate on *dharma*, the first Aim, which meant satisfying the religious, social, and moral obligations (differentiated class by class and caste by caste) that defined correct behavior in all major fields of human activity and operated politically in favor of an order and stability that were advantageous to rulers and priests alike.

But though *dharma* received most emphasis, there was no question of downgrading the other two Aims. These—pursuit of *artha*, material wellbeing, and *kama*, pleasure and love—often strike the Western observer as shockingly unspiritual, but the early Hindu sages knew a good deal about human nature and recognized that economic and emotional starvation were a poor foundation for spirituality. The only reservation they made in the cases of *artha* and *kama* was that they should not be given first priority in life, though, as the *Kamasutra* reasonably pointed out, there were bound to be exceptions. Since *kama* was "the occupation of public women," it was proper that they should consider it as the most important of their Four Aims (*Kamasutra* I 2).

Artha and *kama* were perhaps concessions to the basic human instincts, the sugar on the pill of sanctity. But they were sanctified, just the same. Sex, for the Hindu Indian as for the Taoist Chinese, was a religious duty—not one that would put him straight into tune with the infinite, but certainly one of the least taxing and most pleasurable ways of improving the state of his *karma*.

THE PROBLEM OF LOVE

Whatever the date of the *Kamasutra*, it was a work that must have been of great value to the man-about-town of Gupta times (the fourth and fifth centuries A.D.). In this golden age of Indian history, powerful economic forces were at work and the merchant class, the vaisyas, gained in importance, wealth, and self-esteem. Their sons and daughters had leisure, money, and social ambitions that drove them to acquire *savoir faire*, to study correct behavior in the fashionable as well as the religious sense. Traditionalist writers—as in first-century Rome and the twentieth-century West—complained bitterly about the decline in morals, but only the brahmins listened, though the end result was to be serious curtailment of Indian women's (not men's) freedom.

In the meantime, however, as the *Kamasutra* made clear, girls of the merchant class had considerably more latitude than they enjoyed in any other contemporary society. They might still, as elsewhere, be subject to the "three dependencies"—on father, husband, and then son—but nowhere else were respectable parents recommended to dress their marriageable daughter smartly and send her "where she can easily be seen by all," to "show her to advantage in society, because she is a kind of merchandise" (III 1). However regrettable the reasoning, many daughters in the Gupta period had quite a lively time. There was even a form of marriage that allowed them to choose their own husbands. It is probably true to say that, where other civilizations in general recognized only two kinds of women, the respectable and the unrespectable, India at this time tolerantly accepted several shades in between.

This was partly because early Hinduism, unlike Christianity for example, had no absolute morality, very little concept of *unconditional* right and wrong in terms of human relations. The Aims of *dharma, artha,* and *kama* were directed toward the improvement of each individual's own *karma,* essentially personal and self-centered, and the interaction of one person's behavior with that of another bore as much relationship to the past and future of both as it did to their present. If one person's deeds caused another to suffer, it could always be argued that it was a judgment on the sufferer for failing to observe correct behavior in some previous incarnation; the person who caused the suffering, on the other hand, would probably have to pay for it in some *future* incarnation.

This kind of sophisticated fatalism, so foreign to Western modes of thought, makes some passages in the *Kamasutra* sound remarkably callous today. If a man wanted to marry a girl who was unwilling or undecided, the answer was to get her drunk, or kidnap her, "enjoy her," and then "cause fire to be brought" from the house of a priest and go through a marriage ceremony, "because it is the opinion of ancient authors that a marriage solemnly contracted in the presence of fire cannot afterward be set aside" (III 5). Or if a courtesan "finds that her lover's disposition toward her is changing, she should get possession of all his best things before he becomes aware of her intentions, and allow a supposed creditor to take them forcibly away from her in satisfaction of some pretended debt. . . . After this . . . if he is poor and destitute she should get rid of him as if she had never been acquainted with him" (VI 3).

Yet this brutal realism was counterbalanced by something that had been largely ignored by Ovid and the Chinese sex manuals—recognition that there could be a great deal more to sex than just the mechanics of flirtation and intercourse.

There had been a literature of love ever since the beginning of recorded history, sometimes pallidly romantic as in early Egypt, sometimes cheerfully bawdy as in Greece. But although sex often figured in love poetry, love figured very little in sex literature before the *Kamasutra*. There, however, it was a recurring theme.

By the word "love" the *Kamasutra* did not mean the artificial sighing and yearning, the coquettishness, the simulated passion, the calculated tricks of the amorous trade that were so notable a feature of Ovid's understanding of it, but a great deal more. Clearly, the sage Vatsyayana (or whoever was responsible for compiling the book) not only recognized but sympathized with that curious tangle of emotions, that chemical reaction between man and woman—always commonplace, always unique—that can obsess the mind and nerves of the lover to the exclusion of all else. More than once, the sage interrupts himself in the middle of a discourse on sexual tactics to remind his readers that the rules do not apply for people who are truly in love, or to point out that whatever he may say about the qualities to be looked for in a wife, a man should marry "no other girl but the one who is loved" (III 1).

Yet even while recommending the lover to spurn classifications, the *Kamasutra* was quite unable to resist the temptation to classify love itself—not altogether satisfactorily. It recognized four types. There was simple love of intercourse—a habit, a drug, not unlike the love of a gambler for gambling—and another, separate addiction to specific aspects of sex such as kissing, embracing, or oral intercourse. Then there was the love consisting of mutual attraction between two people, instinctive, spontaneous, and possessive. And finally the kind of one-sided love that often sprang from the lover's admiration for the beauty of the beloved (II 1).

Satisfaction of the first two types of love depended less on harmony between the partners than on physical proficiency, which could be perfected by strict adherence to the rules and techniques

that wise men had evolved over the centuries. True lovers, however, needed no rules to govern them, no teacher but instinct. In
some ways they were above and beyond the rules.

Hindu society, for example, was no more enthusiastic than any
other about one man seducing another man's wife, and the *Kamasutra* was quite emphatic about the conditions which justified
such a course. If the woman could influence her husband on the
lover's behalf, that was all right. It was fine, too, if the woman
could be relied on to help her lover kill her husband, so that they
would both inherit his riches. And so on (I 5). But lacking motives
of self-interest that could be defined in terms of *artha*, mere carnal
desire was not good enough. Seducing another man's wife was
permissible only if the seducer's love was so strong that it was
leading him along the road to destruction. Helpfully, the *Kamasutra* listed the signposts, so that he could take action before the
situation became irretrievable. They were, in succession, "love of
the eye, attachment of the mind, constant reflection"; then came
sleeplessness, loss of weight, rejection of accustomed pleasures,
shamelessness, madness, fainting, and finally death (V 1).

But recognition of love as something on a different plane from
sex, though it lent the *Kamasutra* a distinctively human quality,
at the same time deprived it of subtlety. Separating love from
sexuality forced it into the position of supplying a guide to sexuality only. And a very matter-of-fact one. There is no poetry at all
in the *Kamasutra*, no mellowing use of that romantic-spiritual
language that has encouraged lovers through the ages to believe
that their own feelings are something quite apart from the gross
bodily desires of others. It makes an instructive contrast with the
Chinese sex manuals which, acknowledging no real distinction between love and sex, treated the matter with a cool delicacy that
easily accommodated both.

THE PRACTICE OF SEX

The Chinese manuals had been concerned mainly with what happened in bed, Ovid with how to get there. The *Kamasutra*'s horizons were a great deal wider. Sometimes, indeed, it sounds rather
like some nineteenth-century *Ladies' Household Companion* as it
lists what every young homemaker ought to know. Singing, sewing,
making beds, playing a musical instrument, stringing necklaces,

A prince waylaying a milkmaid; the preliminary to Vatsyayana's "deceitful congress"

dancing, making artificial flowers.... The resemblance ends abruptly. The young Hindu homemaker who desired to please her husband was also expected to study magic and sorcery, cock fighting, quail fighting, and ram fighting; to know the various ways of gambling; and to have some facility with "sword, singlestick, quarterstaff, and bow and arrow" (I 3). In Hindu society, as in all others, pleasing her husband was the first rule of correct behavior in a wife.

Though the earnest student of sex must undoubtedly have found some of the Kamasutra's contents banal, there was much that was illuminating, psychologically perhaps more than physically. Just as the book identified four kinds of love, so it identified seven kinds of "congress." Three of these were between true lovers. "Loving congress" took place between lovers who had long been separated; the "congress of subsequent love" between two people whose love was still in its early stages; and "spontaneous congress" between lovers who were accustomed to one another. The next two categories described intercourse between two people who were both in love with someone else and between a man and a woman where the man, in imagination, transformed his unloved partner into the object of his desire. And the last two covered relationships between a gentleman and a low-class servant (with the strictly functional purpose of relieving the man's sexual need) and what the book called "deceitful congress," where some naive peasant or village girl was seduced by a courtesan or a rake from the glamorous world of the city (II 10).

All the way through the *Kamasutra* there was the same emphasis on naming and classifying. As an aid to memory, this system no doubt had its uses, but it led to some fairly odd juxtapositions, like a file cabinet with too few dividers, taxing not only the author's ingenuity but the reader's patience. There were four kinds of mild embrace, and four that were much more passionate; eight kinds of love bite, eight stages of oral intercourse, and nine ways of moving the lingam (penis) inside the yoni (vagina); four parts of the body that might be individually embraced; three ways of kissing an innocent maiden, and four angles from which it might be done. There were moderate kisses, contracted kisses, pressed ones, and soft ones, and there was also the clasping kiss, when one lover took "both the lips of the other between his or her own." A man with a moustache, said Vatsyayana, should steer clear of this one (II 3), and women from Avanti should never be kissed at all, for they detested the habit (II 5).

Unlike its predecessors, which treated the matter only coincidentally, the *Kamasutra* made something of an issue of sexual dimensions. A man might be a hare man, a bull man, or a horse man, depending on the size of his lingam, and woman a deer, mare, or cow-elephant according to the capacity of her yoni. Matching unions were best, said Vatsyayana solemnly—hare and deer, bull and mare, horse and cow-elephant—but if this was not possible then a slightly tight fit was to be preferred to a loose one (II 1).

If a man with a small lingam found himself having to satisfy a woman with a large yoni, there were certain steps he could take to adjust the imbalance. He could sheath his lingam, base to tip (or beyond), in one, two, or three "armlets" made of thin gold, silver, copper, ivory, buffalo horn or similar material. The *Kamasutra* does not say how these were to be kept on; possibly they were slipped into position before complete erection so that the final expansion held them tight. Or he could coil a thin strand of metal round and round. Or use a *jalaka*, a "tube open at both ends, with a hole through it, outwardly rough and studded with soft nodules and made to fit the size of the yoni, and tied to the waist"; a kind of hollow dildo to be worn over the penis.

The lingam could also be enlarged without the use of mechanical aids, though this meant inducing a long-lasting swelling by means that must have been relatively painful—rubbing it at regular intervals with the "bristles of certain tree insects," for example. If the man viewed none of these suggestions with favor, the alternatives were for the woman either to adopt yoni-constricting positions during intercourse, or to rub on a salve made from the fruit of the *asteracantha longifolia* which was guaranteed to contract the yoni for one whole night. (VII 2).

With a trace of austerity and a faint atmosphere of disclaimer, Vatsyayana reported that "the people of the southern countries" favored inserting an expander *in* the lingam. His description of the method was not entirely clear; it sounds like a practice he has heard of but not witnessed. Essentially, however, it involved perforating the lingam and inserting in the hole or under the skin (the text is confused) any one of a number of strangely named objects. Included among the "wooden mortars" and "places where four roads meet" was the "collection of eight balls." Since much of the later culture of southeast Asia was derived from Southern India, this may well have been an early version of the "tinkling balls" found in Burma, Siam, and China toward the end of the medieval period (see above, page 181).

On the subject of positions for intercourse, Vatsyayana could have learned much from the Master Tung-hsüan. He did, indeed, succeed in outnumbering the Master's 30 positions, but only because he counted congress after the manner of cattle, dogs, goats, deer, asses, cats, tigers, elephants, wild pig, and horses as ten *different* positions. On the whole, the *Kamasutra's* suggestions were unimaginative but acrobatic, and the latter fact was obviously recognized by one of its quoted authorities, a sage named Suvarnanabha, who sensibly recommended practicing them in the bath first. Vatsyayana himself was not so sure; he thought that "congress in water is improper, because it is prohibited by the religious law" (II 6).

Positions such as the "fixing of a nail"—which consisted of the woman stretching out one leg while placing the other on her head—were no doubt popular with lovers who also happened to be contortionists, and there was a peculiarly Indian kind of love talk that required them to be ornithologists as well. Passion, said the *Kamasutra*, was not unlike a quarrel, and it was customary for lovers to strike each other during the course of it, uttering a variety of different sounds the while—thundering, cooing, weeping,

In Gramaneri, said the *Kamasutra,* "many young men enjoy a woman that may be married to one of them."

others "expressive of prohibition, sufficiency, desire of liberation, pain or praise, to which may be added sounds like those of the dove, the cuckoo, the green pigeon, the parrot, the sparrow, the flamingo, the duck, and the quail" (II 7). As well as striking (on the back, shoulders, head, or between the breasts) bruising and scratching were *de rigueur.* Vatsyayana specified eight kinds of nail mark and, discursive to the last, described what a well-bred and well-manicured nail should look like (II 4).

It is apparent that Gupta society, on its jet-set level at least, felt no need to be reticent either about its love or its love-marks. There was a sturdy sexuality about Indian civilization that contrasted strikingly with attitudes in other countries. Even in China, where sex had an equally important place, it was considered a matter for the bedchamber or the brothel, something essentially private and personal. But in India a great deal of life was lived in public; privacy might sometimes be found for the body, but rarely for the mind or the emotions. In any case, sex was natural, enjoyable, a virtuous pursuit of the Third Aim, so why hide it? Which was not quite the same thing as the attitude fashionable in some circles in the West today—sex is natural, enjoyable, good for you, so why not tell the world about it?

FAMILY LIFE

Vatsyayana ended his book with a number of useful recipes, a miscellaneous collection that included aphrodisiacs, anaphrodisiacs, formulae for turning the hair black (or white), for making water look like milk, even for turning red lips pale by applying a salve made from lac (a dark red resin) which had been thoroughly

One of the more intricate postures recommended by the *Kamasutra*

saturated in the sweat from the testicles of a white horse. Absent from this specialized pharmacopoeia, however, were any prescriptions for contraceptives or abortifacients.

There were a number of reasons. Most important, perhaps, was that the *Kamasutra* was essentially orthodox in its opinions. Though it is nowadays misleading to use the devalued word "unnatural" in relation to contraception and abortion, unnatural was precisely what the early Hindus believed them to be—a damaging interference in the pattern of *karma*, a distortion of the complex symmetry of reincarnation.

Sometimes, the Four Aims had a modifying influence on *karma*. It seems, for example, that because a courtesan's primary responsibility to provide love and pleasure made pregnancy undesirable, it was permissible for her to practice birth control. Certainly, early India knew several methods, some of them (such as powdered palm leaf and red chalk taken on the fourth day of menstruation) of doubtful efficacy. But there were affinities with Aristotelian ideas in the recommendation to anoint the vagina with honey, *ghi* (clarified butter), and the seeds of the *palāśa* tree *(butea frondosa* or Flame of the Forest), and as far as it is possible to judge it seems that Indians may have been the first to recognize that salt was an excellent material for discouraging conception. (Its effect is spermicidal.) Courtesans were told to insert in the vagina, before intercourse, "a piece of rock salt dipped in oil." [2]

Despite its encyclopedic intent, there was in fact no reason for the *Kamasutra* to include information that every courtesan learned at the outset of her career and every reason to exclude what it was better for the respectable married woman not to know—birth control methods that could be used without her husband's knowledge. In India, as elsewhere, the man was uncompromisingly the head of the household. Yet there were distinctive differences.

The idea of the "extended family" or "joint family" was by no means new to history. All over the world, for many centuries, married sons had been bringing their wives to live in the paternal home, which had expanded to accommodate them. It was a system that waned as cities grew and became more crowded, but it was still characteristic of the upper classes in China, even if middle- and lower-class families there had begun to splinter into separate households. Nowhere, however, had the system ever flourished as it did in India. Sons, daughters, aunts, uncles, cousins once, twice, and thrice removed—all congregated under one roof or group of roofs, often with living-in servants who brought their own extended families with them. Economically and emotionally, it was a system that featherbedded the weaker members of the clan, protecting them from the hard discomforts of independence and decision-making, insulating them from the chill realism of poverty that, in other societies, so often operated in favor of family limitation. Almost 2,000 years before the Western world discovered it, India knew what social security was all about.

Clearly, one of the dangers of the joint family was that it readily increased to unmanageable proportions, but this was catered for by sacred law operating in harmony with yet another of India's classification patterns. Just as there were four classes in Hindu society and four aims for the virtuous man to pursue, so there were four stages in the life of the individual—an ideal, if artificial division into youth, prime, maturity, and old age. At the end of childhood, brahmins, kshatriyas, and vaisyas were invested with the sacred thread and reborn into society.* From then until the age of 20 a boy was in his student stage, expected to be obedient to his teacher, austere, and celibate. The next stage was marriage and fatherhood. The third, which began in late middle age when his own sons had themselves become fathers, required him to leave his home and become a hermit, to begin the process of freeing his soul from material things. The process was completed when in old age he severed all ties and became a homeless wanderer.

Few men, of course, conscientiously followed this ascetic regiment through to the end, though the *sannyāsin,* the voluntary beggar, has always been a familiar sight in India. But the sense of what ought-to-be flickered like a cloud shadow across the landscape of paternal authority. However supreme a man might be during the second stage of his life, everything afterward conspired to diminish his influence. Most family property was jointly owned, and when the father died it might be divided among his sons who, following the sacred law, could take their portions and depart to set up their own extended families. But long before this, he was expected to abdicate his place in family councils and his administrative control over family affairs, to become a hermit if not in fact, at least to some extent in attitude.

* In more modern times, it has usually only been brahmins who have gone through the sacred thread ceremony and become "twice-born."

There were two striking, and probably unforeseen, effects of this system. In the first place, since a man's sons had implicit religious sanction for easing him out of office when he reached the third stage of life, it was difficult for even a dominating personality to impose a dictatorship on his family; the Indian equivalent of the Hebrew paterfamilias was something of a rarity. And in the second place, despite the very masculine emphasis of Indian society and regardless of legal and social oppressions, the Indian wife and mother could be a figure of surprising power and authority. The silent, subservient Indian woman is and always has been a myth propagated by outside observers who have paid too much attention to laws and not enough to people. As a woman's husband withdrew from responsibility, the respect and obedience that in other societies were accorded to the father of the house were almost insensibly transferred to his wife. However submissive she might appear before strangers, within the family her rule was often absolute.

These later days of her marrige may well have been the happiest time of an Indian woman's life. During the early period of Indian history, it appears to have been customary for girls to be fully adult before marriage, but by the beginning of the present era religious texts strongly recommended marriage just before puberty, and by the medieval period child marriage had become commonplace. There was no single reason for this, but unmarried daughters were a liability, and since Indians (like most other peoples) regarded girls as naturally libidinous and certain to lose their virginity at the merest whisper of an opportunity, it seemed desirable to tie them to a husband before any such disaster could occur. Another factor in increasingly early marriage may well have been an increasing shortage of women. Although India during the first millennium A.D. suffered invasions in the north and small local wars in the south, the absence of extreme fluctuations in population figures [3] suggests that casualty figures were not high enough to have the serious effect they had in China. Famines, however, were a recurring hazard in India, and though they did not slash the population they kept its growth rate down. Pregnant women, newly-born infants, girl children who went short so that their brothers might eat—these were the incidental casualties. More directly, the poor resorted to deliberate female infanticide, as even rich Rajputs still did in the nineteenth century. And, famine apart, as the marriage age became lower the death rate must have risen among girls who were married too young.

In the second and third centuries A.D. the ideal marriage was considered to be one where the bride's age was one-third that of the groom. The law books attributed to Manu proposed eight and 24 as suitable ages.[4] But whether or not theory and practice coincided quite as neatly as this, an eight-year-old bride would not go to live with her husband until she reached puberty at the age of about twelve, and even then she would be introduced to the sexual side of marriage with care. As Vatsyayana said bluntly, "If a woman is forced to submit to rough handling from a man she scarcely knows, she may come to hate sexual intercourse, even to hate the whole male sex. . . ." (III 2). Only after ten days of chaste acquaintance was it suggested that the husband might kiss his wife, proceeding from there by stages strung out over another three days until he felt that she was at last ready for intercourse.

The Indian child bride was usually free from at least some of the problems that confronted her contemporaries in other countries. Her husband, in most cases, belonged to the same class (and, in later times, the same caste) as she, so that their outlook and upbringing were similar. She was also likely to be his only wife. Although polygamy was by no means unknown in India, it was far from common except among royalty and the rich. In some areas—along the Malabar coast, for example, and in the foothills of the Himalayas—there was even a custom of polyandry, which permitted a woman to have several husbands. The great epic, the *Mahabharata*, had as its heroes five brothers who were all married to the same wife, an echo, perhaps, of early custom but one which involved later lawgivers in a great deal of intricate explaining-away. By the first millennium A.D., even polygyny was theoretically acceptable only if a man's first wife was barren, and in most areas polyandry was practiced only in a particular sense—a husband who was sterile could do what the men of Sparta had once done, and "transfer his conjugal rights temporarily to one sexually stronger, from which he could expect beautiful and vigorous children, without the marriage thereby being upset."[5]

The psychological effects even of a monogamous marriage were interesting. Such evidence as there is suggests that Indian husbands, as a rule, treated their youthful wives with much the same tender protectiveness as they so often extended to children, with the result that, instead of forcing them into early maturity (except in the sexual sense) they tended to delay it. The early teenage wife depended on her much older husband intellectually, emotionally, and physically, regarding him, as indeed the religious texts instructed her to do, as a wholly superior being. The differential between 12 and 28 is vast; between 20 and 36 not vast at all. Only, perhaps, when she reached her twenties did the Indian wife begin to discover her own personality and her own potential. And when her sons were grown up and married, her husband contemplating retirement, she still was only in her thirties, able and willing to make her presence felt.

How long this happy situation lasted is not easy to judge, for comparatively little is known about life expectancy in early India. The law books must have envisaged a man's life as lasting for close to 50 years; if he was married at 24 and did not enter into the third stage of life until his grandsons had been born (at least 25 years later), even 50 was an underestimate unless both retirement and renunciation stages were crammed into a very brief period indeed. The likelihood is that only the rich lived as long, and women could expect to die four or five years younger. As a rule of thumb, a woman might possibly expect to outlive her husband by about ten years. And ten appalling years they were, especially in orthodox upper-class families.

Remarriage was forbidden—even, by medieval times, to child widows whose marriages had not been consummated—as were all comforts of the flesh. The widow slept on the ground, was restricted to one simple meal a day (without honey, meat, wine, or salt), banned from wearing colors, ornaments, or perfume and by medieval times expected to shave her head. Her days were devoted to prayer and the performance of religious rites whose object was to insure that she and her husband would be married again in their next incarnation. Her presence was a bane to all except her children; in the social sense, the widow was the specter at the feast.

All in all, it was hardly surprising that some should have chosen to die when their husbands did. Early history in many parts of the world—in Mesopotamia, Egypt, Central Asia, and China—is littered with the sacrificed corpses of man's widows, retainers, favorite horses, faithful dogs, and there is no way of knowing how many went to their deaths voluntarily, out of love or

The ritual of *satī*

loyalty for the departed. In India, however, the custom of suttee, or more correctly *satī* (the word means "a virtuous woman"), was always voluntary, or at least apparently so, for social and family pressures in favor of correct behavior were sometimes sufficiently intense, especially in the medieval period, to propel a widow on to her husband's pyre whether she willed it or not. There are hints in the Vedas that the custom may have been of some antiquity,[6] but it was first recorded in the fourth century and appears to have been fairly rare until medieval times.* Some authorities condemned it out of hand, but others declared that the widow who became *satī* wiped out all her own and her husband's sins by her act of sacrifice, and that the fortunate couple would thereafter enjoy 35 million years of bliss (together) in the nearest Hindu equivalent to heaven.

THE KAMASUTRA IN THE ROUND

According to legend, the first *satī* was the wife of the great god Siva in his earlier role of Rudra. It had taken a good deal of cosmetic surgery to impose an appearance of symmetry on the Hindu religion, which had emerged some time after 500 B.C. as a kind of ecumenical alliance of sects united only in their belief in the Vedas, but by about the third century A.D. the numerous gods and godlings of earlier times had surrendered some of their personality traits and most of their attributes to a new trinity consisting of Brahma the wise one, the creator; benevolent Visnu, the preserver; and Siva, at once paternal and fearsome, a god of fertility who was also lord of ghosts and goblins, king of the dance, and as irrationally destructive as some cosmic vandal.

At much the same time, goddesses began to put in an appearance on the theological scene, where formerly they had been ignored. Ordinary people—especially in southern India, where the masculine primacy of the Aryan invaders never quite succeeded in overcoming the old agricultural attitudes of the indigenous peoples—had always worshiped fertility goddesses, river spirits, and tree nymphs, but Hindu intellectuals, true to the traditions of their nomad-pastoralist ancestors, were for centuries too busy clarifying (if that is the word) the impossibly complex and exclusively male pattern of the ecumenical pantheon to spare any attention for women. Gods, like men, had wives—and that was that.

But when divine wives began to assume importance it was in a unique form. Most aspects of the daily life of India's gods, like those of other countries, bore a recognizable resemblance to the

---

* *Satī* was not unique to India, but characteristic of a number of Indo-European peoples. The Danubian Slavs are recorded as having practiced it in the sixth century, the Western Slavs in the eighth century, and the Serbs in the tenth century.[7]

daily life of India's people, but in the matter of job demarcation between husband and wife there was an unexpected reversal, for the god sat back, calm and aloof, while his wife did the work. She was the *sakti*, the active aspect of the passive god. He *was*; she *did*. It was the Chinese theory of *yin* and *yang* turned back to front.

One of the formerly shadowy figures who now emerged into worldly activity was Siva's wife Parvati. Siva, in a previous incarnation, had been the Vedic god Rudra, and Parvati his wife Satī, "the virtuous one," who had incinerated herself in her husband's sacrificial fire. Now, as his *sakti*, she had as many aspects as he. As the mother goddess Gauri she was the active counterpart of Siva in his role as fertility god; as Kali "the black one," counterpart of Siva the destroyer. Virtually all the facets of Siva and Parvati had a shimmer of sexuality about them, usually creative or destructive, but sometimes flashing out in a blaze of rejection. One form of Siva was "the great ascetic," and one form of Parvati "the inaccessible one."

Early Indian sculpture had, of course, had its fertility symbols, plainly phallic or pleasantly erotic. *Maithuna* figures, representations of two (or more) figures in the act of intercourse, were perfectly familiar in a society which regarded sex as a natural and productive function. The difference was that, in India, it took considerably longer than in other civilizations for such figures to be relegated to the realm of moral delinquency. During the period between A.D. 500 and 900, however, with increasing sophistication and increasing contact with other, more worldly, more opinionated cultures, the Indian *maithuna* sculpture became more seductive, more sexy, and much more self-conscious. It also developed a tendency to retreat into shadowed corners.

This situation was suddenly reversed for reasons that were partly political. Because only the brahmins, the highest traditional class, were permitted to conduct the sacred rites of orthodox Hinduism, religion had taken on class connotations. In time, and inevitably, there was a backlash. No one knows when the new devotional cults came into being, but a major feature of several of them was direct personal relationship between man and god, without the mediation of the priest. The brahmins had concentrated on sacrifice and ritual; the new cults dealt in something that was much easier to understand and immensely appealing to the ordinary Indian—love. The Hindu view of *kama* and the integral sexuality of Siva and Parvati in particular—though Visnu was by no means lacking in enterprise (and, it must be admitted, rather more entertaining in his amours)—made it perfectly natural to think of love in relation to the gods in unambiguously human terms.

The devotional cults were mainly centered on Siva, and they gained in popularity over several centuries until India's rulers found it politically necessary not only to recognize them, but to demonstrate publicly that they recognized them. It was not enough to issue edicts of tolerance to an illiterate people; so, between about the ninth and thirteenth centuries at sites scattered over much of peninsular India, temples were built that were alive with the voluptuous imagery of personalized religion, statements in stone that said as clearly as any twentieth-century election poster that the ruling party was on the side of the people.

Generations of historians, Indians as well as Westerners, have written millions of words vindicating the explicit temple sculptures of India in terms of religious mysticism, creating esoteric mountains out of the molehills of their own embarrassment. Undoubtedly, Hinduism in the early medieval period did develop an element of sexual mysticism, but it is fair to say that, even if India were as "spiritual" as its interpreters so often claim, mystical comprehension would still have remained the prerogative of the very few. The erotic sculptures of such temples as the Kailasanath at Ellora, of Konarak, and Khujarao, may indeed have been commissioned and even created by mystics, but they were enjoyed on a very different plane by the masses who worshiped there. One modern authority even believes that the erotic sculptures at Konarak, which are positioned more or less at eye level and are of coarser workmanship than the essentially religious figures, may well have been intended to attract customers for the *devadāsīs*, or temple prostitutes, whose earnings made a substantial contribution to temple funds.[8] (There were, for example, more than 400 women on the payroll at the Rajarajesvara temple in Tanjore in the eleventh century). Since Konarak, now an island of ruins in a sea of sand, was once a busy and profitable port, this seems perfectly probable.

It is not, however, an explanation that holds good everywhere. At Khujarao, for example, frieze upon frieze of figures rises from ground level to heights well above the immediate vision of the most deprived seaman (or the most disapproving brahmin), every

Right:
The soaring towers of
the Kandariya Mahadev
temple at Khujarao

Below:
An erotic quartet
from the same
temple

figure beautifully executed, graceful, dynamic—perhaps the most elegant series of erotic sculptures the world has ever seen. By the year 1000 when the 83 temples of Khujarao were either being built or about to be built (the ruins of only 20 survive), the Indian temple had become an architectural reconstruction of Meru, the home of the gods, a marvelously engineered sacred mountain with, deep inside it, the dark sanctuary that was at once heart and womb. It has always been a human conceit to visualize the heavenly gods as greater and glossier editions of earthly princes, with their attendants and acolytes, musicians and dancing girls, concubines and courtiers, even sometimes with their comic figures, their caricatures of the crank and the misfit, the long-suffering butt of street-corner jokes. India was no exception. The temple homes of the gods spoke to every passerby of a religion that was, on a superficial level at least, friendly, understandable, popular in the widest sense. The message was there for all to see, even those who were not permitted to pass into the sacred inner temple areas—low-class sudras, outcastes, and (in northern India) women— for in the case of the major temples, the great public buildings of the Cholas and the Chandella Rajputs, the Kesari and the Ganga, most and sometimes all of the erotic sculptures were on the outside walls of the temples. It was there, not inside, that princes and concubines gazed tenderly into each others' eyes, there that courtiers and dancing girls light-heartedly experimented, frozen forever in stone, with some of the more interesting positions recommended by the *Kamasutra,* there that the vainglorious ascetic and the social deviant were maliciously paraded for the amusement of the groundlings in positions of grotesque sexual indignity.

This was the external world of the gods, vivid, alive, tumultuous. In awesome contrast, deep inside the temple in the *garbhagriha,* or "womb house," where the worshiper was reborn, sat the gods themselves, sometimes in fully representational form, sometimes in symbol. The great gods appeared in many shapes, but there was one that was characteristic of Siva—a symbol that, wherever it appeared, spoke unequivocally of him as god of fertility and reproduction. It was the lingam or penis, and sometimes it was combined with the symbol of his consort Parvati, which was the vulva. Long after, the British who ruled India for almost two centuries were to be disgusted to the very depths of their Victorian souls. They might be genuinely reluctant to interfere in the religion of their new subjects, but they could feel only contempt for a people who worshiped a phallus as if it were a god. When they discovered that the reverse was true, they regarded it as a distinction without a difference.

The British response to Hinduism was not the least of the elements that contributed to the long martyrdom imposed on Indian culture between 1757 and 1947, and in some ways the effects still persist today, for those few British who "drowned in the Ganges" (became fascinated by India and shouldered the burden of acting as its missionaries in the West) felt compelled to wrap up more than just erotic sculpture in the clean linen of spirituality. One subject which has not yet succeeded in shaking off these wrappings is the mystic sexual cult of Tantra.

THE JEWEL IN THE LOTUS

Secret languages have a history almost as long as mankind, their purpose one of exclusivity. On the whole, the sentinel's password of early times and the alchemist's use of "gray wolf" for antimony or "dragon's sister" for mercury were probably less impenetrable than everyday specialist language today, which can encompass a whole scientific structure in a single phrase or drown a simple concept in a torrent of polysyllables. When old and new are combined, the result is obscurantism on an impressive scale.

This is what has happened with Tantra. Not only does it have its own particular turns of speech, but, according to one modern adherent, it insists that in books for general publication its more advanced teachings "must be set forth in such a way that no practical use can be made of them. . . . Certain essentials are deliberately omitted and sometimes passages are jumbled so that they cannot be unraveled without qualified guidance; moreover the mystical language in which they are couched yields up the whole of its meaning only to those who have received the teaching that is 'whispered in the ear.' " The purpose of this, apparently, is to deceive "the unscrupulous," who have discovered that the teachings "can be perverted to serve mundane ends," conferring "psychic force" and powerful spells that can "be used for ill." [9]

Tantric texts, as a result, offer a fertile field for scholarly ingenuity. When a ritual requires the deflowering of a youthful virgin, does it really mean a flesh-and-blood virgin, or is it (as the spiritual school proclaims) a synonym for the psychic power that resides at the foot of a man's spine and must be induced to rise to the top of his head? When a magic potion includes among its ingredients blood from a corpse, a leper, the child of an incestuous union, or a woman's menstrual discharge, should it be taken literally or metaphorically? The answer, too often, depends more on the strength of the scholar's stomach than on that of his reasoning. Sometimes he may have doubts, but since the late twentieth century expects to be confused by language an escape route always lies open in the form of philosophic buzzwords and religious psychobabble. Gobble-de-gook and gobble-de-guru became one and the same. According to the cast of the reader's mind, Tantra emerges as disgusting, a spiritual revelation, or blankly incomprehensible.

It is not, of course, simple, but neither does it have to be spoken of in terms of "cosmic genesis," "polarity symbolism," or "union between the phenomenal and the noumenal." No one knows quite what form it took when it first appeared in the early centuries A.D.; modern works are less concerned with the foundations than with the intricate and eccentric edifice that later thinkers built upon them. But to attract followers in any numbers it must have had some relatively clearcut appeal, and its relationship with other religious cults suggests what this may have been.

Essentially, all Indian philosophy was a philosophy of rejection. In Hinduism, the individual's reward for living correctly through unnumbered incarnations was eventual release from the world and its pains, release not into some seductive paradise but into non-existence, the bliss of nothingness. The aim of the second great Indian faith, Buddhism, was the same; *nirvana* was not heaven but extinction.

It was, in fact, the journey rather than the destination that differentiated the major faiths and sects of India. The purpose of every new sect was to get you there quicker. *Hinayana*, or "lesser vehicle" Buddhism, required qualities of lonely self-reliance and personal striving, the vehicle a primitive biplane. *Mahayana*, or "greater vehicle," was less taxing, more reassuring, a prop airliner staffed by helpful *bodhisatvas*. Fastest of all was the supersonic *Vajrayana*, the "thunderbolt vehicle," which magically broke through the spiritual barrier that separated the believer from *nirvana*. Like Buddhism, Hinduism also had its systems, among them *Nyaya* which favored clear thinking and logic as the straightest route; *Yoga*, with its psychic disciplines; and *Vedanta*, which held that meditation could merge the individual soul into the void of the World Soul.

All these systems denied the world. Particularly, they denied all the world's pleasures to those who actively sought release from the cycle of rebirth. The individual who was not prepared to renounce all pleasure had to compromise (as the Four Aims permitted him to do) by living the best life he could and fatalistically hoping that some day his release would come.

What Tantra offered was something quite different. It was an action system, not a study system, and it promised bliss and release in a single lifetime to those who cultivated, instead of abjuring, pleasure, vision, and ecstasy. The argument was that, if the world was an expression of divinity, then what was in it must be divine, worthy to be worshiped rather than renounced. It was an apparently hedonistic creed, and its appeal must have been immense.

Some authorities believe that Tantra, like so many other revolutionary faiths in world history, was a religious expression of political revolt, a protest vote against the social status quo. Many of its practices, certainly, were deliberately aimed at breaking the class/caste system, while others flouted convention in lesser ways by using drugs, magic, and sexual intercourse as part of religious ritual. On the most superficial level, Tantra had the same kind of disrespectful permissiveness that was to attract so many adherents to the Alternative Society in the 1960s.

Hinduism and Buddhism both had their Tantric schools, and there were sharp differences between them. All Tantricists, however, aimed at achieving the nothingness which, in characteristically Indian fashion, they saw as the ultimate reality, the sentient world in which they lived being no more than an illusion. Divine truth was the whole incorporeal universe, the living world only a pale projection of it. What was needed was to shift the focus so that the transparent mirage that was the human soul could be made to coincide with, and merge into, the true eternal substance of the World Soul.

Shifting the focus was, of course, the problem, since it involved redirecting the currents of creative energy in the mind and body of the human aspirant into convergence with the same currents in the World Soul. The scope was vast. Anything that involved human creative energy (or, indeed, *any* positive activity) could be seen in Tantric terms. Fortunately, however, the energy currents did not have to be manipulated individually. Magic and sex, properly used, could simplify the task considerably.

The mantra was a kind of magical sound formula, a syllable or succession of syllables that, if pronounced in the correct manner, served as a lens to concentrate and direct energy. The yantra was its visual equivalent. Tantricists believed that such formulae could be used to force the gods to bestow power on the worshiper, and so speed him on his way to the nothingness he so deeply desired. But not all mantras were coercive. The greatest and most frequently used of all—which had much the same purpose as a preliminary genuflexion in church—was *Oṁ maṇi padme hūm,* whose resonance set up its own subtle vibration in space as it did on the palate. It had (and has) many layers of meaning, but is usually translated in the frankly sexual form of "the jewel is in the lotus," which is another way of saying "the lingam is in the yoni."

Sexual metaphor did not stop at the mantra. In India (though not in Tibet) Tantric Buddhism was almost indistinguishable from *Vajrayana* Buddhism, the "thunderbolt vehicle," and the sexual route to nothingness extended this electrical imagery, however unintentionally, by treating goddesses as lightning conductors that diverted human energy currents straight to the World Soul. By definition, the World Soul was unknowable, but the Tantricist tended to see it as a kind of Siva figure, majestic, all-powerful, aloof, passive. As with Siva, its energy resided in its *sakti,* its counterpart, its feminine aspect, its wife, with whom it was engaged in an eternal embrace—even while she was simultaneously active in the world. Sexually active, of course. It was the only form feminine creative energy could take. The Tantricist who had sexual intercourse with "the goddess," therefore, not only emulated the divine embrace but also became part of it; by becoming one with the *sakti,* he became one with the World Soul itself.

The basic Hindu Tantric rites, for the ordinary worshiper, required the presence of several couples and their guru, who was there to see that ritual sex did not deteriorate into mere self-indulgence and that proper procedure was observed. Even so, the less than devout believer may well have viewed the ceremonial as a pleasant evening's entertainment, the equivalent of a stiff aperitif, a good dinner, and then bed. First there were drugs, taken in solid form, as a drink, or as a smoke. Then came the "five enjoyments," intended, say modern authorities, as a slap in the face for orthodoxy, though it is not entirely clear why they should have been—none of them was taboo in ordinary society in the early days of the Tantric cults; on the contrary, they were all mild luxuries. The first three, fish, meat (sometimes specifically pork), and wine, were all popular on the tables of the rich from the eighth until about the eleventh centuries, and the fourth—cereals, type unspecified—was part of the standard diet.[10] The fifth enjoyment, sexual intercourse, may also have qualified as a luxury, for the general consensus (after much learned debate) was that the one-ness occasionally experienced by a pair of lovers perfectly in tune—which offered a glimpse of the one-ness that might be achieved between the individual soul and the World Soul—was unlikely to result from a union between husband and wife. It was therefore common for the participating couples to exchange partners, or for *devadāsīs*, temple prostitutes who had a special symbolic sanctity, to be imported for the occasion. The primary appeal of Tantra, it must be remembered, was the cultivation, not the rejection, of pleasure as a means to release, and there is no good reason to believe that in the early days these five enjoyments were regarded as anything other than what they appeared to be, even if later theorists converted them into symbols. Christians will remember that it took almost 1,200 years for the bread and wine of the Last Supper to become the body and blood of the Redeemer.

It may be assumed that the vast majority of Tantricists never advanced beyond this basic stage of worship, which encompassed the pleasures promised by the doctrine itself, an element of social defiance (caste and class barriers being deliberately breached in the choice of sexual partners), and a certain spiritual excitement, a feeling of power induced by the uttering of magic spells and the drawing of magic diagrams.

There were some, however, for whom this was not enough, who were wholly committed to achieving what the texts promised, bliss in a single lifetime. There was no rule book, the pattern for each initiate being individually drawn, and for this reason the information is fragmented and often contradictory. But it appears that would-be initiates went through a special ceremony with a partner who had been converted into a "vessel of divine energy" by means of intercourse with an initiate of high spiritual level. These partners, usually women, were known by Buddhists as *dākinīs*, and the right to initiate may originally have been confined to the members of a particular sect.

Once initiated, the *sādhaka* pursued an intensive ritual program, involving prolonged acts of ecstatic meditation engaged in simultaneously with intercourse. This meditation included liturgies, the uttering of mantras, mental visions, yogic postures, and what one authority charmingly describes as "manipulation of the conjoined male and female energies." [11] Only when he was a relative beginner was it necessary for the *sādhaka* to have a flesh-and-blood partner; at a more advanced state "inner realization" was enough. Then, since sexual excitement was felt to indicate the presence of divine energy, some initiates—long before the days of macho or even machismo—ritually worshiped their own erect penises. Others, more advanced still, attained identity with both god and *sakti* and were thus able to indulge in perpetual and blissful intercourse with themselves.

Anatomically improbable though this may sound, it was perfectly reasonable on a secondary level of Tantric theory, that relating to the "subtle body." This idea, that inside every fleshly body there was an ethereal replica consisting of nerves, emotions, channels of energy, intellect, soul substance—whatever, in fact, contemporary knowledge was unable to account for—was fairly common in pre-scientific societies, though it was not always charted with quite the sophistication that the Indians and Chinese brought to it. Tantricists, like Taoists, believed that there was a masculine element in every woman and a feminine element in every man, and visualized the subtle body as containing two nerve channels, one *(lalanā* in Buddhist terminology) feminine, running along the left of the spinal cord, and one *(rasanā)* male, along the right. There were also a number of nerve centers in the body—Hindus knew a basic six, Buddhists four—and these were visualized as being strung out, like lotus-shaped medallions, along a vertical line running from the base of the spine to the top of the head. They were called *ćakras*. When ritual intercourse took place, particularly in one of the convoluted positions that were believed to stimulate the nervous system, the female energy, by complex interaction with the nerve center around the man's navel, helped to convert his activated but unreleased semen into a magical essence *(bindu)*

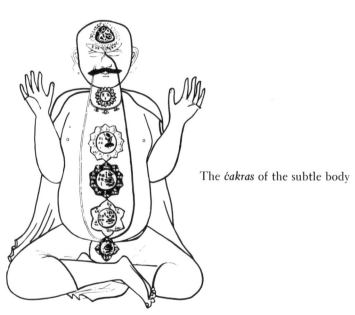

The *ćakras* of the subtle body

The Mongols were (and remained) notorious for their zoophiliac habits. Note the wise precaution of tying the mare's forelegs out of the way.

which then broke through the *lalanā* and *rasanā* channels, opened up a new channel, and whisked up through it to the *ćakra* at the top of the head, "the thousand-petalled lotus," which opened into the void, the eternal bliss of nothingness. Thus the true Tantric adept became one with the dual-sexed World Soul.

There is a particularly interesting parallel here with the Chinese belief that, by means of *coitus reservatus* or *coitus obstructus,* the semen or *yang* essence could be made to ascend and nourish the brain. As ever, the Tantric texts are less than informative, but it seems reasonably certain that Buddhist Tantricists, at least, used respiratory controls not unlike those recommended by the Master Tung-hsüan, while in modern times a Hindu Tantric sect in Bengal has utilized the urethral-pressure method described in *Important Matters of the Jade Chamber* (see above, pages 171–72). As far as can be discovered, however, Hindu Tantricists have never considered it as crucial a part of the ritual as Buddhists, and the reason for this (if any real reason exists) may lie in the origins of the practice. The late Dr. Robert Van Gulik, one of the few modern scholars who has gone deeply into the subject, argued that Indian Tantra picked up the idea of *coitus reservatus/obstructus* from Chinese Taoism in the fifth or sixth centuries A.D. The most likely people to pick it up were Buddhist (not Hindu) missionaries to China. Later, when Tantra developed, it in turn sent missionaries to China, and China began to absorb some of the theories of *Hindu* Tantra. Then again, at the beginning of the fourteenth century, when China was under the rule of the Mongols, another variant of Tantra was exported there, this time an extreme Tibetan form to which the Mongols themselves subscribed, and in which the Chinese no longer recognized any trace of the original Taoist elements.

As in the case of the sex manuals, however, it will never be possible to answer the basic questions about interchange. Whose idea was it? Who thought of it first? Who—*if anybody*—passed on the message from culture to culture, civilization to civilization? Similarity of ideas does not infallibly mean plagiarism.

Stripped of its religious imagery, its spells, its self-hypnosis, its prayers (which differed radically between Buddhists and Hindus), Tantra is like the Bible stripped of its poetry and its quality of revelation. Few religions look attractive in the nude. However, as one modern European scholar remarks, there is more to Tantricism than sex and magic. Hindu and Buddhist critics, he says, "have constantly suggested that the Tantric uses religion as a mantle for sexual desire and debauchery; the Tantrics have constantly answered that the complicated, elaborate, and exceedingly difficult procedure followed by the Tantrics would not at all be necessary to gratify sexual desire, whose objects are much easier to obtain without any [such rigorous] trappings." [12] Which is undoubtedly true.

9.
Islam

There is a felicitous, if rarely recognized irony in the fact that the accumulated wisdom of more than 3,000 years of disparate civilizations—in Sumer and Egypt, Greece and Rome, Syria and Persia, China and India—should have poured for a few brief and productive centuries into the melting pot of Baghdad, the brilliant new capital, the Arabian Nights reality, of the caliphs of Islam. For Baghdad was built, in A.D. 763, almost on the site of Kish, reputedly the very first capital of the world's very first civilization, that of Sumer. And just as the scribes of Sumer had discovered how to pass on the hard won knowledge of their small and circumscribed world by incising it on moistened tablets of clay, so the Arabs of the eighth century A.D. discovered how to correlate and then diffuse all that Europe and Asia had learned in the intervening millennia by writing it down, not on brittle clay or costly papyrus or parchment or flimsy palm leaves, but on durable newly-developed paper made from flax. The intellectually acquisitive Arab mind and the adaptation of a centuries-old Chinese technique together brought about a revolution in scholarship, and subsequently in the whole fabric of Western life, that no one could then have foreseen and few afterward were to acknowledge.

During the last 500 years preceding the birth of Christ, the nomadic peoples of the arid peninsula between the Red Sea and the Persian Gulf had learned to exact their middleman's profit from the lucrative east-west spice trade, but this common interest brought no unity until, after the hegira *(hijra)* of A.D. 622—the flight from Mecca to Medina—the Prophet Muhammad began to preach a visionary, if ragged, composite of Arab, Jewish, and Christian beliefs that came to be known as the religion of Islam, which meant surrender (to the Faith). Its followers were Muslims, or self-surrenderers.

Non-Muslims in the medieval world soon discovered that they, too, had to surrender—to the Faithful, if not to the Faith—so that within a century of the death of the Prophet, Syria, Mesopotamia, the whole of the Persian dominions in the east, the entire Mediterranean coastline of Africa, and virtually all of Spain had capitulated to the men who followed Muhammad.

The Prophet had said, "Search for learning, though it be as far away as China," but his successors found that there was no need to exert themselves in the matter. Paramountcy brought its own reward in the magnetic attraction that drew men of science, philosophers, craftsmen, mechanics, and artists within its field. In Persia, the Arabs fell heir not only to the sophisticated tradition of Persia itself but, through the agency of scholarly heretics who had fled from Byzantium to Jundishapur (then the principal seat of learning in western Asia), to Greek scientific ideas already mellowed and modified by contact with Syrian, Persian, even Hindu modes of thought. To the east, the Muslim conquerors were soon in contact with outward-looking T'ang China, and to the south with the Hindu and Buddhist cultures of India.

Through Islam, the West was almost insensibly to absorb ideas and attitudes originating not only in the Classical world but in the furthest reaches of Asia. It would, in fact, be difficult to exaggerate the importance of the Islamic contribution to science, technology, and the arts in the West. Between the eighth and twelfth centuries Islam held all the learning of the known world in its hand, and from Jundishapur to Baghdad, to Cairo, to Sicily and Spain it passed it on. Greek medicine, forgotten in the medieval West; Hindu numerals (which came to be known as Arabic), the nine digits and a zero that superseded the clumsy Roman system and revolutionized mathematics, scientific experiment, and everyday life; Chinese papermaking, which changed the face of scholarship, and the crossbow, which did the same for war; and a long and luxurious catalogue of adjuncts to gracious living—figured silks, stained glass, damascened metals, canopied beds, carpets, new dye colors, the cusped arch of architecture and the Gothic black letter script, glass mirrors, public baths, secular hospitals, the lute, the kettledrum, and the exotic and escapist tales that were to inspire Boccaccio and Chaucer, von Eschenbach and la Fontaine.[1] But because the serried ranks of Church and state were solidly opposed to ideological contamination, most of what the West accepted from Islam lay in the realm of practical ideas and inventions rather than in that of the mind, in useful discoveries that seemed to exist independently of the idea-systems from which they emerged. "Arabic" numerals had nothing to do with theology, and Turkish armorial devices—such as the double-headed eagle so inappositely adopted by the Holy Roman emperors—were merely a convenient way of distinguishing one animated suit of armor from another in a scrimmage.

Even so, some thought processes and attitudes slipped through, unnoticed or unrecognized, helping to change the mind of Christendom as material acquisitions changed its face. The results were occasionally surprising. Very curiously indeed, the Arab love song—product of a society that remains today the last bastion of female subservience—was to provide the stimulus that transformed the West's image of woman (see pages 259–66). But even before that, the monogamous Christian male learned of the delights of polygamy and the harem, and evolved his own system along less fettered lines. The medieval period introduced into Western history not only the "Lady" of the chivalric ideal, but the extramarital convenience of the mistress. And before that, too, the importance of eunuchs in the Near East and more particularly in the Byzantine church helped to convince the Church of Rome that the "voluntary" celibacy it required of its priests was mild and civilized by comparison. As indeed it was.

THE   DEVELOPMENT   OF   THE   HAREM

Life in Baghdad was very different from life in the desert, even if the desert for which the new *jeunesse dorée* felt such romantic nostalgia was not quite the idyllic and starry-skied haven of their imaginings. But although they might be as innocently sentimental about the land of their fathers as most exiles, they took a worldly view of the problems of love and sex. Polite society knew only two kinds of women—the courtesan, usually a singer, usually a foreigner, witty, beautiful, talented, and inconstant, and the respectable lady, hemmed in by prohibitions, an inaccessible idol to be worshiped from afar.

She had not always been so. Before the days of the Prophet, although subject to a great many legal disabilities (depending on her tribe), she had enjoyed a degree of personal freedom. Segregation was neither wholly possible nor even particularly necessary in the deserts of Arabia, and the custom of women veiling their faces does not appear to have been obligatory. But all this had changed with the Islamic conquests of a wider world, for though the Prophet himself had tried to improve the lot of women, his purpose had been undermined by the requirements of city life and the long-established customs of the civilized Near East. The Arab incomers observed the usages not only of their new subjects, but also of their cultured neighbors over the border. Byzantium, hated and admired, became their first social preceptor, with unfortunate results.

Byzantium's own heritage could scarcely have been more mixed, for over the centuries its population had come to include Armenians, Syrians, Greeks and Jews, Macedonians and Italians. Its laws were Greco-Roman, its religion Christian, and its social attitudes Mediterranean. With such a background, its view of women was bound to be unfavorable. Their principal duties—with the notable exception of ladies of the imperial family—were to stay out of sight and to bear children. Unmarried girls were often kept in a seclusion so complete that they were not even seen by servants, and there was a provision in the marriage ceremony for the happy couple to have a few moments alone so that the groom could draw aside his bride's veil and see her face for the first time. One scholar, with commendable solemnity, remarks that Byzantine marriages were not always consummated, and that it was not unusual for a new husband, once alone with his wife, to inform her that for his soul's sake he proposed to live with her as if they were brother and sister, or even that he proposed to retire into a cloister and recommended her to do the same.[2]

Byzantium was not wholly at fault for Arab women's adoption of the veil. The Prophet had decreed that his own wives should be veiled as a mark of respect, and this had been enough to persuade upper-class converts to Islam also to shroud their faces, a protection that took on meaning in the rowdy, undisciplined city. But

Muslim polgamy and Byzantine segregation were to interact in a way that proved disastrous for women.

In pre-Islamic times polygamy appears not to have been widespread among the Arab tribes; it was an institution that flourished mainly where there were frequent wars, a wide range of class distinctions, a continuing supply of slaves, and a regular supply of money. Muhammad, however, chose to encourage polygamy among his followers, partly, it has been suggested, to increase the number of the Faithful, but partly also as a way of providing social security for the widows and orphans left destitute by the slaughter at the battle of Uhud. The Koran is notoriously difficult to interpret, and the relevant verse is susceptible to a different reading, but his followers took his meaning to be that they were at liberty to marry wives up to a maximum of four, as long as they felt themselves capable of treating all four with impartial kindness. Anyone who did not was recommended to restrict himself to one wife and an unspecified number of concubines.[3] In the event, most ordinary Muslims found it less taxing to make do with one wife and change her regularly; repudiation was no more of a problem than it had ever been.

One of the most important religious thinkers of Islam, Ghazālī (1058–1111), conveniently summed up in his book of *Counsel for Kings* all the pains that had been visited on women as a result of Eve's transgression in the Garden of Eden (a legend as important to Muslims as to Christians). The list shows clearly enough the position of women in Islam and shows, too, that what was in essence *social* custom had the sanction of religion behind it.

"As for the distinctive characteristics with which God on High has punished women, [the matter is as follows]:

"When Eve ate fruit which He had forbidden to her from the tree in Paradise, the Lord, be He praised, punished women with eighteen things: (1) menstruation; (2) childbirth; (3) separation from mother and father and marriage to a stranger; (4) pregnancy; (5) not having control over her own person; (6) a lesser share in inheritance; (7) her liability to be divorced and inability to divorce; (8) its being lawful for men to have four wives, but for a woman to have [only] one husband; (9) the fact that she must stay secluded in the house; (10) the fact that she must keep her head covered inside the house; (11) [the fact that] two women's testimony [has to be] set against the testimony of one man; (12) the fact that she must not go out of the house unless accompanied by a near relative; (13) the fact that men take part in Friday and feast day prayers and funerals while women do not; (14) disqualification for rulership and judgeship; (15) the fact that merit has one thousand components, [only] one of which is [attributable] to women, while nine hundred and ninety-nine are [attributable] to men; (16) the fact that if women are profligate they will be given [only] half as much torment as [the rest of] the community at the Resurrection Day *; (17) the fact that if their husbands die they must observe a waiting period of four months and ten days [before remarrying]; (18) the fact that if their husbands divorce them they must observe a waiting period of three months or three menstrual periods [before remarrying]."[4]

Although such rules of conduct had to appear publicly to be obeyed, the women's quarters in the lower-class Muslim household—their *ḥarām*, or sanctuary—involved no more than a token segregation. Poor men could not afford to lock up their wives and daughters. But it was a different matter for the better-off. The Prophet's ban on discriminating between wives had led to a custom of allocating a separate room, apartment, or even house to each wife, and this, besides taking up a good deal of ground space, also made it easy for the women to yield to any temptation that happened to offer. Muslim husbands had no higher opinion of the wives' morals than Chinese or Indians, Greeks or Romans—"it is a fact," said Ghazālī, "that all the trials, misfortunes, and woes which befall men come from women" [5]—and they soon followed the Byzantine example of keeping their women virtual prisoners. All in all, it was hardly surprising that when Arab love songs developed into a distinct genre so many of them should have serenaded a lady who was remote, unapproachable, and unattainable. And hardly surprising that the composers should have taken the opportunity of shaping that lady into the ideal creature of their own imaginings.

THE   ARAB   LOVE   SONG

When the early Muslims conquered Persia, they experienced a revelation that was not only intellectual but emotional and ab-

---

* Item 16 looks more like a blessing than a punishment.

sorbed influences that were not only major but sometimes apparently quite minor—but only apparently. One channel through which these were transmitted, was, perhaps surprisingly, the professional storyteller who flourished in the cities of the Near East, as ready to tell his tales to passersby on street corners as to the caliph in his court. The repertoire of these men, especially the Persians among them, was astonishingly varied. They drew on the Bible and the Vedas, recounted the exploits of Greek heroes, Roman warriors, and Egyptian queens, told of angels and djinns, winged horses and magic carpets, of treasure houses on earth and dancing girls in paradise. Their word pictures had a wild, exotic glamor that took possession of the Arab imagination.

Newly adjusted to the romantic vision, the Arabs found it (in the flesh) in the seductive slave singers who were among the prizes of conquest. Self-possessed, exquisite, highly trained, cultured, these girls soon developed into a fashionable elite that exercised a civilizing influence all the way from Persia to Spain.[6] The fact that their charming foreign accents were unable to cope with the archaic words of traditional Arab songs proved not to matter very much, for lyrics based on the rough life of the desert and rhythms matched to the camel's tread were out of place in the city, and the simple love songs the girls themselves preferred soon captured the Arabs' ears as the storytellers' romances had captured their imagination.

The new kind of love lyric helped to crystallize a sensuous image of woman, and not only of the slave singers, who were, after all, relatively few in number and an upper-class luxury. The orthodox Muslim lady, immured in her *harām*, also acquired a novel and enigmatic charm. As a result, two forms of love song developed and two schools of love itself.

The slave singer, a willing courtesan, was the primary target of the love-desire school, whose adherents were experienced, debonair, and dissipated. It was up to the lady to ravish the gentleman with her wit and beauty, while he courted her with style, finding his pleasure in the hunt itself and feeling perfectly free, once his object was achieved, to set off in pursuit of a different quarry. The courtesan may also have enjoyed the game for its own sake, but she appears to have been more interested in following (however unknowingly) Vatsyayana's advice on profit-taking. The poet Djâhiz complained that "most of the time she lacks sincerity and uses treachery and cunning to exhaust her victim's fortune, then

Eighth-century dancing
girls; a highly
formalized representation
from Baghdad

she abandons him." [7] Money was of the greatest importance to
her, because if she had enough of it she was permitted under
Muslim law to buy her freedom.

In the love-desire game, the courtesan's only serious rival was
the 18-year-old boy, whose attraction the Arabs felt as keenly as
their predecessors the Persians and Greeks had done. Both were
objects of a hedonistic, impermanent devotion that was no new
phenomenon in the civilized world. In effect, love-desire, even as a
cult, was far from being unique to the Arabs.

But "pure love" was something quite different, very much a
masculine game designed to satisfy intellectualized masculine
emotions. The courtesan was at least a person, however mercen-
ary, whereas the heroine of the "pure love" lyric was not a person
at all, only a focal point. Thanks to the veil and the harem (ḥarām), the respectable lady's face, figure, charm, and wit were all
unknown quantities to her poet-lover. Indeed, it seems likely that
many heroines of these lyrics were not even aware of the poetry
they inspired. They were shrouded figures, sometimes seen at a
distance, known to their admirers perhaps only through the boasts
of husbands or brothers.

Love was of the mind, sex of the body, and the Arabs saw no
reason to confuse the two. What the "pure love" school did was

turn to account the segregation of women, so that instead of denying love it supplied it. Chastity, the first rule of the game, became so important that it would have been a betrayal for the lover to satisfy his passion even if he could. The second rule, fidelity, was expected to be observed for life, while the third required absolute subjection of the lover to the beloved, even if it made him die by inches, a victim "weeping for love of his assassin," as the poet Djamil put it.[8] Although, to begin with, the poets were quite prepared to divulge the name of the woman they adored, by the eighth century this was frowned on, and Djamil's successors could find no release for their torments of love and jealousy except in poetry and art. Because of this, "pure love" came to be seen in the light of "ennobling love," as a creative, spiritual source of inspiration.[9]

It was this final form of "pure love" that was to be introduced into Europe with peculiar social results. But before that happened, pilgrims and Crusaders had begun to contrast their own loveless and monogamous marriages—business arrangements that took little account of personal chemistry—with the tempting delights of the harem.

Or what looked, to the ignorant outsider, like the delights of the harem. The insider had reservations.

THE GRAND SERAGLIO

The sheer administrative problems of a society polygamous on its higher levels were seen at their most complex in the royal household. China had experienced them and rationalized them a thousand years before. There, the king had been expected to have one queen, three consorts, nine second-rank wives, 27 third-rank wives, and 81 concubines (figures arrived at through an age-old system of number magic), and it had become necessary for several court ladies to be employed as "sex secretaries." It was their responsibility to ensure that the king had intercourse with the right partner on the right day and at the right frequency; lowest rank first, working up in sequence to the queen, who had the pleasure of his majesty's company once a month when his vital essence had been fortified by the *yin* of her inferiors. The secretaries kept diaries using special red writing brushes, and the expression "records made with the red brush" came to be synonymous with "secrets of the royal bedchamber." The day and hour of each consummation were noted in the records, and as a kind of cross-reference every royal bedfellow was given a silver ring to wear on her right hand before she was taken to the king, the ring being switched to the left hand after intercourse. If the girl conceived she was given a gold one instead.

By the T'ang period (A.D. 618–907), when the Muslims of Baghdad were still only beginning to come to grips with the problem, the Chinese royal seraglio was numbered in hundreds and the sex secretaries needed real actuarial talent to organize the schedule and keep track of the date and hour of every union, as well as menstrual periods, signs of pregnancy, and associated data. For magical as well as security reasons, the possibility of one girl substituting for another was a continuing headache; in the early eighth century, girls who had slept with the emperor were rubber-stamped afterward. The stamp said, "Wind and moon [sexual relations] are forever new," and was smeared with a cinnamon ointment that made it indelible.[10]

Neither Indian rulers nor Muslim caliphs ever seem to have gone to quite such extremes. Indeed, according to the *Kamasutra*, Hindu rulers even succeeded in retaining the right to choose whom they went to bed with. Typically, however, Vatsyayana skimmed over the subject in favor of advising young men how they, too, could go to bed with the royal women, provided they succeeded in smuggling themselves past the guards and into the *zenana*. It was not, he admitted, the safest of enterprises, but if a man was determined on it, then "he should first ascertain whether there is an easy way to get out. . . ." [11]

Perhaps because Europeans had little direct contact with the courts of China or India until well after the end of the medieval period, the polygamous habits of the emperors of China and maharaj-i-rajas of India made relatively little impression on the Western imagination. But contacts with the Muslim world during the Crusades gave the peoples of Europe a very exotic picture indeed of the private lives of the caliphs of Baghdad. And although that fount of seraglio romance, *The Thousand Nights and One Night*, was not to be translated into a Western language until the beginning of the eighteenth century, the tales contained in it—drawn from Persian, Indian, Greek, Hebrew, and Egyptian sources—were already part of the common currency of the storytellers at the time of the Crusades. Even so, the myth of the harem did not achieve its fullest splendor until the days of the Ottoman Turks, who in 1453 overwhelmed the few thousand remaining defenders of the once glorious empire of Byzantium and rode into Constantinople itself, the last lonely bastion of the Eastern Roman Empire.

This is hardly the place to retail the extraordinary saga of the Ottomans. Much in-depth psychoanalytical and socio-biological research needs to be done before it will be possible to make a valid assessment of the effect, not only on the Near East but on the whole of Western history, of the sultans' own parentage and sex life, the long celibacy of the military elite (the janissaries) and the emasculated state of many of the chief civil administrators of the empire, the eunuchs. But it seems clear that in no other society can sexuality on the one hand, and its suppression on the other, have had such a continuing influence at the level of political and diplomatic decision.

The Ottomans, originally a nomadic people related to the Mongols, appear not to have embraced the delights of the harem until after the conquest of Byzantium, but when they did they found it necessary to perpetuate the extreme state of segregation favored by their Arab predecessors. Not until 1909, when Abdul Hamid II was finally deposed and deported with a mere three wives and four concubines for company, did anything solidly factual become known to the outside world about the secret and jealously guarded precincts of the harem of the Grand Turk.* Before then, the Grand Turk's harem, like that of the caliphs of Baghdad, had been a reservoir of mysteries, serving outsiders as a kind of erotic grab bag of wish-fulfilment fantasies. No one *knew* what went on in the harem. As N.M. Penzer said in the first comprehensive study of the subject, the West for more than 400 years thought of it as a place where the sultan passed his days "surrounded by hundreds of seminaked women, in an atmosphere of heavy perfume, cool fountains, soft music, and over-indulgence in every conceivable kind of vice that the united brains of jealous, sex-starved women could invent for the pleasure of their lord." [12] But it was not quite like that.

---

* "Harem" is an abbreviation of *harēmlik*, meaning "women's quarters" or "sanctuary," a Turkish version of the Arabic *harām*. The male domain was the *selāmlik*. The Italian word *seraglio*, an adaptation from Persian, properly refers not just to the harem but to all the buildings in the royal enclave, including the *selāmlik*. The Indian word *zenana* is the equivalent of harem.

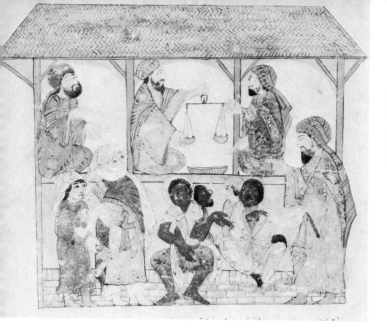

Zabid (Yemen) was an important market for the sale of slaves imported from Abyssinia in the thirteenth century.

Containing between 300 and 1,200 concubines with their attendants and guards, their Mistress of the Robes, Keepers of the Baths, the Jewels and the Storerooms, their Reader of the Koran, and their Manageress of the Table Service, the harem could scarcely afford to be languorous, even if the emotional atmosphere was often steamy. Most of the girls had been bought in the slave markets of the Mediterranean and the Black Sea or presented directly to the sultan by their captors,* and each had her appointed place, depending on her age, status, and how far she had progressed with her harem education. A new girl would be placed under the supervision of one of the departmental heads to go through an apprenticeship in embroidery, coffee-making, music, or accountancy, and if she never caught the sultan's eye was liable to remain an embroiderer or coffee-maker or instrumentalist or book-keeper until she was pensioned off and sent to live, with the superseded harem of the previous sultan, in the Eski Serai, the "Old Seraglio." But if the sultan's eye did chance to light on her with approval, she was immediately set apart and allocated private rooms and attendants, and when the summons came (if it did) she was hurried off to the harem baths to be shampooed, massaged,

---

* The Mongols were more organized than the Turks in the matter of harem-stocking. According to Marco Polo, Kublai Khan annually sent for four or five hundred girls from a particular province, famous for its beauties, and had them assessed on a points system (21 being top marks) until the number had been whittled down to 30 or 40, who shared his bed in rotation for the subsequent year. Runners-up were presented to his noblemen.[13]

and perfumed, to have any body hair removed, her nails tinted, and her hair washed and dressed. Then, suitably clothed and jeweled, she was taken, with such laboriously contrived secrecy that the entire seraglio must have known about it, to the sultan's bedchamber. It was the first, and sometimes the last, step on the ladder to genuine power, to the envied if not always enviable position of Sultan Valideh, Mother of the [next] Sultan.

A wife or concubine might lose favor and be repudiated, but the sultan's mother held a place of unique honor. It was she, not the Grand Turk himself nor his favorite bedfellow, who ruled over the whole complex institution of the harem, and her authority stretched much further than that—even to the boundaries of the empire if she were strong and her son weak. Hers was the position that every beauty in the harem aimed at and plotted for, and it could not be achieved until after the death of the sultan who had fathered her child.

Muslim custom diverged in many ways from that of Europe and Byzantium, and not least in the matter of succession and

The women's baths

inheritance. Christian society was founded on legitimacy and the right of primogeniture, and its preoccupation with rank and political expediency forced royal families in general to marry within the restricted circle of other royal families, and noble families to marry within the nobility. In some periods, it may be fairly assumed that more bastards were born than legitimate heirs (see pages 276-77), but it was the heirs who had the rights, whether or not they were worthy of them.

In Muslim ruling households, however, where a large harem was as much a symbol of power as crown, orb, and scepter in the West, it would scarcely have been possible to restrict breeding within such narrow boundaries. Most concubines were slaves, and most children of the ruling house were therefore born of slaves. Of the 38 Abbasid caliphs who ruled Islam in the early medieval period, 35 were the sons of foreign slave girls.[14] The legitimacy that so preoccupied Christians could scarcely be an issue in the Muslim world.

Arab tradition followed the line not of primogeniture but of tribal seniority (*califah*) in its succession, with the result that if the most dynamic member of the ruling family happened to be a younger son it was not only his elder brothers who became targets for assassination when the throne fell vacant, but his uncles as well. The Turks, however, when their turn came, accepted that it should be a son who had first claim to the succession, although the question still remained—which one?

There was a system of seniority in the harem based on the Koranic tradition of four wives, although it was unusual for an Ottoman sultan to go so far as to marry. A concubine who bore a son was customarily elevated to the rank of *kadin,* which gave her many privileges, especially if she were fortunate enough to be the first of a new sultan's women to do so. The position of a *kadin* was not immutable. An astute and determined Second *Kadin* could oust the First, if she played her cards well, and win a place in the harem inferior only to that of the Sultan Valideh, the sultan's mother—with whom she would usually find herself in a permanent state of war. But if she were clever she could achieve more than that; she could ensure that her own son stood highest in the favor of the sultan himself, a vital step toward the succession, and essential if she had any maternal feelings. For until the seventeenth century the alternative to succession was death.

The absence of any law of primogeniture meant that the succession was usually settled in a bloodbath; indeed, in the latter part of the fifteenth century this became compulsory when Muhammad II issued the Law of Fratricide, which decreed that the son who succeeded to the throne should at once—if he had not already done so in order to insure his succession—execute all his brothers. The object was to eliminate, at the same time as the unfortunate princes, all possibility of future sedition or secession. Though ruthless, it was not altogether foolish. If the 19 brothers of Muhammad III had chosen to unite against him, for example, far more than 19 men would have died in the ensuing struggle. Muhammad's successor, however, Achmet I (1603–17), reacted against the practice and replaced it with one that, however unintentionally, had far worse results all round. Now, claimants to the succession were merely locked up in a small building known as the Cage until their turn came, with only a handful of women and attendants to keep them company.* The Sultan Ibrahim was caged from the age of two until he succeeded at 24; Suleiman II for a total of 39 years; and Osman III, in the eighteenth century, for 50. The Cage was not only a living death, but a guarantee that any sultan who emerged from it would be a weak one, out of touch with humanity, the empire, and the world.

In every way, therefore, it was in a *kadin's* interest to insure that her son appeared in a favorable light in the sultan's eyes, and if she were intelligent and farsighted enough she reinforced her efforts in that direction by buying the support of the viziers, the janissaries, the chief eunuchs, and the influential Grand Mufti of Islam. Many of the Ottoman emperors owed their thrones, and the continuing right to sit on them, more to their mothers' abilities and efforts than to their own.

Some of the *kadins* would have made their mark in any period of history, most of all, perhaps, Roxelana Sultan, who even persuaded Suleiman the Magnificent to marry her, the first sultan for well over a century to enter into the state of legal matrimony. The

---

* The women were usually rendered sterile by removal of the ovaries. Sometimes the seraglio physicians fitted them with contraceptive pessaries instead, probably as a regular routine at the end of each menstrual period. Though Arab contraceptive medicine was relatively advanced—Avicenna's medical encyclopedia was the standard work of reference from the time of his death in 1037 until 600 years later—it appears to have been customary to leave such pessaries in position for days, or even weeks at a time.[15] If a mistake did occur, any child born in the Cage was unceremoniously drowned.

interesting result was that the reputedly depraved Grand Turk thereafter lived a far more respectable and connubial life than his Christian contemporaries, Henry VIII of England with his succession of wives, and Henri II of France with his succession of mistresses. Roxelana, a Russian, had considerable political acumen and strongly influenced Suleiman in his intricate maneuverings against his favorite enemy, the Holy Roman emperor, Charles V of Spain. Two reigns later, Safieh, a Venetian of noble birth who had been captured by a Turkish corsair, herself directed the movement of Ottoman fleets and armies while her master, the sultan, occupied himself with his other *kadins* and concubines; she ultimately achieved the rank of Sultan Valideh, but made herself so unpopular that she was murdered in her bed.

Some *kadins* succeeded in escaping not only from the harem but even from the control of the palace. An indulgent new sultan, having slaughtered his brothers, occasionally married their mothers off to local worthies. One such earned a nickname that emerges irresistibly in translation as "The Filthy Sultana." The description appears not to have referred to her standards of personal hygiene but to the fact that, when her husband died, she decided it would be a pity to waste her training and talents and therefore set up in business as Constantinople's most exclusive procuress, selecting girls, educating them, and then hiring them out to reputable clients—among whom she chose not to include the Sultan Muhammad IV. He put in an order for one and was refused.

Sadly, very little is known about the more intimate aspects of harem training. Girls were presumably carefully instructed as to the individual tastes of different masters. Some sultans had an unquenchable appetite for virgins and never summoned the same girl twice. Some made use of women concubines for dynastic reasons, while preferring boys when only pleasure had to be considered. Some, like the regrettable Ibrahim, were devoted to nameless orgies, though as far as it is possible to judge—and with the exception of the occasion on which he consigned his entire harem of 280 concubines to the Bosphorus, tied up in weighted sacks—these seem to have been comparatively harmless. Mirrors in the bedroom, a high intake of aphrodisiacs, and a favorite game in which he played the stallion while his girls pretended to be mares, form the total of his recorded eccentricities.

The only reasonably well documented item of interest concerns the mode of a concubine's entry into the imperial bed. When she was brought to his room, the sultan was already between the sheets, but protocol had to be observed even here. The girl did not simply slip in beside him, but instead crept humbly under the coverlet at the foot of the bed and wriggled her way up toward the head until she found herself level with him. This was not a system unique to the Ottomans, some *nouveau-riche* insistence on deference at all times, for the imperial seraglio of China held to the same routine as late as the last quarter of the nineteenth century.[16] Possibly the idea occurred independently, or perhaps it was transmitted in one direction or the other by the Mongols, who in the fourteenth century ruled a vast stretch of territory that included not only China but parts of the Near East as well.

Beyond that, it can be deduced that sexual techniques in the Ottoman harem did not differ greatly from those generally used in the Muslim world. The Near East had its own *Handbooks of the Jade Chamber*, its *Kamasutra* and *Ananga ranga*, some with titles that translate a little clumsily, perhaps—like *The Book of Exposition in the Science of Coition*, or *The Book of the Zone of Coition-Boon*—others exaggeratedly poetic. *The Perfumed Garden for the Soul's Recreation*, for example, an Arabic work whose date is variously ascribed to the sixteenth or early fifteenth centuries, is a highly practical and sometimes funny book couched in the most explicit terms.

The Perfumed Garden does not, in fact, differ very much from the *Kamasutra*, although it is longer—mainly because of the lascivious stories scattered through it for the purpose of illustrating tricky problems of sexual psychology—and specifically designed to assist "the man to whom erection offers difficulties." [17] The author, Shaykh Nefzawi, who wrote it at the instigation of the vizier to the Bey of Tunis, was no stranger to the Indian sex manuals and said so. Indeed, having worked his way through all the standard Near Eastern positions for intercourse to reach a paltry total of only 11, he remarked that the people of India had "advanced further than we in the knowledge and investigation of coitus" and went on to list no fewer than 25 additional Indian positions. Whether Vatsyayana would have recognized them is open to question. Some of them appear to have come from Chinese rather than Indian sources.

Nefzawi ended his discussion of positions by describing one particularly "grand exploit" which he said originated in India. "The woman being stretched out on her back, the man sits down on her chest, with his back turned to her face, his knees turned forward and his [toe] nails gripping the ground; he then raises her hips, arching her back until he has brought her vulva face to face with his member, which he then inserts, and thus gains his purpose." Doubtfully, the Shaykh added, "This position, as you perceive, is very fatiguing and very difficult to attain," and then, more decisively, "I even believe that the only realization of it exists in words." [18] He was probably right.

But right or wrong, it was unlikely to have been realized in the bedchamber of the Grand Turk, for besides requiring the woman to have a cast-iron chest and a rubber spine, it could never have been achieved without practice. And practice with a man, other than the sultan himself, was the one thing that harem training could not include. Every girl in the harem belonged to the sultan alone, and only he could provide the one thing lacking in that training—practical experience.

THE EUNUCHS

Even with the best will in the world, which few of them possessed, sultans who had other business to attend to could scarcely have been expected to bed every one of their concubines more than once or twice in the year. A thousand to one was unmanageable odds even by Taoist standards. This meant that the harem was bored, frustrated, and correspondingly difficult to control and guard. As had been customary since long before the days of the Ottoman Turks, the task was confided to those who were believed (not altogether accurately) to be best fitted for it, the emasculated men known as eunuchs.*

Essentially, the principle was simple enough. A man who had been shorn of some or all of his external sex organs was equally shorn of his capacity to take advantage of the opportunities offered by service in the harem. But there was more to it than that. Ever since the time of Cyrus the Great, who had rationalized the

---

* A word derived from the Greek, meaning "he who has charge of the bed."

matter in the sixth century B.C., it had been widely held that eunuch slaves, separated from their families and unable in the nature of things to form any new family ties, would give their loyalty without stint to "those who were in the best position to make them rich and to stand by them if ever they were wronged, and to place them in offices of honor." Despite their disability, they were not "any less efficient horsemen, or any less skilful lancers, or less ambitious men," and "no one has ever performed acts of greater fidelity in his master's misfortunes than eunuchs do. . . . Recognizing these facts, Cyrus selected eunuchs for every post of personal service to him, from the doorkeepers up." [19]

Despite Xenophon's eulogy, however, Cyrus was not the first Near Eastern ruler to employ eunuchs. The custom may well have evolved from the ancient—and in some regions modern *—legal practice of castrating men found guilty of rape or adultery. According to Assyrian laws dating back to between 1450 and 1250 B.C., a husband who caught his wife with another man was at liberty either to kill them both, or merely to cut off his wife's nose and castrate the man.[21] That this punishment was inflicted with a degree of frequency is suggested by the fact that there were a number of eunuchs among Assyrian royal officials, while others were employed in the harem to guard the four royal wives, 40 concubines "and others" incarcerated in it, being forbidden to approach them more closely than seven feet, or to speak to them at all if they were inadequately clothed.[22]

The Persians who succeeded to the Assyrian empire appear to have been the first to castrate prisoners in cold rather than hot blood, though Herodotus mentions that they chose only the handsomest youths [23]—which suggests that these, at least, were not designed for any conventional harem. Darius even required Babylon and the rest of Assyria to send him 1,000 talents of silver and 500 castrated boys as tribute, and the custom of importing eunuch slaves appears to have expanded from then on.

From Persia, the idea of employing castrati in royal service may well have spread to China, if it had not already evolved there. Chinese history and tradition both say that branding, maiming,

---

* In San Diego, California, between 1955 and 1975, 397 sex offenders chose to be castrated rather than serve a long jail sentence. In Denmark between 1929 and 1959, 300 prisoners or detainees made the same choice. In Britain, chemical suppressants of the sex urge are preferred. The World Health Organization strongly opposes the whole idea.[20]

and execution were the criminal punishments used in early times, and that it was usual for those who had suffered castration (called "the palace punishment") to be compelled to serve in princely families thereafter. When the supply of castrated criminals fell short of demand, boys were brought in and "shaved" for duty. Even so, the Chinese restricted the use of eunuchs to the imperial family, where they were used in the harem, and sometimes as private executioners.[24]

In the Greek world, also open to Persian influences, castration was a more commercial proposition. One man of Chios, called Panionius, "made his living by the abominable trade of castrating any goodlooking boys he could get hold of, and taking them to Sardis or Ephesus, where he sold them at a high price," [25] and Rome, too, had its "barbers." There, castration was favored not only by the priests of the new religions but, according to the satirists, by the lovers of certain enterprising ladies (see page 249). The Emperor Domitian at last prohibited it, at the same time cannily imposing price control on such eunuchs as remained in the slave-dealers' hands.[26]

In Christian Byzantium eunuchs really came into their own. The violent record of imperial succession led its rulers to choose ministers and even Church patriarchs who were believed to have been freed from family ambition by their inability to father children, and eight of the chief posts of the empire were reserved for them. The result was that parents with several sons began to have one or two of them castrated, on the principle that they would be able to exert influence on behalf of their uncastrated brothers. And this was precisely what happened. The most notable case was that of John the Orphanotrophus. "If ever a man was shrewd, he was," remarked Michael Psellus,[27] and he was certainly shrewd enough to maneuver first one of his brothers and then a nephew onto the imperial throne itself. Unhappily, though Michael IV remained grateful to him, Michael V did not. John was sent into exile, and the emperor, with apt cruelty, made eunuchs of all the other male members of his family as well.[28]

Western Christendom never adopted the habit of employing eunuchs, except in the Papal Choir of the Sistine Chapel (until Leo XIII put a stop to it in 1878) and on the Italian operatic stage. The reasons were complex. Politically, only the great states needed to delegate responsibility to (theoretically) incorruptible administrators; rulers in the fragmented West were more closely in touch with their lands and their peoples. Eunuchs were therefore not needed on levels of power, nor were they needed to guard women in societies where women had some degree of freedom. Further, the Western Church always remembered (as the Eastern did not) the verse in Deuteronomy saying, "He that is wounded in the stones, or hath his privy member cut off, shall not enter the congregation of the Lord" (23 1), and this typically nomadic view, inherited from the ancient Hebrews, was reinforced by the equally nomadic prejudices of the barbarian tribes who played such a key role in the development of the medieval West. It seems that the original Hebrew attitude may have traveled to India with the Aryan invaders, for the Vedic and Hindu faiths regarded eunuchs as utterly unclean, an opinion that rubbed off even on the later Muslims (the Mughals) who ruled India from 1526 until 1806. The Indian *zenana* was guarded by elderly men and armed women, and eunuchs were few and far between.[29]

Muslims were in general oblivious to color distinctions, but not when it came to eunuchs. In the seraglio, it was black eunuchs (six to eight hundred of them) who had charge of the harem, and white who served in the sultan's own quarters, the *selāmlik*. But this division of labor had an entirely practical basis. The fact was that no one could be sure that white eunuchs were genuinely impotent. Black eunuchs from Africa were shaved of all their external sex organs (and had to urinate with the aid of a quill); white eunuchs, who came in the fifteenth century mainly from Hungary, the Slav lands, and Germany, and later from Armenia, Georgia, and Circassia, had usually lost only their testicles. It had been known from Greek times, and probably before, that castration did not eliminate sexual desire, and that a castrate who had preserved his penis was, under certain circumstances, capable of having erections for some time afterward, depending on the state of his heart, his circulation, and his prostate gland. Richard Burton, the Victorian traveler, reported that a eunuch's wife had told him that her husband could even be aroused to a kind of ejaculation (presumably of fluid from the prostate) after a protracted period of erotic stimulation.[30]

Greece knew it, and Rome knew it. In his attack on the habits of Roman women, Juvenal said.

There are girls who adore unmanly eunuchs—so smooth,
So beardless to kiss, and no worry about abortions!

But the biggest thrill is one who was fully grown,
A lusty black-quilled male, before the surgeons
Went to work on his groin. Let the testicles ripen
And drop, fill out till they hang like two-pound weights:
Then what the surgeon chops will hurt nobody's trade
but the barber's.*

(Slave-dealers' boys are different: pathetically weak,
Ashamed of their empty bag, their lost little chickpeas.)
Look at that specimen—you could spot him a mile off,
Everyone knows him—displaying his well-endowed person
At the baths: Priapus might well be jealous. And yet
He's a eunuch. His mistress arranged it. So, let
them sleep together.[31]

But what no one was entirely clear about was whether it was possible for amputated genitals to grow again. It seems that harem physicians in the Near East kept a wary eye on the eunuchs, but in China this precaution was overlooked until one chief eunuch in the eighteenth century made the mistake of being insolent to a senior imperial official. This gentleman took his revenge by informing the emperor that "although the eunuchs had originally been castrated, yet the mutilated organs must, in many cases, have grown to such an extent as to render recastration necessary. He had heard such a thing had occurred in the Ming dynasty [there is no record of it], and the result had been licentiousness and disorder in the palace between the eunuchs and the ladies. . . . To prevent such a scandal occurring again [he] begged that the whole of the eunuchs might at once be inspected, and that those whose organs had partially grown might have them 'swept clean.'" Ch'ien-lung assented, and the result was that many of the eunuchs were forced to undergo another operation, and many of them died of it.[32] Chinese eunuchs, like Africans, were completely shaved, and the possibility is that the "knifers," the emasculating surgeons, on this occasion removed stumps left by the earlier operation, rather than new growth.

There were four ways of castrating a man. He might be shaved of both penis and testicles, or have only the testicles removed.

---

* One effect of castration was to eliminate the growth of bodily hair.

Sometimes, in the case of a very young boy, the testicles were simply crushed, twisted, or compressed, causing permanent injury to the seminal glands. And sometimes only the penis was removed, leaving the testicles and the power of procreation but no way of exercising it (until the days, first of rubber and then of plastic surgery). Standards of surgery and hygiene varied considerably, as did the mortality rate. In the seventeenth century on the Upper Nile, the main source of supply for fully-shaved eunuchs in the West, only one in four could be relied on to survive.[33]

Rome knew two extremes. The novitiate priests of Cybele ceremonially castrated themselves on the *dies sanguinis*, the "day of blood." Latin sources are not explicit about the ceremony, but it seems probable that it followed the lines laid down in Syria when, to the insistent sound of music and chanting, priests and novitiates cut and slashed themselves, dervishlike, before the temple. Then, when religious excitement was at its most frenzied, the novitiate flung off his clothes, grasped the ceremonial sword, and with a single blow castrated himself.[34] By a few centuries later, the Romans themselves had developed a rather less hit-or-miss method, using a special clamp of the type shown in the illustration. The penis was drawn through the oval ring to keep it out of harm's way, while the scrotum and testes were pulled through between the arms of the clamp, so that when everything was locked in position the serrated edges gripped the folds of skin joining the scrotum to the body. It took only a single stroke of the knife to cut away scrotum and testes, and the cut edges were then either sewn up or cauterized.[35] This method must have reduced the mortality rate quite considerably; indeed, it appears not to have been much more dangerous than a modern vasectomy, even if considerably more painful. Most fatalities occurred as a result of removal of the penis, the urinal opening having to be stopped up

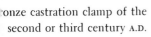
ronze castration clamp of the second or third century A.D.

for three days while scar tissue formed.[36] Fully shaved eunuchs usually suffered from a weak bladder for the rest of their lives.

What the eunuch did with the family jewels—"the precious," as the Chinese called them—offers an interesting sidelight on human psychology. Paul Valéry once said that historians of the French revolution spent their time bombarding one another with severed heads, but the Syrian worshippers of Cybele did better. Genitals in hand, they ran through the streets until they could run no more, and then sent them flying through the nearest house-holder's window.[37] Whether Roman citizens objected to this prac-tice is not recorded, but it appears that in Rome Cybele's priests, more sedately, buried "the precious" in the ground in some kind of fertility rite. The Chinese eunuch, in contrast, was loath to part with what he had lost, and treated his precious very much as a child treats his tooth after an extraction, keeping them "in com-mon pint measures hermetically closed, and placed on a high shelf," so that they might, when the time came, be buried with their owner in his coffin. He had other reasons, too. Even in the late nineteenth century it was apparently necessary for him to show his qualifications for promotion by presenting his pickled precious to the chief eunuch for inspection. If he had carelessly left them with the knifers, he had to pay heavily for the privilege of reclaiming them, although sometimes he might borrow or hire a set from a friend.[38]

The eunuch of popular imagination is often a repellent, sinis-ter figure, high of voice and flabby of flesh, with a taste for sweet-meats, bright colors, and strong rhythms, and a disposition that is acquisitive, cruel, and vengeful. The emasculated state may have encouraged such characteristics where the tendency already ex-isted, but, to judge from Byzantine examples, they seem not to have been particularly strong in men who were voluntarily—or at least not forcibly—castrated. In the eunuch who had the right to be resentful, however, an unwilling sacrifice to a system that first mutilated him and then scorned him for that same mutilation, they may have developed as a natural compensation for the ordi-nary social relationships that had become almost impossible to realize.

The eunuchs of the harem left no memoirs, but something of the agony of a full-grown man violently castrated still echoes in the writings of two of the most famous eunuchs of history, Ssu-ma

Ch'ien (145-c. 90 B.C.), Grand Historian of the Han court, and the great French logician and teacher, Peter Abelard (A.D. 1079-1142).

Ssu-ma Ch'ien was "sent to the silkworm house" for the crime of attempting to mislead the emperor, and eight years after the event he could still write, "I sit in a daze and lost, abroad I know not where I am going. Whenever I think of this shame the sweat drenches the clothes on my back. I am fit only to be a slave guarding the women's apartments: better that I should hide away in the farthest depths of the mountains. Instead I go on as best I can, putting up with whatever treatment is meted out to me, and so complete my degradation." 39

Abelard, brutally castrated by the uncle of his beloved Héloise, recorded that at first he "felt the misery of my mutilation less than my shame and humiliation." In the end, however, he was able to sublimate it. Writing to Héloise twelve years after, he asked her to remember "God's mercy for us . . . the wisdom whereby he made use of evil itself and mercifully set aside our impiety, so that by a wholly justified wound in a single part of my body he might heal two souls. . . . So when divine grace cleansed rather than deprived me of those vile members which from their practice of utmost indecency are called 'the parts of shame' and have no proper name of their own, what else did it do but remove a foul imperfection in order to preserve perfect purity? . . . Join me in thanksgiving, you who were made my partner both in guilt and in grace." 40

Both men were intellectuals, and both, after the first shock of pain and revulsion, had some escape into the private refuge of the mind. But the eunuchs of the harem were trapped in the mesh of social intercourse, with no way out. Whatever they may have felt for their fellow-sufferers, to others they were over-sensitive—sometimes excessively affectionate, more often withdrawn and hostile.

There is no way of judging what would have become of the slave eunuchs if they had remained "whole" men. It seems likely that those who were charged with guarding the harem of the Grand Turk would have been set to guarding tribal cattle instead. Those who became able administrators might have become village headmen. What is almost certainly true is that their emasculation made of the quicker-witted eunuchs far more effective officials than they would otherwise have been, for they owed no clemency to the people with whom they dealt. Without the cold and calculating avarice that was his defense against the world, the chief black eunuch (known as the Kislar Agha) would probably never have become the most feared and bribed official in the whole of the Ottoman empire, a member of the council of state, the only person permitted to approach the sultan at any hour of the day or night, inspector of the religious endowments of the imperial mosques, commander of the *baltaji* (halberdiers), a pasha of the highest rank, and, of course, superintendent of the harem. He was rich, and he was hated. And when the time came for him to die, he knew the ultimate bitterness, the ultimate reminder of his impotence. All his possessions automatically reverted to the sultan.

The rule of the eunuchs lasted for as long as that of their masters, until the first decades of the twentieth century. But although in the late nineteenth century it was calculated that not less than 8,000 eunuchs a year were being imported into Arabia, Egypt, and Turkey,[41] by the 1930s N. M. Penzer was able to trace only two or three of "these strange beings" in the whole of Turkey, and was told that "these were the last of them." [42]

Osbert Sitwell did better in China during a visit in 1933-34, spending most of an afternoon drinking tea with 20 who had formerly served in the Imperial Palace of the Forbidden City. Talkative, withered, sad old men now, he said, seeing out the last of their days in a Refuge for Distressed Eunuchs next door to the fashionable Pa Pao Shan Golf Club.[43]

PART FOUR

The Expanding World,
A.D. *1100–1800*

Although the Christian Church still disapproved, quite im-
partially, of both sex and women, the twelfth century began
to see a change. Woman, who for so long had been a cipher,
was transformed—by the game of courtly love that had developed from the "pure love" of the Arabs, and the importa-
tion of the cult of the Virgin Mary from Byzantium—into the
"Lady," pure, unattainable, virtuous, admirable. It was a
change only in image, but it was to prove revolutionary, especially when reinforced by the sixteenth-century Reformed
churches' emphasis on the family, and the seventeenth-century scientific discovery that man's semen was not, as had
been thought since the days of Aristotle, the crucial element
in procreation. Woman became not an incubator, but a
mother. The nineteenth century was to blend morality and
motherliness into a new image of "the angel of the house"—
with surprising political results.

In the meantime, Spain had swept Latin America clear of
the sodomites who had reputedly infested it, and repeopled
the land with a tougher race of mixed blood. Britain had
injected a new mixed-blood community into India, while simultaneously shaking Hinduism to its foundations by legislating to protect women. And white Americans had begun to
transform their early cultural prejudice into color prejudice
with the aid of laws against love.

10.
Europe, 1100–1550

"Noble sir, which would you prefer: that people spoke ill of your lady and that you found her good, or that she were well spoken of, and you should find her bad?" In fourteenth-century France, the correct reply to this loaded question was, "I should prefer to hear her well spoken of, and that I should find her bad." [1]

Two hundred years earlier, such an answer would have surprised the questioner very much indeed—shocked him, even—for no self-respecting early Crusader would have considered rating a woman's reputation above his own comfort. Yet the Crusades themselves, in which the attractions of war, religion, and loot were irresistibly combined, had the unforeseen effect of helping to transform the woman of the Age of Churlishness into the lady of the Age of Chivalry.

The period between the early twelfth and late sixteenth centuries was a notable one in the history of women, perhaps the most critical since the neolithic era, although at its end they were no better off legally, financially, or physically than they had been at the beginning. The only perceptible difference was in their image. At the beginning they had been despised, not only by men but often by themselves; at the end, they were respected, even admired. It does not, perhaps, sound like very much of a revolution, but it was this reversal of attitude that made all subsequent changes possible, even if the psychological and genetic adjustments necessary after more than 5,000 years of inferiority were to mean that it took several hundred more before the most radical of them came about. Some, of course, have not come about even yet.

Today, an image is a commodity that can be bought off the rack on Madison Avenue, a product of computer simulation where even happenstance has been reduced to a differential equation. But that was not how the change in women's image was achieved. It was the accidental result of a concatenation of circumstances that, separately, might have had no effect at all. And although the change may have been recognized at the time, its implications for the future certainly were not. Man, in effect, made the same error as neolithic woman had made when she failed to check his grow-ing self-importance. This time, man's mind was fixed on his own spiritual exaltation, and he indulged *her* growing self-importance because he thought (if he thought about it at all) that it was of no consequence. For very specific reasons, he turned "the Lady" into a symbol of virtue and failed to see that the time might come when her new status would have to be recognized in practical terms.

There are almost as many theories about man-woman relations in the medieval period as there are historians, and it is difficult to reconstruct precisely how it came about that woman was allowed to join the human race. The story here moves into the realm of personal chemical reactions. It also moves into a period where certain aspects of literature and life were so closely involved that, from a distance of several centuries, they are almost indistinguish-able. But Thomas Aquinas, Peire Vidal, and Chrétien de Troyes were no more representative of everyday life in the twelfth and thirteenth centuries than Marshall McLuhan, The Who, and Rosemary Rogers are of the late twentieth. Courtly love was the great theme of late medieval literature, and the great theme, too, of upper-class life. But no one knows how closely the two really matched.

Of the factors, many still unidentified, that helped to trans-form woman into lady, some stand out. One was certainly the maturing experience of the Crusades themselves. Fully half the knights of France, according to modern estimates,[2] set off for the Holy Land or northern Spain on public or private crusade during the 30 years following 1097, and after a slightly slow start England and Germany also hastened to export their more bellicose citizens in large numbers.* Those who reached the Levant—even those who traveled no farther than Spain or Sicily—found themselves dazzled by the sheer exoticism of Islam, which even in disarray remained far more advanced, far more civilized, than anything the crude barons of the West could have envisaged. Only the First Crusade was to prove an unqualified success, but the warriors of the Church militant suffered a sea change and took home with them more subtle booty than they realized. It was nothing as grand as a new vision of life, no more than a handful of ideas and impressions, an increased awareness and receptivity, but it was enough to make them amenable to changes that had already begun to take place in Europe.

While the Crusaders were experiencing the impact of Islam at first hand, men who had remained at home—too old or too young, too sensible or too cynical to join in the imperial adventure—were finding a different excitement in the rediscovery, partly through the work of Muslim scholars, of the science and wisdom of the Classical world, with its old-new attitudes, its old-new philosophy, and the conditional humanitarianism that the Greeks had known and the Romans forgotten. Much of this arrived filtered through the mesh of Muslim Spain, which also transmitted the literary forms that were to have a direct effect on the position of women in Europe.

The absence of so many of the more intolerant members of society, and the presence of others who were in the process of discovering a new mildness and rationality, offered a golden opportunity to the women of the upper classes. Until the end of the eleventh century they had been completely dependent on their fathers, their husbands, and then their sons. The fact that even God thought of them as irresponsible minors was confirmed by His insistence that their fathers and husbands should be accountable for them in His sight. But during the Crusading period many wives were left of necessity in charge of their absent husbands' demesnes and soon discovered that estate administration, taxes, tithes, even politics were rather less impenetrable mysteries than

---

* By the time of the Third Crusade, malingerers were sometimes presented with the medieval equivalent of the white feather, a distaff and wool, "as a hint that whosoever declined the campaign would degrade himself as much as if he did the duties of a woman." [3] Which was by no means fair to women. Quite a number of them—including, it was said, prostitutes by the thousand—went along for the trip.

they had always been led to believe. They also discovered the pleasures of company when they took disputes to the fount of authority, the ducal or royal court, which also happened to be the center of contemporary society, of fashion and wit, gossip and intrigue. And while the Church could scarcely have been said to encourage them in these activities, it did help to stabilize their legal position; the eleventh-century husband who tired of his wife had found it easy to repudiate her, but when marital law passed into the hands of the ecclesiastical courts—who loathed divorce even more than they loathed marriage—this practice came to an abrupt end.* There was one other trend, too, that in time was to influence the attitude of both Church and man. In Byzantium, the Virgin Mary had long been an object of devotion, and her cult was brought back to Europe in the early twelfth century by pilgrims, Crusaders, and merchants. For many long centuries, the Western Church had equated woman with Eve, the architect of man's downfall; when Eve at last gave way to Mary in the fourteenth century, all women benefited.

Most of these influences converged, at different times, in the extraordinary game that evolved during the first half of the twelfth century, the game of courtly love, which began as a literary conceit but was soon to move over into the world of reality; the classic case of life imitating art. Courtly love was class-conscious, escapist, soap-opera-sentimental, a kind of idealized affair between a high-born lady and a romantic squire, a pretty daydream to while away the idle hours, but it introduced a new code of behavior that was to have a direct and potent effect on the status of women.

WOMAN INTO LADY

Historians have always been intrigued by courtly love, not least because it was a fundamentally irreligious idea that emerged and flourished at a time when the power of the Church was at its peak. Until the nineteenth century, it was commonly held to have developed from a reverence for woman that was thought (erroneous-

---

* Except, of course, in the case of couples of high estate, where marriage and divorce were religious/political bargaining counters.

The lady of courtly love was often shown in association with a unicorn, a fierce beast which instantly became meek at sight of a virgin. It was used, in art, as a symbol of chastity.

ly) to have been characteristic of the German and Celtic peoples, but this view was displaced by another which saw the troubadours as members of a Catharist conspiracy against the papacy and their love songs as a vehicle for heretical ideas.* This theory, in turn, gave way to another, that "love service" was no more than an aspect of feudal vassalage. Then, as anthropologists began to take an interest in history, to one that courtly love was an expression of a matriarchal society intent on abjuring Christian precepts in favor of archaic sexual mores. And ultimately, when psychoanalysis appeared to have the answer to everything, that it was a collective fantasy born of infantile mother fixation.[4]

But the courtly lover and his lady were neither religious misfits nor suitable cases for treatment. Hundreds of millions of people today read thousands of new romances and thrillers every year.

---

* Since the Catharists, in fact, believed that all carnal pleasure was sinful and even marriage no more than an organized debauch, the arguments in favor of this view were necessarily intricate.

The medieval world was not so generously served, but it solved the problem to everyone's satisfaction (except that of the Church) by acting out its dreams according to the rules of the new game that was introduced just when "love" was sufficiently possible to be attractive, but sufficiently improbable to be a challenge. And, like so many other novelties of the period—including chess, with which it had a lot in common—the love game owed much, if not quite all, to the Arabs.[5]

There was one essential difference between Muslim society and that of the Christian West, and it was because of this difference that European women acquired the mask of virtue. Arab women were strictly segregated, Western women scarcely at all. The idea of ennobling love had, in fact, been built on the foundation of the harem's walls, so that the true personality of the beloved woman scarcely impinged on the poet's image of her—and this placed the European male at a serious disadvantage. The unconsecrated spirituality of ennobling love, which seems genuinely to have caught his imagination, was far from easy to achieve when its object was not only visible and audible, but, as far as it is possible to judge, willing and accessible as well. Consciously or unconsciously, the poets of southwestern France, where courtly love had its genesis in Europe, set about trying to find some bastion that would substitute for the walls of the harem.

What seems to have happened was this. In Muslim-influenced Spain, the original Arab traditions retained their clear identity. Mocadem of Cordova (c. A.D. 900) was the apostle of love-desire, Ibn Sara one of the many exponents of pure love, and the eleventh-century poet and thinker Ibn Hazm—who claimed that "the union of souls is a thousand times more beautiful than that of bodies"[6]—the most distinguished advocate of ennobling love. When the love songs crossed the Pyrenees into France, however, they lost some of their point although the society that had begun to develop there was sufficiently lively, colorful, and aware of the riches of Islam to find them attractive. Fashions were changing, drab tones giving way to bright, short robes to long, dull foods to spicy. Education was spreading, so that in almost every aristocratic family there was at least one person who had actually read a book, and many who had learned to find enjoyment in games that exercised the mind. "Taste," irrational and erratic as ever, had revived after a long hiatus as a new factor in class distinction. The fine

The rich and leisured cou of Burgundy, c. 1410

music and singing of the Church had begun, tentatively, to be imitated on a secular level. And lords of the manor gave permanent employment to scholars, who drew up charters, kept accounts, and added to the intellectual tone of their masters' courts.

There was a second center of the new culture in northern France, between Normandy, the Loire valley, and the Ile-de-France, but it was made of sterner stuff, pugnacious, dogmatic, ready to accept the new convention of courtly love when it arrived in its fully-evolved form—ready, indeed, to add strength and drama to it—but not relaxed or romantic enough to breathe into it the first vital spark of life. The credit for that, as far as is known, belonged to a southerner, one of the most libertine seigneurs of his day, Guilhem, seventh count of Poitiers and ninth duke of Aquitaine, the most powerful nobleman in western Christendom.

Guilhem (1071–1127) must have been well acquainted with Hispano-Arabic love poetry and philosophies of love. He was married to Philippa of Aragon (even if he seems to have paid her little attention), while one of his sisters was the wife of Alfonso VI of Castile, and another of Pedro of Aragon. The story goes that, comfortably adjusted to a life of sensuality and seduction, Guilhem found his activities seriously curtailed by the advent of a preacher, Robert d'Arbrissel, who succeeded in converting many of the ladies of his court to a belief that the fires of hell were being stoked for adulterers. Guilhem, deeply troubled, devoted his mind to the problem, and the result of his meditations soon became apparent in his poems. Frank eroticism had formerly been their style, but this now gave way to something that strongly resembled the ennobling love of Ibn Hazm—without the chastity. Love, Guilhem argued, was not an abasement but an exaltation, not a sordid sin but a divine mystery, and the lady within whose gift it lay was a goddess to be adored. Some scholars believe that his change of view came from the heart,[7] although the aura of cynical expediency is not easy to dissipate, but whatever the truth he appears to have convinced his ladies, who were happy to take on the unfamiliar role of goddess. And even if, in cold fact, the new love was just as adulterous as the old, it sounded a good deal more refined.*

Guilhem's blend of love-desire and ennobling love soon became a favorite theme of wandering scholars, singers, poets and *jongleurs* (general entertainers), and a kind of formula began to develop. The subject was attractive but limited, short on plot and even shorter on tension, but this proved easy enough to rectify, since whereas great lords in their crowded courts had little difficulty in finding a great lady on whom to bestow their love, it was a different matter in the countryside. Especially for the ladies themselves, who often lived a monotonous existence with their lord and his entourage away from home and only youthful squires and impoverished knights for company. Such ladies—who were the troubadours' paying audience—wanted to hear love songs that had

---

* Love was considered in medieval times as a gift freely given (which remains true enough today), and this by definition excluded it from marriage, a business contract in which personal considerations played no part.

Ladies at lesser courts were neither as winsome nor as well-dressed

some meaning for *them*, and the troubadours obliged by evolving the convention of a great lady loved by a romantic hero of lower rank, who struggles to become worthy of her, and with whom at last she falls in love.

As a story line it had a good deal of potential, but it seems to have landed some of the troubadours in trouble. It was customary for the love songs to be written in the first person, and this made it rather too easy for the lady to assume that the troubadour himself was the lover, telling her in verse what he dared not say in prose. In imminent danger of becoming peripatetic gigolos, the troubadours (some of them, at least) began to look round anxiously for a harem-substitute bastion capable of being scaled by man but not demolished by woman.

It was a *jongleur* of the generation after Guilhem who provided the answer, a Gascon named Marcabru. A dedicated and virulent misogynist who detested the moral laxity that characterized the early days of courtly love, he hammered home the point that beauty and rank alone did not justify placing woman on a pedestal, but that virtue was also a prerequisite—an impeccable sentiment slightly marred by the implication that, if this view prevailed, the pedestal-makers would soon find themselves out of business. But it was just what the troubadours had been waiting for. A lady might be ready enough to abjure her rank for a lover, but it was remarkably difficult for her to disclaim moral virtue. And no gentleman, of course, would have asked her to.

The convention of courtly love existed at three levels—that of the men, and sometimes women, who composed the songs; that of the troubadours (who might also be composers) who disseminated not only the songs but the whole idea-system surrounding them, fulfilling much the same function as the media today; and that of the fashionable world, which played the new game of love according to the rules set down in the lyrics.

It was the poets, subject to a multitude of influences including feedback from both troubadours and courtiers, who set the tone. And they, too, responded to Marcabru's passionate advocacy of virtue. Their reasons do not seem to have been his, however. What he wanted was for flesh-and-blood women to mend their ways and their morals; it was the women themselves he was concerned with. The poets were more interested in their own souls. Virtue was the attribute that, by elevating woman to some immaculate plane, cleansed their love of all taint of carnality and left it free to soar into the realm of the spirit. Virtue became the European harem.

In the songs, at least. What happened in the love game played by the fashionable world is not so clear. It seems probable that, for most of the way, it followed the pattern of the songs, which scarcely changed between the middle of the twelfth and the end of the thirteenth centuries. The heroine was a lady of high birth married to a powerful seigneur, and what worried her lover was not her husband but her high estate. He strove to become worthy and succeeded in attracting her love. For the sake of her reputation, however, their love had to be kept secret, which made it a kind of mystery and set the couple apart from others, even if not from the horde of minor characters who helped or hindered in their intrigue, playing the same roles as they had done in the Arab love songs—confidants who acted as messengers, smoothed out problems, and lent themselves to deceptions; mischief-makers who placed the lovers in danger through indiscretion, disapproval, or simple ill will.

It is at this point that the facts become hazy. The troubadours never sang of love consummated. Some explicitly disclaimed any desire to possess their ladies. Others, stretching credibility, sang of a chastity that could survive any test, just as Djamil had done 400 years earlier. He had seen no harm or danger in embraces, kisses, even in passing the night in bed (talking) with his beloved.[8] Andreas Capellanus, in France in about 1186, wrote that *amor purus* "goes so far as the kiss and the embrace and the modest contact with the nude lover, omitting the final solace, for that is not permitted to those who wish to love purely." [9]

Whatever the songs and treatises on love might say, it would be naive to suppose that all courtly lovers and their ladies, having trodden the ordained path of courtship, love talk, illicit assignations, kisses, embraces, and admiration of each other's naked perfections, stopped there. On the other hand, the new preoccupation with virtue did leave the options open. It seems likely that in the south of France, Guilhem's original ingenuity in combining love-desire with ennobling love maintained its attraction for several generations of lovers, for the fusion of the two satisfied the needs of both body and spirit, in proportions that could be adjusted to suit individual taste. In this case, virtue was an escape route for those who wished to play the game without taking the final gamble. But in the north, where the moral climate was harsher, the grip of the Church stronger, and the penalties for the woman caught in adultery more likely to be imposed, virtue probably triumphed, in life as in the lyric.

LADY INTO ALLEGORY

Within less than half a century, disregarded Woman had been transformed into honored Lady, in effigy if not in the flesh. Pygmalion reversing his priorities. But she was honored only for her virtue which, in the circumstances, hardly qualified as a compliment. There was still nothing whatever to suggest that she might have qualities of her own, least of all a brain. This, however, by another strange literary caprice, was an omission that was soon to be rectified.

It was, appropriately enough, Guilhem's granddaughter, Eleanor of Aquitaine, who helped to establish the ideal of courtly love in northern France when she married Louis VII in 1137, but it did not entirely suit the northern temperament, which preferred good meaty adventure stories to undiluted sentiment. Eleanor and her daughters therefore turned their attention to encouraging a synthesis of the two.

For some centuries, the north had relied for its entertainment on the *chansons de geste* (songs of action), which were long assonant poems delivered as a kind of recitative to a simple musical accompaniment and dealt mainly with the exploits of warriors and heroes, feudal lords, and Christian chevaliers of the time of Charlemagne. In the early twelfth century, the *roman* (romance) also developed, a tale in rhymed verse designed to be declaimed to a small audience and usually taking for its theme a quest or voyage through a dream world which was the scene of marvellous adventures in love and war. The early *romans*, reflecting the rediscovery of the Classical world, were historical dramas with such titles as the *Romance of Alexander*, the *Romance of Thebes*, and the *Romance of Troy*, but for political reasons it became desirable to find subjects nearer home. Eleanor, by this time (1170) married to Henry II of Normandy and England, was instrumental in bringing into fashion the Celtic myths of Arthur and his knights of the Round Table, an 'ideal' ancient society which lent itself admirably to being gilded with modern dreams and embroidered with the symbols of courtly love. She herself patronized many distinguished troubadours, including Bernart de Ventadorn, while her daughters, notably Marie de Champagne, followed in the family tradition. It was Marie's chaplain, Andreas, who produced the famous *Art of Courtly Love,* a treatise that owed something to Ovid as well as to Aquitaine, and it was Marie, too, who urged Chrétien de Troyes to fuse tales of love with tales of action, to turn love into an adventure, and the knight into a knight-errant. This was the real beginning of the institution of chivalry.

It was natural enough that the lady-as-inspiration should have found an early place in the knightly ethos, but in northern France and Germany, less subtle than the south, the idea lost some of its spiritual content and became a semimagical means of improving the knight's prowess in the field, lending strength to his arm and precision to his aim. Love service deteriorated into lip service. In Germany, for example, the knight considered fidelity as the primary virtue—to God, to his suzerain, and to his Lady, in that order. What the *Minnedienst* (the service of love) required of him was to carry his Lady's favor, to strive to be worthy of her, to conquer in battle for her, and to expect no reward from her other than a word of commendation. If some mischievous nineteenth-century time traveler had whisked the Lady away and replaced her with the Regiment or the Flag, the medieval knight would probably not even have noticed.

Courtly love had endowed the Lady with virtue, chivalry with the insignia of command. The *roman* was subsequently to help envelop her in an atmosphere, a mist—certainly nothing more substantial—of attainments that had formerly been part of the masculine preserve.

It was Jaufré Rudel, a contemporary of Marcabru, who opened the way. A member of the nobility, he was best known for his poems of "love from afar," which appear to have been misinterpreted by a thirteenth-century biographer who romanticized Jaufré's own life and identified his distant love as the Countess of Tripoli (in Syria), a fabled beauty of whom Jaufré was said to have heard from pilgrims returning from the Holy Land. After writing her a sequence of songs of courtly love, he left France on the crusade of 1147, hoping at last to see her for himself. But he fell ill on the voyage, and when he landed he was dying—though he had the felicity of expiring in his lady's arms. Most of this touching tale was myth, but although modern scholars are divided it seems that the true object of Jaufré's love was not the "Countess of

Tripoli" but the Holy Land itself and that he conceived of pure love as an ideal of life with which all other ideals could be compared, provoking the same hopes and torments and bringing the same joys. There was thus nothing to prevent the Holy Land, or Divine Grace, for example, from being poetically represented by a beloved Lady.[10]

But if it was Jaufré Rudel who first used the Lady as a metaphor, it was Guillaume de Lorris and Jean de Meun who, in the thirteenth century with the *Roman de la Rose*, turned the whole idea of allegory into a medieval cliché. The first part of the *Roman*, written by Guillaume de Lorris in about 1230, described how a lover approached the mysterious garden of love and saw a rose (representing a Lady) which ravished his heart. The agonizing question was, should he pluck it? For 4,000 verses the arguments raged among a number of allegorical figures representing the sentiments and vicissitudes of love—Leisure and Courtesy, Gaiety and Hope, Beauty and Wealth, Sweet Speech, Danger, Slander, Fear, and Shame. Reason also appeared on the scene, and so did Venus.

Guillaume de Lorris' text stopped short with nothing resolved, and 40 years later Jean de Meun elected to finish it, taking another 18,000 verses to do so. The tone of his part was very different, eloquent, witty, sexually cynical, a glorification of seduction where Guillaume de Lorris' verses had been tender and refined, an almost innocent inquiry into the rights and wrongs of using the artificial arts of courtesy in the serious context of love. Guillaume de Lorris had exalted the idea of woman; Jean de Meun, a trenchant realist, treated her with the contempt that, in practice, was still the lot of women who were not sufficiently noble, rich, and beautiful to qualify as heroines of courtly love.

The *Roman de la Rose* was the most read book of the late Middle Ages—partly, no doubt, because of the bitter controversy that raged over Jean de Meun's contribution to it—but it scarcely dented the Lady's noble image, for most people were perfectly awake to the difference between the ideal and the real. What happened instead was that literature and art became fixated by allegory. It was not altogether surprising. Few people, even today, have the capacity for abstract thought, and the practical burghers and merchants of the later medieval period felt themselves drowning in the tide of new ideas that covered every subject from cosmology to child care. Allegory cut their metaphysical problems down to size.

For simple artistic and esthetic reasons, some of the allegorical figures had to be women, and the results were often surprising. It might be understandable to represent Chastity, Nature, and Leisure as feminine, but Dame Reason was a less obvious conjunction in the climate of the times. In art, the Lady of chivalry and courtly love was even shown as a personification of such traditionally masculine attributes as Justice, Science, the Arts, and Geometry. If it had all been a passing phase, it might not have mattered, but for more than 200 years writers and artists refused to be parted from the allegorical mode, and by that time the *atmosphere* of the attributions had begun to stick. No one really believed that women were masters (or mistresses) of the principles of geometry, or justice, or reason, but the constant repetition of such associations was enough to influence, quite profoundly, the increasingly sensitive area of women's status.

The Lady of allegory and courtly love was not real. She was an icon colored by man to suit his own aspirations, and it was he—not she—who derived spiritual benefit from the relationship. But the idealization of this strange, beautiful, virtuous, bloodless creature of man's imaginings introduced a new stage in the relationship between men and women, and there was also a more immediate effect on the fleshly medieval ladies who acted as stand-in for the image. Though the game of courtly love may have ennobled their reputations, but not their spirit, it did require them to mend their manners. As men became more chivalrous, ladies became, if not always more virtuous or chaste, at least more gracious. And they must undoubtedly have derived a good deal of private amusement out of the whole romantic daydream of *l'amour courtois*.

Magnanimity, Temperance, and Justice

The Byzantine
Madonna

The Virgin of Mercy. "Our Lady" as protectress
of churchmen, rulers, and merchants

Mary
Mother

MARY

The coincidence in timing between the genesis of courtly love and the sudden expansion of Mariolatry in Europe was too close to be entirely accidental, yet also too close for one to have been a direct response to the other.

Until the early twelfth century, Mary had been just one of the saints in the Western Christian calendar, but soon after her cult was brought back from Byzantium she attracted the passionate adoration of Bernard of Clairvaux, the great French churchman who was responsible for reforming the Cistercian order. Under St. Bernard's influence, hundreds of new Cistercian abbeys were founded all over Europe, their monks dedicated to the Virgin, wearing white in honor of her purity, and building special lady chapels to her in their churches. By the thirteenth century, poets and troubadours had begun to confuse the Virgin with the Lady, the sacred love with the profane, and even those who contrived to keep them separate, like Dante Alighieri in Italy, did so more by literary technique than spiritual intent. The Virgin became Notre Dame, *Our* Lady, a stately and unmistakably aristocratic figure much more at home in the princely courts of the West than she would ever have been in the inn at Bethlehem. But under the fourteenth- and fifteenth-century influence of the Franciscans, she shed her mantle of disengagement to become a warm, compassionate mother to the poor and the wretched of the earth. The Holy Family, which had had no place in the gospels, found one in the social milieu of fifteenth-century Europe.

Mary's increasing popularity owed much to the troubadours,

to the Cistercians and Franciscans, and to the noblemen, merchants, and burghers who commissioned works of art and architecture in her honor. She was warm, and loving, and good, less the Mother of Christ than the mother most men would have liked to have and hoped their sons' mothers might be educated to become. But not until the Counter-reformation in the latter part of the sixteenth century did she arouse any similar enthusiasm in the scholars who were responsible for orthodox Church doctrine. The saintly Madonna and the secular Lady were two views of an ideal which, in the opinion of the Church, had no relevance to the human situation. Mary as Virgin would have suited the Church very well, but her increasingly diversified cult kept slipping through its doctrinal fingers. Though the laity, to whom faith was something quite apart from logic, were quite ready to accept Mary as, simultaneously, Virgin, Bride of Christ,* and Mother, this combination of roles presented certain intractable theological problems, as well as some that were more practical. While the Christian-in-the-street persisted in regarding Mary less as a saint than as an ideal of womanhood, she remained a thorn in the flesh of the Church's policies, an inhibiting factor in all its dictates about the rightful position of women. With increasing frequency, it found itself forced into the dialectically weak position of having to make an exception of Mary, because she was "different."

MARTHA

Thomas Aquinas, the "Angelic Doctor" of the thirteenth century, stated the position on women that even the Reformed—the Protestant—churches were still to hold to more than 400 years later. Since woman had been created from Adam's rib, he said, she was obviously destined for social union with man and should thus exist neither in authority or servility. She was his partner, but only in matters where she was biologically indispensable; in other words, procreation. In the wider sphere, another man was a much better partner than she could ever be. Man, after all, was the head of the family for the very good reason that it was only in him that "the discretion of reason" predominated, and his superiority was dem-

---

* And more. Godfrey of Admont (d. 1165) argued that she was bride to the two other members of the Trinity as well.[11]

onstrated even in the act of intercourse, where he took the active and therefore nobler part, while she was passive and submissive.[12] *

Matrimony, in the view of Thomas Aquinas as in that of his fellow theologians, had only two recommendations. First, of course, it was the only situation in which children could be conceived without sin. And secondly, it kept men out of other sexual troubles. These, in descending order of magnitude, were bestiality (zoophilia), sodomy (homosexuality), nonobservance of the proper methods of coitus "either in the employment of undue means [artificial aids?], or by resorting to other monstrous and bestial modes of intercourse [presumably anal or oral]," masturbation, incest, adultery, seduction, and plain everyday fornication.

Kisses, touches, and caresses were not sinful as long as they were not motivated by lust (one of the rare occasions on which the Church and the troubadours found themselves in agreement), while "nocturnal pollution" was sinful only if it resulted from a state that was itself sinful, such as gluttony, hard drinking, or the deliberate cultivation of lascivious thoughts.[13] One modern theologian slyly points out that nocturnal emissions "consequent upon speculative thoughts about carnal acts, such as necessarily engage the moral theologian from time to time, are not sinful as to their cause." [14]

This reference to "lascivious thoughts" was particularly interesting in the context of the medieval period, when there was a plague of incubi and succubi, male and female demons who invaded the lives and the beds of living people. As early as the ninth century, Hincmar, archbishop of Rheims, had recorded how a demon might sometimes deceive a woman by taking on the appearance of the man she loved and told of a nun who was tormented by the visitations of an incubus until a priest exorcized it.[14] Not much more was heard on the subject until the twelfth century, when incubi began to figure prominently in the chronicles. Bernard of Clairvaux had one particularly difficult case to deal with, of a woman who had been visited nightly for six years by a demon who took his pleasure with her, always without waking her husband. Neither prayers nor pilgrimages had any effect. Bernard gave her his staff to take to bed with her, but on this occasion

---

* The teachings of St. Thomas Aquinas have remained the basis for theological study in the majority of seminaries so that his opinions are given new life in every generation of the priesthood.

the incubus merely retreated outside the door and stood there yelling fearsome imprecations. On the following Sunday Bernard summoned the entire population of Nantes to church and told them the story, then called down anathemas on the demon and forbade him ever again to molest a living woman. History does not record whether it was the anathemas or the publicity that had the effect, but one of them did. The woman was not troubled again.[15]

It is difficult to avoid the impression that the late medieval plague of incubi was directly related to the spread of courtly love, even if the incubi themselves failed to adhere to its rules. Fashions on the upper levels of society inevitably filtered down to the lower, where the fashion for ladies to have lovers was transformed from a literate daydream into an illiterate night vision, a classic wish-fulfillment fantasy. The fact that the succubus, the female demon who visited men, attracted none of the horrified fascination of the incubus, suggests that although men were accustomed to wet dreams there was some new outside influence that was inducing the same in women—or at least inducing them to confess to it. It was a matter that gravely worried the Church. Thomas Aquinas and others were convinced not only that demons were at work but that they were capable of impregnating the women they visited. The method was ingenious. The demon, in the form of a succubus, would visit a man and receive his seed; then, transforming himself into an incubus, would visit a woman and transmit the seed to her.[16] Artificial Insemination by Donor, in fact, 700 years ahead of its time.

Fantasies about incubi were not originally connected with witchcraft, but they may well have been connected with the kind of woman who later came to be regarded as a witch. Even during the great European witchhunt of the sixteenth and seventeenth centuries when, under torture, "witches" gasped out allegations against anyone whose name came to mind—public figures, usually, like magistrates, teachers, innkeepers, merchants [17]—the number of women witches far exceeded that of men. In the Swiss canton of Lucerne between about 1450 and 1550, for example, 32 witches were accused, and only one of them was a man; while in the English county of Essex between 1560 and 1680, when 291 witches were tried, only 23 were men, 11 of whom were closely connected with a woman.[18] The women involved in such cases were usually married women or widows aged between 50 and 70 (old for the time), sharp-tongued, ugly, very often following the profession of village midwife, a calling that naturally attracted suspicion at a time of high infant mortality, especially since witches were known to need a regular supply of unbaptized babies for their banquets. The *Malleus Maleficarum* (1486), the first great handbook of the witch inquisitors, had no more difficulty than a modern psychoanalyst in accepting that this type of woman might readily believe she had had intercourse with the Devil himself, a huge, black, monstrous being with an enormous penis and seminal fluid as cold as ice water.

That the elderly housewives of the late medieval and early modern world attracted none of the respect and admiration vouchsafed to their younger and more decorative sisters was only to be expected. But that so many should have suffered the fatal malevolence of the witchhunters was another matter. It was as if the higher the ideal of woman, the greater the sin of the defector. The figures calculated by modern scholars anxious to play down numbers rather than magnify them are sobering. In the single Swiss canton of Vaud, 3,371 witches died between 1591 and 1680. In the little town of Wiesensteig in Germany, 63 women were burned in the year of 1562 alone. In Obermarchtal, 54 people— seven per cent of its inhabitants—went to the stake in two years, and in Oppenau 50 out of a population of 650 in only nine months.[19]

Fortunately, most of the world's Marthas lived and died less eventfully, especially in cities where hatred of antisocial women was circumscribed by woman's privacy and man's preoccupation with his own affairs. It was not incubi that troubled the wives of the merchants of Paris, for example, so much as their husbands' determination to turn them into reflections of the great and virtuous ladies of the court, and to induce in them the chaste, submissive humility of Mary Mother.

The early days of chivalry had started a fashion for "courtesy books" that would teach rough knights how to comport themselves in a civilized manner, and by the end of the fourteenth century bourgeois women were also becoming a target for improvement now that it was recognized that they were not, by their very nature, ineducable. One of the most interesting and earliest of these books was written by a late fourteenth-century merchant known to history only as the Goodman of Paris, an elderly man with a fifteen-year-old wife. One of his main concerns was that when she remarried after his death, as he fully expected

Housewifely Martha

her to do, she should not disgrace him in the eyes of her second husband by showing herself a slovenly housewife, so he wrote at encyclopedic length about her religious and moral duties, about household management, and cookery, and deportment, and manners, and how to make a man comfortable.[20] It was the Book of Proverbs and Ischomachus and the Lady Pan Chao all over again, with a dash of Mrs. Beeton thrown in. A good wife who can find? But what was new about the Goodman's book was that it was not something to be learned by rote; its hundreds of pages were meant to be read and referred to. The spread of literacy among the middle classes had begun, and it was to be as revolutionary for women as for men. Previously, word of mouth and personal experience had been the only teachers, memory the only work of reference. Now—and even more explosively when printing was introduced into Europe in the late fifteenth century—the mind was beginning to be freed from the bonds of parochiality. One person's word was no longer automatically law because other people spoke, too, and they might speak differently.

But although man's attitude to woman had changed more in the 300 years between 1100 and 1400 than in all the 3,000 years of civilization that had gone before, the new emphasis on virtue and morality had some unhappy side effects, especially among practical-minded burghers who locked up their money and saw no reason why they should not do the same with their wives.

The chastity belt appears to have been developed in the fourteenth century, possibly in Italy, though its name of "Florentine girdle" is not conclusive; it has always been customary to blame foreigners for inventions that appear to belong on the shady side of respectability. The belt may originally have been designed as a protection against rape, a common hazard in medieval times, but it proved a godsend to husbands who still subscribed to the age-old belief that women were natural wantons.

The belt of medieval times was usually constructed on a metal framework that stretched between the woman's legs from front to back. It had two small, rigid apertures that allowed for waste elimination but effectively prevented penetration, and once it was locked over the hips the jealous husband could take away the key; jokes about spare keys became part of the repertoire of satirists

The faithless wife takes money from her husband's purse to give it to her lover, who already holds the key to her chastity belt.

and caricaturists. Chastity belts still figured (for men as well as women) in surgical instrument catalogues until at least as late as the 1930s, though their purpose by that time was to prevent masturbation—one of the most popular models was devised by a mid-nineteenth-century Edinburgh doctor, John Moodie, who swore that half the women of Scotland used dildoes, a practice as dangerous as it was immoral. By his day, caoutchouc, or soft rubber, had become available, and his design of an ivory or bone grating embedded in a rubber pad was presumably a little less uncomfortable than earlier types.[21] *

MARY MAGDALENE

Chastity belts or no, French and German historians are accustomed to refer to the fifteenth century as the age of bastards, and it may not be a coincidence that this was also the century during which brick fireplaces, flues, and chimneys came into general use, and alcove beds in the communal hall gave way to warm, private sleeping chambers.

Among aristocratic families bastards were regarded as a normal occurrence, treated as part of the household, cared for with legitimate children, and left pensions or sums of money (rather than property) when their fathers died. In most of Europe, such children could be legitimized if their parents subsequently married, but not in England, which decided against the idea in 1235 and remained adamant about it right up until the 1960s. This may have had something to do with the fact that the English were slow to latch on to the notion of the mistress, and seem more often than not to have made do with domestic servants and prostitutes when they wanted a change from their wives; the barons would take no hand in encouraging a man to marry women such as those.

In 1500 as in 1900, foreigners thought the Englishman undemonstrative. "Although their dispositions are somewhat licentious," remarked an anonymous Italian visitor, "I have never noticed anyone, either at court or among the lower orders, to be in

---

* Tribal societies still use extreme methods to ensure chastity. Some modern Nubian women willingly submit to a surgical operation when their husbands have to be away for any length of time. It involves infibulation (sewing up) as a shield against penetration; the operation can be reversed when the husband returns.[22]

love; whence one must necessarily conclude, either that the English are the most discreet lovers in the world, or that they are incapable of love." But he added, "I say this of the men, for I understand it is quite the contrary with the women, who are very violent in their passions." [23] True or false, cases of married women involved in adultery appeared by the hundred in church registers and manorial court rolls though the population ratio of 133 men to 100 women that persisted from 1430 to 1545 may have had more to do with this than woman's lasciviousness. Adultery in the countryside was often a matter of impulse. Edmund Paston reported the sad case of a favorite servant of his. "It happed him to have a knave's lust, in plain terms to swive a queen, and so he did [in a field]. It fortuned him to be espied by two ploughmen of my mother's . . . wherefore there is no remedy but he must go." Fashionable ladies and gentlemen in the cities were more circumspect. That irrepressible gossip, the seigneur de Brantôme, recounted how one French lady always insisted on adopting a woman-superior position when she was in bed with her lover, so that if anyone accused her of allowing a man to "mount" her, she could protest her innocence with absolute truth.[24]

On a more professional level, the Englishman who lived near London could visit the brothels of Southwark, safe in the knowledge that they were under the respectable jurisdiction of the Archbishop of Canterbury and the Bishop of Winchester. Private enterprise prostitution had flourished in Europe since time immemorial, and nothing its rulers could do succeeded in stemming the tide. Indeed, when St. Louis (Louis IX of France) tried to put an end to it, the irate bourgeois of Paris complained that it was no longer safe for their wives and daughters to appear upon the streets.* But as towns, cities, and prostitution simultaneously expanded, it became something of a public scandal.

The Church was not in a position to ban prostitution, and did not in fact want to. Even St. Augustine had said that, though the institution was sordid, immodest, and shameful, "yet remove prostitutes from human affairs, and you will pollute all things with lust; set them among honest matrons, and you will dishonor all

---

* In 1976, citizens of Leicester and Southampton, in England, were still complaining that their wives and daughters could not walk along the streets without being solicited, not, this time, because of a lack of prostitutes, but because prospective clients were apparently unable to distinguish between them.[25]

things with disgrace and turpitude." Thomas Aquinas added his mite by comparing prostitution with "the filth in the sea or the sewer in a palace. Take away the sewer, and you will fill the palace with pollution. . . . Take away prostitutes from the world, and you will fill it with sodomy." [26] So the Church took out shares in the business and gathered the girls tidily under its soutane.

Temple prostitution came to Europe. There was a Church brothel in Avignon where the girls spent part of their time in prayer and religious duties and the rest of the time servicing customers. Christians only. No Jews or heathens were permitted to cross the threshold. Pope Julius II was said to have been so impressed by the Avignon example that, at the beginning of the sixteenth century, he founded one just like it in the Eternal City itself.

At the same time, dedicated to each-way betting, the Church urged all prostitutes to give up their evil habits. Mary Magdalene was to be their example, a whore who had repented and followed Jesus,* and a number of "Magdalene homes" were built for fallen women who had seen the error of their ways. Local citizens appear to have regarded these as a deserving cause, so much so that the Soul House in Vienna (founded 1384) received enough endowments to make it the richest institution in the city. It caused a sad scandal when, in 1480, one of the women superiors and a large number of inmates suffered a multiple relapse.

As well as ordinary brothels, religious and secular, there were institutions known in Europe as bath houses and in England by the more evocative name of "stews." The old Roman custom of hot baths had long ago died out, but the Crusaders had reintroduced the idea of public bathing from the Muslim world, even if in a slightly amended form. The baths in the stews were generally large enough to accommodate half a dozen people in vertical proximity, but there were some designed for a horizontal two. Dry rooms and beds were available for those whose tastes ran to the more conventional. Paris was said to have 30 such establishments at the beginning of the fifteenth century.

The number of "public women" in Rome in 1490 is believed

---

* In fact, Mary Magdalene was a composite of three women in the Gospels, none of whom was a whore. However, the Church needed saints who could be models for the world's sinners, who could prove that penance was the road to salvation and even to sainthood.[27]

to have been about 7,000, which was a reflection of the fact that the Eternal City was inhabited mainly by men; the women lived in houses belonging to monasteries and churches, and it was quite usual to see them parading the streets in company with priests. In Venice, according to the chronicler Sanudo, there were 11,654 *filles de joie* in a population totalling 300,000, and some, in Renaissance times, played a role very much like that of the hetairai in Greece. Aretino said of one that she knew by heart "the whole of Petrarch and the whole of Boccaccio and innumerable verses of Virgil, Horace, Ovid, and a thousand other authors," and although this may have been something of an exaggeration, the Renaissance courtesan was perfectly competent at singing, playing an instrument, declaiming a poem, and sometimes even writing one. Tullia d'Aragona, in the sixteenth century, produced a treatise in the Platonic idiom, while others, less ambitious, turned their reception rooms into salons for prelates, gentlemen, and humanists. To live in this style, of course, they had to be realistic about their fees. Veronica Franco asked four to five crowns for a kiss, and 50 for what Montaigne called the complete transaction, while Tullia d'Aragona forced a German client to disburse a hundred crowns for a whole night with her. It is impossible to translate sixteenth-century into modern money, but Veronica's kiss cost roughly as much as a domestic servant earned in six months.[28]

Patronage of brothels and ordinary prostitutes seems to have faltered in the early days of the sixteenth century with the epi-

Indoor brothel/bathhouse of the fifteenth century

Outdoor bath in the late sixteenth century

A sixteenth-century sufferer from syphilis imbibes a remedy compounded (by the workers next door) from the hardwood, guaiacum. A picture on the wall reminds him of the reason for his plight.

"Aretino's postures" had a wide, though surreptitious, circulation

demic spread of syphilis, a disease whose history remains obscure. Busily passing the buck, as always, the French called it the Neapolitan malady, the Spaniards the French disease, and the Germans the Spanish scabies. Many medical historians believe that it was introduced from America because much of Europe suddenly became infected within 18 months of Columbus's return from his first voyage to the Indies in 1493. If this is true, his 50 crew members must have had a very strenuous time when they got back. The alternative explanations are that a formerly harmless European organism mutated suddenly and became pathogenic; or that syphilis had existed in a relatively benign form and flared up for no apparent reason; or that only the epidemic proportions were new, and that many of the references in medieval literature to "lepra" did not describe leprosy (which they often, in fact, did not fit) but syphilis itself.[29] Whatever the truth, in the sixteenth century syphilis became, and has remained, one of the most unpleasant scourges of society.

THE RENAISSANCE

There is a popular myth—for which, like so many of the myths of history, the Victorians were mainly responsible—that the Italian Renaissance was a new dawn not only in culture but in the history of women. It was, said Burckhardt, impossible to understand the life of the upper classes if one did not take into account the vital fact that women enjoyed a position in every way equal to that of men.[30] If he had said that a few women were accorded the same kind of excessive courtesy as the noble ladies of the rest of Europe had begun to enjoy in the twelfth century, and that some were remarkable for their culture, he would have been less open to criticism. Certainly, there was no sign of equality except for the very few until the sixteenth century (the Renaissance is generally regarded as having begun in the fourteenth), and then only in certain cities in northern and central Italy, and only on the highest levels of society.

Renaissance Italy was very much a man's world, and an individual man's world. He saw himself as a creature of destiny, larger than life, noble, romantic, with an infinite capacity for heroism or tragedy. It was a theme that permeated the arts and overflowed into society and politics, and the long procession of historians who have been dazzled by the virtuosity and sheer stylishness of Renaissance Italy glorify it almost as if it were a spiritual coming of age. But inseparable from such a cult of individuality was a narcissistic egoism, a search for self-expression that could breed nothing but ruthlessness. The real uniqueness of Renaissance man was in the patina of urbanity with which he overlaid it. The Middle Ages had invented the knight. The Renaissance invented the gentleman—a gentleman with perfect manners and no morals whatsoever.

Sex—or, more accurately, talking about sex—was one of the most popular outlets for self-expression in the fifteenth as in the late twentieth century. Sometimes it was possible to go too far. Aretino, for example, a kind of literary licensed jester to the Med-

Aretino's wheelbarrow position

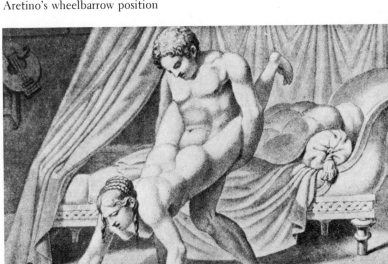

ici pope Clement VII, cuckolded too many husbands and wrote some sonnets that were altogether too explicit and found himself banished from the papal court. He soon bounced back, however, living like a prince on the Grand Canal in Venice, sharing his palazzo with his women and his boys, keeping open house, holding enormous banquets, and organizing what he called feasts of love.

It was hardly surprising that nudity should have come into fashion in art and sculpture, though not in the flesh as some would have wished. It was illogical, said Lorenzo Valla. "We allow women who have a beautiful head of hair, a beautiful face, a beautiful bosom, to show off those parts of their bodies; why are we so unjust to those whose beauty resides not in those parts but in others?" [31] Some of his contemporaries agreed with him that women were overdressed, though not for the same reasons. The Renaissance was a period of great riches in Italy, for the maritime cities had made substantial profits out of the Crusades, and Venice in particular continued to do so out of the spice trade, but men seldom stopped complaining about the extravagance of women, which almost matched their own. In Florence alone over the half century between 1343 and 1396, seven different sets of sumptuary laws were passed in an attempt to regulate the number of gowns a woman might possess, the length of the train she could wear, the cost of her fabrics and ornaments, even the depth of her decolletage—though the last had more to do with class distinctions than economy.

By the fifteenth century, however, Renaissance man was becoming more interested in male than in female nudity. The Greek influence showed not only in the somewhat ambiguous adolescent nudes of Verrocchio, Botticelli, and Leonardo, but in the increasingly bisexual tastes of Italian men. Brantôme, on his first visit to Italy, heard of a husband who, enamored of a beautiful youth who was, by a happy chance, in love with his wife, persuaded her to summon the boy to their home. The day came, the young man arrived, and when he and the wife were in bed the husband emerged from hiding and held a dagger to the young man's throat, threatening to kill him (as Italian law permitted) unless the young man gave him what he wanted.[32] An early variant of the badger game.

But although the Italian Renaissance tried to relive the Greek experience, and although it was fascinated by Plato's view of love (newly discovered through the *Symposium,* which reached Europe later than his other works), its cultivation of pederasty had very little of the tone of the Greek original. It was nearer to what the late Middle Ages had learned to call buggery.

The original buggers were heretics, not homosexuals. The Manichaean heresy of the third century had spread disruptively in the East but quietly in the West, and had become well established in Bulgaria, from which it spread in a slightly different form to Provence, Germany, northern France, and Italy. To the Church, Manichaeanism was the most dangerous heresy, and it became easy to speak of Bulgars and heretics as if they were by definition the same; in this way, Bulgari or Boulgres, corrupted into Bugari and Bougres, became part of the language in western Europe. In the district around Albi in southern France, the Bulgarian/Manichaean heresy culminated in Catharism, otherwise known as the Albigensian heresy and believed by the Church to be spiritually and socially disastrous. All that most people knew about the Albigenses was that they regarded propagation of the species as wrong, forbade sex altogether to the highest ranks (the Perfecti), but simply forbade the lower ranks to conceive children. The heretics, the *bougres,* were thus sexual deviants from the Christian line, and sexual deviation allied with a ban on conception could only mean homosexuality and/or heterosexual anal intercourse. (No one seems to have thought of *coitus interruptus,* possibly because it was common, if unconfessed, among orthodox Christians.) Heterosexual anal intercourse was, in fact, a standard if reprehensible contraceptive method in France in the medieval and post-medieval period, as it had been in Classical Greece; Brantôme says that several husbands of his acquaintance used their wives "more by the rear than the front, and only made use of the front in order to have children." [33]

Of the three nations which today remain pillars of the Catholic Church in Europe, France in post-medieval times treated religious doctrine with the same adaptability as it has always done; Italy with a cynicism that later history has completely effaced; and Spain with the passionate conviction of the convert and the missionary. Spanish laws against sodomy or buggery (the words became interchangeable) were both ruthless and ruthlessly enforced, in Spain itself and on the unfortunate inhabitants of the New World (see pages 289-301). It may have been a reaction to the Arab occupation, when *bardajes* (catamites, or passive homosexual partners) were a familiar sight and it was generally believed that no pilgrimage to Mecca was complete unless the pilgrim whiled away the journey by having intercourse with his camel boys (and his camels), but the stringency with which the laws were administered seems to have had some effect on the Spanish people. Despite the temptations of the long sea and land journeys involved in the conquest of Latin America, only two cases of homosexuality were recorded among the conquistadors, one involving sailors who served under a German captain and may themselves have been German, and the other five Italian soldiers in Venezuela, who were duly "strangled and burnt, with general applause" at the orders of their Spanish commander.[34]

The Spanish anti-buggery laws applied, as they did in England and other parts of Europe, to zoophilia as well, and attracted the death penalty. The priest and chronicler Jerónimo de Barrionuevo expressed a conventional mystification over the necessity for it when he recorded the execution in 1659 of two farmers, one of whom had fallen in love with his she-ass and the other who had "lain with his sow." Yet all the while, remarked Barrionuevo, "there are women around at three for a farthing." [35] Such cases were, however, extremely unusual, as were known cases of heterosexual anal intercourse, which also attracted the death penalty. Spain believed itself relatively free from all variants on what was generally regarded (in Spain) as the Italian vice. As Francisco Gomes de Quevedo sardonically remarked, "Those [women] who have a Genoese for a lover may have a Spaniard as another, without jealousy of the first, because each of them works in a different area. . . ." [36]

Homosexual or heterosexual, the man of the Italian Renaissance had mixed feelings about women, even if he cultivated and exercised his smooth tongue in long discussions about ladies and love. Like his predecessors of the Middle Ages, he was happy to flatter and admire the beautiful, the charming, and the rich, while treating the less well endowed with superficial courtesy and those of the lower classes with the same cursory contempt as he had always done.

But the overall picture, however indefinably, *had* changed. Petrarch (1304–74), "the first modern man," was representative of the days when the change was just beginning. Though he had once written of Laura that she was "all virtue, all beauty, all nobility, bound in one form in wondrous unity," [37] he said in his later years,

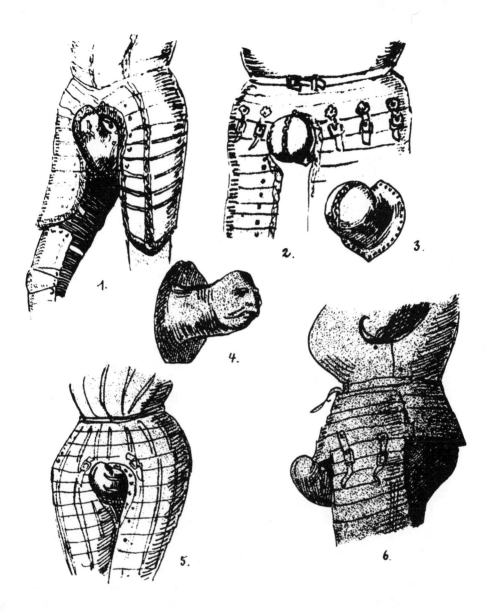

1. 2. 3. 4. 5. 6.

The protective codpiece worn by the tight-breeched
Europeans of the fourteenth, fifteenth, and sixteenth
centuries, although related to the Highlander's sporran,
the tribal penis sheath, and the baseball player's jock-
strap of later times, had a panache all its own. As well as
protecting, it displayed—even from under a full suit of
armor.

"Woman ... is a real devil, an enemy of peace, a source of provocation, a cause of disputes, from whom a man must hold himself apart if he wishes to taste tranquillity. ... Let them marry, those who are attracted by the company of a wife, by nightly embraces, the screaming of children and the torments of insomnia. ... As for us, if it is in our power, we will perpetuate our name through talent and not through marriage, through books and not through children, with the cooperation of virtue and not with that of a woman...." [38]

Two hundred years later, though many men would still have agreed with him, such an attitude no longer had the old quality of revealed truth. The Church's view of beauty as an instrument of perdition had finally been overthrown. Virtue was no longer the optimistic dream it had once appeared. Some women did have the warmth of Mary Mother, others the intellect of the allegorical images. As women began to play a recognizable role in religious and even political life, and as wives showed themselves capable of shouldering responsibilities, men became faintly aware of the legal disabilities under which they labored. By the end of the period no decisive victories had been won (and none *were* to be won for another 300 years), but the groundwork had been laid.

In Castiglione's early sixteenth-century book of manners, *The Book of the Courtier,* one of his characters says, "Who does not realize that without women we can get no pleasure or satisfaction out of life, which but for them would lack charm and be more uncouth and savage than that of wild beasts? Who does not realize that it is only women who rid our hearts of all vile and base thoughts, anxieties, miseries, and the wretched ill humors that often accompany them? And if we really consider the truth, we shall also recognize that in our understanding of great issues, far from distracting us, they awaken our minds...." [39] That last sentence could never have been written before the days of courtly love, of allegory, the worship of Mary Mother, and the education of Martha.

11.
Imperial
enterprises

When Mark Twain said that fluid prejudice was the ink with which all history was written,[1] he must have had his native continent in mind, for when the Spaniards collided with the pre-Columbian civilizations of America—separated from Europe not only by 5,000 miles of ocean but by well over 2,000 years of technical sophistication, political development, and Judeo-Christian philosophy—rational judgment was the first victim of the encounter. Cannibalism, human sacrifice, incest, drug abuse, drunkenness, sodomy, adultery, robbery, murder.... The only sin with which the Spaniards did not instantly saddle the Incas and the Aztecs was heresy, and that was because they could not, by definition, be pagans and heretics at the same time.*

During most of the sixteenth century, however, it was not the rational judgment of the Spaniards that exercised the minds of statesmen and theologians, but that of the Indians. If the American Indians were, as the sins of which they were accused seemed to imply, no better than brute beasts—"irrational" (or "non-rational") creatures was the preferred euphemism—then it was morally permissible, even desirable, for the Spaniards to appropriate their land, their property, and their persons. "Irrational creatures cannot have dominion ... because dominion signifies rights. ...

---

* The roster of sins sprang readily to the European mind. For almost fifteen centuries it had been customary to attribute all of them to any sect that failed to conform to majority practice.[2] When Columbus encountered cannibalism in the Antilles, and Cortes human sacrifice in Mexico, the others automatically followed.

[Since] irrational creatures cannot have rights, it follows that they cannot have dominion." [3] It was an ideology custom-built for the imperial adventure. But unfortunately, when the Spanish pope Alexander VI Borgia had issued the bulls *Inter cetera* of May 1493, giving Spain sole dominion over most of the New World, he had made it a condition that the inhabitants should be instructed in the Catholic faith, and this was something "irrational creatures" were regarded as unfit to receive. As a result, there was a basic conflict between the interests of Church and State, with the Church and its missionaries arguing that the people of the Americas were not irrational, merely misguided, while the Spaniards who flocked to the Indies in search of gold and silver found it more convenient to think of them and treat them as brute beasts.

The controversy flourished. Exponents of the "irrational" theory dismissed as biased Pope Paul III's 1537 pronouncement that Indians were "truly men," and ignored the great Spanish theologian Francisco de Vitoria when he acidly pointed out that, if the sin of sodomy could be used to justify Spain's depredations in the Indies, it could equally well be used to justify France if she chose to declare war on Italy.[4] The irrationalists, like so many of their predecessors and successors in public debate, knew that loud and frequent repetition was the most convincing argument of all. As Bartolomé de las Casas, the Dominican Apostle of the Indians, bitterly remarked, their "infamies have flown almost all over the world . . . because it is an old habit to believe more easily what is evil than good." [5]

Advocates of Indian rationality were at a disadvantage in their search for proofs to refute the allegations that had so swiftly gained currency, the Gothic horrors that had such spine-tingling appeal for the peoples of the Old World. Cannibalism and human sacrifice could not be explained away; no recognition of their religious logic would ever overcome the early conquistadors' gut reaction to the all-pervading reek of blood. In other matters there were language difficulties and literacy problems, aggravated by the impetuous bigotry of such men as Archbishop Zumárraga in Mexico and Bishop Landa in Yucatan, who seized and burned many of the religious and legal records of the pre-Columbian period. Even the Indians who were prepared to answer questions were of little help, trying "to soothe the Spaniards and flatter them, answering questions as they think the questioner wants them answered, and not with the truth" [6]—a habit still prevalent in peasant societies today.

When the most reliable information was correlated, it transpired that sodomy, incest, adultery, rape, murder, and theft were just as illegal in the dominions of the Aztecs and Incas as they were at home in Spain; that drunkenness, admissible in Spain, was a crime among the Aztecs; that the Incas, just like the Spaniards, thought of prostitution as a necessary evil; and that human sacrifice was rare among the Incas and cannibalism almost unknown.

But it was too late to distinguish between the law makers and the law breakers, and it has remained too late ever since. The image of the Latin-American Indian, like that of the European lady of courtly love, had been irrevocably shaped by other people's words and for other people's reasons.

"ABHOMINAL AND UNNATURAL LECHERY"

Four centuries later, much of the "evidence" of pre-Columbian sodomy has an unconvincing ring about it, a repetitiveness that is, at the very least, suspicious. The people of Panuco on the Gulf of Mexico were "great sodomites," reported an anonymous conquistador in 1519, and the town council of Vera Cruz (encouraged by Cortés) confirmed in 1522 that this was true of the whole of Mexico. In fact, said López de Gómara in 1552, no one in all the Indies could be absolved of it. Two years later, Augustin Zaraté confirmed that the Peruvians were at it, too, though in 1569 López Medel, with unnatural gentility, refused to go into detail about the "nefarious and widespread customs" of the Mexicans and Guatemalans because he did not wish "to offend chaste ears." But López de Velasco had no such inhibitions five years later about the people of Puerto Viejo in northern Peru.[7] And so it went on.

A few of the chroniclers took their task more responsibly, even if they suffered from a kind of willful pro-Indian credulity that sometimes devalued their judgments, and it is possible to build up a rough picture of sexual habits in the Spanish Indies from their writings, some of which have only come to light in recent years. What the picture shows is a series of societies momentarily frozen by the chroniclers at one stage or other of the transition from tribalism, with its relaxed attitude towards sexual variation, to the kind of authoritarian civilization that insists on uniformity.*

There were three major centers of culture in the Americas when the conquistadors arrived, two of them young and authoritarian—the Aztecs in the valley of Mexico and the Incas in Peru—and one old and disintegrating, the Maya of Yucatan, the stout peninsula that marks the division between the Caribbean and the Gulf of Mexico. Of the three, the Maya civilization is the least well documented, but appears to have been the most widely disseminated.

The Maya were among those who recognized adolescent homosexuality, and, indeed, favored it over heterosexuality. Until a boy was old enough to marry, it was usual for his parents to provide him with a male companion, a slave boy, to meet his needs, and he was discouraged from meeting them in any other way. If he had intercourse with an unmarried woman, he was liable to a fine, and if the girl was a virgin, a shotgun marriage swiftly followed.[9] According to this view, marriage was the important relationship, and heterosexual activity outside it more of a threat than homosexual exchanges. The Maya, however, also recognized and tolerated—as the Aztecs and the Incas did not—the type of adult homosexuality that is permanent and genetic.

As luck would have it, it was the Maya that Spain encountered first of the civilizations of the New World, and it was either from them or from the tribes in their diffusion area that they deduced sodomy throughout the length and breadth of the Indies. Not that their error was surprising. They had no idea of the extent of these new lands, and as they explored the islands of the Caribbean and the whole thousand-mile length of the narrow isthmus that stretches from Yucatan to Panama, it must have seemed as if they had indeed discovered a new world inhabited entirely by sodomites. Homosexuality was one thing at home in Spain—a secret, surreptitious, private vice, and recognized as such—but here they encountered a matter-of-fact public acceptance of it that shocked

* One study of modern tribes (made in 1952) showed that two-thirds of them considered adolescent homosexuality as normal and acceptable, and other researchers have found it institutionalized among the Cubeo on the Amazon, and the Mohaves and Zuñi, among others, in North America.[8] Modern psychiatry recognizes, in fact, that a homosexual phase is by no means uncommon in adolescence, but most of the world's great civilizations have always either ignored or actively suppressed it.

them very deeply indeed. "Look to what degree they boast of such a guilt. . . . They carry as a jewel, made in gold relief, a man mounted upon another in that diabolic and nefarious act of Sodom." [10] Fernandez de Oviedo, royal supervisor of gold smelting in South America in the second decade of the sixteenth century (only 20 years after Columbus made his first landfall), was so disgusted when one such ornament was brought to him that he did not simply smelt it down but "broke it with a hammer and smashed it under my own hand." [11]

Balboa, too, encountered it in 1513 among the chiefs at Quarequa in Panama. Here, he said, was "the most abhominal and unnaturall lechery," practiced by "the Kynges brother and many other younger men in womens apparell, smoth and effeminately decked, which by the report of such as dwelte abowte hym, he abused with preposterous Venus." Balboa dealt summarily with the offenders, throwing forty of them to his dogs. Homosexuality could be contagious, but he hoped he might have arrested its spread, for he thought that "this stynkynge abhomination hadde not yet entered among the people." [12]

Cortés, however, was sure that it had, and his march from Vera Cruz to the Aztec capital of Tenochtitlan was notable for the frequency with which he advised all and sundry to "give up the worship of idols and make no more human sacrifices," and to commit "no more robbery or sodomy." [13] When he said as much to Moctezuma himself, the emperor was politely surprised. Aztec law included the death penalty for homosexuals, male and female, as well as for transvestites, and it was a law enforced by regular witchhunts.[14] Nor was this antipathy to the homosexual anything new in Mexico. The peoples of pre-Columbian America had no equivalent of hell, no threat of eternal damnation to deter the nonconformist; the only deterrent was earthly punishment, and the nastier the punishment the greater the deterrent. The Aztecs' predecessors had applied a moderately nasty one to homosexuals. In the case of "the one acting as a female, they removed his entrails from the bottom, tied him down to a log, and the boys from the town covered him with ash until he was buried; and then they put a lot of wood and burned him. The one acting as a male was covered with ash, and tied down to a log until he died." [15] It would perhaps be a mistake to deduce from this that the passive or "womanish" partner was more harshly treated than the male;

the pre-Columbian tendency to favor suicide in preference to life suggests that they may have regarded the quicker death, however brutal, as the lesser evil.

In Peru, far to the south, anyone who committed sodomy was condemned to be "dragged" (presumably through the streets at the end of a rope) and hanged, and then "burned with all his clothes" to symbolize complete destruction.[16] The same penalty was applied to zoophiliacs, who were less of a rarity in Peru—where they had more scope, in the form of semidomesticated llamas and vicuña—than in Mexico, where the only domesticated livestock were turkeys and dogs.

And Peru was also unlike Mexico in that, outside its great centers of population, there were scattered communities that rarely saw an outsider from one year's end to another. It appears that homosexuality may formerly have been fairly widespread, particularly in these outlying districts, but by the time the Spaniards arrived it had been ruthlessly suppressed. The Incas, like most authoritarian rulers, disliked what did not fit into the majority pattern and took every opportunity to wipe out "the abominable sin" as they expanded their dominion into the more remote mountain valleys and along the narrow coastal plain.[17] The Inca himself "ordered that a careful search was to be made for the sodomites and when found they had to be burned alive in the public square, not only those proved guilty, but also those indicted by circumstantial evidence, however slight. . . . Even the name was odious to them and they never uttered it; any Indian . . . who in anger or in dispute with another used it as a term of abuse was regarded as disgraced, and for many days looked upon by the rest of the Indians as something vile and filthy for having used such a word." [18]

Cieza de León, one of the more balanced sixteenth-century writers on the Incas, estimated that in the Chimú area—a river culture on the northern coastline, surrounded by desert—fifteen women were left to every one man after the Incas had exterminated all the sodomites there.[19] (He does not say whether this unhappy event was followed by a proportionate increase in lesbianism.) In fact, although the Chimú area appears to have had a long record of sexual unorthodoxy (see page 296), it seems likely that the Incas were at least as interested in destroying their highly sophisticated, and therefore competitive, culture as in arriving at a "final solution" to the problem of sodomy.

About 300 miles north of Chimú, in the district of Puerto Viejo, now part of Ecuador, sodomy was said to have been practiced publicly and proudly before the days of the conquest, "despite the fact that among [the people] there were women in abundance and some of them beautiful." There was a legend about its beginnings, "a story of some giants who landed on the coast at the point of Santa Elena in the vicinity of the city of Puerto Viejo. . . . As they had no women of their own and the Indian women of the neighborhood were too small for them, or else because the vice was habitual to them . . . they practiced the unspeakable sin of sodomy, committing it openly and publicly without fear of God or personal shame." Cieza de León heard this story some time in the 1540s, which gives added piquancy to the climax. For when "all the giants were together engaged in this accursed sodomy, there came a fearful fire from heaven to the accompaniment of a great noise, in the midst of which a shining angel appeared holding a sharp, bright sword with which he slew them all at a single stroke." [20] Any resemblance to the fate of Sodom and Gomorrah was no doubt purely coincidental.

Even so, legends of giants from the sea are part of the common currency of coastal mythology and often enshrine some vestige of ancestral memory. Sex-starved castaways thrown up on the Peruvian coast were probably not uncommon; sailors from the far west are believed to have made landfalls on the Pacific strip of South America as early as 2500 B.C.[21] It is perfectly possible that active homosexuality should have been introduced to the formerly heterosexual inhabitants of Puerto Viejo by such strangers, possible, even, that it should have become as fashionable there as its pederastic version in classical Athens. In any case, it seems to have been slow to die out. As late as 1580, Pedro Gutierrez de Santa Clara, son of a Jewish convert and a Mexican Indian mother, reported gloomily that still, in his day, the people of Puerto Viejo practiced sodomy "in their rites and ceremonies and in their drunkenness." [22]

IN THE MANNER OF VIPERS

When the Spaniards in the New World talked of sodomy, they nearly always meant it in the sense of homosexuality. They would scarcely have needed to be voyeurs to recognize the implications of young men wearing skirts, beads, and bracelets and occupying themselves in "the usual chores of the house such as sweeping and washing and other things customary for women." [23] But the other main branch of sodomy, heterosexual anal intercourse, was a private matter requiring more intimate research, and although the Spaniards found out about it soon enough they seldom wrote about it specifically, except when it appeared unusually provocative—when combined with polygamy, for example. "The chief Behechio had thirty wives of his own, and not only for the [kind] of copulation married men usually have with their women, but for other bestial and nefarious sins. . . . The chief Goacanagarí had certain women with whom he copulated in the manner vipers do it. Look what unheard-of abomination, which he could only have learned from such animals. . . ." [24]

It seems possible that by the time the conquistadors arrived heterosexual anal intercourse may—in response to Aztec and Inca suppression of the homosexual variety—have become more common than it had been before, although it seems never to have been altogether *un*common. The evidence, however, is tenuous. Early American art and religion were not very much concerned with sex, and the law books more with its public than private aspects. But there survives from one area of Peru a remarkable collection of ceramic drinking vessels that would (if they could be regarded as representative) throw a mildly startling light on the sexual habits of the pre-Columbian Andean peoples.

The Chimú who had been massacred in the course of the Inca drive against sodomy were the successors of a civilization known as the Moche (or Mochica), which had flourished during the first millennium A.D. on much the same cultural level as Sumer 3,000 years earlier. With their dead, the Moche buried grave goods, and those that have been dug up show that the people of the area were superb craftsmen and unusually fine potters; indeed, their talent for three-dimensional portraiture has rarely been surpassed. Characteristic of the period were stirrup-spout pots, globular in shape, with a hollow arched handle on top molded into a drinking spout at the apex. These pots lent themselves to decoration, and Moche potters seem to have had a marked fondness for what museums classify as "erotic subjects."

A few years ago, one distinguished authority on Peruvian art (Rafael Larco Hoyle) published a monograph on these pots, many

A stirrup-spout vessel illustrating anal intercourse

of which belong to his family's private collection, and an equally distinguished authority on pre-Columbian attitudes of mind (Dr. Francisco Guerra) analyzed their subject matter, with illuminating results.[25] Of something over 100 stirrup-spout pots, he found that:

31 percent illustrated heterosexual anal intercourse
24 percent the penis
14 percent oral intercourse
11 percent conventional heterosexual intercourse
6 percent zoophilia
5 percent male masturbation
4 percent the vulva
3 percent homosexual anal intercourse
1 percent lesbianism
1 percent uncertain *

Did conventional heterosexual intercourse, in the days of the Moche, come a very poor third to anal and oral intercourse, with homosexuality and lesbianism scarcely in the running?

There is unfortunately no archeological law which says that what goes down must come up, and the hundreds or thousands of pots that still remain buried might tell a different tale. In fact, all that can be legitimately deduced from the specimens excavated is that the Moche were not unalterably devoted to sex in the recumbent, man-superior position. They may have used anal intercourse as a method of contraception, or as a way of satisfying the man when the woman's vagina had become dilated by child-bearing. And there is a possibility, though perhaps a remote one, that Peruvian methods of circumcision may have been clumsy, reducing sensitivity so that a man could find full satisfaction in intercourse only when his glans was tightly constricted.

Something else the pots indicate is that the potters (who appear to have been women) had a strong, if unsubtle, sense of humor. In the 24 percent of pots featuring the penis it usually appeared as the drinking spout; in some cases the filling hole was surrounded by perforations so that there was no alternative to

---

* Just how uncertain can be seen from the fact that one pot "shows a most realistic digital stimulation of the vagina in a woman by a castrated man, although the active party could also be described as a woman engaged in a lesbian practice."[26]

drinking from the spout. In a few specimens, the spout was molded into the shape of the vulva, and there were two pots with two spouts, one penis-shaped and one vulva-shaped, giving the drinker a choice between *fellatio* and *cunnilingus.*

It is perfectly possible that these *jeux d'esprit* do have something to say about the realities of life in the valleys of Chicama, Moche and Virú in the middle of the first millennium, but that they are not to be taken too literally is suggested by the zoophiliac examples, which show women having intercourse with a jaguar, a dog, and, in three cases, cormorants.

SINNERS AND A SAINT

Whether or not sodomy was commonplace at the time of the Spanish conquest, the Church was compelled to assume that it was, and it armed its priests with appropriate questions to be asked in the confessional.

"When your wife [had her menstrual period] did you have intercourse with her? And at the time you both joined was it with lewdness and not in the proper vessel? And by chance did you execute any other lecherous things and filthy pleasure, which are not mentioned here? Remember all of them, to confess and declare all." [27]

The confessionaries, like the penitentials, covered as many permutations of sexual sin as possible. Few documents, perhaps, convey more clearly the view of sex as something vulgar and sordid than the confessionary designed for use among the warrior Tarascan tribe of western Mexico in 1697.

> Are you a married woman, or a widow, or a virgin, or
>   have you lost your virginity?
> How many times?
>
> Did you want anybody?
> Are you relatives?
> In what degree are you relatives?
>
> Have you sinned with a woman?
> Were they your relatives?

Did you commit sin with some woman using both parts?
Have you kissed any woman?
Was she your mother, the one who gave you birth?

Have you committed sodomy?
Have you touched the lower parts of a man with pleasure, wishing to commit a sin?
Have you committed sin with any beast?
Have you committed sin with a woman while she was
lying down like an animal on four feet, or have you
put her like that, wanting to sin with her?

And how many have sinned with you?
And was one your father, the one who begat you?
And was one your elder brother?
And was one your younger brother?

And have you sinned with another woman as if you
were man and woman? [28]

In 1583, the reform-minded Third Provincial Council of Lima,
Peru, approved the kind of sermon that was to be preached to
Indian converts.
"If there is any one among you who commits sodomy, sinning
with another man, or with a boy, or with a beast, let [it] be known
that, because of that, fire and brimstone fell from heaven and
burned the fine cities of Sodom and Gomorrah and left them in
ashes. Let it be known that it carries the death penalty under the
just laws of our Spanish kings. . . . Let it be known that the reason
why God has allowed that you, the Indians, should be so afflicted
and vexed by other nations* is because of this vice that your ancestors had, and many among you still have. . . . God will finish you,
and he is already doing so if you will not reform. Take away drunkenness and feasts which are the sowing ground of these abominable vices, remove the boys and men from your beds, do not sleep
mixed up like pigs, but each one of you by himself, do not sing or
say dirty words, do not entice your flesh with your hands, because
this is also a sin and deserving death and hell." [29]
But although the Church had a low opinion of its Amerindian
flock, by a strange quirk the sodomites of Mexico succeeded in

_____
* A surprising statement.

acquiring something that none of their fellow-sinners in the whole Christian world had ever possessed—a patron saint. In 1732, one José Manuel García del Valle y Araujo, chaplain of a hospital in Mexico City that had been founded by Cortés for the treatment of syphilis, published a *novena* or nine-day prayer which, if addressed to St. Boniface, Martyr, would persuade him to intercede for the sinner so that God would rid him of "the dishonorable vice." That St. Boniface's intercession was in reasonably popular demand is suggested by the fact that the *novena* continued to be reprinted at intervals until well into the nineteenth century. What the eighth-century saint himself—no friend to homosexuality among his contemporaries—would have thought of the spiritual charge placed upon him in Mexico remains a matter for speculation.[30]

POPULATION PROBLEMS

The Spaniards' sanctified loathing for sodomy had its origins, even if they did not recognize it, far back in the Hebrew past and the divine command to "be fruitful and multiply"—which was very much what the Incas and Aztecs also appear to have been aiming at in their sex legislation.

The Inca had a clearly formulated population policy, and they needed it, for in the course of only 60 years they had extended their empire from a heartland no larger than California today until it stretched all the way from Quito (Ecuador) in the north to the center of Chile in the south, a matter of some 2,500 miles. They built roads, agricultural terraces, and irrigation systems, introduced staple crops into the empty lands, and sent governors, garrisons, farmers, and priests to establish Inca civilization in the conquered territories. It was an authoritarian rule, but a rational one, and the legal system, though bloodthirsty enough, tried to temper punishment not with humanitarianism, but with basic common sense. A man who raped a virgin was to die by stoning. But "if she wanted to marry him, he should not die but must marry immediately." [31] *

* Until 1978, Italian law also provided that a man who raped a girl should go unpunished if she later agreed to marry him. It was an article subject to much abuse, having become the recognized legal instrument in much of southern Italy by which a man could virtually force a girl to marry him.

Marriage and hard work were the cornerstones of Inca policy. In every town there was supposed to be a judge to deal with "idlers and lazy people, to punish them and to make them work." Lords and headmen were expected to "have fifty women for their service, to increase the number of people in the kingdom." [32] And, like it or not, no man was permitted to remain a bachelor.

The Inca was father of his people, and it was his responsibility to provide his "daughters" with husbands, a responsibility that appears to have been taken seriously. Once a year the Inca himself conducted a kind of mass betrothal ceremony in Cuzco, and his representatives did the same in the outposts of the empire. Since each newly married couple was presented with a piece of land and a house that had been built for them by the community and furnished by their relatives (the Aztecs had a roughly similar system), it was necessary for them to be adult enough for the responsibilities involved, and the marriage age was between 18 and 20 for the girl, and 24 for the man, which was late by European standards of the time. None of the authorities seem able to agree on the Inca view of virginity. One seventeenth-century bishop of Quito complained that women still could not be persuaded to "care for their virginity *ante nuptias,* which among all nations in the world is respected and honored; on the contrary they take it as an affront, and consider themselves unhappy if no one has wanted them." As a result, Indians did not get married "unless they have had evil intercourse first for several months with the one who is going to be their wife, to know by experience if she is going to be adequate." [33]

Because the principal wife was bestowed by the Inca there was no question of her ever being divorced or of a secondary wife being promoted to her place when she died. (In practice, a custom that must have discouraged mayhem in the harem.) A husband was permitted to take a replacement first wife, if he wished, but a widow had to marry either her brother-in-law or no one—a kind of levirate system that reinforced the opinion of some sixteenth-century thinkers that the Incas were descended from one of the lost tribes of Israel. It was usual for the eldest son to take over responsibility for the rest of his father's ladies.

The Inca's own harem was stocked by much the same method as Kublai Khan's (see p.240 f/n). Government officials paid regular visits to centers of population, large and small, and selected the

prettiest ten-year-old girls to be taken away from home and educated in special convents. These girls were the *acllacuna*, the
"chosen women," and when their education was complete, after
four or five years, their qualities were reappraised. The Inca made
his own choice from among them, distributed some of the others
to men he wished to honor, and despatched the rest to become
"Virgins of the Sun," nuns sworn to perfect chastity and liable to
death if they lapsed—though one of the conquistadors reported
unkindly that "if one was pregnant and swore an oath that the sun
was the father of her child, she was spared." [34] The chastity requirement seems not to have been eternal, however, since the
Virgins formed a useful reservoir of beauty and talent that could
be drawn on in emergency, as when the Incas endeavored to pla-
cate the Spanish invaders by presenting them with gifts of the
kind they thought would be most appreciated. Some chroniclers
report that those who acted as confessors* to the Virgins had to
be "either eunuchs or men who had proved perpetual chastity,
and they were usually old men," and another says that "they killed
them very cruelly if they had dishonest conversation" with the
women.[35] Which suggests the Incas may have had the same problem with their bronze eunuchs as the Turks with their white ones.

The custom of taking the most beautiful girls in the empire
out of general circulation was, of course, a matter of religious
rather than population policy, but it was also politically useful for
the Inca's concubines to be drawn from among the chosen women
of the Sun god cult. The Inca himself claimed to be a direct
descendant of the Sun, and appears to have been obsessed by the
need to display his credentials. At every opportunity, sun-symbol-
ism was stressed, and purity of descent emphasized, a purity that
was maintained—as it had been in Egypt 3,000 years earlier—by
incest. The Inca could marry only another descendant of the Sun,
and that meant his sister.

Among the people, of course, incest was unpleasantly punished
whenever it came to official notice, as it was among the Aztecs and
many of the tribal societies of North America. Most Amerindians
also disapproved strongly enough of rape, adultery, and abortion
to enact severe penalties, although the tribals were more lenient,

---

* Pre-Columbians did practice a kind of confession, though its object was to relieve the
mind rather than seek absolution for the soul.

and the Maya imposed the death penalty for adultery only if the sinners made a habit of it.

The population problem in Peru was concerned with speeding up the normal peaceful rate of increase. The Aztecs had the much more serious problem of replacing people who were disappearing as fast as water down a drain because of the demands of human sacrifice.

War, to the Aztecs, was a cosmic duty, but it was not the kind of war familiar in Europe. In Mexico, the main object of all concerned was to take prisoners. When a battle began, archers and javelin-throwers loosed their weapons, and then the ranks broke and the warriors rushed in with sword and shield. The battlefield disintegrated into a series of private dogfights as each man did his best to defeat another and hale him off to the sidelines, where noncombatants were waiting with ropes to tie the captives up. When serious war was impracticable, the Aztecs would set up a friendly War of Flowers with some neighboring state, a kind of chivalric tournament designed to produce not winners but losers who could become sacrificial victims.

The Aztecs themselves usually came out on the right side but, even so, perpetual war must have made serious inroads in their numbers. It was the surrounding peoples who suffered more severely, however. The scale of human sacrifice is generally agreed to have been considerable, even if it never again reached the improbably high peak claimed for 1486, when 20,000 victims were said to have been slaughtered in a matter of only four days. Some anthropologists suggest an annual rate of a quarter of a million victims, or an average of just under 700 a day,[36] which in sacrificial terms—and since the ritual took place at a number of temples (no one is quite sure how many)—sounds not unreasonable.

But in population terms it was utterly unreasonable. Although there were special festivals at which women and children died, all the sources make it clear that the usual victims were young adult males. To subtract this class from a population of 25 million at a rate of 700 a day (or even less) must, in a comparatively short time, have played havoc with the age and sex balance of society and, of course, with its fertility. The Aztec world view, however, shared by the surrounding peoples who were called upon to sacrifice their young men, was that the choice lay between total extinction and pacification of the gods by mass sacrifice. It scarcely amounted to a choice.

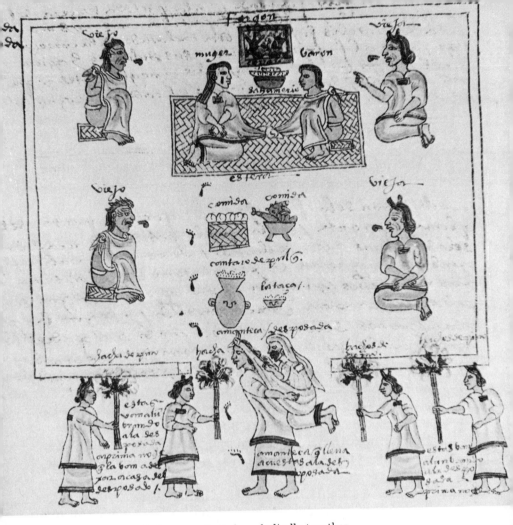

edding of an Aztec couple, their garments tied symbolically together

The Incas looked ahead, the Aztecs dared not. As a result, they followed no revolutionary population policy, but adhered to the traditionally expansive measures that had proved satisfactory in the days before sacrifice became a fetish in the last decades of the fifteenth century. They penalized nonproductive sex and imposed the death penalty for abortion. They encouraged marriage at an earlier age than the Incas (14 or 15 for the girl and 20 for the boy), but if it did not work had no real prejudice against divorce and remarriage. And they practiced polygamy, hoping, no doubt, if they thought about it at all, that this would help to redress the sacrificial balance. But one king of Texcoco, the proud possessor of 2,000 concubines, succeeded in fathering only 144 children, a very poor return on his investment, and no contribution at all to an expanding population.[37] It is actively misleading to talk, as some historians do, of polygamous families becoming "exceedingly numerous." [38] Axayacatl's total of 22 children, Auitzotl's 20, Moctezuma's 19, and Tlacaeleltzin's 17 might have been impressive in the context of monogamy, but they were derisory in the context of "a great number of wives." All that these figures suggest is that a good deal of reproductive capacity must have gone to waste. In fact, the poorer classes, monogamous by necessity, probably showed a higher rate of increase than the polygamous rich. But polygamy at least provided security for many women who, because of the sacrificial drain on manpower, would not otherwise have had the opportunity to marry.

MEXICALI ROSE

Some women, of course, did not want to marry, and there were a number of trades either reserved for them or open to them. They could become tailors or weavers, spinners or manuscript painters, they could be cooks, healers, midwives—or prostitutes. Despite their attitude toward adultery, the Aztecs had nothing against prostitutes,* and even gave them an important if subsidiary role in religious ceremonies.

Forty years after the conquest, the Franciscan father, Bernardino de Sahagún, conscientiously interviewing Amerindian informants about the Mexican past, extracted from some of them a delightful description of the fast ladies of Tenochtitlan, slightly qualified, perhaps, in deference to his priestly sensibilities, but making it very clear that the *auianime* of Mexico, the *harimtu* of Babylon, the green-bower girls of China, the hetairai of Greece, and the *qiyân* of Baghdad, were all sisters under the skin.

The public woman "goes about selling her body, starting when young and not leaving off even when old, when she gets drunk and careless. She is beautiful and polished, but shameless deep down ... lewd, and indelicate, talkative, and very vicious in the carnal act.

"She grooms herself with great care, so carefully that she looks

---

* Unlike the Incas, who forbade them in towns and villages but conceded them the countryside, designating them by the inappropriate name of "women of the uninhabited places." [39]

like a rose by the time she has finished. To prepare herself, she first looks in a mirror, then takes a bath, washing herself very well and freshening herself so as to appear pleasing. Then she uses a yellow cream called *axin* to give herself a pale, glowing complexion, and at the same time tints her face with rouge, because she is dissolute and worldly. She also colors her teeth with cochineal, and lets her hair hang loose to make it appear more beautiful. . . . She scents herself with nice perfumes and goes about chewing *tzictli* [chicle, the raw material of chewing gum], clacking her teeth like castanets. She enjoys walking about in the streets and squares, looking for immoral people; she goes about laughing—she never stops—but her heart is always uneasy. . . . She has the habit of calling out to people, of making gestures, looking at men, winking, beckoning with her hand, glancing slantwise, smiling at everyone, until she picks up the one she likes best." [40] The girls' charges do not appear to have been recorded for Mexico, but in Nicaragua in the 1540s the going rate was ten cocoa beans.[41]

Although there were brothels in Central America, the Spaniards were initially a little confused about them, placing them—because of their acquaintance with the stews of Europe—in what appear to have been perfectly innocuous bath houses. These were rather like the saunas of Scandinavia. There was a fire on the outside of one wall, and the bather crept into the building, which was quite small, and threw water against the hot stone. Immersed in steam, he (or she) then indulged in vigorous self-flagellation with grass stalks, and finally subsided quietly on to a mat to recover. The object was simple cleanliness, personal and ritual, but it was a combination that had no meaning for the Spaniards, who reported that "many Indian men and women bathed naked and committed inside many obscenities and sins in this bath." [42]

In civilized Tenochtitlan, prostitutes may just have drifted into the business, but in tribal areas it was different. Among the Sinaloa on the Arizona border, for example, a new prostitute had to be consecrated at a great festival, "at which all the chiefs of the locality gather and dance naked, and after all have danced with her they put her in a hut that has been decorated for this event, and the chiefs adorn her with [shawls] and bracelets of fine turquoise, and then the chiefs go in one by one to lie with her, and all the others who wish follow them. From this time on, these women cannot refuse anyone who pays them the agreed amount. Even if

they take husbands, it does not exempt them from obliging anyone who will pay them." [43]

THE BIRTH OF THE MESTIZO

The Spaniards who conquered so much of central and southern
America were honored sons of their native land, adventurers who
set off for the New World with official goodwill in search of
wealth for their country and themselves. They were not there,
individually, to stay—though many of them did—nor to settle,
though many of them were forced to. Usually, they thought of
themselves as doing a tour of duty overseas, and there was a regular traffic back and forth across the Atlantic that maintained links
with home. It was a colonial situation that was to recur more than
once in later centuries, notably in the case of the British in India.

To begin with, Spain forbade wives to accompany their husbands, and the inevitable consequence was free sexual intercourse
between Spanish men and Amerindian women, though "free" was
not always necessarily the same as "willing." Sometimes the contacts were casual, between soldiers and village girls; sometimes
legalized, between officers and women of high birth; sometimes
not legal but relatively permanent, as in the case of Cortés and
Malinal (Doña Marina, as the conquistadors called her), the slave
girl without whose help Mexico might never have been conquered.

The children of these liaisons inherited some of the characteristics of both parents, including a degree of immunity to the
European diseases that were to destroy, more effectively than the
systematic slaughter of the Spaniards, so many millions of the
native population. In Mexico and Yucatan before the conquest,
there are believed to have been about 25 million people; immediately after the conquest, these had been reduced to under seven
million. By 1650, only one-and-a-half million Indian-speakers
(pure-blooded indigenes) remained. Peru, with ten million inhabitants when Spain started counting, had only about two million
pure Indian-speakers in 1650.[44] It was the *mestizos,* part Indian,
part Spanish, who were the ones genetically equipped to survive,
and it was they who were to found the new hybrid races that have
inherited central and southern America today.

THE OTHER INDIES

In the real India, that southern promontory of the great Eurasian landmass, things were to turn out rather differently. When Vasco da Gama set foot on the subcontinent in 1498, six years after Columbus discovered America, he was landing not in a new world but in a very old one. His achievement was to pioneer a sea route from western Europe to the source of the spices that played such a large part in the economy of the late medieval period, a route that would enable Portugal to break the Turkish-Venetian monopoly based on the land route.

India had suffered many earlier invasions through the mountain passes of the northwest and by the fifteenth century had become something of a spiritual, cultural, and political jigsaw. Since there was no way by which a non-Hindu could convert to Hinduism (Hindus were born, not made), India, unlike China, was unable to absorb invaders, who remained half-assimilated, with their own social customs, often their own languages,* and, unless they chose to subscribe to one of the minority faiths such as Buddhism or Jainism, their own religions. It was not they who adapted to Hinduism, but Hinduism that slowly and unobtrusively adapted to them. This was to remain true when the Portuguese and, later, the Mughals, and finally the British came to exercise sovereignty in India.

* The Indian constitution still recognizes 13 major languages today, and there are well over 300 minor ones in everyday use.

The Spaniards left their mark on the Philippines as on Latin America. Nineteenth-century *mestizo*.

The contrast with the American Indies was to be striking. Whereas the Spanish adventure changed the genetic structure of almost all Latin America, in India the Portuguese, the Mughals (who were Muslim by faith), and the British, all added separate and independent pieces to the existing jigsaw. The substantial Muslim presence was ultimately to lead to the trauma of partition in 1947, and the creation of the new state of Pakistan; the Portuguese and the British, by interbreeding with pure-blooded Indians, were to create within the country's own frontiers a new group of invaders—predominantly Christian Eurasians.

In 1510, 16 years before the Muslim adventurer Babur founded the great Mughal empire that was to become a universal symbol of luxury, taste, and riches, the Portuguese captured Goa—on the middle of the west coast—and began to create a more workaday empire based on trade, sustained by mastery of the sea routes, and held (or so they hoped) not by military force but by a special kind of loyalty based on Christian fellowship and an increasingly *mestiço* population.

Christian conversions were slow to begin with, but when the Jesuits arrived in 1542 the struggle for souls became intensive. Temples were demolished, priests deported, sacred books destroyed, and before very long Hindus, Muslims, and Jews who lived in the vicinity of the Portuguese enclaves were forced to turn to Christianity simply because they had been deprived of the means to practice their own religions. Nor did those who clung to their faith escape the onslaught, for the decrees of the Ecclesiastical Councils at Goa (given legal sanction by the viceroy) penetrated far into private life. Non-Christians were forbidden to celebrate marriages in public. *Satī*, the rite of "the virtuous woman," was banned. Monogamy was imposed on all; a man with more than one wife had to repudiate all but the first, and if he had only concubines then he was required to marry one of them. In effect, although the Church forbade its missionaries to make forced coversions, what they did instead was enforce the sexual and personal morality of Western Christendom on nonbelievers in Goa. And when the Inquisition arrived in 1560 the arguments in favor of conversion became irresistible, for, as the English historian C.R. Boxer puts it: "The burning of Hindu widows in suttee was replaced by the roasting to death of Jews in the *autos-da-fé* celebrated at Goa." [45]

Once established, however—even on such terms as these—Christian fellowship proved easier to maintain than the *mestiço* population, which, according to the theory of Portugal's first Governor in the East, Alfonso de Albuquerque, should have been loyal to Portugal while regarding India as its home. To begin with, it had looked like a promising idea. Portuguese soldiers and traders were as ready to bed with Indian women—especially dancing girls and temple prostitutes (retired)—as Spaniards were with Amerindians. They were prepared to marry them, too, especially as there was a kind of semi-official sanction allowing a man to have, at the same time, one wife in Portugal and another in Goa. And it was only the missionaries who complained when they went further and bought "droves" of slave girls, "just as if they were sheep," and slept with all of them. Between 15 and 20 seems to have been par for the *zenana* of an ordinary European or Eurasian artisan.[46]

It was in succeeding generations that the trouble started. Albuquerque's vision was not shared by those who followed him. *Mestiços* were regarded as soft, effeminate, useless even as cannon fodder; in 1634, any *mestiço* who wished to enlist in the army had to bring a certificate from his priest guaranteeing that he was either the son, or at least the grandson, of a European-born Portuguese. On the administrative level, things were not much better, and in the long run Eurasians often felt more resentment toward Portugal than loyalty.

Nor did the Eurasian strand in the population widen as Albuquerque had hoped. One reason was that the indigenous peoples of Goa numbered about a million, while of the 2,400 Europeans who sailed from Portugal every year during the sixteenth century less than half survived the rigors of the journey to reach their destination and start fathering *mestiços*. But more decisive was the fact that in Goa, unlike Spanish America, the indigenous population did not succumb to mass slaughter either by its new masters or by European diseases (to which its own Indo-European heritage had given it reasonable immunity), but survived with perfect sangfroid. With no advantage of numbers comparable to that in Spanish America,* the Eurasian population remained small,

---

* Or, indeed, to that of Portuguese Angola, which today has a strong Eurafrican class largely because, at the height of the slave trade, pure-blooded Angolans were being drained out of the population at a rate of 20,000 a year.[47]

and in the course of time became smaller still. Many of its more ambitious members crossed the border into the wider world of British India, while others merged back into the native Indian scene. By 1956, there were only just over 1,000 recognized *Descendentes* in a total Goan population of over half a million.[48]

What the Portuguese succeeded in doing during the period of their presence in India was injecting into the existing jigsaw of races and religions a very small new piece whose genes were predominantly Indian, but which was Portuguese in custom and language, and Roman Catholic in morality, sex, and frequently faith.

What the British, in turn, were to do during the period of expanding dominion that began in 1757 and ended with independence in 1947, was not only to create a far more substantial Eurasian population (and one with staying-power) but change the face of Hinduism itself.

Originally, the British hoped to avoid disrupting the traditional pattern of Indian life, but there were some manifestations of popular Hinduism that they found themselves unable to stomach. As early as 1795 they began to legislate against female infanticide, classifying it as murder, but it was remarkably difficult to suppress. As one Rajput landowner explained to Sir William Sleeman in the middle of the nineteenth century, it was a matter of custom. "A family commonly destroys the daughter as soon as born, when the father is from home and has given no special orders about it, taking it to be his wish as a matter of course." [49] In 1870 the government was still trying, with limited success, to enforce registration of births and verification of the continuing well-being of newly born female children.

Satī was another source of trouble. Long before the British had ever become involved in Indian affairs, the Mughal emperor Aurangzeb had legislated against it, for it was as offensive to Muslims as it was to Christians. But the practice continued, particularly (as with female infanticide) in the aggressively masculine Rajput states; in 1780, 64 wives accompanied the Raja of Marwar to the hereafter. Aware of its religious significance, the British approached the question of *satī* cautiously, sending a police officer to supervise the ceremony and insure that the *satī* was voluntary and that the woman concerned was over 16 years of age and not pregnant. The unfortunate effect of this was to invest the occasion with government sanction, and the number of *satīs* officially reported in Bengal rose from 378 in 1785 to 839 in 1818. At last, in 1829, the government took its courage in both hands. *Satī* was declared illegal in Bengal, and in Madras the following year; anyone assisting was to be held guilty of culpable homicide. But it persisted in more isolated regions until the 1860s, and as late as 1932 the London *Times* reported an attempted *satī* at which the widow was saved by police action—and three other people were killed in the process.[50]

Laws, of course, are effective only when people are aware of them, and only when they are enforceable. British attempts to put an end to Hindu polygamy—which was, in any case, rare—proved ineffectual; not until the days of Indian independence, in 1955, was it finally and unequivocally declared a crime.[51] Nor was the Hindu Widow Remarriage Act of 1856 much more successful, granting a permission, of which most people remained unaware, to do something that tradition wholeheartedly condemned. The same was true of education for women; in 1939 there were still only about three million girls attending school, which represented roughly two per cent of the female population.[52]

But whether the many, or only the literate few, recognized the specific impact of new laws on traditions that had always seemed an inalienable part of Hinduism, the revelation that right could be changed to wrong by simple decree was shattering to the mass of India's people—above all, perhaps, because it so often struck directly not at brahminical philosophy but at the sacrosanct foundations of family life. Hinduism, the rock on which Indian society rested, was never to be quite as stable again.

The British had not ventured on the social-sexual legislation that proved to have such far-reaching results for Hindu society without a good deal of painful argument and a good deal of hesitancy. Appearances to the contrary, they would rather have forsworn the dangers of activity in favor of the placid comforts of inertia. And this was very much the attitude they adopted in the matter of relationships between themselves and Indians.

Like the Portuguese, they had at one stage considered the possibility of deliberately building up a Eurasian (Anglo-Indian) community. But, as one epigrammatist put it, necessity was the mother of invention and father of the Anglo-Indian, and official action would have been superfluous. For the first 70 years of British rule in India, Englishwomen were scarce, and when they ar-

A British expatriate in India, presiding over a musical performance in his harem, and smoking tobacco through a rosewater hookah.

rived in numbers—disapproving strongly of relations with "native women"—they still had little influence on the sexual enterprise of young bachelors newly out from Home and even less on the licentious soldiery, a strong presence in the country especially after the drama of the Indian Mutiny of 1857.

Between Eurasians in British India and in Portuguese Goa there was one important difference—their group survival potential. The Christianity that had been imposed on so many pure-blooded Indians in Goa was caste-less, so that there was no barrier between them and the Eurasian. The Eurasian could, if he (or she) wished, marry a Christian Indian and be reabsorbed into the Indian background, socially and genetically. But in the great bulk of British India, Hindu by faith, the Eurasian was by definition an outcaste—and was therefore quite unable, either by marriage or conversion, to return to the pure-blooded Hindu Indian community. As a result, Eurasians came to form a self-conscious and quite substantial class of their own, and the British gave them mildly preferential treatment, making calculated use of them on the lower technical and administrative levels especially (because they were thought to be trustworthy) on the railroads and in the police.

HOME FROM HOME

The imperial adventures that shaped so much of the history of the modern world were embarked on with a kind of tough-minded innocence that still, hundreds of years later, looks impressive, however disastrous its results may often have been. In the welter of dates and battles and treaties to which history is reduced on the printed page, it is not always easy to recognize that the people involved were motivated as much by personal feelings as political considerations. It was the Spaniards' personal sexual imperative that repopulated the thousands of miles of central and southern America that their political imperative had depopulated. It was the personal sexual imperative of the British that created a whole new ethnic group in India. It was self-indulgent humanitarianism that led the British to suppress practices such as *satī* and female infanticide, so contributing to deep and lasting changes in the whole 2,000-year structure of Hindu society. And in North America, Australia, and South Africa, it was the narrow-minded logic of a handful of settlers that ultimately transformed impersonal cultural prejudice into highly personal color prejudice and so laid the foundations of a whole vast edifice of racial conflict.

The Europeans who began to arrive on the east coast of North America in the seventeenth century settled in at first almost as a tribe among tribes. They were numerically few, anxious to avoid trouble, and they had no incentive of silver or gold, silk or spices, to make war with the Indians worth while. They regarded the redskins as savages, parleyed with them sometimes, traded with them often, and did not begin to slaughter them for almost 200 years.

Because so many of them were Puritans of one shade or another, there was no question of casual sex with the natives—or anyone else (see page 328). Although some of the immigrants were sturdy irreligious bachelors despatched half-willingly to the New World in the seventeenth century very much as their predecessors had been despatched to the Crusades in the eleventh, their sexual enterprise, though by no means quashed, was seriously hampered by the high moral tone of their fellow colonists. The Pilgrims and the Puritans, the Huguenots, Quakers, Rhinelanders, and Moravians who formed the ramrod spine of the new body politic had come to America to create a society in which they would no longer be oppressed minorities, but a majority with all a majority's power. It was their view of morality that mattered now, and by the time 20,000 Puritans had flocked to the new colonies (as they did between 1630 and 1650), they were in a position to impose it.

The Puritans had their faults, but color prejudice was not one of them. Color prejudice in the West, in fact, is a modern phenomenon. While is not entirely true to say, as one modern scholar does, that "the notion of physical repugnance on the part of the European when faced by people totally dissimilar in appearance is no more than a myth," [53] the composite of responses nowadays classified as "color prejudice" certainly did not gain real strength until the nineteenth century.

What the early Europeans in North America (and Australia and South Africa) suffered from was *cultural* prejudice, and this conditioned their attitude to the indigenous peoples in a quite specific way. The Spaniards in South America, the Portuguese in Asia, the British in India, were all transients, there to rule, to fight, to administer, to trade—but not to settle. They recognized themselves as foreigners in a foreign land and though they might often hate and fear the country, the climate, and the people, they knew that some day they could go home. Because of this, their attitude to the natives, though sometimes marred by a virulence approaching hysteria, had an oddly detached quality about it. But the situation of Europeans in North America, British in Australia, and Dutch in South Africa, was quite different. Their voyage had been made on a one-way ticket, and they carried the image of "Home" with them in their baggage to be reconstructed on foreign soil. Their attitude to the people they found in the new lands was shaped by a passionate need to protect the way of life, the cast of thought, the centuries of civilization on which their own identity depended, and this was to apply just as much to African slaves in America as to the indigenous peoples; more, perhaps because the contacts were closer.

It was little more than coincidence that their new neighbors' skin color marked them unmistakably as intruders in the European landscape; the settlers would have felt just the same about Kashmiri Brahmins, as light-skinned as Europeans and often a good deal more handsome. But when the new settlers were sufficiently well established to have time to look about them, they began consciously to recognize the need for defense. If this was to be *their* country, it had to be *their* culture. The culture represented by dark skins had not belonged in white Europe, and did not belong in white America.

The danger was cultural, but the only way to deal with it was on a mundane level. The bans on intermarriage that were imposed in Virginia in 1691 and Massachusetts in 1705 must have seemed, at the time, like a rational way of warding off invaders, a sensible response to something that appeared to threaten the inviolacy of the European tradition. What the Europeans in America did was adopt the ghetto mentality, cutting white and colored people off from each other as effectively as the Jews had cut themselves off from the Gentiles almost 2,000 years before, and by much the same means.* But this time, because color and sex were so obviously involved, and because there was a general tenor of superiority that appeared to be more anti the outsiders than pro the insiders, the effect was greater and more far-reaching. What was essentially a clannish exclusivity took on the appearance of calculated and personal insult.

That rejection of the colored peoples was less a matter of private preference than public policy is clear enough from eighteenth-century history. There were a great many white Americans who paid no heed at all to the boundaries others were so officiously intent on drawing. Thomas Jefferson, for example, had a long affair with his daughter's mulatto maid, Sally Hemings, who bore him five children, and thousands of his countrymen equaled or surpassed his record. In some ways this was unfortunate for the future of race relations. In the South, particularly, owners and plantation overseers continued to treat the more attractive women slaves as men had always treated women slaves, through all the centuries of recorded history and in all the countries of the known world. Though it has often been made to appear that this was some new form of cruelty springing from a deep well of racial hatred, it was, on the contrary, a very old one whose source was possessiveness. The eighteenth-century Southerner, however unattractive he may look from the viewpoint of the twentieth century, was simply a man of his time—a time that was still, except in a few areas of a few great cities, rough, ruthless, and wholly self-seeking.

* In the 1970s, the New York Board of Rabbis still barred from membership any rabbi who officiated at a mixed marriage, while even the reform-minded Central Conference of American Rabbis called on its members not to officiate at such events.

The modern WASP sometimes condemns his ancestors for not having known better. But, in terms of their time, there was no reason *why* they should have known better. The modern black sometimes condemns his ancestors for not having fought back. But, in terms of their time and situation, they *could* not have fought back.

The ban on intermarriage meant that where there was love, there was also resentment. It also reduced sexual contact to the level of client and prostitute, or rapist and victim. In the South, too, there was a clearcut racial equation: black skin = slavery, slavery = inferiority, therefore black skin = inferiority. It was not altogether surprising that when, in the nineteenth century, new "scientific" theories about race and new discoveries in biology set their baleful seal on the color prejudice that had gradually evolved out of cultural prejudice, many white Americans should have over-reacted.

NATURAL MORALITY

Of all the major candidate countries for imperial occupation, only China was to escape. By a series of historical accidents, in fact, China was to have a more immediate impact on the West than the West on China. The Confucian theory of "natural morality," though it suffered a sea change on the way, was to inspire new ideas in the influential French rationalists of the eighteenth century.

It was the Jesuits, Catholicism's most militant and cleverest apostles, who coincidentally supplied their irreligious contemporaries in the West with the materials of revelation. Evangelical fervor had fueled the Jesuits' long journey to China, and it was this that led them to present China to Europe in the most flattering *secular* light, for they recognized that the Confucianism by which the Ming and, after 1644, the Ch'ing (Manchu) dynasties ruled was not a religion at all but a moral code that might be reconciled with Christianity and so bring the whole vast empire into the Christian fold—if Rome was prepared to make a few concessions. Rome was not.

Although the Jesuits may in many ways have been over-sanguine, the social customs that Confucianism had imposed on

China did appear to have resemblances to those of the West, especially on a personal and domestic level. The position of Chinese women, for example, had been one of subordination rather than subjection while Taoism was strong, but when the Ming came to power in 1368 and adopted neo-Confucian principles female seclusion and full separation of the sexes began to be practiced in earnest. When the Portuguese missionary Gaspar da Cruz arrived in Canton in 1556, he reported that respectable ladies did not appear on the streets, but only "some light huswives and base women." [54] He (and others) thought that the reticence and submissiveness of Chinese women were in essence the same as had been shown in happier and more devout times by the women of the Christian West.

Matteo Ricci's description of marriage customs at the end of the sixteenth century might have applied just as well (with a few minor adjustments) to the continent of Europe as to China. "These people usually marry at an early age," he said. "Marriage contracts are arranged by the parents of both parties but without the consent of those to be married, though at times they may be consulted. Those who belong to the upper social classes marry within their class, and equal family rating within the class is required for legitimate marriage [this was true enough in Europe, too, though less as a matter of legality than of custom]. All men are free to have concubines [for Europe, read mistresses or prostitutes], and class or fortune means nothing in their selection, as the only standard of preference is physical beauty. . . . Among the lower classes wives are bought and sold for silver and as often as a man may wish." [55] Even that was not unknown in Europe until as late as the eighteenth century, though the authorities did not approve and the price was not always calculated in silver. One Scotsman is recorded as having bought another's wife for twopence a pound.[56]

But Ricci failed to identify the way in which China still differed fundamentally from the West, even if it was not to do so for much longer. This was in its attitude toward sexuality. What foreign observers saw was the inhibited neo-Confucian facade rather than the uninhibited Taoist attitudes that lay beneath. Talking about, making a display of sex was sinful because it was vulgar, for Confucianism was as much a code of manners as of morals; historically, Confucius himself has an excellent claim to be accounted the world's first true gentleman. But the practice of sex had spiritual as well as physical meaning, even when what the modern world calls "love" was absent, and it remained actively beneficial provided it was enjoyed in the seclusion of the bedchamber.

Taoist sex, however, was a cultivated pleasure whose benefits depended on stylish and stylized practices that, in turn, depended on knowledge—and it was during the Ming period that this knowledge began to disappear. The new Confucian bureaucracy did not regard sex as immoral, but it did regard sex manuals as such, and they were no longer given official tolerance. When the Taoist canon was printed in 1444-47, all references to sexual alchemy were expunged from it, and even before that the Buddhist canon had been bowdlerized of its Tantric sexual content.

A few new manuals continued to appear though they had very limited circulation. Based largely on the classics, they had little to add to what had first been said more than fifteen hundred years before. The *Admirable Discourses of the Plain Girl,* however, devoted a few not very helpful sentences to the matter of penis size and rigidity, sensibly condemning the excessive use of drugs as improvers, and concluding rather sanctimoniously that if the emotions of man and woman were in harmony and their spirits in communion, everything would be all right on the night. The *Plain Girl* also reminded readers that a woman whose vulva was located unusually near the front of her body was "suitable for cold winter nights. For a man can have intercourse with her under the embroidered coverlet of a square bed by lying on top of her." In the heat of summer, however, a woman whose vulva lay further back was to be preferred, "for a man can have intercourse with her sitting on a stone seat under a reed canopy, inserting his penis from the rear, while she is inclined before him with her knees bent." (This, it may be noted, was not the same as bringing the Flowering Branch to the Full Moon, which meant anal intercourse.)

By the beginning of the seventeenth century, even quite distinguished literary scholars were not only ignorant of the detail in the sex manuals but cynical about their value. Wang Chieh, for example, thought (from what little he had heard) that the practices they recommended were both dissolute and likely to damage a man's sexual performance. He had little patience with those who, believing that longevity and wisdom could be achieved through sex, looked for help to aphrodisiacs made from the genitals of animals whose sex drive was proverbial. "I have not yet," he remarked, "seen a lizard develop the elixir of life, or a beaver become an Immortal, or a seal ascend to heaven!"

More surprisingly, the authors of such famous erotic novels as the *Chin-p'ing-mei* seem to have been as ill-informed as the literati. Though they dealt, often in great detail, with all the usual sexual permutations—including fellatio ("playing the flute"), homosexuality, lesbianism, and anal intercourse—they did so in terms that would have been understood in any other country in the world, giving no place to what should have been a natural theme for the Chinese eroticist, intercourse as a means of strengthening a man's vital essence and prolonging his life.[57]

There was, however, one part of the country where the manuals retained their popularity until the very last days of the Ming, and that was in the prosperous area south of the Yangtse river where writers, artists, wealthy merchants, and retired imperial officials congregated, preferring a congenial freedom to the stiff and politically sensitive atmosphere of the capital, Peking. In Chiang-nan, as the region was then known, both gracious living and Ming culture reached their greatest heights. But Chiang-nan society in the last decades before the fall of the Ming had certain resemblances to French society in the last decades before the revolution. Elegance and polish had reached such perfection that the path of good taste appeared to have come to a dead end. The only place oversophisticated scholar-artists could find to go was into the gutter, and they plunged in with an abandoned and insalubrious splash. Poets turned to pornography, couched in back-alley slang and burdened with orgiastic detail, utilizing the great Taoist sex manuals in such a way that they appeared utterly obscene. The heroes and heroines of such works usually came to a tragic end, either through excessive consumption of aphrodisiacs or from simple exhaustion. But the sadism so characteristic of French pornographers even before the days of de Sade never really appeared in Chinese works; scatology—no more attractive but rather less lethal—was Chiang-nan's substitute.

As well as pornographic novels, the artistic community produced a new kind of erotic album consisting of illustrated poems. These were much less provocative than the novels, though not without sociological interest. Dr. Robert Van Gulik tabulated the sexual activities illustrated in a dozen of them—about 300 pictures in all.[58] They make an interesting comparision with the Moche pottery list given on page 298, above.

25 percent heterosexual intercourse, man-superior position with minor variations
20 percent woman-superior positions, with the woman sometimes facing toward the man's feet, sometimes his head
15 percent woman reclining with her legs raised and supported by a chair, bench or table, the man standing in front
10 percent woman kneeling for rear entry
10 percent heterosexual anal intercourse
5 percent man and woman lying side by side, facing
5 percent man and woman crouched close, or woman sitting on man's crossed legs, in a bathtub or on a cushion
5 percent cunnilingus
3 percent fellatio
1 percent less conventional positions—one man with two women; inverted or 69 position; woman rocking in a swing
1 percent lesbianism

About half the prints show the lovers only; in the other half there is an audience of women, one or more, who are probably intended to represent wives or concubines there to watch or assist.

When the Ming dynasty collapsed, it was the end of the sex manuals and the erotic albums—even, for a while, of the pornographic novels—for, as conquerors so often do, the Ch'ing dynasty imposed rigid controls and a rigid censorship. The controls encouraged the Chinese to do what they had earlier done under Mongol rule, to keep their private lives obsessively to themselves, and the censorship finally obliterated the sources of traditional knowledge about the variations and refinements of sex. As a result, though sex was never to become morally reprehensible in China as in the West, it tended to deteriorate into an uninstructed routine designed to fulfil the Confucian requirement for sons. It was not a sin, but the next-worst thing—a duty.

Yet although China relinquished the sexual mores of two

thousand years almost without realizing it, the Japanese—more volatile, more resistant to conformity—helped to perpetuate them, even if in a form that after eight centuries of naturalization was more Japanese than Chinese. Those few foreigners who visited the country between the sixteenth and nineteenth centuries were astonished to find how little the pleasure quarters of the major cities resembled the seedy entertainment districts of the West. Because the Japanese had no reason to be ashamed of visiting courtesans, and because the brothel quarter supplied the informal social intercourse that was denied elsewhere by strict class divisions and the subordination of women, it was bright, well regulated, animated, welcoming with its cherry trees, its paper lanterns, its atmosphere of relaxation. In the older cities of Kyoto and Osaka, the pleasure quarters were long established, and when the new military capital of Edo (now Tokyo) was being planned at the beginning of the seventeenth century the authorities wisely set an area aside expressly to house the courtesans. In 1657 this quarter was rebuilt on a new and larger site, where it remained until 1958, when all Japan's red light districts were closed down (mainly as a result of pressure from women's groups).

By the mid-eighteenth century, Edo's pleasure quarter (Yoshiwara) had become known as "The Nightless City," and was almost a self-contained town with its own theaters and tea houses, its own shops and tradesmen, its own festivals and customs, even its own fashionable dialect, and three thousand courtesans among its inhabitants—elegant creatures clad in rich and formal garments embroidered with gold and silver, intricately quilted, their flowery kimonos bound by elaborate sashes and their hair heavily burdened with ornaments and clasps. The would-be patron was expected to make an appointment through one of the tea houses that acted as booking agencies for courtesans and theaters alike, as well as being favorite meeting places and restaurants which supplied another kind of entertainment, that offered by the dancers, singers, and musicians known as *geisha*. (In Osaka and Kyoto they were *geiko*.)

Although the *geisha* was to gain a reputation in the West as a kind of delicate and exotic courtesan of the most refined type, she was in fact an intensively trained singer and dancer who resorted to prostitution only occasionally and in face of the deepest official disapproval. The *geisha* was not even necessarily female; there was still at least one male *geisha* performing in certain of the larger restaurants of Tokyo in the 1950s. Nor was the female *geisha* necessarily beautiful. It was musical talent that made a *geisha*, to the continuing disappointment of Western visitors brought up in the Madame Butterfly tradition.

The pleasure quarters of Kyoto, Osaka, and Edo were the "Floating World" that formed the inspiration not only for handbooks with such titles as *Forty-eight ways of having commerce with harlots*, but for distinguished writers and artists, providing men like Saikaku and Chikamatsu with plots, and Hokusai and Kunisada with images for the prints that were subsequently to have such a far-reaching influence on the style of the Impressionists. Japan today is remarkably, if often inconsistently, permissive in its attitude toward sex and eroticism, blacking out pubic hair in imported girlie magazines, yet showing strip shows on peak time television. With its warring heritage of Japanese, Chinese, and Western cultures, of Shinto, Taoist, Confucian, and Christian attitudes toward sex, it could hardly be otherwise.

The pleasure quarter of Kyoto in the seventeenth century

12.
Europe and America, 1550-1800

Was Elizabeth I of England—the Virgin Queen, Good Queen Bess—a feminist? If she had been, even as pugnacious a churchman as John Aylmer might have though twice about categorizing women in general as "wanton flippergibs," and the occasional good one as "an eel put in a bag amongst five hundred snakes," so that, even "if a man should have the luck to grope out the one eel from all the snakes, yet he hath at best but a wet eel by the tail." [1]

Fortunately for the bishop, Elizabeth, like the great majority of women who preceded her in the historical halls of fame, was very little interested in the condition or wellbeing of others of her sex. It was not simply that women in positions of power were too engrossed in playing a man's role in a man's world. Much more important was the fact that—with the exception of a handful of saintly psychotics like Joan of Arc—virtually every one of them owed her distinction to the accident of having been the daughter, wife, widow, or mistress of some great man. It was from this relationship that, in the eyes of others, they drew their authority, and to this relationship that, in their own minds, they looked for guidance. The great women of history, however distinguished they often became in their own right, were still essentially extensions of the great men of history.* They did not stand—quite—on their own feet.

---

* The cynical reader might be forgiven for wondering whether things have changed very much. Queen Elizabeth II (daughter), Queen Margrethe (daughter), Indira Gandhi (daughter), Sirimavo Bandaranaike (widow), Maria Estela Perón (widow). But it takes more than 300 years to overturn the traditions of 5,000, and at least Britain's Margaret Thatcher and the late Golda Meir of Israel made it on their own, while a great many other women have reached secondary levels of power.

Soon after the Elizabethan era ended at the beginning of the seventeenth century, however, things began to change in Europe, not as a result of any passionate new feminine awareness, but because of the complex interaction of a variety of social forces. Humanist philosophy and the first faint stirrings of rationalism both had something to do with it. So, too, had the wars and revolutions of the seventeenth and eighteenth centuries, many of them of the localized and oddly personal kind that have always offered the illusion of equality to everyone, man or woman, prepared to bear arms.* The fishwives who marched on Versailles in October 1789 experienced the same heady feeling of achievement as the *précieuses,* the bluestockings of a hundred years earlier when they turned their salons into centers of cultural and political influence. But although the *poissarde* and the *précieuse* were only remotely representative of the majority of women, it seems probable that neither could have fulfilled her public role if it had not been for the subtle changes that had begun to take place in society in the sixteenth century as a result of the Reformation, the Counter-reformation, and the increasing enterprise of the bourgeoisie.

PROTESTANT MARRIAGE

At first—and, indeed, for a long time—it looked as if the Reformation and the Counter-Reformation were about to undo all that the previous three centuries had achieved in the realm of man-woman relationships.

When the religious reformers of the early sixteenth century rebelled against the rule of the Pope, they went back—anxious to clear away the rubble of generations of theological debate—to the scriptures and found there a whole new view of life. High on the list of topics that engaged them were clerical celibacy and vows of continence, which they saw not only as badges of papal servitude but as a direct contravention of divine law. In the battle to justify marriage for the clergy, they coincidentally upgraded it for the

---

* As they still do. The girls of the Bader-Meinhoff gang are the direct descendants of women like Chai Ho-ku, the Triad leader of the 1850s, and of Ch'iu Erh and Su San-niang, viragos of the T'ai P'ing; those who fought in the FLN campaign in Algeria the spiritual great-granddaughters of the women of the Paris Commune.[2] History shows, however, that when the battle is over, so too, more often than not, is the equality.

laity as well. Not for the reformers the traditional Catholic view of wedlock as a necessary evil.

To Luther, virginity was undesirable, continence abnormal, and—stealing a 400-year march on Freud—chastity actively dangerous. Though he could not quite rid himself of the Augustinian view that sex was sinful, calling it "a medicine" and comparing it with a "hospital for the sick," he had no doubt that marriage was as necessary to the nature of man as eating and drinking.[3] Calvin, whose own sexual urges appear to have been less intense than Luther's, took a more constructive view, seeing woman not just as a child-bearer and a vessel for the relief of man's sexual desires, but as the inseparable associate of his whole life.

If marriage was so important, then it was clear to the reformers that a bad marriage was a disaster. The Catholic Church, when it had acquired jurisdiction in the matter in the twelfth century, had insisted that the contract was for life, a sacrament involving the grace of God, but when the reformers went back to the Bible they could find no justification for this view. Separation without remarriage was, admittedly, the only form of divorce that had been specifically sanctioned by Christ, but Luther chose to regard this as advisory, not mandatory. In his view, adultery automatically severed the matrimonial bond, and if a woman refused conjugal rights to her husband it could be construed as desertion. For one partner to prevent the other from leading a godly life also constituted grounds for divorce.

Since they did not see marriage as a sacrament, the reformers' general inclination was to return marital jurisdiction to the secular authorities, even if not completely. It remained the duty of the theologians to advise the civil power on the principles that should guide their judgments. Of the Protestant countries of Europe, England was to remain the odd one out until as late as 1857; Henry VIII's matrimonial adventures had involved the new Anglican Church, whose head he had declared himself to be, so deeply in manipulation of the divorce laws that there was no question of handing the matter over to the civil courts, in his day at least, and reform later went by default.

The other face of the reformers' enthusiasm for marriage was absolute and uncompromising disapproval of any kind of extramarital sexual activity. Where the Catholic Church's ambivalence about marriage had come to express itself in a certain leniency toward bachelors when they erred, the reformers said flatly: "There is no necessity that men must either debauch matrons or be fornicators; let them marry, for that is the remedy which God hath appointed." [4] But although marriage was the only acceptable outlet for sex, at least the reformers had progressed beyond the stage of regarding it primarily as a matter of procreation. Sex was permissible if it stemmed from "a desire for children, or to avoid fornication, or to lighten and ease the cares and sadnesses of household affairs, or to endear each other" [5]—a list which did, indeed, cover most eventualities. It also made mistresses and prostitutes superfluous. Said one seventeenth-century divine, it was worse for a whole city to be polluted with houses of ill fame than for a few honest wives and maidens to run the risk of violation, for such establishments, far from reducing the evil, created habits of lust and encouraged rather than prevented attacks upon virtuous women. [6] Luther himself opposed the reopening of brothels in Saxony, though when it came to closing some in Halle he turned jesuitical and advised against rushing it, in case it might do more harm than good. [7]

If the reformed religions had not swallowed their scriptural sources whole, they might have made a genuine contribution to the improvement in women's status that had begun in the late medieval period. But, ignoring the 2,000 years of social development that had passed since the Hebrew law books were written, they resurrected all-powerful fathers, "good wives," and subjugated children from the pages of history and placed the patriarchal household of the Old Testament squarely before their converts as a model for the devout. In effect, they upgraded the position of "wife" without upgrading the women who held it.

The results were interesting, and particularly interesting in America, where for a while it was possible to cultivate the reformed view of sex and marriage in almost laboratory conditions, uncontaminated by the old attitudes, the old habits of Catholic Europe.

THE PILGRIM PATRIARCHS

The Puritan view of the family was remarkably well suited to founding a new society under adverse conditions. The Jamestown

settlers had gone down before the assault of carelessness and con-
trariness, but the efficient, humorless, cantankerous Puritans of
New England prided themselves on their foresight and were prepared to go to extreme lengths to impose the discipline they knew
the circumstances demanded. Inevitably, they overdid it.

Their views were to a large extent partly conditioned by the
certainty that all God's creatures, even the Chosen, were born to
an inheritance of sin. They were as full of it "as a toad is of poison.
Thy heart," said the Reverend Thomas Shepard, preaching at
Cambridge, Massachusetts, "is a foul sink of all atheism, sodomy,
blasphemy, murder, whoredom, adultery, witchcraft, buggery [un-
accountably, he left out cannibalism and incest]; so that if thou
hast any good thing in thee, it is but as a drop of rose water in a
bowl of poison." [8] It was a heavy burden, and one that could not,
for Protestants, be shrugged off in the confessional. Thus it was
the duty of the strong-in-faith to help their weaker brethren—
whether they liked it or not—to fight temptation.

The fight began within the ruthlessly disciplined family, presided over by a father whose role was stand-in for Jehovah. Obedience, solidarity, and fruitfulness had all been enjoined on the
children of Israel, and these were the rocks on which Puritan families—and America itself—were built.

Right from the start, of course, there were problems. Although
the Fathers who sailed on the *Mayflower* had providently taken
their wives and children with them, 13 of the 18 wives died during
the first winter, and for several decades afterward men seriously
outnumbered women.

Where men were deprived of women, and where many women
were suspect, sexual sin was rife, and the Puritan assessment of
human weakness seemed to be justified. In the tradition of the
time, punishment was harsh. Fornicators were flogged, and then
had to make public confession in church; adulterers were similarly
treated, and sometimes branded as well; the pillory or the stocks
were the penalty for parents whose first child was born too soon
after the wedding day; an infant born on a Sunday was often
refused baptism because it was believed that it must have been
conceived on a Sunday. The weak-minded might be burned as
witches, or hanged—like the teenage servant, Thomas Granger of
Duxbury—for having carnally abused a mare, a cow, two goats, five
sheep, two calves, and a turkey. And a petty criminal, innocent for

once but harried beyond the bounds of reason, might be put to death because one piglet in a sow's litter had a human look about it, as well as "one eye blemished just like [his] . . . which occasioning him to be suspected, he confessed." 9

In a society where the word of the elders was law—and law in a way it had never been in Catholic Europe, where Church and state had never, quite, been one—sensible women stayed out of sight. But too many changes had taken place since the days of the first patriarchs for them to accept the role of cipher. Puritan morality had three direct effects on the American future. It produced a mental state of Victorianism fifty years before Victoria herself mounted the throne on the other side of the Atlantic. It taught American women how to control their menfolk by sickly-sweet virtue and purity that sometimes reached caricature proportions, while yet appearing to submit to them like good Old Testament wives. And it gave extraordinary importance to the concept of "the family."

The Puritans' fight to maintain their own dour moral standards was bound to be a losing one. But they were the firstcomers in effective, if not in factual terms, and they were forceful enough and bigoted enough, and possessed of a sense of self-preservation powerful enough to enable them to impose their ways on several generations of later colonists, even those of milder faith. For a long time they were assisted by the fact that new immigrants were predominantly Protestant. A traveler in 1700, making his way from Boston to the Carolinas, would have encountered assorted Congregationalists and Baptists, Presbyterians, Quakers, a variety of Puritan radicals, Dutch, German and French reformed church followers, Swedish, Finnish, and German Lutherans, Mennonites and radical pietists, Anglicans, a few Rosicrucians—and some Roman Catholics and a handful of Jews.10 Because of this, the Puritan ethic had a disproportionate influence on the whole future of the United States. Senators and Congressmen today, struggling (whatever the state of their faith and/or marital relationships) to project an image of dedicated family men, at work, at rest, at church, at play, owe this particular electoral hazard to the early New England settlers who wove the public demonstration of family solidarity into the American ethos. In no other country in the world is a politician expected to drag his wife and children onto the public podium with him.

THE   FAMILY   IN   EUROPE

The Puritans took themselves and their ideal of the family, as a kind of package deal, to America. But in Europe it was not so simple. Neither the family nor its members could be arbitrarily detached from the long tradition of Judeo-Catholic laws and customs.

Historians differ radically over the past history of the European family, especially in the medieval period. Some favor a quantitative approach to research, though their results, like the statistics on which they are based, are of debatable value. Computer analysis of household listings and parish registers from one hundred widely divergent English communities over a period of three hundred years has produced a mean figure of 4.75 persons (plus one servant) per household [11]—which is as illuminating as saying that the average height of 50 seven-foot giants and 50 four-foot pygmies is five feet six inches. Other sources, in fact, make it clear that there were a good many households consisting of single women or widows, and that somewhere between the peasant cottage, with its parents and children, and the great houses of the nobility with their vast concourse of relatives, near and distant, all with their own servants and retainers, there lay a substantial number of homes accommodating father, mother, and children, as well as younger brothers and sisters of the parents, orphaned nephews and nieces, and perhaps a widowed cousin or two.

Recently, one English scholar has identified three separate stages in the development of the family from the fourteenth century until today.[12] First there was the extended medieval family, with little privacy, little opportunity for establishing close personal ties (even between husband and wife), and limited scope for individualism; its members shared their lives, their table, and their beds.* In about 1550, however as the structure of society changed and the merchant classes gained in independence and self-assurance, this untidy and unbusinesslike arrangement gave way to a more authoritarian, smaller unit, with fewer temporary members. The result might have been a greater feeling of stability for those

---

* It seems likely that the practice of bundling, common until the later days of the eighteenth century in America and parts of Europe, in which betrothed or about-to-be-betrothed young couples retired to do their courting—fully clothed—in bed, may have been a survival from this period.

In the satirists' view, the husband was not always the master. Prints on the theme of "who wears the pants?" (shown here lying on the floor) were commonplace in the fifteenth and sixteenth centuries.

who remained, but the conditions were not right. The mortality rate in the sixteenth century remained high, and life expectancy was no greater than it had been long ago in the paleolithic era. The average age at death was between 25 and 30. A child might have two or three stepmothers *and* stepfathers between birth and adulthood; a young woman could be twice married and twice widowed before she reached the age of 20.

By the mid-seventeenth century, however, the situation was beginning to improve. A moderately affluent Englishwoman could now expect to live to 32, and the upward gradient was maintained until, by the end of the eighteenth century when the plague had disappeared, she might survive to almost 50.[13] At the time, of course, no one thought in such crudely specific terms, but there was a general slackening in the awareness of mortality, a fading of the Dance of Death nightmare that had thrown its tarnishing shadow over the bright Renaissance dream.

Apt—apparently—to the moment, in about 1640 a third type of family began to develop, characterized in its later days by a new warmth, a new emotional stability, and a new individualism; the nuclear family consisting of only parents and children. With equally neat timing, there was a sharp drop in the bastardy rate that seemed to confirm the emotional solidarity of the new, tightly-knit family unit. If this had been confined to England, it might have been attributable to the Cromwellian revolution, but the figures were unnaturally low in France, too, and did not begin to rise again until the second quarter of the eighteenth century.[14]

It seems that what may well have happened was that all Europe was subtly influenced by the religious upheavals of the sixteenth century, so that the whole of society, and particularly the family, was afflicted by a kind of nervous defensiveness that led it to withdraw into itself, just as the Chinese did under the Mongols and, later, the Ch'ing.

Despite the disreputable courts of, notably, Charles II and (until Madame de Maintenon took the matter in hand) Louis XIV, despite even the fact that Don Juan first saw the light of day in 1630—in Molina's play *El Burlador de Sevilla y el Convivado de Piedra*—and the Earl of Rochester published poems and plays that would bring a blush even to the cheek of the 1980s, Europe at this time was in many ways remarkably straitlaced. Its arbitrary violence and the sometimes unattractive frankness of its language were legacies from earlier centuries, but the habits of people outside court circles were showing the effect of the Reformation itself and the Catholic Counter-Reformation, which had attempted to restore severity to rulings softened by carelessness, custom, and the dictates of humanity.

At the twenty-fourth session of the Council of Trent (which sat, off and on, from 1545 until 1564), the Church of Rome restated the sacramental nature of marriage, introduced new requirements of parental consent to marriage and the publication of banns, announced that clerical celibacy would in future be enforced, that virginity was still a more blessed state than marriage, and that paintings calculated to excite lust would henceforth be frowned upon—which put an effective, if temporary stop to Italian artists' preoccupation with the erotic nude. (Overreacting, Pope Paul IV ordered the naked and tortured figures of Michaelangelo's *Last Judgment* in the Sistine Chapel to be modestly shrouded in loincloths and robes.)

What very gradually percolated down to the great mass of worshipers, of course, was not the doctrinal detail but the buzzing atmosphere of religious frenzy, which, in days when the memory of Protestants drowning Anabaptists and Catholics massacring Huguenots was only too fresh, was enough to pin any sensible man to the straight and narrow path of conventional morality, social and sexual. He seems to have stuck to it for almost a hundred years, until long after the theologians had cooled down again.

But whatever the reason for the development of the new, small, tightly-knit family, it was not simply a question of longer life expectancy offering the prospect of a longer and more settled marriage. For what, in fact, happened was that as life expectancy increased so also did the average age at marriage. One development canceled out the other.

Later marriage appears to have grown out of necessity. Formerly, the nobleman's eldest son, his heritage not in doubt, could marry when he liked, or when a suitable heiress presented herself. Second and subsequent sons, forever dependent on their brother's generosity, were equally free. The peasant, in contrast, married when his feudal landlord permitted. But the young men of the new merchant class, like the plebs of Rome so long before, had to postpone marriage until they could afford it. By the seventeenth century they were postponing it until they were at least 25 or even 30, and some postponed it permanently. In medieval times, only five per cent of Europe's population had remained single; now, the figure was nearer 15 per cent. A more far-reaching development, however, was that men now looked for wives not, as in the past, ten or 20 years younger than themselves but in their own age group. As man's average age at marriage rose, so did woman's. In America, with its shortage of women and unique population problems, 16 to 18 remained the rule, but statistics from eighteenth-century Venice, the Netherlands, Bavaria, France, and elsewhere in Europe show that most women did not become wives until they were in their mid-twenties.[15]

The probability is that practical and hardworking husbands had problems enough without adding emotionally immature wives to them. When a self-made man married—and not only a self-made man, for middle-class customs filtered both up and down— he wanted an efficient housekeeper, a rational partner, an unpaid concubine, and a competent mother for his children. Love still had very little to do with marriage, but in such a relationship there was new scope for a kind of mutual dependence and placid affection.

From the woman's point of view the change was revolutionary. Marriage, like any other close relationship, involves a continuing interaction between personalities in which the stronger may not always dominate, but always distorts, the weaker. A mature husband can scarcely avoid imposing his own attitudes, opinions, and desires on a wife still too young to have discovered her own identity. But when women began to marry later, fully adult and possessed of a sense of individuality, when their husbands no longer spoke from some Olympian platform of age and experience, the whole ambience of married life began to change. Unless she was by nature mild and suggestible, a wife became less easy to force into the mold of her husband's choice and rather less uncritical in what she passed on to her children. Some marriages may have been the worse for it, but marriage as an institution was probably better—and so, undoubtedly, was woman's image of herself.

NATURAL MORALITY—EUROPEAN STYLE

The rising age at marriage and the longer period of premarital chastity (however nominal) had their inevitable result, particularly since the latter stages of the change coincided with "the age of enlightenment," that eighteenth-century era of skepticism, gaiety, license, and rational inquiry. Ironically, the early philosophers of the period found their model in Jesuit writings about China and were particularly impressed by Confucian principles, which they misinterpreted with the greatest innocence and enthusiasm. "Action in harmony with the human spirit and natural morality" sounded just like what they were looking for, and if "natural morality" meant, to them, an extremely un-Confucian relaxation of discipline, a *carte blanche* for self-expression, it was perhaps a pardonable error.

Since most philosophers were men, their definition of what constituted "natural" in the sexual field was predictable enough. Rousseau, neatly compromising between chauvinism and commiseration, said that "woman was made to yield to man and to put up with his injustice," [16] and the illegitimacy statistics of the eighteenth century suggest that this view was widely shared.

A great many illegitimate births, of course, went unrecorded, but there is a useful series of records in the municipal archives of the French seaport of Nantes—kept, as in a number of other cities, for the practical purpose of establishing the name of the father so that he could be charged with the hospital lying-in costs.[17] At the beginning of the eighteenth century only three per cent of the children born in Nantes were illegitimate; by the end, the figure had risen to ten percent.*

This does not necessarily mean that extramarital activity had increased in the same proportion. It seems likely that men may have become more careless. During the course of the century, society became more mobile, and the French farmworker, for example, gradually began to spend a large part of the year away from home looking for work. His sex life would often consist of casual encounters, in which he felt no need to exercise the care that would have been necessary with a girl in his own village.

On the other hand, it was in the eighteenth century that the condom began to come into use as a contraceptive. It was the great Italian anatomist, Fallopius, who claimed to have invented it—though as a protection against syphilis, not conception. In a work published in 1564, two years after his death, he explained how the uncircumcised could guard against infection by fitting a small linen sheath over the glans, and then drawing the foreskin over it. By the eighteenth century, condoms—still advocated as an armor against syphilis, but beginning to be used (as Casanova said) "to put the fair sex under shelter from all fear"—were made usually from sheep gut, sometimes from fish skin, and were stocked and sold in brothels as well as by a few specialist wholesalers such as London's Mrs. Philips, who was prepared to supply "apothecaries, chymists, druggists etc" as well as "ambassadors, foreigners, gentlemen, and captains of ships &c going abroad."[18]

It is imponderables like these that make statistics difficult to interpret, but on some points the Nantes figures are unequivocal. There, at least, the footloose farmworker was not the most prolific begetter of illegitimate children. Sailors came much higher on the list. So, in the early part of the century, did respectable householders; more than half the unmarried mothers who, between 1726 and 1736, gave their occupation as domestic servant named

---

* Interestingly, in the English seaport of Dover 200 years later, in 1975 and the era of the Pill, 9.19 per cent of all births were illegitimate.

Despite the statistics, French artists persevered with idealized representations of family life among the poor.

their employer as father. Later, however, gentlemen and merchants, lawyers and shopkeepers alike all began to prefer the semi-official mistress, safely segregated from the family in a rented room or apartment. This trend (and the expression "kept woman") came into being after 1750, and by the 1780s only nine per cent of the Nantes maidservants who became pregnant blamed their employers for it. When Beaumarchais wrote *La folle journée, ou le mariage de Figaro* in 1784, he intended it as an attack on the rich man who seduced his innocent servant, but, as satirists so frequently are, he was already behind the times.

Nantes was probably representative of a good many cities in Europe, though not of the great capitals, which had a life of their own. Because of the sheer complexity of Paris and the bird-of-passage atmosphere of so many of its *arrondissements*, it is impossible to draw parallels. But in a slightly different area of the subject, some of the figures noted by men like Buffon are enough to suggest a striking level of social instability. In 1745 there were 3,233 children abandoned to foundling homes; by 1766 the number had risen to 5,604. In 1772, roughly 40 per cent of the children born in Paris were forsaken in this way—7,676 out of a total of 18,713.[19] Not all illegitimate children finished up in foundling homes, of course, and not all children who finished up in foundling homes were, except in the most exact legal sense, illegitimate. Thérèse Le Vasseur, for example, who lived with Jean-Jacques Rousseau for many years, bore him five children whom he was convinced he would never be able to provide for; refusing even to set eyes on them, he had all five deposited in a home. Most of the foundlings, however, were the children of unmarried mothers, or of poor parents who could not afford to care for them, or of the increasing number of couples among the artisan classes who chose to live together temporarily, without benefit of clergy, and had no wish to be burdened with the products of their union. But even at a time when children were considered as much a bane as a blessing, the number of the unwanted was dangerously high, an indicator not only of the urgent need for effective contraceptive knowledge but of a rootlessness and resentful poverty that were to help bring about the revolution of 1789.

THE DIVINE MARQUIS

If the court at Versailles had been France in microcosm, the eighteenth century might (just) have merited the title so often given to it of "the century of the woman." Madame de Pompadour, the Dubarry, and Marie Antoinette certainly set a cracking pace, although this scarcely begins to explain why, in the last decades before the deluge, even the toughest of men should have succumbed to the prevailing feminine mode of paint and powder, satins, silks, jewels, and manners as exquisite as they were hollow. It was not the peacocking that was new—men had gone broidered and gemmed for at least three centuries—but the theatrical superficiality. The fashionable world was a stage, and all the men and women merely players; the fashionable plot a libertine love affair with strongly narcissistic undertones.

Libertinism was a game for the idle and a game very much like the love-desire of the early Abbasid caliphs (see pages 235-36), except that the lady was as often a noblewoman as a dancing girl. An *affaire* had four stages—selection, seduction, subjection, and separation—and although second-rate *roués* like Casanova might regard the third as the sweetest, the real sophisticate knew that the point of high drama came with the final rupture, the moment of cruel truth.

There was a calculated viciousness about the love game that comes through clearly in the literature of the period, written, most of it, by men who did not belong to court circles but had some opportunity to observe them. The genre that was to culminate in the novels of the Marquis de Sade, the Provençal nobleman who gave his name to the sexual perversion known as sadism, had in fact begun in England in 1747-8 with Samuel Richardson's *Clarissa, Or the History of a Young Lady*, a moral tale in epistolary form that traced its heroine's progression, downhill all the way through seven volumes, from seduction to disorderly house to debtors' prison to deathbed. England was the home of the Gothic-horror school, still young in Richardson's day but already characterized by melancholy ruins, moldering caverns, and brooding silences broken only by the cry of the lone screech owl, and *Clarissa* struck exactly the right gruesome note. At one stage, she dreams that her cruel lover carries her into a churchyard and there "stabs her to the heart, and then tumbles her into a deep grave ready dug, among two or three half-dissolved carcases; throwing in the dirt and earth upon her with his hands, and trampling it down with his feet." [20]

Richardson's tale of the persecuted innocent proved enormously successful, not only in England but in France, where it inspired a number of imitators. Diderot owed something of *La Religieuse* to it, and so did Rousseau's *La Nouvelle Héloïse*. So, too, did one of the handful of really great eighteenth century novels, *Les Liaisons Dangereuses* by Choderlos de Laclos, whose characters—Valmont, the perfidious Don Juan figure; Madame de Merteuil, the witty, malicious courtesan; vain, silly Cecile; and spineless Danceny—were not merely pegs on which to hang a dubious moral, but real people observed with rare psychological insight.

All these novels were works of extreme sensuality, largely concerned with the torture, physical or mental, of innocent girls, and perfunctorily justified by the argument that virtue triumphed in the end, even if only in the last paragraph, and even if only in the heroine's ascent to heaven clad all in white and accompanied by massed choirs of angels.[21] Most of the authors, with the exception of Laclos, wrote frankly for money, and the genre would not have survived if there had been no audience for it. But although the cynical morality of Versailles might suggest that the court formed the main market—such books having a special appeal for men whose public role was one of enforced deference to the ladies—this was not the case. When the Marquis de Sade (anonymously) published his first novel *Justine, ou les malheurs de la vertu* in 1791, court circles had more urgent matters to attend to, and by the time of *Juliette, ou les prospérités du vice* (1796) they had disappeared altogether. But de Sade's success was great. Rétif de la Bretonne, who was admittedly prejudiced, claimed of *Justine* that the revolutionary leader Danton "read it for kicks," [22] and it seems likely that the bourgeoisie enjoyed the more degenerate specimens of the *littérature galante* as much for the illicit sexual excitement they offered as for their exposure of the depravity of the *ancien régime*.

De Sade, in fact, had spent most of the years between 1777 and 1790 in prison for half-poisoning a number of prostitutes by giving them a dangerous overdose of the aphrodisiac *cantharides* (Spanish fly), and much of what remained of his life was also passed behind bars, first in a variety of prisons and then in a lunatic asylum. But he made up for what he lacked—first-hand experience, literary style, wit, judgment—with the kind of imagination that was capable of writing a novel specifically designed to illustrate every conceivable form of sexual perversion and, particularly, the pleasure to be derived from the infliction of physical suffering. The persecuted maiden had never been as thoroughly persecuted in all the long centuries of her literary and mythological existence as she was by de Sade. The unfortunate Justine was tied down, spreadeagled, for bloodhounds to savage; she took refuge with a surgeon, who tried to vivisect her; she fell into the clutches of a saber-happy mass murderer; and was finally released from the vale of tears by a thunderbolt sent down by Nature, justifiably weary of her incorrigible virtue. The general scenario (minus the virtue) is familiar enough in the late twentieth century, but in the 1790s it was something new—not just in the extremist quality of its violence, but in de Sade's justification of it.

He was a staunch believer in the "natural harmony" that the rationalists had adapted from Confucianism a few decades earlier, and, like Diderot and others, used it to justify the brutal "realism" of his work. Writing of Gilles de Rais and others of his kind, he said: "Fools object .to me that these men were monsters. Yes, according to our customs and our way of thinking; but . . . they were only instruments of [Nature's] designs; it was to fulfill her laws that she endowed them with characters both barbarous and bloody." [23] Where he departed irrevocably from his predecessors was in his stated conviction that the world was evil, not good, and that to conform with natural harmony meant practicing vice, not virtue. It was certainly a convenient theory, for in the light of it de Sade's novels became perfectly (if nastily) logical. Virtue led to misery and ruin, vice to prosperity, and there was no need to ruin the plot with a traditional happy ending.

Justine was banned in France in 1814, the year of de Sade's death, and *Juliette* a year later. One almost inevitable result was that the Divine Marquis (as he came defiantly to be called) gained a much stronger hold over the minds of later French and Francophile writers than his dull and repetitive style warranted. Romantics, Decadents, Surrealists all admitted his influence; Baudelaire, Lamartine, Swinburne, D'Annunzio, Nietzsche, Cocteau, all admired him. Whether this was because the bloodied horrors of his imagination fed some private need in themselves, or whether it was because he had emptied a metaphorical slop-bucket over the outraged head of bourgeois respectability, has never been entirely clear.

SEMINAL THEORIES

Where the sixteenth and seventeenth centuries had been a period of physical adventure, the eighteenth sizzled with intellectual activity, and one of the things it discovered was the answer to the 10,000-year-old question of *how* sexual intercourse produced children. Curiously enough, despite the fact that even the most unobservant must have recognized, during the span of more than 400 generations, that children as often resembled their mothers as their fathers, it had always been believed that woman's contribution to the reproductive process was minimal.

In the Western world, it was the Greeks who first propounded the theory that man's seminal fluid was the essential element in procreation and that woman was only an incubator. Aristotle, in the fourth century B.C., thought the fluid was a kind of soul-substance * that blended with woman's menstrual blood to produce the living child. He compared the process with that of turning milk into cheese. "Here, the milk is the body [the material element], and the fig juice or the rennet [the seminal fluid] contains the principle which causes it to set." Galen, 500 years later, said there was no difference between sowing the womb, and sowing the earth, and his Christian contemporary, Clement of Alexandria, defined seminal fluid as something that was almost, or about-to-become man.[25] Between them, they put a high philosophical premium on semen, and Clement's view, in particular, helps to explain why the Church regarded it in an almost mystical light, so that expending it for any purpose other than procreation was a sin in its own right as well as in the more general context of permissible and impermissible sex.

If semen was almost-man, then it was directly related to God, which would have made it blasphemous for a Christian to quibble about its quality. Things were different in Asia. The Chinese, more realistic despite the abstract nature of Taoist thought, made a positive effort to improve it by means of regular infusions of *yin* (see page 170). But it was the Hindus, closely followed by the Arabs, who gave serious attention to quality control.

As recently as 1950, an unusually well-qualified psychologist interviewed a number of high-caste Hindus in a village near Udaipur and discovered what they knew about semen. He learned that it was not easily formed. To make a single drop took 40 drops of blood and 40 days, though the process might be hastened by careful attention to diet—milk, butter, wheat flour, rice and fine sugar (all expensive foods, it may be noted), were good, while maize, coarse sugar and spices were to be avoided. The man who claimed to be the village's champion sexual athlete recommended raw eggs and honey beaten in milk.** Good-quality semen was like rich creamy milk, and a satisfactory store of it was a guarantee of health and wellbeing, any surplus being stockpiled in

---

* The idea of the soul having an almost-tangible, almost-visible reality was common in the ancient world; sometimes it was thought of as an essence, sometimes as the "breath of life," sometimes as an unseen shadow.[24]

** The Arabs held much the same view. *The Perfumed Garden* recommended honey, eggs, meat, and fine sweetmeats, but did not mention milk, for the Arabs, having few cows (sacred or otherwise) relied mainly on sheep's milk and did not hold it in very high esteem.[26]

An electric alarm to warn of nocturnal emissions. Expensive

Cheaper. A spiked ring, to warn the sleeper of imminent erection

Cheaper still. Distinctly tinny in quality

a reservoir in the head which had a capacity of just under seven ounces.[27]

It all sounds charmingly naive, but it was, of course, nothing of the sort. The Hindus equated sexual activity and seminal potency with a general level of good health, and, in a country where people regularly died by the millions of starvation, it would have been very strange indeed if they had not emphasized the importance of diet. They also recognized quite specifically (as the Chinese did by implication, and the Western world did not) that after an ejaculation it takes some time for seminal potency, as distinct from seminal fluid, to build up again; modern research suggests about 40 hours.[28] And though the idea of a reservoir in the head may appear quaint, it is perfectly logical in the context of the "subtle body" system of Tantric belief (see page 226).

But however much the inhabitants of the great Eurasian landmass might diverge on detail, they were unanimous in the belief that semen should never be carelessly expended. The Chinese thought it weakening on all levels; Indians knew supplies were limited; and the West, true to its hellfire tradition and its exaggerated respect for the dignity of almost-man, held that wastefulness

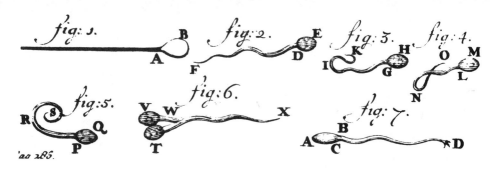

Animalcules; "an infinity of animals like tadpoles"

would result in every imaginable kind of physical retribution. "Wastefulness" covered homosexuality, masturbation—an appalling sin in Victorian times—and coitus more than once a week. Sinibaldi, the Italian who in 1642 produced the first of Europe's standard works on sexuality, the *Geneanthropeia* (translated in 1658 into English, somewhat bowdlerized, as *Rare Verities, the Cabinet of Venus Unlock'd*), threatened gout, constipation, a hunched back, bad breath, and a red nose. Two hundred years later, it was revealed in a vision to Ellen White, founder of the Seventh Day Adventists, that masturbation would turn a man into a cripple and an imbecile. And for more than 50 years after that, the medical profession consistently promised masturbators the reward of blindness and/or epilepsy, and, on a more grandiose note, complete moral and physical bankruptcy for the overactive Casanova.

From the days of Aristotle until the seventeenth century, there was no doubt in any Western mind that semen was the active ingredient in conception (which was true enough, though not quite in the Aristotelian sense). At the beginning of the Christian era, the Alexandrians had discovered the ovaries, but took them to be an unimportant feminine version of the testes, producing a derisory quantity of sluggish seminal fluid that could be compared neither in virtue nor vigor with the male product. One sixteenth-century Spanish anatomist included this information in his *Story of the human body* only with the greatest reluctance, hoping that "women might not become all the more arrogant for knowing that they also, like men, have testicles." [29] But in the seventeenth century came the microscope.

First, in 1672, the young Dutch surgeon Regnier de Graaf discovered the egg, the ovum, and realized that it traveled from the ovary to the womb. But what started it moving? He decided it must be the *aura seminalis*, the pungent vapor from the male

The minuscule human beings that were visible (to the eye of faith) in spermatozoa under the microscope.

seminal fluid. Three years later, Antony van Leeuwenhoeck put some seminal fluid under the microscope and discovered it was alive with miniature tadpole-like creatures, which he christened animalcules.

Decades of argument followed. De Graaf's followers (the ovists) argued that the egg contained a tiny model of the parent, just waiting to be developed. Van Leeuwenhoeck's followers (the spermists) had the same idea—only they located the model in the head of the sperm. If either was right, of course, it meant that neither parent was more than an instrument of predestination. According to the "box theory," if the germinal particle (egg or sperm) contained a preformed human—complete, as Leibniz pointed out, with its soul and its allocation of Original Sin—then each little preformed human must also contain within it another of the same, which must contain another, and another—and so on, *ad infinitum*. The whole future human race packed into a series of Chinese boxes.

The air became thick with theories of reproduction, but none of them accommodated the possibility of both parents contributing substantially to the physical and intellectual heredity of the child. They did, however, encourage many scientists in the diligent pursuit of microscopic research, with useful results over a wide spectrum—including proof that the Church had been right about the Virgin Birth. A virgin greenfly was discovered to be capable of producing nine young in a day by her own unaided efforts, and if a greenfly could do it . . .

By the middle of the eighteenth century, botanists had proved (genuinely) that plants, at least, owed something to both parents, while the ovist-spermist controversy, if it had done nothing else, had cast serious doubts on the old belief that reproduction was a purely seminal miracle. Some scientists, committed to neither side, even began to look at half-castes and recognize that it was more than mere coincidence that black + black = black, and white + white = white, but black + white = khaki. Gradually it came to be accepted that a child derived its characteristics as much from its mother as its father, but it was not until 1854 that anyone succeeded in observing the fusion of sperm and egg that proved the truth of the matter—and even then it was not human sperm and egg, but those of the frog.[30]

The discovery of woman's enhanced role had some unexpected

side effects. During the first half of the nineteenth century, a new doctrine of racial superiority was evolved, based on unsound history and specious biology but swift to gain currency, particularly in Germany, where anti-Semitism was in full flood, and America, where the abolition of slavery was a major issue. Joseph Arthur, Comte de Gobineau, set it out—at length—in the 1850s in his *Essai sur l'inégalité des races humaines,* and Darwin's *The Origin of Species,* in 1859, appeared to confirm that some races might indeed be superior as a result of natural selection. The combination of this belief with the fact that children were now known to inherit characteristics from both parents meant that mixed marriages became a matter of serious concern and theorists on both sides of the Atlantic busied themselves proving that cross-breeding infallibly resulted in deterioration of the superior strain. The word "miscegenation" first reared its unappealing—and philologically confused—head in 1864, in a Democratic dirty-tricks booklet entitled *Miscegenation: the Theory of the Blending of the Races, applied to the American White Man and Negro.*

Fortunately, there were other effects. If God had endowed women with the right to contribute to their child's heritage, they *could* not be as unequal as men had always thought.

PART FIVE

Shaping the present,
1800-1980

The Victorian resurrection of courtly love was largely responsible for transforming middle-class ladies into sweet, untouch-
able guardians of morality, whose distaste for sex led to an
explosive increase in prostitution, an epidemic spread of venereal disease, and a morbid taste for masochism. The ladies,
dismayed by the evidence of vice and intemperance of which
they heard even in their ivory towers, decided that only they,
pure and moral, could set society to rights. They demanded
and ultimately won the right to vote. In the meantime, another struggle was in progress, one that aimed at spreading
contraceptive knowledge; it was seriously hampered by the
morality lobby's belief that the only sanctified form of contraception was abstention. The artificial ideal of the Victorian family was sustained until well into the twentieth
century, most influentially by Hollywood rather than the
Church, but the published researches of Kinsey and others,
increasing familiarity with psychoanalytic theory, and simple
economic reality ultimately helped to undermine it. Even so,
it still survives, despite the revulsion against traditional relationships expressed in Women's Liberation, Gay Liberation,
and the free sex movement, and despite the fact that, in legal
terms, the sexes have in many countries been brought almost
into equilibrium. In social terms there still remains some
way to go.

13.

The Nineteenth Century

Though it may sometimes seem as if the nineteenth century could scarcely have existed without the stout little lady in black bombazine who presided over so much of it, Victorianism was a phenomenon that was unique neither to the nineteenth century nor to the British Empire. Even China suffered from its own particular brand—stimulated as much by fear of Western imperialism as by neo-Confucian prudery—while in both America and Germany it began earlier than it did in Britain, in the first case partly as a product of Puritanism, and in the second as a response to the political disruptions and new aspirations of the eighteenth century. Somewhat later, France, struggling through the sixty years of crisis that preceded 1848 (and with more to come), looked for private ideals to compensate for political betrayals, and in Britain the new and self-conscious middle classes, criticized by their betters for vulgar commercialism, thriftily blended old philosophies with new intellectual fashions into a system of morals and manners that suited their social ambitions.

Because there was a steady cultural commerce between Europe and America, it was natural enough for the new attitudes to take a similar form, and someone, some day, will perhaps succeed in explaining why they took the form they did—why the elegant neo-Classical style of the eighteenth century, counterpointed by frivolous fancies for *chinoiserie* and Gothick, should have given way in the nineteenth to a starched pomposity that found its light relief in the raging melodrama of the Romantic movement, in which anything exotic (and especially anything to do with the Middle Ages) was like caviar to the gourmet. "Serious" Gothic, quite different from the artificial Gothick of a few decades earlier, was most aggressively visible in literature and architecture and later cast its ornate pall over every aspect of design and decoration, but it had much farther-reaching effects than that. When the frockcoated and increasingly bewhiskered gentlemen of the Victorian era, in the grip of this strange medieval nostalgia, cultivated the stilted and excessive courtesy toward "the ladies" that they fondly believed reflected the chivalric ideal, they also—though without malice aforethought—reduced them once more to the status of spectators at the tournament of life. What Harriet Martineau said of American men in the 1830s was equally true of Europeans—they gave women indulgence as a substitute for justice.[1] And regrettably, women encouraged them, finding it pleasant to be worshiped, cherished, and deferred to, flattering to be considered vulnerable, virginal, and remote; pure angels to whom a man might turn for respite from the rough, cruel world of business realities.*

It was a game that two could play, and wives were urged to reciprocate by treating their husbands as a cross between God and Sir Galahad. As Mrs. Sarah Ellis said in a book addressed to the women of England in 1842, it was essential to recognize "the superiority of your husband simply as a man. . . . In the character of a noble, enlightened, and truly good man, there is a power and a sublimity so nearly approaching what we believe to be the nature and capacity of angels, that . . . no language can describe the degree of admiration and respect which the contemplation of such a character must excite. . . . To be admitted to his heart—to share his counsels, and to be the chosen companion of his joys and sorrows!—it is difficult to say whether humility or gratitude should preponderate in the feelings of the woman thus distinguished and thus blest." But the plush of Mrs. Ellis's prose concealed a spiky little aside that would seriously have displeased her predecessors—

---

* It was an attitude that developed a sharp twist in twentieth-century Germany. Hitler, captivated by the view of man as the Teutonic knight and woman as Gretchen at the spinning wheel, ensured that the maternal type of woman was better treated by government than in any other country, while making every attempt to block the employment of career women. Women themselves showed a sacrificial willingness to be Gretchens, and to bear children, as instructed, for the glory of the Reich.

the Book of Proverbs, Ischomachus, the Lady Pan Chao, Saint Jerome *et al.* For although she made it clear that male superiority was part of the natural order of things, she added that this was so *in spite of* the fact that a wife might have "more talent, with higher attainments" than her husband.[2]

WOMAN'S PLACE

Times were undoubtedly changing, but woman's place was to become worse before it became better. Social pressures reinforced life's tendency to imitate art.

Before the Industrial Revolution, the history of Europe had featured the Aristocracy versus The Rest, but now the middle classes began to replace the aristocracy in the structure of power. Economic success, however, was meaningless without social success, and the nineteenth century became obsessed by its upward struggle on the ladder of gentility. In America the struggle was lateral rather than vertical; everyone was equal, but everyone aimed to be more equal than everyone else.

One index of success was that the mistress of the house should have servants to do everything for her, and the triumph of the middle classes is vividly illustrated by the relevant employment statistics. Of the 16 million male and female inhabitants of England and Wales recorded by the 1841 census, just under a million were in domestic service. Ten years later, of the three million women and girls aged ten or over who worked for a living, 751,641 (one in four) were domestic servants. By 1871, the figure had risen to 1,204,477, showing a rate of increase double that of the population as a whole. Throughout the nineteenth century, and indeed until 1914, domestic service was the largest single employment for Englishwomen, and the second largest overall.[3]

The middle-class wife who had been freed from household drudgery was ill-equipped to deal with her leisure. She and her husband both believed—and the books of etiquette that flooded the market confirmed it—that she was living like a lady, but they were wrong. Ancestry apart, there was one essential difference between the middle-class wife and her nobly-born predecessor. Lady This and the Countess of That had made positive, if often frivolous, use of their leisure, enjoying a varied life that was possible largely because their husbands or lovers were free to escort them wherever they wished to go. Middle-class husbands, however, were tied to their place of work, and their wives and daughters were left to their own devices. Some filled the time with good works, but the majority drifted through their days shopping, gossiping, idling, and cultivating ladylike manners.

In *Women in America*, in 1842, Mrs. A. J. Graves commented on the women who, "in their ambition to be considered ladies, use their fair hands only in playing with their ringlets, or touching the piano or guitar," and in the same year Mrs. Ellis, in *The Women of England*, complained that "the number of languid, listless, and inert young ladies who now recline upon our sofas, murmuring and repining at every claim upon their personal exertions, is to me a truly melancholy spectacle." But where fashion and etiquette— "the barrier which Society draws round itself, a shield against the intrusion of the impertinent, the improper, and the vulgar" [4]— conspired to make women idle, idleness itself developed into a kind of disease that undermined both physical and nervous health; by no means all the Victorian ladies who relapsed into a picturesque decline did so merely for the sake of being interesting.

The husbands of these wilting creatures helped to exacerbate the situation by protecting them from any kind of harsh reality. Even in America, said James Fenimore Cooper in 1828, the genteel wife lived "retired within the sacred precincts of her own abode . . . preserved from the destroying taint of excessive intercourse in the world." A dozen years later, a London court of law confirmed that a husband was justified even in kidnapping a refugee wife (whose morals were admitted to be impeccable) and keeping her under lock and key because "the happiness and honour of both parties place the wife under the guardianship of the husband and entitle him . . . to protect her from the danger of unrestrained intercourse with the world, by enforcing cohabitation and a common residence." [5]

It was unfortunate that the world from which the ladies had to be protected should have included the world of medicine. A doctor might—in the presence of a chaperone—be consulted, and the patient might even indicate, on a lay figure, where she felt pain, but only in the most extreme case was it permissible to make a gynecological examination. Then, the concessions that had to be made to the lady's modesty were of a kind that would probably lead to a modern doctor losing his license; standard practice appears to have been to make the examination under a sheet in a darkened room. Yet many physicians encouraged this morbid modesty. One, a professor in Philadelphia, was quoted in *Godey's Lady's Book* in 1852 as saying that he was proud that in America "women prefer to suffer the extremity of danger and pain rather than waive those scruples of delicacy which prevent their maladies from being fully explored." He thought it was evidence of "a fine morality." [6] Such an attitude not only prevented doctors from doing their job properly but also prevented women from learning anything about their own anatomy and physiology. Menstruation, for example, was rarely mentioned and was thought of by doctors and women alike as a disability; as late as 1878 the *British Medical Journal* ran a six-months' correspondence on whether hams could be turned rancid by the touch of a menstruating woman. The Victorians were also convinced that "the full force of sexual desire is seldom known to a virtuous woman," [7] and medical men—unlike pornographers, whose acquaintance (it may be assumed) was with unvirtuous women—seem to have been inadequately informed about female orgasm and the function of the clitoris.

Chivalry, gentility, delicacy, and ignorance all combined to pin the middle-class woman to her home, and even the discovery of the female role in reproduction did not at first mend matters because although equality had at last entered into the equation it was a biological equality that applied, not to the woman, but to the mother. And the emphasis on motherhood, with all its domestic connotations, was reinforced by one of the most widely publicized academic controversies of the nineteenth century, that concerning *jus maternum*.

Jus maternum, or "the law of the mother," was not altogether a new idea, but it was propounded in 1861 by the Swiss jurist and historian Johann Jakob Bachofen in the kind of philosophical-scientific language that the Victorians found quite irresistible. Bachofen denied man's "natural" superiority over women, and claimed, with a wealth of historical and anthropological detail, that when humanity was still close to nature and maternity the only recognizable parental relationship, women had ruled, but that when the spirit conquered man took over. Bachofen's ideas attracted powerful support, notably from the American ethnologist Lewis N. Morgan, who combined Bachofen's theories with his own observations among the Iroquois to produce a neat picture of how sex and family life had developed during prehistory. There had been, he believed, complete promiscuity in the earliest stages, then collective marriage in the time of the hunting-gathering communities. Since in neither situation was it possible to identify a child's father, it was the mother's relationship that was decisive and the mother's influence that was predominant.* Only when agriculture developed, allowing even a small family to become self-sufficient through ownership of private property, did monogamy become the rule and woman subordinate to man.

Progressive circles welcomed these theories with the greatest enthusiasm. The direct connection between private property and female subordination was especially appealing, and *jus maternum* became part of the socialist catechism as well as an article of faith for early feminists and a cliché in any discussion about woman's role in society. But none of it did much for woman as woman, even if "the mother" was raised almost to the status of goddess.**

Despite all this, the idea that woman's place was in the home was not an invention of the Victorians. It was simply that they happened to be the first who found it necessary to put it into words, for woman in the nineteenth century was on the verge— though only on the verge—of real independence, a state impossible to achieve without economic self-sufficiency or its potential.

The battle for financial independence was not to be won until well into the twentieth century. It was not, at first, a matter of great concern to the upper classes, where marriage settlements, separation settlements, and allowances, were all discreetly negotiable and even the most errant wife was unlikely to starve. But the doctrine of "woman's place" seriously hampered even the unmarried among the middle classes, who might have found employment in the outside world if the doctrine itself had not persuaded employers that offering work to the genteelly literate would be self-defeating. In 1861, out of the 2,700,000 women and girls over

---

* It took a while for scholars to spot the major flaw in this reconstruction, which was the confusion between matrilinearity (in which society traces descent and inheritance through the mother's line) and matriarchy, where the mother wields power. Subsequent research was to show that matriarchy was historically rare, and that in matrilinear societies the mother's nominal rights and powers were usually exercised by her closest male kin—father or eldest brother.

** At the same time, the mother-goddesses of history came to be credited with rather more power than they ever seem to have possessed.

15 who were "gainfully employed" in England and Wales (26 per cent of the female population), precisely 279 were clerical workers.[8]

The laboring poor were, until the twentieth century, not much concerned with "woman's place" because they could not afford to be. In their case it was industrial capitalism that was the hindrance. The Industrial Revolution had wrecked the long, stable tradition of peasant family life, the system in which women had been much more aware of their own value than on any other level of society because they had played an essential role in a hardworking family group. The women of the lower classes had seldom had independence, but they had been possessed of a good deal of freedom. Industry, however, changed all that. The working woman became, like her husband and children, a wage slave and a low-paid one, receiving sometimes less, sometimes slightly more than half what a man received for the same work. In the mid-nineteenth century, the average American male employed in the cotton industry earned $1.67 a week, the female $1.05. In England, a male spinner was paid 14 to 22 shillings a week, sometimes more, while a female powerloom weaver received only five to ten shillings. The French printer's wage might be two francs a day, but a woman rated only one.[9]

The cheap labor system, in effect, paid women too little to live on, but at the same time gave them an unfair advantage over men in the search for work. There was undoubtedly a rough historical justice in this, but the principle of paying the rate for the person, rather than the rate for the job, played havoc with the theory of "working-class solidarity." Man's resistance to woman as wage-earner is only now beginning to fade. Even so, real equality will not have arrived until the day when the average man ceases to distinguish between his wife ("who is earning good money") and the women with whom he has to compete for his job.

FALLEN   WOMEN

It was not altogether surprising that the gentle and submissive Victorian wife should have been thought of as undersexed. Her repressed upbringing, the refinement and "spirituality" that were forced upon her, and her ignorance of physiology all helped to make her so, and even a woman who was not physically revolted by intercourse needed very delicate handling if she were to enjoy the experience. It was a task for which few Victorian husbands were equipped. They had their own problems, their own inhibitions, and making love to "the angel of the house" in the awareness that she was concealing a gently-bred disgust was scarcely conducive to a satisfactory performance.

St. Augustine, however—in unholy alliance with the medical profession—came to the rescue. The Church Fathers had believed that sex, even in marriage, was permissible only if procreation might result, but although Catholic Church doctrine had accepted this, and though it colored the whole of Catholic thinking on the subject of sex (and consequently on many other aspects of daily life), its real effect had been limited as much by difficulties of mass communication as by natural instinct. The curious result was that nineteenth-century Protestants, conscientious students of improving works of theological literature, came to pay rather more attention to St. Augustine than their Catholic predecessors had ever done. Few Victorians went as far as the American Dr. Alice Stockham, who claimed in 1894 that any husband who required marital intercourse except with a view to conceiving children was making his wife into a private prostitute,[10] but there was a general consensus that men should not impose their animal desires on their wives any more than was absolutely necessary—once a month for preference, once a week if the situation were desperate, and never during menstrual periods or pregnancy.

This should not be taken to mean that Victorian wives were neglected. In 1871, the English middle-class family averaged six children, and 177 families in a thousand had ten or more.[11] The ban on intercourse during pregnancy and menstruation, however, imposed celibacy on the average husband and wife for roughly six years out of the first twelve of their married life—which does not appear to have distressed many wives but placed a serious strain on their husbands.

Fortunately or unfortunately, disapproval was a state of mind more common among women than men. Whatever the domestic pressures may have been, most Victorian husbands were aware of no social pressures that forced them to curb their sexual instincts. Indeed, many of them felt they were doing their wives a favor by taking those instincts elsewhere. In resorting to prostitutes they even had religious justification. St. Augustine, during his meditations on the subject of sex in the Garden of Eden, had concluded that (had it not been for the unseemly episode of Eve, the serpent, and the apple) intercourse should have been cool, calculated, and free from all "unregulated excitement"; it was only after the Original Sin had been committed that lust and passion entered into the equation (see pages 141–42). Nineteenth-century doctors took this to its logical conclusion. Coitus, they declared, though harmful in excess, was an acceptable health risk provided it was carried out plainly and without any extravagant expenditure of emotion. In other words, sex with a prostitute, where neither love nor passion was involved, was "generally attended with less derangement" than sex with a wife.[12]

Prostitution flourished as never before. Unfortunately, statistics are unreliable; there were too many people with too many moral and political axes to grind. Police estimates erred on the conservative side. In Paris in the 1860s the police admitted to 30,000 prostitutes, a figure that, in the context of social conditions in which they arrested over 35,000 beggars and vagrants during the course of a single year (1868), seems unnaturally low. Unofficial sources put the number at nearer 120,000.[13]

Opinions about London were even more divided. In 1839, the chief of the Metropolitan Police claimed that London had only 7,000 prostitutes, while Michael Ryan, reporting on behalf of the Society for the Suppression of Vice, reckoned nearer 80,000.[14] Ryan's figure may not have been quite as wildly exaggerated as some historians believe. The Metropolitan area was only a part of Greater London, which had a population of two million in 1841 and a substantial number of prostitutes who stayed out in the suburbs; the police themselves still had no detective force and relied on the observation of the uniformed man on the beat; and while the professional prostitute had no particular reason to stay out of sight of the police, the part-timer or amateur anxious not to attract attention (except from a customer) was restored to instant propriety when the familiar uniform hove into view. Since 350 people out of every thousand may (as a rule of thumb) be taken to be males between the ages of 15 and 60, and since one prostitute for every dozen active males seems to have been average for the major nineteenth-century city, a figure of 50,000 prostitutes in Greater London would have been perfectly possible in the 1840s.

For a while, Vienna had been the sex capital of Europe with, in the 1820s, 20,000 prostitutes in relation to a total population of 400,000—one girl to every seven men.[15] Apologists point out that many of the girls worked strictly for the tourist trade, and this could also have been said, in a slightly different sense, of New York, a city of immigrants and transients. In the 1830s, New York was reputed to have 20,000 prostitutes, and the social reformer Robert Dale Owen calculated that, making allowances for a five-day week and time off for menstruation, if each of them received three clients a day then half the adult males in the city must visit one of them three times a week.[16] This picture of bustling eroticism was probably optimistic, for the high mobility of New York's population offered encouragement to amateurs, girls who, needing money, took as many clients as they could find for a few days or weeks and none at all for the rest of the year. It was very different in San Francisco at the time of the Gold Rush, where the population exploded from under a thousand in early 1848 to more than 25,000 in 1852, a figure that included close on 3,000 prostitutes who had made the business trip from New York, New Orleans, France, England, Spain, Chile, and China, and only the merest handful of "respectable" women. The competition was much too stiff for the amateur.

In Cincinnati, there were 7,000 prostitutes in a population of something over 200,000 in 1869, and Philadelphia had 12,000 to a population of around 700,000. The Philadelphia figure, in fact, was considerably depressed by the nearness of Atlantic City. As one English journalist wistfully remarked in 1867: "Paris may be subtler, London may be grosser, in its vices; but for largeness of depravity, for domineering insolence of sin, for rowdy callousness to censure, they tell me Atlantic City finds no rival on earth." [17]

DEMI-MONDAINES AND DOLLYMOPS

The girls who became prostitutes in the nineteenth century usually did so because they needed the money. At one end of the scale there was the independent-minded career woman who knew that, without any capital other than herself, only prostitution and the stage offered the prospect of making a good living; at the other, the young widow or unmarried mother able to earn little but almost certain to be separated from her child if she applied for the parish relief that would save them both from starvation. The Victorians' worship of motherhood had strict limitations.

Somewhere in between were the majority, the London garment workers and the girls from the tobacco factories in Louisville, earning below-average wages (even for the time) and having to supplement them in order to live. Even so, it often required something more to push such girls over the edge, and one sexual lapse was all that was needed—in an era when that was all it took to make a "fallen woman." In 1888, the U.S. Commissioner of Labor obtained from 3,866 professionals in Boston, Chicago, Cincinnati, Louisville, New Orleans, Philadelphia, and San Francisco, details of their previous occupations. 1,236 had gone straight into the business as soon as they were old enough, but 1,155 had first done hotel or domestic work, 505 had been seamstresses or garment factory workers, 126 saleswomen or cashiers, 94 textile factory workers, and so on down the scale to a mere 11 telephone or telegraph operators.[18] Excluding the girls with no previous occupation, 1,100 had been employed in some kind of work where they were segregated from the public, while 1,500 came from service or similar industries where a perfunctory but disastrous seduction was only too easily possible.

The prostitute who, having accepted the inevitable, decided to aim for the top, needed more than beauty. Personality and ambition were the two most important qualifications. Nor could she hope to go far in Milwaukee or Manchester. It was great cities like Paris and Vienna that held out the lure of money and success.

Paris, in the febrile period of the Second Empire, had the glossiest courtesans. The *demi-monde,* the society that clung to the fringes of the imperial court, was wide open to girls who might not have birth or breeding, or even the beauty and brains characteristic of the great courtesans and *hetairai* of the past, but had learned to cultivate charm of an often brash but always voluptuous kind. Madame de Pompadour, a hundred years earlier, would have thought them extremely vulgar, but they would have excelled, a hundred years later, as Hollywood starlets. They had no difficulty in finding protectors among the bankers, financiers, army officers, and aristocrats of all nationalities who flocked to the

La Païva

Cora Pearl

gas-lit stage of Second-Empire Paris. Russian grand dukes, Turkish pashas, South American millionaires, paid their bills. It was a German mine-owner who built her astonishing house for Moscow-born La Païva (Thérèse Lachman), with its onyx staircase, marble tub, and jeweled faucets, while Cora Pearl (born Emma Crouch) owed to the emperor's cousin Prince Napoleon, known as Plon-Plon, and to the young Prince of Orange—among others—the income, if not the inspiration, that enabled her to dance nude on a carpet of orchids and bathe before her dinner guests in a silver tub full of champagne. "If the Frères Provençaux [restaurant] served an omelette with diamonds in it," remarked the Duc de Gram-

Looking the girls over
in a better-class brothel
in Paris, 1910

mont-Caderousse, "Cora would be there every night." [19] No one
was bothered by her Cockney French, her stable-boy's vocabulary,
or her frank self-interest.

There was nothing quite like the Paris *demi-monde* elsewhere.
London had its equally dashing ladies, but none of them expected
to be received in polite society; it was only the more discreet
courtesans who succeeded in maintaining a facade of respectability that allowed even the highest circles to acknowledge them
without loss of face. Lily Langtry remains the classic example.
Washington, too, had its ladies, the "female lobbyists" who stayed
in town only for as long as Congress was in session, and then
departed, bag and baggage, when the legislators did.

New Orleans was unique. In 1850, 116,000 of the whole Loui-
siana population of 134,000 people lived in the city, where sexual
supply and demand were coordinated in the most exemplary fash-

ion. French, Spanish, American, and mulatto blood ran in the
veins of most of the girls who had been trained, almost from infancy, to become not wives, not mothers, not prostitutes, but mistresses. A gentleman in search of companionship was recommended to attend one of the formal quadroon balls, where he
could choose a girl who appealed to him and then enter into
negotiations with her mother. If he were well off he might set the
young lady up in a pretty little house for a relationship that would
continue until he married (someone else); the more impecunious
might have to settle for visiting the girl at her home, with occasional use of a bedroom, and light refreshments as part of the deal.
This businesslike system received its death blow in 1897, when in
response to agitation on the part of the city's more straitlaced
inhabitants an ordinance was passed restricting prostitution to a
specified district which, in honor of Sidney Story, the alderman
who had thought up the idea, came to be known as Storyville.

Only a girl of real quality could expect to have her own house,
whether on upper Rampart Street or on the new boulevards of
Paris. The next rank down looked to the high-class brothel as the
peak of attainment. In the early nineteenth century, the most
luxurious brothel in the world was agreed to be "The Fountain"
in Amsterdam, which in addition to private rooms had a restau-
rant, dance hall, cafe, and a billiard room where the girls successfully distracted their opponents by playing in the nude.[20] But
despite the mythology, only a small proportion of the world's prostitutes were to be found in brothels—in Berlin none at all, for the
hundred that had existed in 1780 had been whittled down during
the course of a long morality campaign to a mere 26, which were
finally closed in 1844.[21] Elsewhere in Europe—notably in France
and Belgium—police regulations made it extremely difficult for a
girl to leave a brothel once she had been registered there, so that it
became a prison, denying her the freedom that was one of the
greatest attractions of prostitution as a career.

London had relatively few brothels in the mid-nineteenth century, but New York was better served. In 1866, the Superintendent of Police admitted to the existence of 621 when Bishop
Simpson of the Methodist Episcopal Church unwisely proclaimed
that there were as many whores in the city as there were Methodists.[22] The most exclusive, perhaps, was Josephine Wood's on
Clinton Place. The girls wore evening dress, the only drink was

champagne, the house was furnished with crystal chandeliers and deep-pile carpets, and the butler checked the credentials of every client, none but aristocrats being permitted to cross the threshold. It was a far cry from the "cow yards" of San Francisco, whose show place at the end of the century was a bright new barracks of 450 rooms which its owners had carefully stocked with nymphomaniacs, on the sound principle that a happy worker was a good worker. They wanted to call it the Hotel Nymphomania but were refused permission. It became the Nymphia, but not for long, falling victim in 1903 to the indefatigable Father Caraher's clean-up campaign.

Technically speaking, the Nymphia was a lodging-house brothel, making its profit out of rents rather than out of the girls' earnings. This was a system that operated in many cities. The girls liked it because they had more freedom than in an orthodox brothel, while being relieved of the major problem of the independent prostitute—finding a landlord prepared to give them house room. Better still, however, was to have a home quite separate from work and to take clients to what were known as "accommodation houses," "houses of assignation," or "*maisons de rendezvous*," which rented rooms by the hour. Some of these houses were used not only by prostitutes but by married women who had trysts with their lovers. In London they were often located in the fashionable West End, over elegant little millinery shops or in the back premises of such establishments as "Beautiful for Ever," Madame Rachael's expensive beauty parlor, while in New York the better class of business was centered on Fifth Avenue where the busiest time was during the afternoon shopping hours.*

Professionals, of course, first had to find their clients, and there were well-known pick-up points in most cities. The more flamboyant girls, gowned in satins and feathers, were usually to be found in the saloons and corridors of the theaters or in the more select

---

* The modern equivalent of the Hotel Nymphia is the "Eros Centre" popular in northern Europe. In 1977, Rotterdam embarked on a floating one; bars, clubs, and movies ashore, and the girls accommodated in brothel boats close by. One veteran streetwalker remarked when the plan was first agreed: "Imagine the tidal waves four hundred hookers will produce. Better stay off the quays or you'll get your feet wet." The imaginative apogee of the *maison de rendezvous*, however, is to be found in Japan, where there are more than 25,000 of them (all legal and properly inspected), designed to nourish romantic fantasy; there are palaces from the Arabian Nights, haunted mansions, and Rhineland castles. These serve not only professionals, but lovers unable to find privacy anywhere else on the most tightly-packed islands in the world.[23]

type of casino (a dance hall rather than a gambling house). The Portland Rooms in London were selective; entry was refused to gentlemen unless they were wearing dress coats and white waistcoats. If it was late, with theaters and casinos closed, the place to go was a "night house," a kind of glorified tavern from which such undesirables as drunks and common streetwalkers were firmly excluded. Although the night houses made their profits from drinks—Kate Hamilton's off Leicester Square specialized in champagne and moselle at outrageous prices—it was the girls who frequented them who attracted the paying customers, and landlords since the eighteenth century had found it profitable to publicize the charms of their habituées. Between 1760 and 1793, for example, a London tavern-owner named Harris published an annual register describing the faces, figures, manners and special talents of the Covent Garden Ladies who patronized his house in Drury Lane; 8,000 copies are said to have been printed and sold every year. More widely informative were publications such as *The Rangers' Magazine*, which in the 1790s ran a "monthly list of the Covent Garden Cyprians; or the man of pleasure's vade mecum," and the short-lived erotic periodical *The Exquisite*, which provided much the same kind of information for the roué of the early 1840s under such headings as "Sketches of Courtesans," and "Seduction Unveiled." * Sometimes even the most impeccable sources could prove useful. In the early 1830s, any New Yorker with his wits about him could find out all he needed to know from *McDowall's Journal* which recorded the Reverend John R. McDowall's investigations into vice in the city and state in such conscientious detail that it became known in interested circles as the Whorehouse Directory. But it was New Orleans, inevitably, that scooped the pool, first with the *Green Book, or Gentleman's Guide to New Orleans*, and then, when Storyville came into being, with the *Blue Book*, which began publication in 1902, was available at hotels, railroad stations, tobacco stands, and landing stages, and was packed with advertisements extolling the charms of brothels, madams, and girls. Diane and Norma claimed to be known on "both continents," but even if their knowledge of geography was limited their knowledge of sex was not. Anyone whom they failed

---

* In 1961 (in *Shaw v. Director of Public Prosecutions*), publishing a list of prostitutes' addresses was held to be criminal under the headings of "a conspiracy to corrupt public morals" and "an act tending to the public mischief."

The French dollymop expected to be entertained in a private room at one of the more select restaurants.

to satisfy, they said confidently, "must surely be of a queer nature."

What most publications could not do was list amateurs like the dollymops, London's equivalent of the Paris *midinettes*, pretty little sempstresses or milliners or nursemaids who were ready to be picked up by a personable young man or wealthy older one, and could be cajoled into bed in return for a fee paid in flowers, chocolates, trinkets, and entertainment under the bright lights. Nor did they deal with the hordes of streetwalkers, the ravaged professionals and desperate part-timers of all ages who picked up their clients riskily in the street and were paid (if they were lucky) after a hasty encounter in some dark doorway or alley.

The risk, however, was not always on the prostitute's side.

THE WAGES OF SIN

The Victorians' indulgence in indiscriminate sex produced an appalling increase in venereal disease. Prostitutes were the main transmitters, naturally enough, though not always because they were irresponsible or negligent. It was insidiously easy for them to spread gonorrhea, for example, since it is quite common for women to feel none of the early symptoms and so to pass on the disease without being aware of it. Men, on the other hand, within two or three days of infection experience pain and a discharge from the urethra that, untreated, can develop into blockage of the flow of urine. In the case of syphilis, however, men may have been at least as responsible for disseminating it as prostitutes, who knew as much about the disease—if they were professionals—as most doctors.

The first and second stages of syphilis are characterized by symptoms that appear sporadically and disappear of their own accord. As little as a week or as much as three months after infection there may be a swelling of the lymph nodes, usually in the groin, and a small lump develops that can turn into an ulcer. Weeks or months after these symptoms have cleared up, there may be a skin rash and another mild swelling of the lymph nodes, but these too disappear even without treatment. Only with the third stage, which need not occur until after a lapse of years, does the permanent damage become apparent, sometimes in a loss of coordination that produces the characteristically jerky walk of the advanced syphilitic, sometimes in delusions or insanity. It was easy enough for a careless or ignorant Victorian to dismiss the early symptoms as unrelated minor ailments and to pursue a normal sex life, infecting not only previously clean prostitutes but his own unfortunate wife—and his unborn children.

The medical profession was virtually powerless in the face of the new epidemic. Doctors did not even know that gonorrhea and syphilis were two different diseases but took the first to be an early stage of the second and treated both with mercury, which was painful, protracted, and frequently ineffective. Nor could they tell whether a cure was complete. Many gonorrhea patients were given a clean bill of health when they were still highly infectious.

The number of sufferers increased and continued to increase. In the 1830s and 40s in Vienna, between six and seven thousand women (mostly prostitutes) were admitted annually to three public hospitals to be treated for either syphilis or gonorrhea, while in London in 1856 three major hospitals dealt with 30,000 cases (men and women) between them, and half the surgical outpatients at another were also venereal disease sufferers.[24] In Paris in the 1860s, 60 percent of the prostitutes sentenced to the women's prison of

Saint Lazare could be relied upon to be infected, and in the course of only three months in 1865 the Garde Impériale lost 20,000 duty days through hospital treatment for venereal disease. It was claimed that in Copenhagen in the last quarter of the century one man or woman in three at some stage contracted one of the major venereal diseases, and in America in 1914 a pessimistic expert estimated that over half the male population of the country had had gonorrhea.[25]

In most countries, the public health authorities tried to control the problem by controlling prostitutes. And indeed, if they had succeeded in subjecting all prostitutes to regular medical inspection they might ultimately have reduced the incidence of venereal diseases in the population at large.* But there were too many amateurs and part-timers, and the task was impossible, even in continental Europe where registration of prostitutes was compulsory and the authorities at least had somewhere to start. Britain and America did not even have that. In fact, when the British government—responsible for an empire that depended on armed forces who were becoming riddled with venereal disease—brought in the Contagious Diseases Acts of 1864, 1866, and 1869, it ran head on into trouble.

The Acts were mainly designed to remove known transmitters from circulation and to enforce regular inspection of women working at major naval installations or within 15 miles of any major garrison town, excluding London. For the first time, this made it necessary for the police to keep a register of prostitutes—and to decide who should appear on it. They had no problem with the admitted professionals and brothel inmates, whose own health and prosperity inclined them to favor regular medical inspection, but the ignorant amateurs and already-infected streetwalkers who could afford neither a cure nor the loss of earnings it entailed—the women who most needed to be identified—were a very different matter. Short of catching them in the act of accosting passersby, the police had no alternative but to rely on hearsay and information supplied to them confidentially. In the numerous miscarriages of justice that occurred, malice and genuine mistake seem to have played roughly equal parts.

---

* As an indicator, Italy banned state-supervised brothels in 1958, and by 1960 there were twice as many people infected by syphilis as there had been in the year before the ban was imposed.

There was a public outcry against the Acts, a strange confrontation between brothel owners and procurers on the one side and ladies of paralyzing respectability on the other. Improbably, it was the former who supported the restrictions and the latter who condemned them as an infringement of prostitutes' constitutional liberties. From the viewpoint of the late twentieth century, there is a certain piquancy in the fact that Josephine Butler, wife of a clergyman and secretary of the Ladies' National Association, should have criticized vaginal inspections as an affront to the modesty of girls for whom they were an everyday occurrence (even if not usually under medical supervision). But the ladies were rationalizing their objections. They might claim that it was unjust for men to make laws penalizing women for being what man's uncontrolled desires had made them,* but what they were really expressing was hate and fear of prostitution itself. Medical inspections that removed infected girls from circulation could do nothing but strengthen the whole institution. What the ladies wanted was its abolition.

It was the godly who triumphed. The Contagious Diseases Acts were suspended in 1883 and repealed three years later, and the agitation that brought this about was also partly responsible for the Criminal Law Amendment Act of 1885, which made illegal, not prostitution (taking money for sexual services), but procuring and brothel-keeping.[26] Formerly, the British police had acted only if a prostitute—or a houseful of them—could be said to be "annoying" people. It was a system that had worked quite well, even if the police themselves were sometimes surprised at what could annoy an evangelical Victorian. But afterward, organized prostitution became a crime—with the inevitable result that the criminal classes moved in.

In America, too, the godly succeeded in preventing the establishment of licensed and regulated prostitution, except for brief periods in New Orleans, between 1870 and 1874, and San Francisco in 1911-13.** As a result, the U.S. War Department, as concerned as the British War Office over the health of its servicemen, had to deal with the problem in its own way. This consisted

---

* An argument that combined one irreproachable sentiment with one extreme over-simplification. Prostitution was the product of a whole social system, dominated legally by men but owing a great deal to man-woman consensus. The still fashionable belief that "men make prostitutes" did, in fact, have some contemporary truth in the late nineteenth

partly of issuing condoms to all sailors going on shore leave, a realistic approach that met with virulent opposition because it appeared less as a prophylactic measure against venereal disease than an outright encouragement of contraception, currently a heated issue.[27] During World War I, soldiers serving overseas were also supplied with condoms—and even recommended to use them for what was known in polite society as "fraternizing"—but at home the authorities made a determined attempt to wipe out illicit sexual activity. The decree that all brothels within five miles of a navy base had to close brought the vivid saga of Storyville, New Orleans, to an abrupt end in 1917. But although historians still express horror over 280,000 cases of venereal disease being reported in the U.S. army and navy between September 1917 and February 1919,[28] this figure represented a remarkable improvement compared with the situation only a few years earlier. The American forces numbered almost five million men, all at the age of peak sexual activity. Yet whereas in 1914 it had been estimated that one man in two had at some time suffered from gonorrhea (an extremist view, perhaps), now only one man in 17 in the armed forces had contracted *any* of the venereal diseases.

The Germans were equally successful. At the beginning of the war, eminent scientists informed the High Command that sexual abstinence should be made obligatory and brothels closed, but it was decided that this would be dangerous for morale. Military brothels soon sprang up behind the fighting lines, often in caravans that advanced and retreated as the army did. Red-light brothels were for NCOs and private soldiers, blue-light ones for officers, and there were no concessions to leisureliness or grace. A sergeant from the Medical Corps was posted at the entrance to check pay books and health certificates, to note the name and unit of each customer, to supervise a brief medical inspection, dispense prophylactic medicines and ointments before and after each visit— and collect a fee on Madame's behalf. The girls averaged ten cus-

century, but over a wider spectrum of history it is truer to add that prostitutes also make customers.

** Prostitution is officially a crime in much of the United States today, although there are estimated to be at least half a million prostitutes—and almost as many laws concerning them. The legal situation is chaotic. They can "loiter" in Chicago but not in New York; their clients can be arrested in New Jersey, but in most of Nevada men are encouraged to patronize state-inspected houses of prostitution. And so on. . . .

tomers each between about 4 P.M. and 9 P.M. At the peak of the
off-duty rush hour, ten minutes per man was all that was allowed
before the duty sergeant bellowed out "Next! " [29]

At this time, German scientists knew as much about venereal
disease as any in the world. In Berlin in 1900, it had been officially
admitted that 16,000 people were under treatment for either
gonorrhea or syphilis, but unofficial estimates were, as usual, much
higher. One contemporary authority claimed that 37 per cent of
all the men in Hamburg and Berlin contracted syphilis between
the ages of 15 and 50, and that on the average, *every* male could
be said to contract gonorrhea more than once.[30] Whether or not
these figures were inflated, they were enough to frighten a people
who set a high value on Teutonic physique, and it was in Germany
that the first important advances in syphilis research and treatment took place.

In 1905, syphilis spirochetes were identified by an East Prus-
sian zoologist named Fritz Schaudinn, and in 1906 a bacteriologist
in Berlin, August von Wassermann, evolved a system of blood
testing that made diagnosis more reliable than ever before, though
since spirochetes were not found in all patients or at all stages of
the disease it was not infallible. In 1909, in Frankfurt-am-Main,
the chemist Paul Ehrlich discovered that an arsenic derivative
(which he called salvarsan) effected a magical cure, and although
there were a number of unpleasant accidents during the early
days—dosage technique being complicated—an improved version
overcame most of the problems. Today, antibiotics and sulphonamides have replaced arsenic in the treatment of syphilis, but it can
still be cured only during the first and second stages; by the third
stage, the tissues have suffered irreversible damage.

It took longer to find a cure for gonorrhea. In 1879 a young
laboratory assistant at Breslau discovered the guilty microbe,
which made it possible to say decisively whether a patient had
been cured or was merely undergoing a remission, but it was not
until the introduction of sulphonamides in 1935 and penicillin in
1941 that a swift cure became possible. Microbes, however, have as
powerful an instinct for self-preservation as human beings, and
strains of gonococcus have now developed that are resistant to
both treatments and actually seem to thrive on penicillin. Some
antibiotics still work, but the World Health Organisation is justifiably nervous. In an era of casual sex, when the Pill and the loop

have superseded the dual-purpose condom, and when gonorrhea cases are being treated at a rate of three million a year in the United States and 100 million worldwide, the failure of curative and control drugs could have the most serious consequences.*

THE CRAZE FOR VIRGINS

One unsurprising but unfortunate corollary of the Victorians' terror of venereal disease was a growing demand for virgin prostitutes—who could be assumed to be clean. (There was even a myth, tragic for the woman, that intercourse with a virgin could effect a cure.) Up to £100 was charged in London in the early part of the century, although by the 1880s the going rate had dropped to £5, which reflected not a slackening in demand but an increase in supply—as well as a burgeoning suspicion that not every *virgo intacta* was as intact as she appeared.

Enthusiasts had always claimed that there was a special pleasure in deflowering a virgin, because of the emotional thrill, a blend of aggression, possessiveness, and mild sadism. A few modern historians, following the erratic Dr. Dühren,** consider defloration of virgins as a particularly English vice, but history proves otherwise. At some periods, it has even been institutionalized, most commonly in the form of *droit de seigneur,* which granted the king or feudal landlord the right to bed a new bride before her husband did. This is recorded as far back as Sumerian times. One episode in the *Epic of Gilgamesh* refers to the annoyance of the people of Uruk over their king's insistence on clinging to tradition by demanding still "to be first with the bride, the king to be first and the husband to follow," and the practice persisted in Europe, off and on, until the eleventh or twelfth century. In France, by the thirteenth century, it was being referred to as a custom of former

---

* In Eastern Europe, there has also been a resurgence of venereal disease in some areas, notably Lithuania, despite punitive measures that make it a criminal offense to infect another person even unwittingly, to refuse treatment, or to drink alcohol during treatment. The guilty party is also required to pay for the treatment of the person he or she has infected. In Russia, anyone found guilty of knowingly infecting another person is considered to have committed "premeditated bodily harm of a serious nature" and is liable to three years' imprisonment or up to one year in a forced labor camp.[31]

** Who, as Iwan Bloch, in the early years of the present century wrote a study of *Sexual Life in England Past and Present* that remains a model of misinterpretation.

times, but it seems probable that a prince or landlord who felt so inclined was still perfectly able to enforce it.[32]

Where a man did not exercise the right, the gods or their representatives often did. In Rome, before a marriage was consummated, the bride lowered herself on to a sculptured phallic symbol representing one of the lesser gods of fertility, while in Cambodia a thousand years later it was customary for Buddhist priests to deflower each girl before her marriage.[33]

Bridal virginity has been a preoccupation of most societies throughout history, but although it is usually associated with questions of legality and legitimacy there is much to suggest that the specifically sexual aspect was also important, particularly in places such as Sparta, Crete, and Rome, where the wedding ceremony incorporated a kind of formalized representation of kidnapping for the purpose of rape—which, psychologically, is a more extreme version of defloration.* Indian Muslims, at some stages of history, are recorded as practicing public defloration as proof of the bride's premarital chastity, while both they and the tribal Kurd were accustomed to display a cloth stained with hymeneal blood for the same reason. In both cases the avowed object helps to mask a strong element of masculine boasting over the act itself. Muslims appear to have been particularly fascinated by defloration. In the Islamic Paradise, the believer was promised 10,000 virgins who, deflowered each night, had their virginity miraculously restored on the following morning.

In effect, deflowering a wife and deflowering a prostitute, however different in theory, were not so different in practice. The realistic Chinese made just as much of a ceremony out of the defloration of a courtesan as they did out of marriage, and the fee and the banquet cost the lucky man almost as much.[35]

It was a nineteenth-century English journalist who was largely responsible for fostering the impression that his fellow countrymen specialized in defloration. In 1885, W. T. Stead ran a series of

---

* Virginity is still important at the eastern end of the Mediterranean. In 1978, continuing to put a price tag on it, an Athens court awarded 350,000 drachmae (£5,000 or $9,500) to the parents of a 16-year-old girl who had been seduced by her foreign languages teacher. The sum was estimated to represent the amount the parents would have to add to her dowry "in order to compensate a man of her own economic and social standing for the loss of her virginity." [34]

daring exposés of the white slave trade* in the *Pall Mall Gazette*,
under the title "The Maiden Tribute of Modern Babylon" (Babylon being the nickname for the part of London's West End in
which the entertainment and prostitution industries were centered). Stead was what would nowadays be called an investigative
journalist, prepared to contribute to the making of a story as well
as its reporting. His most dramatic coup was to buy a girl, a virgin,
from her mother and carry her off to Paris, an enterprise that cost
him three months in prison despite the fact that he had hurriedly
handed the girl over to the Salvation Army.

All that he had succeeded in proving was that it could be
done—not that it was done regularly. But his claim that, in London, the rape of virgins was a highly organized and efficient business curdled his readers' blood in a most satisfactory way. There
was nothing the Victorians enjoyed more than a horror that did
not touch them personally.

Most of the girls, said Stead, were too young to understand
what was happening to them, and the trade was, of course, considerable, since a virgin's first encounter with a customer left her a
virgin no longer. Some brothels specializing in virgins found them
at the great railroad termini where trains from the country came
in; others found London's parks a more profitable hunting ground.
It was not too difficult to persuade nursemaids or shop girls to
sacrifice their virginity in exchange for a golden guinea, although
they sometimes began to regret it when the moment of truth
approached. Because of this, virgin brothels were often set apart
from other houses and well insulated for sound.

Some brothels had their own doctors to supply the certificates
of virginity that customers habitually asked for. And not only the
certificates, but very often the virginity itself.

Most virgins have a tab of membrane, the hymen or "maid-
enhead," that partly obstructs the entrance to the vagina. This
membrane, when the vagina is fully penetrated for the first time,
is often torn or stretched, and depending on its diameter and

---

* "White slavery" was to a large extent a fiction of lady novelists. In thickly populated
Europe, there were enough willing recruits to prostitution to make kidnapping unnecessary,
and the women who were smuggled across the frontiers were usually voluntary emigrants.
But in America, San Francisco's Chinese women had been slaves, in every sense, since the
1850s, while toward the end of the century procurers began to entice women into the
country from Poland, Ireland, Puerto Rico, and Cuba and use their dependence to force
them into prostitution. By 1900 it was big business, with an estimated 50,000 procurers and
ponces making a living from it.

The reality. The skinny, frightened virgin offered
by bawd to client

thickness (which varies from woman to woman) begins to bleed,
sometimes copiously, sometimes scarcely at all. Bleeding is, in
fact, a largely unreliable guide to virginity, but tight entry and
clear traces of blood have always signified maidenhood to the
man, and it has always been in the interests of women to know
how to simulate them. Such knowledge was age-old, though it
seems to have faded for a time in early medieval Europe before it
was revived by the distinguished doctors Avicenna and Albertus
Magnus, whose lists of "the signs of virginity and/or its corruption" turned out (quite unintentionally) to be an invaluable guide
for the barbers, bathhouse keepers, and retired prostitutes who
supplemented their earnings from the proceeds of virginity restoration.

To produce convincing bleeding, all that was needed was to
insert in the vagina a scrap of sponge soaked in blood that was
released by pressure during intercourse; a small fish bladder filled
with blood produced a more dramatic effect but was probably
rather more difficult to handle when it was being placed in position. Either method, however, was infinitely superior to two of the
other ideas sometimes suggested—bloodsucking leeches and fragments of broken glass. Contracting the vaginal opening was less

easy. Stitchery might sometimes have to be resorted to, but more often a powerful astringent was used; the steam from vinegar, myrrh water, and an infusion of acorns or sloes were the chief recommendations. In some brothels, professional virgins were patched up several times a week, and not only in London, but in Paris, Berlin, New York, San Francisco, and New Orleans, where some houses at the turn of the century offered defloration as part of the floor show.*

There were some customers for whom an adolescent virgin was not enough. They wanted a younger one. In France, the laws against debauching minors were sufficiently stringent to discourage child brothels, but London had them in the eighteenth century, even if the children involved usually seem to have been 14 or 15 years of age—which, in eighteenth-century terms, was very nearly adult. More disturbing in the first half of the nineteenth century were the freelance 12-year-olds from the slums of the great cities who had been sent out by their parents—if they had any—to earn their bread, and no questions asked. Raised in the appalling conditions of New York's Five Points and London's Seven Dials, most of these children had learned the facts of life as naturally as they had learned to walk and talk, and many of them slipped easily enough from the role of observer to that of practitioner. Some were taught by their fathers or brothers, as they still are today where families sleep six to a bed.[36] Incest, that ancient tabu, had become part of a social morality that was meaningless where survival, and the needs associated with it, overrode all other considerations.

As the century progressed and men demanded more esoteric forms of sexual titillation, the demand for child prostitutes increased. Josephine Butler may not have been far wrong when she claimed in 1869 that of 9,000 prostitutes in one of England's great seaports, "a late enquiry showed that 1,500 were under 15 years of age and of these a third were under 13 years of age." ** The

---

* Virginity restoration is known nowadays (in Tokyo, at least) as "hymen rebirth." Between thirty and forty thousand such operations are estimated to be carried out in Japan every year, mostly on girls about to be married; more than 80 per cent of Japanese men still demand a virgin bride. Plastic surgeons use sheep gut to construct an artificial hymen, and the date of the operation has to be carefully calculated as the sheep gut dissolves within a month. A delayed wedding means the operation has to be done again.

** In 1977, New York City police estimated that there were 20,000 runaway teenagers under 16 on the city streets, many of them available for commercial sex. In Chicago, rings of girl prostitutes, many of them 12-year-olds, were at work. In Los Angeles, up to 3,000 girls and boys under 14 were engaged in prostitution.[37]

children who embarked on their apprenticeship by darting out of doorways to tug a man by the sleeve were ideal recruits for the specialist brothels that flourished in both London and New York in the last decades of the century. Some made convincing innocents when they were patched up and given a little acting tuition. Others were reservd for clients who found a special kind of excitement in lying with a girl who was young in years but, as the Victorians repellently put it, "old in sin." It is debatable whether these children's lot was any worse than that of their contemporaries who, for much of the century, had slaved in the mines or factories for up to 18 hours a day, starting at the age of five. But it was an oddly tragic anomaly that the trade in child prostitutes should have blossomed just when legislators were making a long overdue attempt to control the exploitation of their contemporaries in more conventional types of employment.

ATHENS REDIVIVUS

It was not, of course, only girls—adolescent or adult—who attracted intimate attentions in the late Victorian and Edwardian periods. Boys did, too. In England, there was even an earnest fellowship of minor poets known as Uranians* who favored pederasty in the Greek tradition, educated men who took working-class boys under their protection with the aim of loving, helping and guiding them.[38]

But relationships were seldom as pallid or high-minded as this. More common was what the Reverend Charles Parkhurst encountered in New York in 1892 after he had made the tactical error of damning the city administration for a "lying, perjured, rum-soaked and libidinous lot" without first marshaling his proof. A Grand Jury summons sent him hurriedly off on a tour of the city's haunts of vice in search of it. The detective he hired as guide showed him round the Tenderloin and Haymarket, took him to saloons, brothels, and Chinese opium dens, and, as a grand climax, to the Golden Rule Pleasure Club on West Third Street, where, in separate cubicles in the basement, sat a number of youths with their faces painted, high falsetto voices, girls' mannerisms, and girls'

* From Urania, another name for Aphrodite.

Toulouse-Lautrec recorded life not only in the theater and the brothel, but in the Lesbian cafés of Paris. Here, the best-known of them; the *A la souris* in 1897. The dog, Bouboule, was notorious for his dislike of the customers.

names. The detective explained what the boys did, and the Reverend Mr. Parkhurst beat a precipitate retreat.[39]

Age apart, homosexuality as a commercial proposition was a late feature of the nineteenth-century prostitution explosion, especially in Britain and the States. In France it had begun rather earlier. Although the French had gone on burning homosexuals long after they had given up burning witches—until as late as 1725, in fact—the Napoleonic Code had eased the laws considerably so that by the 1860s homosexuality and lesbianism were, if not commonplace, at least tolerated. There were hundreds of male prostitutes in Paris, including one famous one called André who, according to Edmond de Goncourt, made as much as 1,800 francs during the season of the Opéra balls.[40] (A skilled craftsman at this time earned between two and four francs a day, Cora Pearl 5,000 a night). Some were instantly recognizable, dressing in women's clothes and wearing false bosoms made from sheeps' lights (lungs), first boiled and then cut to shape. "One of them complained to me the other day," said the Parisian doctor François-Auguste Veyne, "that a cat had eaten one of his breasts which he'd left to cool down in his attic." [41] Others were less easy to identify, and the results were sometimes unexpected. The brothers Goncourt recorded that a bureau chief in the Ministry of War was introducing so many soldiers of the Garde Impériale to a particular coterie of rich men that the government began to suspect a military conspiracy.[42]

In Germany 40 years later an even more dangerous conspiracy was suspected. There were growing rumors at the turn of the century that the imperial court was being run by a clique of homosexuals who were cutting the emperor off from his more responsible (i.e. heterosexual) advisers, and the rumors were intensified when a certain Count Günther von der Schulenburg sent out circulars to aristocratic homosexuals *(Urnings)* suggesting they might care to join the combination friendship society and defense league he was hoping to set up.

In 1906, Maximilian Harden, publisher of the Berlin periodical *Die Zukunft*, decided to open everyone's eyes, including those of the emperor, to the dangers of an *Urnings'* alliance. These people formed, he said, "a comradeship which is stronger than that of the monastic orders or of Freemasonry, which grips tighter and makes a link across all the walls of creed, state, and class, which unites the most remote, the most foreign, in a fraternal league of offense and defense. Men of this breed are to be found everywhere, at courts, in high positions in armies and navies, in the editorial offices of great newspapers, at tradesmen's and teachers' desks, even on the Bench. All rally together against the common enemy." [43]

It was the old international conspiracy theory—usually applied to Jews, but also, at various times, to such sects as Freemasons and Rosicrucians—in a new guise and all the more alarming because, where Jews were easy to recognize, homosexuals very often were not. Harden's campaign successfully crushed Germany's *Urnings*—and at the same time taught the public all there was to know about homosexuality. Despite the efforts of Magnus Hirschfeld, the famous Berlin sexologist who regarded homosexuals as a "third sex" and believed they should be protected by the law, not persecuted, there was a general reaction against them. The man in the street learned to identify them and boycott them, and to sneer at them as "175-ers," after Paragraph 175 of the German Penal Code, which provided against male homosexuality.

The position of England's homosexuals was rather more ambivalent, for the English had reduced to a fine art the technique of ignoring homosexuality in people they liked or respected, while condemning it utterly among outsiders (foreigners and the British working classes) and mavericks (such as Oscar Wilde). Although in sexual matters the Victorian Englishman suffered more from self-delusion than hypocrisy, in the case of homosexuality he came very near the edge.

Part of the reason for this was, no doubt, that until as late as 1861 the death penalty had been enforceable—according to the letter of the law, if not in practice. As with all legal systems where "the law" is a product of evolution and precedent, there were a number of inconsistencies and gray areas. "Public" practice of sodomy required the presence of a third person, but sodomy itself had not always been precisely defined. In the eighteenth century, some unfortunates were arrested for little more than transvestism. In 1828, however, a new Act was passed dealing with offenses against the person, which restated the principle that "every person convicted of the abominable Crime of Buggery committed either with Mankind or with any Animal, shall suffer death as a Felon," and further remarked that whereas formerly offenders accused either of buggery or rape had often escaped by reason of the "Difficulty of the Proof which has been required of the Completion of

Gay dancers on a
New Orleans street
corner

A WELL KNOWN NUISANCE

those several Crimes," in future it would not be necessary "to prove the actual Emission of Seed, but that the carnal Knowledge shall be deemed complete upon Proof of Penetration only." [44] In 1861, the death penalty was reduced to imprisonment—anything from life down to ten years—with homosexual assault subject to a shorter sentence.

This was only coincidentally a concession to homosexuals. Between 1826 and 1861 Parliament had been engaged in whittling down the number of capital offenses from 200 to only four (treason, murder, piracy, and offenses against the Dockyards Protection Act),[45] and the reprieve for homosexuals came far down on the list. But for a while those who were sensible enough to keep quiet about their proclivities probably felt themselves safer than ever before.

Then came the disastrous day in 1885 that saw the passage of the Criminal Law Amendment Act. This had been introduced into Parliament to provide for "the protection of women and girls, the suppression of brothels, and other purposes" and initially made no mention of homosexuality. Possibly the clause that was inserted at a late stage, and adopted without any real discussion, was an ill-phrased attempt to cover male as well as female prostitution, but what it said was that "any male person who, in public or private, commits or is party to the commission of, or procures or attempts to procure the commission by any male person of any act of gross indecency with another male person" was liable to up to two years' imprisonment with or without hard labor.[46] This meant that even a private, consenting homosexual relationship, and even one that stopped well short of full intercourse, now came under criminal law. It was a blackmailers' charter, and has remained so ever since, despite the legalization in 1967 of homosexual relations between consenting adults (except those in the army, navy, or police).

The 1885 law had an effect that was quite the reverse of what had been intended. The low-profile homosexual was now endangered not only by imprisonment, but by the fact that, the sentence being relatively light, charges were more readily brought and the publicity resulting from a court case could be at least as damaging as imprisonment itself. The professional, however, had no reputation to lose and saw a two-year sentence as derisory in comparison with anything from ten to life.

The male prostitute had always had an easier time than women in the sense that he was less easy to identify, even when he went soliciting. As long as he refrained from turning out in drag, the police tended to leave him alone, even in areas where, according to one facetious tourist guide of the 1850s, any out-of-town yokel could go to see a veritable three-ring circus of Margeries, Pooffs, and Mary Anns. "The Quadrant, Holborn, Fleet Street and the Strand are full of them. Not so very long ago signs and bills were hung in the windows of respectable hotels in the vicinity of Charing Cross with the notice: 'Beware of paederasts!' They usually gather near the picture shops, and are recognisable by their effeminate appearance, fashionable clothing, etc.... The Quadrant is visited by a great number of the most notorious [of them], who parade there in search of their 'prey,' just like so many feminine prostitutes." [47]

This seems to have been something of an exaggeration. During the 50 years that spanned the middle of the century, there was a limited demand for homosexual prostitutes simply because social pressures tended to steer the bisexual in a heterosexual direction, leaving only the four or five per cent of genetic homosexuals to fill the role of customer. Some Victorians undoubtedly faced up to their bisexuality and deliberately suppressed the homosexual side, but it seems clear that the great majority of men with latent homosexual tendencies remained unaware of them.

It is difficult to estimate the prevalence of homosexuality at this period because in both Britain and America there was a fashion for intense male friendships that not only sublimated the homosexual urge but in many instances probably disguised the practice. Provided they fell short, as Herman Melville put it, by as little as one degree "of the sweetest sentiments entertained between the sexes," [48] they were considered perfectly acceptable, and even admirable. By the 1880s, however, on the eve of the *fin-de-siècle* reaction against the stuffy respectability of the preceding decades, the younger generation began to cultivate the unconventional. The English public school, which kept boys in monastic seclusion until their middle teens, had always been a nursery of homosexual experiment that had usually ended with the pupils' schooldays. Now, it continued into adult life. W. T. Stead made a valid point when he wrote, at the time of the Oscar Wilde scandal: "Should everyone found guilty of Oscar Wilde's crime be imprisoned, there would be a very surprising emigration from Eton, Harrow, Rugby, and Winchester to the jails of Pentonville and Holloway. Until then, boys are free to pick up tendencies and habits in public schools for which they may be sentenced to hard labor later on." [49]

Eton and Harrow were often followed by the all-male residential colleges of Oxford and Cambridge. Only in the 1970s, when it at last became safe to confess, did it become clear what a strong homosexual undercurrent there had been in upper-class education for almost a century. Clear, too, just what a danger blackmail had been when many of the top posts in diplomacy, government, and administration were filled by men who had grown up in this environment.

THE ENGLISH VICE

Frenchmen in the nineteenth century referred to homosexuality as *le vice allemand* (the German vice) and, with an equally cavalier disregard for accuracy, to flagellation as *le vice anglais*, but sexologists in both countries, inspired by a kind of inverted jingoism (or *hurrapatriotismus*), accepted the attributions with the greatest goodwill and set about providing chapter and verse. Ignoring such awkward exceptions as de Sade, Rousseau, and the religious-erotic flagellants of medieval Spain, the English happily concluded that it was the public school that was largely responsible for turning gentlemen into deviants. Trained from infancy by nannies and schoolmasters who believed that to spare the rod was to spoil the child, upper-class boys (they argued) found it habit-forming and continued in their adult years to need a good beating to set the blood coursing through their veins.

In fact, if being regularly whipped in childhood was all that was needed to make a flagellant, the practice would have been less an upper-class sport than an international pandemic. Except in India and among certain tribal peoples, the majority of history's children were treated with a harshness almost inconceivable today. Clearly, it made some difference who wielded the rod; a boy whipped by a young nanny or nursemaid about whom he had childish sexual fantasies, or by a schoolmaster whom he adored in adolescence, may well have found flagellation a powerful stimulant in later life. But in the great majority of cases, this particular deviation appears to have depended, as it still does, on some innate urge toward masochism.

Masochism was first defined at the end of the nineteenth century by the Austrian police doctor and psychiatrist, Richard von Krafft-Ebing, whose *Psychopathia Sexualis* (1886), a study of pathological sexual behavior in which the more lurid details had been carefully translated into Latin, soon became the bible of all pornographers who could afford a good Latin dictionary. Since the Marquis de Sade had given his name to the type of sexual pleasure derived from inflicting pain, it seemed reasonable to Krafft-Ebing to name the alternative pleasure of being hurt, humiliated, or dominated, after *its* most distinguished advocate, the Ritter Leopold von Sacher-Masoch, a fellow Austrian of some academic distinction who in 1870 had begun publishing novels and short stories on the theme of men who needed to have women inflict pain on them.

The most famous of Sacher-Masoch's stories was *Venus in Furs,* which established once and for all the essential weapons in the masochistic armory. Wanda, cruel, imperious, and fur-clad, entices her lover Severin into a trap, has him tied up, and then appears before him with a whip in her hand. Furs, whips, and satanic (but always aristocratic) beauties were a recurring theme in Sacher-Masoch's work. "The beautiful woman bent on her adorer a strange look from her green eyes, icy and devouring, then she crossed the room, slowly donned a splendid loose coat of red satin, richly trimmed with princely ermine, and took from her dressing table a whip, a long thong attached to a short handle, with which she was wont to punish her great mastiff. 'You want it,' she said. 'Then I will whip you.' Still on his knees, 'Whip me,' cried her lover. 'I implore you!' " [50]

Tennyson's "divinely tall and most divinely fair" heroines took over from small, wistful girls in the middle of the nineteenth century, and Charles Dana Gibson's long-legged autocrats came to epitomize the voluptuous man-eater of popular imagination.

Sacher-Masoch was by no means the first of the literary flagellants. There was, indeed, a long tradition of *femmes fatales* who dominated and even, like the praying mantis, killed the men they loved or coveted. And the men quite enjoyed it. Until the nineteenth century, there had been no precise stereotype of the predatory feminist, although "a wild imperious majesty" was *de rigueur*,[51] but the Victorians' muddled blend of public courtliness and private guilt made it necessary to create one.

"I love the majesty of human suffering," said Count Alfred de Vigny (who was not called upon to experience it to any significant extent), but while his contemporaries recognized the nobility of the sentiment they failed to observe its actuality in the slums and sweatshops of the Industrial Revolution. Many of them, as if to compensate for the sadistic negligence that was responsible for so much human misery, subjected themselves to a special type of artificially masochistic make-believe. The materials were readily at hand in the Gothic image of courtly love, where the lover suffered deeply because of the untouchability of his beloved, and this idea was inflated to unnatural proportions during the course of the century. There had been a brief fashion for the *homme fatale* (after the style of Byron) at the beginning of the century, but this gave way in the middle decades to the fatal woman whose power lay in pain, who was the antithesis of the Victorian "angel of the house," and by whom the man who dominated timid, deferential women at home was in turn reduced to abject subjection.*

In literature, the French at first led the field on the subject of *le vice anglais*. It was Théophile Gautier who crystallized the *femme fatale* with his own slightly eccentric picture of Cleopatra—queen, voluptuary, woman of sublime cruelty and barbaric insight, who each morning ordered the slaughter of the lover with whom she had spent the night.[53] His followers additionally favored Nyssia (a kind of oriental Lady Macbeth), Herodias, Helen of Troy, and the Queen of Sheba. On a less rarefied plane, Prosper Merimée established Spain as the breeding ground of the run-of-the-mill *femme fatale*, although toward the end of the century Russia came to be preferred.

Even so, it was that perfect English gentleman, Algernon Charles Swinburne, who produced the most exotic examples of "beauty fresh from hell."[54] Swinburne—whose obsessive masochism is still described in biographical dictionaries as "intemperate living"—believed that man should aspire to be "the powerless victim of the furious rage of a beautiful woman,"[55] a woman, perhaps, like "Dolores, Our Lady of Sensual Pain," who had:

> Cold eyelids that hide like a jewel
> Hard eyes that grow soft for an hour;
> The heavy white limbs, and the cruel
> Red mouth like a venomous flower . . .

and in whose ambience:

> Pain melted in tears, and was pleasure;
> Death tingled with blood, and was life.[56]

It was certainly a cut above Sacher-Masoch.

But the literary luminaries in the masochistic pantheon were romantics, to whom the *femme fatale* wielding the whip meant more than the pain itself. They lived in a special kind of dream world, richer and more immediate but no more real than that of

---

* Times change. Whereas the arrogant imaginary woman acted as a sexual stimulant to the Victorian male, the flesh-and-blood feminist today often alarms her lover into impotence.[52]

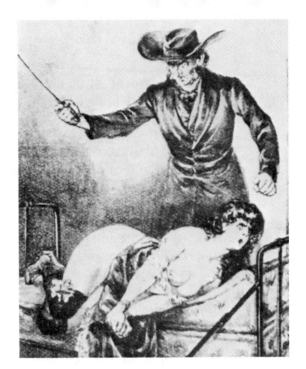

The artistic quality of the flagellation manuals was not high.

the modern horror-movie buff or the woman who commutes between bingo halls and criminal courtrooms in search of excitement. There was, however, another kind of masochist, to whom flagellation was a functional necessity.

The functional masochist was sometimes a tired sophisticate, sometimes repressed and under-sexed, sometimes the kind of coarse-grained bully whom Hippolyte Taine, the French philosopher and critic, described as a "human animal [that] finally satisfies itself with noise and sensuality." Taine blamed the excessive consumption of alcohol and red meat for the Englishman's addiction to the rod,[57] but the reasons were psychosomatic. For certain types of people, acute physical pain has the power to stimulate instead of depressing the nerves involved in sexual response. Rage can have the same effect, so that the functional type of masochist easily tips over toward sadism. (The portmanteau word for pleasure inseparable from pain, inflicted or received, is algolagnia.)

Imagination and private arrangement were frequently enough for the romantic masochist, but the functional type needed his brothel even if, during periods of deprivation, he sometimes had to console himself with one of the pornographic works in which the English specialized—*Lady Bumtickler's Revels, Madame Birchini's Dance,* or *The Romance of Chastisement;* or revelations of *school and bedroom. By an expert &c.** Some flagellation manuals were written specifically for brothel proprietors or independent prostitutes who liked to cater for all tastes. It was recommended that they "keep a small book containing a series of birch scenes, written in a dramatic form, which, when your visitor calls, you should put into his hands, and ask which of them he would most like to enact." [58] Once this was settled, there was the matter of clothing to be decided. The *Exhibition of Female Flagellants* frowned on complete nudity and recommended partial nakedness as a better way "to obtain the highest degree of [customer] satisfaction." Furs were good, but a nun's habit also went down well, as did gold-threaded silk stockings, spangled shoes, or an all-white outfit made of silk and lace and finished off with white garters.

Sexual flagellation, according to the inimitable Dr. Dühren, requires "great delicacy and a certain *savoir faire.*" [59] At the beginning of the nineteenth century, London's Mrs. Collet was famous for her *savoir faire,* but she was soon cast in the shade by Theresa Berkley (or Berkeley), a true perfectionist who believed that a workwoman was only as good as her tools. At her house near Portland Place, she kept her rods in water "so that they should be green and supple. She had a dozen tapering whip thongs, a dozen cat-o'-nine-tails studded with needle points, various kinds of thin supple switches, leather straps as thick as traces, currycombs and oxhide straps studded with nails, which had become tough and hard from constant use, also holly and gorse and a prickly evergreen called 'butcher's bush.' During the summer, glass and Chinese vases were kept filled with green nettles." [60] Mrs. Berkley catered for more than the make-believe masochist.

But her great invention (in 1828) was the Berkley Horse, or Chevalet, which was essentially an extending ladder (adjustable to the customer's height), propped up and comfortably padded. The client was tied to it so that his face projected through one space and his genitals through another. The "governess" stood behind and administered the whip to back or buttocks, according to taste, while a scantily dressed girl sat in front and massaged his cock and bollocks.** The Berkley Horse proved extremely profitable, its

---

* There was a good deal of "etcetera" in Victorian publishing. Until the commercial dust jacket became common, voluble authors often incorporated a blurb or sales pitch into the title itself.

** Still perfectly respectable words in the 1830s.

ingenious designer making (it was said) a net profit of £10,000 ($20,000) in eight years, a substantial sum for the time.

One of the better-known early flagellation manuals, *Venus Schoolmistress, or Birchen Sports* (1788, repr. 1898), divided male addicts into three classes—those who enjoyed being whipped by a woman, those who preferred to whip the woman, and those who derived their excitement simply from watching (something a brothel owner could always arrange for a paying customer). In other words, masochists, sadists, and voyeurs, all of them classified by modern psychoanalysts as suffering from sexual perversion.

But it could also be argued that most Victorian sex approached perversion in the psychoanalytical sense. The other face of the Victorians' enormous self-assurance was a sense of vulnerability and a nervous guilt that infused even simple heterosexual recourse to prostitutes with an element of intellectual and moral masochism. Gustave Flaubert summed up all the obscure, uneasy sexual contradictions of the nineteenth century when he said, "A man has missed something if he has never woken up in an anonymous bed beside a face he'll never see again, and if he has never left a brothel at dawn feeling like jumping off a bridge into the river out of sheer physical disgust with life." [61]

14.

The Great Debate

"When the women of this country come to be sailors and soldiers," said Senator George H. Williams of Oregon in 1866, "when they come to navigate the ocean and to follow the plow; when they love to be jostled and crowded by all sorts of men in the thoroughfares of trade and business; when they love the treachery and the turmoil of politics; when they love the dissoluteness of the camp, and the smoke of the thunder, and the blood of battle better than they love the affections and enjoyments of home and family, then it will be time to talk about making the women voters. . . ." [1]

Victorian legislators, in fact, had no shortage of motives for refusing to give women the vote. Ranged on Senator Williams's side were men who opposed, on principle, any change in the *status quo;* others who hated the prospect of feminine intrusion into the comfortable world of whiskey-and-cigar politics; others, still, who feared the electoral result of extending the franchise to millions of new voters whose party allegiance could not be predicted (though it was generally expected to be conservative). But these were unstatesmanlike attitudes that had to be expounded on the public platform with some care and delicacy, and, as a result, for more than fifty years most of the voices opposed to woman suffrage merged into a chorus whose refrain was concern for woman's "special" position and "special" morality.

It was a refrain that fell sweetly on women's ears. One of the most lucid advocates of the doctrine of "separate spheres" was, in fact, a woman—Catharine Beecher, sister of Harriet Beecher Stowe and the Reverend Henry Ward Beecher, America's most conspicuous parson. As Miss Beecher saw it, the division of society into men and women was a "natural" one (as opposed to division into classes, which was "unnatural"), and politicians and philosophers, far from trying to obliterate it, should seek to discover "new ways to maintain the boundaries between men and women in an urban environment where both might be performing similar functions." * When it came to mapping out the spheres, it was clear that man's included the responsibility for government, and for that reason the vote should belong to him alone.[3]

As an argument against woman suffrage, this would have been perfectly tenable even in modern terms if Miss Beecher had not promptly invalidated it by pointing out that women could influence public affairs very satisfactorily without recourse to the ballot box, by the simple expedient of influencing the opinions and outlook of those who *did* have the vote—their husbands and sons. What she smugly advocated, in effect, was the exercise of power without responsibility, but no one seems to have criticized her for wanting to have it both ways. This was because Victorian men had maneuvered themselves into the position of believing (or seeming to believe) that women were, by nature, morally superior to men, and in duty bound to exercise an elevating influence over them.

This curious idea was a product of nineteenth-century Romantic medievalism. When Mr. Gladstone remarked in the late 1880s that he could not countenance any extension of the franchise to women because he had too much respect for them "to trespass upon the delicacy, the purity, the refinement, the elevation" of their natures by involving them in the vulgarities of political life,[4] no one found it in the least extraordinary. Certainly not the women to whom he referred. For while there is little evidence to suggest that the original lady of courtly love was ever taken in by the myth of her own spiritual virtue, her Victorian successors swallowed it with uncritical unanimity, assured of it by their fathers, their husbands, by social reformers and by the Protestant

* It was a problem that had already arisen in a non-urban environment. Modern studies of the sunbonneted wagon-train pioneers who helped to open up the American West, sharing the heavy labor with their menfolk and displaying remarkable stamina under the most trying conditions, make it apparent that they fought all the way to retain their purely feminine roles and duties, regarding themselves not as partners but as long-suffering conscripts for whom the day of discharge could not come quickly enough.[2]

churches, who had long ago jettisoned the Catholic view of women and were as anxious to recruit feminine labor as the ladies
were to find occupation; good works were the nearest thing to a
career open to the majority of middle-class women. Even the popular English novelist, Mrs. Humphry Ward, who was eminently
capable not only of standing on her own feet but on those of any
mere male (no matter how distinguished) who was foolish enough
to irritate her, seriously believed that "the special moral qualities
of women" would be tarnished if they became involved in "the
ordinary machinery of political life," and that votes for women
would be no more than a prelude to anarchy, "breaking up all the
social values—weakening all the foundations of the social edifice." 5

Mrs. Humphry Ward and Catharine Beecher were clever and
self-sufficient, and they reached their conclusions by due process of
reason, however insecurely based. But they drew support on both
sides of the Atlantic from a great army of women who were content with things as they were and instinctively adopted and used
the fictions of woman's "special" position and "special" morality
as a last-ditch expression of resistance to change, a final means of
rationalizing (or spiritualizing) fear of the independence, of the
need to compete, that now lay just over the horizon. Susan B.
Anthony, after 50 years of campaigning for women's rights, admitted resignedly in 1902 that women in general were more conservative than men. This she attributed to "the narrowness and isolation of their lives, the subjection in which they have always been
held, the severe punishment inflicted by society on those who dare
step outside the prescribed sphere, and, stronger than all, perhaps,
their religious tendencies through which it has been impressed
upon them that their subordinate position was assigned by the
Divine will and that to rebel against it is to defy the Creator." 6
There was a good deal of truth in this, despite the element of
special pleading, and it made life extraordinarily difficult for the
radical minority. "It is not man as man," said the South African
propagandist Olive Schreiner, "who opposes the attempt of
woman to readjust herself to the new conditions of life: that opposition arises, perhaps more often, from the retrogressive members of her own sex." 7

But what is particularly interesting today about the long argument over woman suffrage in the late nineteenth and early twentieth centuries is that it was not only the reactionaries who took

Left: "Oh, woman! Masterpiece of creation, queen of humanity, mother of the human race. . . . Take my boots off!"

Right: "Take that away! . . . It is impossible to work with such a row going on. . . . Ah! Monsieur Cabassol, it is your first child and I swear it will be the last!"

"woman's morality" as their watchword, but the radicals as well. The no-change lobby claimed that women should *not* have the vote because they were special; for the very same reason, the suffragists claimed that they *should*. And they made no concessions. "The dangerous experiment," they declared, had already been tried "of enfranchising the vast proportion of crime, intemperance, immorality and dishonesty [viz. men], and barring absolutely from the suffrage the great proportion of temperance, morality, religion and conscientiousness [viz. women]. . . . In other words, the worst elements have been put into the ballot-box and the best elements kept out." [8]

It was an attitude that could scarcely have been expected to please even the averagely intemperate male, but it was to be perpetuated throughout the whole subsequent history of man-woman relationships. Up to, and including, today. Anita Bryant (women-as-guardians-of-morality) and Kate Millett (women-as-superior-beings) still display the two sides of the same traditional coin.

The suffrage movement did not develop along quite the same lines in Europe and America, Europe being more directly influenced by class and tradition, while the freer social system of America was offset by the complicated structure of its political institutions. Until 1882 in Britain, for example, any real property acquired by a married woman before or during marriage legally belonged to her husband; and until 1884, in most of the country, there was still a property qualification for voting. This meant that before 1882 the only substantial class of women who would have been able to exercise the vote, if it had been granted, would have been property-owning spinsters or widows, and only those who lived in cities. For this reason, among others, the early period of the suffrage movement in Britain was notable less for women's involvement than for men's, and more for an emphasis on "natural justice" than specifically *women's* rights. Later generations have praised the Utilitarian philosopher John Stuart Mill for moving that women be included in the franchise when the Reform Bill of 1867 was under discussion; but Mill also believed in an educational qualification for the vote, a kind of examination paper that would decide whether a voter should be allocated one vote or more (one for the ignorant laborer, six for the lawyer or clergyman).[9] Women's education being what it was at the time, he was offering the great majority of women a prize of no more than nominal value. Even so, principles of equity (the natural argument, to the modern mind, for woman suffrage) did receive an airing in Britain as, year after year, the question was debated in Parliament and, year after year, came to grief in the face of party indifference.

In the nineteenth century, as now, reform groups seeking political representation had to win support from those who already possessed it, and in Britain, a small country with a unified culture, an ingrained respect for the parliamentary tradition (now somewhat eroded), and a legislative system that, in the last analysis, allowed even the most revolutionary change to be pushed through by only a few hundred men, this challenge did not appear insuperable. Everything encouraged the suffragists to adopt an orthodox political approach. Even Emmeline Pankhurst and her daughters, emotional social reformers rather than rational advocates of the vote, embarked on their spectacular career conventionally enough as members of a pressure group designed to influence the Labour Party in favor of women's suffrage. When their impatience led them into direct action they did rather more damage to their cause than to the people and property they attacked. Even so, by 1914 the majority of parliamentarians had ceased to oppose votes for women; only the party manipulators remained to be converted. In 1918, women over 30 were granted the vote. Ten years later, when it had become apparent that women voters were simply women voters rather than the components of some vast Female Conspiracy, the qualifying age was dropped to 21.

The situation was quite different in America. There it was not equity but emotion that was the keynote, not (as many men claimed) because women were wholly governed by emotion, but because it was a more viable proposition in the context of time and place.

The disadvantage of a written constitution is its inflexibility; the trouble with safeguards designed to protect against bad causes is that they also erect barriers against good causes. Suffragists in America were faced with a far more intractable problem than their contemporaries in the compact nations of Europe. To amend the United States constitution and so make woman suffrage mandatory throughout the country, it was necessary to muster solid support within the states themselves. Every state that could be persuaded voluntarily to adopt woman suffrage not only improved the standing of its own women but could be expected to subscribe to the three-quarters majority necessary to push through an amendment to the federal constitution. One of the suffragists' primary aims, therefore, was to bring about reform on a local level. In most of the areas classified as "territories," simple legal enactment sufficed to extend the suffrage, but in the states themselves (and by the post-Civil-War years there were three times as many of these as territories) such reform required the passage of a constitutional amendment, which entailed not only a beneficent legislature but a state referendum showing a "constitutional majority," which was usually larger than a simple majority. The suffragists thus had to win the support, not of hundreds of men, but of millions, and lacking either powerful state organizations or the support of the traditional party bosses, who could see no electoral advantage for themselves in the enfranchisement of women, they had little choice but to try to influence the whole climate of public opinion. As one modern American scholar has pointed out, in any culture where religion is important, and where it is "largely an affair of the heart or of the intuitive qualities of the mind . . . so far it will be believed that the rational faculties are barren or perhaps dangerous." [10] In Victorian America, feeling was more prized than thinking, and the suffragists therefore embarked on their formidable task with an appeal, not to reason or justice, but to emotion.

W I T H   F R I E N D S   L I K E   T H E S E . . .

Since American men had long been accustomed to viewing their womenfolk in an excessively sentimental light, the suffragists should have been off to a head start.* And to begin with they seemed to be. The first organized demand for woman suffrage had been made at a convention at Seneca Falls, New York, in 1848, and a mere 21 years later—in 1869, when the National Woman Suffrage Association and the American Woman Suffrage Association were only just being born—women were granted the vote in the frontier territory of Wyoming.

Even at the time, this success was mysterious. Wyoming was the roughest and most lawless of the new lands, infamous for its bad men, its bad towns, and the hell-on-wheels of the railroad that had pushed from Cheyenne in 1867 to Laramie in 1869. Men outnumbered women by six to one. Yet every woman over 21 was granted not only the vote but the right to serve on juries, to hold her own property if married, and to be paid (if she was a teacher) on the same scale as a man.

There was a good deal of startled speculation about frontier egalitarianism, but the truth seems to have been that responsible settlers hoped to counteract Wyoming's gunslinging image by making a demonstration of respect for those citizens who most clearly symbolized respectability and morality. It was a risky experiment, but it worked. As Chief Justice Hoyt admitted a dozen years later, "With all my prejudices against the policy, I am under conscientious obligations to say that these women acquitted

---

* They were later to find men's attitude an acute irritant, even a hindrance. As Harriot Stanton Blatch complained just before World War I, "We are up against a hard proposition in the American man. . . . In England . . . the police put us off the streets; they send us to jail! . . . In America, they blandly admit us before the legislative committees, listen to all we have to say, treat us with perfect courtesy . . . and never so much as bother to answer our arguments. . . . [It's] highly insulting!" [11]

A Mormon family group in the 1880s; husband, four wives, and seven children

themselves [on juries] with such dignity, decorum, propriety of conduct and intelligence as to win the admiration of every fair-minded citizen of Wyoming. . . . After the grand jury had been in session two days, the dance-house keepers, gamblers, and *demimonde* fled out of the city in dismay, to escape the indictment of women grand jurors! In short I have never, in twenty-five years of constant experience in the courts of the country, seen more faithful, intelligent and resolutely honest grand and petit juries than these." [12] The effect was so immediate that the first elections under woman suffrage saw a substantial *drop* in the numbers voting, since the roughnecks stayed away from the polling places in case their presence should offend the ladies.[13]

Scarcely three months after Wyoming blazed the trail, the territory of Utah also granted the vote to women. This time, respectable suffragists reacted more with dismay than delight, for Utah was predominantly Mormon, and the Mormons were polygynists.

Although the sexual proclivities of Joseph Smith, founder of the Church of Latter-Day Saints, appear to have been less than puritan, by the time the Mormons came under the aegis of Brigham Young their polygyny, like their whole way of life, had strongly Old Testament overtones. Piety, sobriety, industry, frugality, fidelity, and asceticism were the rule.* Birth control, abortion, and intercourse during pregnancy, menstruation, and lactation were banned. Female obedience (as in all polygynous societies) was rigidly enforced. The Mormons, in fact, were aggressively straitlaced, but to outsiders their multiplicity of wives branded them as the worst kind of sinners. It was genuinely painful for suffragists struggling to sell morality as a qualification for the vote to see that vote handed on a platter to the most immoral group of women in the country.

Woman suffrage in Utah, however, as in Wyoming, was an exercise in masculine politics. Although the vote may have been given to women partly to counteract the general view that the Mormons held their wives in servitude, it was more directly aimed at insuring the maintenance throughout the territory of the influence of the Latter-Day Saints. The new railroad was expected to bring an increasing flow of new settlers, who would in time outvote the Mormons—if only men had the vote. But when the vote was extended to women, the numerical advantage was bound to be on the side of the Saints. Although only about 25 per cent of them are believed to have practiced polygyny, those who did (marrying converts when the supply of Mormon-reared girls ran out) considered three, four, or five wives as reasonable; Brigham Young had 27.

The first Utah experience of woman suffrage ended 17 years later, when Congress passed the Edmunds-Tucker Act of 1887 which, designed to break up the Mormon system in Utah, abolished woman suffrage at the same time. But when Utah was admitted to the Union in 1896 its constitution included votes for women, even though polygyny was no longer legally permissible, and even though the non-Mormon threat had failed to materialize. In the year of admission, nine out of ten citizens of Utah were members of the Church of Latter-Day Saints.[15]

The Mormons were an embarrassment to suffragists but not, on the whole, as much of an embarrassment as some of their allies closer to home—people like George Francis Train, whose more reputable exploits included going around the world in 80 days

---

* Which certainly contributed to long life for those who could bear a long life on such terms. A recent study argues that abstention from tobacco, alcohol, and extramarital sex are directly responsible for the fact that between 1950 and 1969 the Mormon rate of deaths from cancer—lung, esophageal, and cervical—was 22 per cent less than the average for the whole of the United States.[14]

(which gave Jules Verne and Mike Todd, if no one else, reason to be grateful to him), and the irrepressible Claflin sisters, whose advocacy of free love, short skirts, and occultism (not to mention magnetic healing, excess profits tax, vegetarianism, and world government) put them, in the early 1870s, about a hundred years ahead of their time. With the financial backing of Commodore Cornelius Vanderbilt and a useful apprenticeship in quack healing, spiritualism, and blackmail, the girls became the world's first lady stockbrokers and, when that palled, proprietors of the weekly newspaper that was first to publish Marx's *Communist Manifesto* in the United States. Victoria was even nominated by the Equal Rights party as a candidate for the presidency, with Frederick Douglas, the first black ever to be put up for the office, as vice-presidential running mate.

It was the personal view of Victoria and Tennessee that anything men could do they could do better, and Victoria, who had looks, charm, and the most unblushing effrontery, proved that, at least as far as publicity was concerned, this was certainly true. The National Woman Suffrage Association was an irresistible arena, and Elizabeth Cady Stanton and Susan B. Anthony and their respectable cohorts stood by her, pale but resolute, even when she campaigned not only for woman suffrage but for free love at its freest and a kind of highly personal anarchism that offended every tenet of the American Way of Life—and made a mockery of the entire feminine morality thesis. Victoria's public career lasted for only five years but her connection with woman suffrage did the movement considerable damage by associating it directly with sexuality and scandal. The defeat in 1875 of a suffrage bill in the Michigan legislature was directly attributable to her involvement in the Beecher-Tilton trial, an alienation-of-affection suit so full of salty detail that it kept the country enthralled for 16 glorious weeks. With friends like these, the suffrage movement scarcely needed enemies.

But it went ahead and made them just the same.

MORALITY ON THE WARPATH

This was not so obvious in the new states where progress was slow but reasonably satisfactory. The frontier lands hoped, as Wyoming had done, to attract family settlers by demonstrating how highly they esteemed respectability, and where the political scene had not yet congealed into irresistible forces and immovable objects it was possible to make a good case for giving women the vote. By 1900 four states had granted woman suffrage, and things looked promising in several more.*

The suffragists' vanity was flattered by these compliments to their worth, which confirmed what they had always believed. But by the turn of the century the complexion of the movement had changed. The earlier suffragists had contented themselves with disseminating the generalized radiance of feminine morality; the later ones transformed this into a harsh glare of rectitude. The result was that, while they gathered many new women into the fold, they alienated a great many of the male voters whose approval they needed if woman suffrage was ever to be achieved.

To begin with, the suffrage movement had associated itself with a number of constructive reforms, calling not only for the right of women to enter the universities and the professions, to hold property, and to receive custody of their children in divorce cases, but, in the wider sphere, for peace, the abolition of slavery, and social welfare legislation.

They had also called for temperance. American women were much more passionately involved in the temperance movement than their contemporaries in Europe, and although many supported it primarily in response to the dictates of the Church, others had a more personal interest. Americans had always put away an impressive quantity of beer and spirits, from home-brewed ale to whiskey, rum, and essence of lockjaw (otherwise known as applejack). Just before the War of Independence it was estimated that the colonists were downing close to four gallons of rum per head per year.[16] As time passed, less and less liquor was brewed at home and more and more had to be paid for, with distressing financial effects. But an even stronger argument against drinking, in women's view, was that it frequently acted on men as a sexual stimulant, and this, to women who had been brought up to think of sex as, at best a submission, and at worst a degradation, was intolerable. The intercourse forced on them by drunken husbands was rendered no more acceptable by the knowledge that, if the

---

* By 1914, 11 of the last 18 states admitted into the Union had statewide woman suffrage—but none of the first 30.

men had not spent all their money on liquor, they would have gone to prostitutes instead.

Few reasonable people would have denied that America's drinking habits would have benefited from reform, and the early suffragists' pleas for temperance were not extremist enough to offend those who believed that the tone of society could do with improvement and were prepared to accept that giving women the vote might help to bring this about.

In the 1870s, however, while the suffrage movement was still reeling from the effect of the Claflin sisters, the Women's Christian Temperance Union was founded—a misnomer, since it was prohibition, not temperance, that was its aim. The WCTU declared its intention of putting an end not only to drinking (and smoking) but to prostitution as well, and under the dynamic leadership of Frances Willard in the 1880s and 1890s set about refining the whole moral climate of the nation and reforming the character of the coarse and vulgar male. Since there appeared to be no way of attaining these objects unless women had the vote, the WCTU lined itself up with the campaign for woman suffrage.

The activities of the WCTU were diffuse. A lady who was too shy to run an anti-Rum booth at the county fair could help at a temperance kindergarten instead, or make up posies of flowers (with Bible texts attached) for Sunday distribution to every prisoner in the local jail. As a result, it was possible to attract many members who might otherwise have held back, and every woman who joined the WCTU could also be counted as a recruit to the cause of woman suffrage.

When Frances Willard died in 1898 and the WCTU faltered, the suffrage movement revived again, but it was not the same as it had been. Despite the continuing single-mindedness of Susan B. Anthony and a few other elder stateswomen, too many new recruits had been influenced by the example and experience of the WCTU, which had given them other hobbyhorses besides woman suffrage, and a strong sense of righteousness. Carried away by their own morality campaign, they were convinced that what they disapproved of had to be wrong. They would not—could not—make allowances for normal human frailty.

Not surprisingly, many potential supporters took fright. Men who had no particular objection to woman suffrage, as such, had the greatest possible objection to the scrutiny of their own manners, morals, and habits that the temperance-suffrage ladies promised as a sequel. The liquor interests, too, swore that if women were given the vote prohibition would result.* And they proved to be right. In the state of Washington in 1910 the temperance ladies agreed to hold their tongues for a while in deference to the "whiskey vote"; woman suffrage was passed in 1911; and prohibition came to Washington four years later. Between 1914 and 1917, seven Western states adopted prohibition; all of them were woman suffrage states.[17]

The woman suffrage movement alienated other potential supporters—the liberal-minded—by taking up a position on immigration. It had been clear since the 1870s that the strongest opponents of woman suffrage, apart from the vested political and liquor interests (and those "religious bigots" who believed that if women were allowed to vote "St. Paul would feel badly about it" [18]) were first-generation immigrants still saturated with European-Catholic ideas about woman's role. In the early years of the twentieth century, America's great immigration crisis was in flood, and this provoked a resurgence of the same kind of culture-protectiveness that had marked the nation's earlier history, with Italians, Russians, Poles, Hungarians, Greeks, and "Asiatics" added to the roster of outsiders. The white, American-born, middle-class women who formed the backbone of the suffrage movement became increasingly WASPish. In 1904, for example, Ida Husted Harper, referring slightingly to the political contribution made during the previous 35 years by "the majority of negroes, Indians and immigrants who have been enfranchised during that time," asked her readers to judge "whether women as a body could not bring something to offset these last acquisitions. Those who fear the foreign vote and the colored vote should remember that there are more native-born women in the United States than foreign-born men and women; more white women than colored men and women." [19] It was the white woman's vote that would insure a "pure America." **

* They had grounds for this beyond the propaganda of the American WCTU. In 1893, women in New Zealand had been granted the vote partly through the efforts of the local WCTU and partly as the result of a political miscalculation on the part of the prime minister. In the same year, the WCTU and their teetotal ("wowser") male allies also won what looked like the first battle in the prohibition war, an enactment that gave local electors control over liquor licenses in their own areas to the extent of forbidding the sale of liquor entirely.

** Ironically, Australia in 1902 had followed New Zealand in granting votes to women, and in its case the sequel had been, not an imminent threat of prohibition, but an Immigration Restriction Act framed to implement a "white-Australia" policy.

The suffragists won in the end, partly because by 1915 they had gained powerful support from trade unionists and social reformers, but more, perhaps, because the particular aspects of morality which they chose to stress suddenly found a large and willing audience during the course of World War I when the austerities of prohibition and the patriotic logic of immigration restriction ceased (temporarily) to appear reactionary and became, instead, symbols of hundred-per-cent clean-cut Americanism. By a malicious twist of fate, it was not until after the imposition of immigration restrictions (in 1917) and the ratification of prohibition (1919) that the Nineteenth Amendment was ratified and woman suffrage became part of the American Constitution. It was August 1920, 72 years since the demand had first been made at Seneca Falls.

THE   AFTERMATH

By 1920, New Zealand, Australia, Britain (on a restricted basis), and America had all granted women the vote; so, too, in the course of radical political change, had Finland (in 1906) and Norway (in 1907). The years immediately after the war saw women's suffrage introduced in Austria, Canada, Czechoslovakia, Germany, the Netherlands, Poland, and Russia. Turkey, a dictatorship in which the vote was irrelevant, had by 1926 outlawed many of the old masculine privileges, banned polygamy, and ordered women to cease wearing the veil.

The end of World War II brought woman suffrage to Albania, France, Hungary, Italy, Japan, and Yugoslavia, and the new state of Israel adopted it in 1948. Almost simultaneously, independence began to be granted to many of the old imperial possessions, and between 1949 and 1956 women in India, Indonesia, Pakistan (temporarily), Ghana, Chad, Dahomey, Mali, and Senegal all won the vote as a result.

Today, women in more than two-thirds of the world's countries are entitled to vote in national elections. But the picture that is so often held of brave women around the globe fighting for the abstract right to justice and equality, and being granted it in return for their noble and self-sacrificing work during war, revolution, or the struggle for independence, is in many ways misleading, a comfortable fiction that, like so many other historical fictions concerning relationships between the sexes, was a product of friendly collusion. It suited both sexes to emerge with their haloes intact.

Certainly, some suffragists did fight for justice and equality; but some demanded "equal rights" for themselves so that they could take a hand in restricting the rights of others. Some governments did introduce woman suffrage because war had made nonsense of the main arguments against it; but others used war as a grand-gesture reason for introducing a measure that had become desirable for old-fashioned party political reasons. And often, in the case of the new nations, women demanded and governments granted woman suffrage because it appeared to them as one aspect of the state of advanced Westernization that they were overridingly anxious to achieve.

The motives, perhaps, did not matter very much in the context of such a radical social development, except insofar as they illustrate that revolutions are not always accomplished by revolutionaries. What was important at the time was that the vote appeared as a symbol representing the end, at long last, of 5,000 years of masculine supremacy.

THE YEARS BETWEEN

It took almost 40 years for women in Britain and America to realize that it *was* only a symbol. Another revolution was needed, and it was not to occur until the 1960s.

During the intervening decades it was difficult to see things clearly. There was a General Strike in Britain in 1926, the Wall Street Crash in America in 1929, the continuing Depression of the 1930s, the World War of 1939-45, and the long slow years of recovery in Europe, longer for the victors than for the vanquished. Yet the social changes were striking, particularly for women. Though, as G. K. Chesterton drily remarked, "Twenty million young women rose to their feet with the cry, 'We will not be dictated to,' and promptly became stenographers," the new prospect of independence that had opened up in front of the twenties generation included the prospect of real independence—if they wanted it.

No one, however, encouraged them to want it. All the new

Hollywood romance rampant. Valentino in *Son of the Sheik*

toys and diversions of the postwar era were showered upon them. Cosmetics, lightweight clothes, cheap jewelry, phonograph records, holidays by the sea, dance halls, restaurants, coffee shops, tea rooms, and above all the cinema, conspired to absorb the brief spending power of those whose working lives were expected to last only for the few years between school and marriage. Men had possessed women, and women had been possessed by men, for more than 5,000 years, and it was to take more than a vote and a salary to break the marriage habit.

It was Hollywood, from the days of its first widespread popularity in the 1920s until television undermined its influence in the 1950s, that most consistently, conscientiously, and stylishly sustained the image of marriage as woman's natural goal, the romantic culmination of her life. Many package deals have been sold to the public, before and since, but never as effectively as Hollywood sold the package deal of glamour, romance, and marriage. Long after "the modern woman" had jettisoned the ideas and habits of her Victorian grandmother, Hollywood was still conditioning her to the belief that woman's place and destiny were in the home. Not because she had, as in the past, no option, but because she was willingly tied there by the magical power of love. Hollywood's view of love was by no means new; there was a literary thread going as far back as the days of the troubadours, if not much further. But where literature—even in the cloying romantic novels of the nineteenth century—had recognized it as a rare chemical reaction between favored individuals, Hollywood presented it as the birthright of all nice people, and the white wedding as a guarantee of its lifelong validity.

The conditioning extended to men, too. Fighting morale during World War II was more successfully maintained by Betty Grable and Alice Faye than by any bite-the-bullet general or cigar-chewing statement. It was Hollywood that supplied the marching songs, provided the image of the girl next door, assured every cinemagoer that when it was all over things would be just as they had been before—only better.

The reaction hit America first because its 12 million veterans returned home, not as Europeans did, to a civilization aged and matured by six years' direct contact with danger, but to one that had hardly been touched. The GIs might almost have been of a different generation from the wives and girl friends who were to be their lives' companions. Peace proved more challenging than war, and the early years of marriage, never easy, more traumatic than anyone could ever have foreseen. But old traditions died hard, especially the Hollywood-Victorian tradition that the state of marriage was itself, in some mysterious way, sufficient recompense even for a lifetime of incompatibility, recalcitrant children, petty backbiting, financial stress, and endless boredom. The great majority of ill-matched middle-class couples were prepared to face anything but the scandal of divorce, the admission of their own failure, and while their families were growing up they grimly held together "for the children's sake."

Although the "baby boom" lasted for more than ten years after the war, conveying a widespread impression of domestic contentment, the cracks had already begun to show. According to the Kinsey reports of 1948 and 1953 [20], 70 percent of men had visited prostitutes, and 40 percent of husbands been unfaithful to their wives. Thirty-seven percent of men and 19 percent of women had had at least one homosexual contact in their lives. One farmhand in six had experimented with zoophilia. Although these figures may well have represented an improvement on earlier centuries, they appeared nothing less than shocking to a generation conditioned to the Hollywood ideal of love.

Scientists of the mind found their services in increasing demand. Between 1946 and 1956 the membership of the American

Psychological Association increased by 241 per cent. Psychoanalysis became the fashion, and theories developed by Freud at the turn of the century became familiar, if ill-understood, commonplaces, leading large sections of the population to become neurotic about their neuroses. Freud's view of women was that they were far more masochistic and narcissistic than men, that they were rigid and unchangeable by the age of 30, and unable to match the high moral character of the male; all this because the infant girl discovered at an early age that she lacked a penis.* The truth or falsity of such propositions scarcely mattered. What the popularity of psychoanalysis did was encourage the discontented to explore their own internal problems, instead of seeking to arrive at some domestic *modus vivendi*. Deeper knowledge of self did not contribute much to a more tolerant understanding of others.

The dam was not to break until the mid-1960s, as the culmination of a process that had unexpectedly begun in Britain ten years earlier, when the last relics of wartime austerity were finally swept away and a generation of teenagers who had lived out the whole of their lives under gray restriction discovered a new world, the world of the here-and-now, and took it noisily into their own hands. The cult of youth that developed was only one aspect of an extremely complex social revolution, but it was reinforced by the nostalgia and envy of a great many older people who felt that the war had robbed them of their own youth.

It was the children of the postwar "baby boom" who, on both sides of the Atlantic, became the rebels of the late 1960s and early 1970s, rebels against what they regarded as the dreary political, social, and sexual orthodoxy of their parents. Despising the conventional, they hastened to evolve their own convention (one notable for its mental and physical untidiness); although tiresome while it lasted, it had the salutary effect of forcing their elders to scrutinize the standards to which they themselves, often unthinkingly, adhered. In America in 1965, there was one divorce to every four marriages. By 1977, there was one to every two.

---

* This theory, which Freud evolved between 1900 and 1910 (just when the moralist-feminists of the Western world had begun to show their claws in earnest), had unmistakable class connotations. Poor children might run about naked, but the well-brought-up little girl of Victorian and Edwardian times very rarely *did* discover that she lacked a penis. It was axiomatic in upper and middle-class households that children should never see each other in the nude, or in the process of relieving themselves.

In the past, many unsatisfactory marriages had survived because women had clung to them, but by the mid-1970s this had ceased to be true. The feminist movement, which effectively began with the foundation in 1966 of the National Organization for Women and was given a particular direction and style by the need to compete for political attention with the civil rights and anti-Vietnam war campaigns, was a very different proposition from the earlier suffrage movement. And a major reason was that, where permission to vote and permission to earn had failed to change women's view of themselves, a single medical development of the 1960s had spectacularly succeeded.

BIRTH CONTROL

For thousands of years women had been swallowing powders and potions in the hope of preventing conception. The Pill, at last, was an oral contraceptive that really worked. But its importance was far greater than that. Since the act of taking it was quite dissociated from the act of intercourse, it aroused none of the moral, political, social, or esthetic uneasiness that had proved such a long-lasting heritage of Victorian attitudes to birth control.

Although Church and state had always taken account of the question of birth limitation, it became a major public issue only in the nineteenth century. For this, "the best-abused man of the age," the economist Thomas Robert Malthus, was directly if unintentionally responsible. In 1798, he published an *Essay on the Principle of Population* that was designed to refute the optimistic belief of Rousseau and, more particularly, William Godwin (widower of Mary Wollstonecraft, the "first modern feminist"), that an increasing population and social ownership of land were a formula for Utopia. Malthus claimed that population would always outstrip the available resources, and could see no way of changing this prospect, only of controlling its development by means of a system of checks and balances that would necessarily operate against the poor, the numerical majority.

Malthus's theories might not have had any great impact if there had not followed, in 1801, the first comprehensive British census, which showed that the pace of population growth had wildly outstripped the predictions of both politicians and statisticians. Suddenly, the population question turned into the population problem. Europe was alarmed, for its food production resources were already strained, but America was unconcerned and remained so until the end of the century. As Thomas Jefferson remarked at the time, "In Europe the object is to make the most of their land, labor being abundant; here it is to make the most of our labor, land being abundant." [21]

European theorists drew several conclusions from Malthus's gloomy document. In the first place, if the poor, the vast majority of the people, continued to multiply, even the rich would suffer. In the second place, there was no hope of improving the condition of the poor themselves unless there was a diminution in their numbers. And in the third, that the solution was to encourage the poor to limit the size of their families. Malthus, a clergyman for several years before he was appointed Professor of Modern History and Political Economy at Haileybury, the East India Company's training college, in 1805, disapproved of birth control, however, and a great many people shared his view. Steeped in the Augustinian belief that marital sex was a sin unless procreation was its end, they could not reconcile the idea of contraception with their Christian consciences.

The French, curiously enough, had already succeeded admirably in achieving just such a reconciliation, with the result that, almost a century before the rest of Europe and against all the laws of probability, the birth rate in France had begun to decline in the 1790s. As far as demographers have been able to discover, this occurred as a sequel to the theological controversies that raged in the seventeenth and early eighteenth centuries, notably that associated with Cornelius Jansen, who preached that contemporary Catholic dogma had become so lax that it now represented all that St. Augustine had condemned. Jansenism was extremely influential in parts of France, but its horror of illicit sex (in the Augustinian sense) was such that it often skirted around the subject; further, as a heretical sect, it encouraged its followers to stay away from the orthodox confessional. The unforeseen effect was to shift the responsibility for everyday morality from the Church confessional to the individual conscience so that it became notably easier to view married sex as the concern, not of the priesthood, but of husband and wife alone.[22] Throughout much of the eighteenth century, infanticide and the abandonment of un-

wanted children to foundling homes persisted, but increasing social unease and the series of disastrous harvests between 1773 and
1789 that caused prices to soar and wages to plunge finally led
many of the poorer and middle classes to take deliberate steps to
limit their families; *coitus interruptus* appears to have been the
system generally used. Although the population of France continued to increase, it did so at a much slower rate than in the rest
of Europe.

The nineteenth century had other than religious reasons for
finding the idea of contraception distasteful. It did not, for example, accord with the middle classes' romanticization of motherhood. Nor did it suit the temperance ladies, many of whom
wanted not only to be freed from the burden of childbearing imposed on them by drunken husbands but, even more, to be freed
from the burden of intercourse itself; the one form of contraception that met their requirements was abstinence, and at the center
of the first "voluntary motherhood" movement was the right of a
woman to refuse her husband. The women who were opposed to
the demands of the suffragists, who believed in "separate spheres"
and divided human conduct into the "natural" and the "unnatural," could scarcely have been expected to view contraception
as anything other than "unnatural," while committed suffragists—
loudly professed guardians of morality—were quite unable to support any practice that would lead lovers to "indulge their passions" without proper moral fear of the consequences. And the
medical profession, of course, conservative as the classes on whom
its income depended, readily confirmed that "a woman on whom
her husband practices what is euphemistically called 'preventive
copulation' is necessarily brought into the condition of mind of a
prostitute," and that she had "only one chance, depending on an
entire absence of orgasm, of escaping uterine disease." [23]

In most of Europe, contraception became a public issue before
it had established itself as a widespread private custom, and, as a
result, general acceptance was long delayed. Its advocates, defen-
sive in face of moral and medical opposition, rarely advocated it
for their own class, though in the 1870s and 1880s the middle
classes were to take to it for selfish economic reasons while continuing to disapprove of it for others. The most vocal exponents of
birth control, as things turned out, were Malthus's own followers
who, unable to discover any other way of warding off the over-
population he had foreseen, rejected one part of his teaching and

became outright advocates of contraception for the masses. Coincidentally, they succeeded in alienating the first generations of Marxists, already repelled by the Malthusian implication that the working classes, through lack of sexual discipline, were responsible for their own misery, and in no mood to heed the Neo-Malthusians' claim that birth control, in the long run, would prove to be the cure for low wages and poverty. Marxists knew that the same result would be achieved far more rapidly by destruction of the whole capitalist system.

From the humanitarian point of view, this was unfortunate. Nineteenth-century women of the laboring classes were in desperate need of contraceptive advice. It was on them that the whole burden of the family rested; they who suffered most from the appalling conditions in which the workers of the new cities lived. They passed their days in suffocating, ear-blasting weaving sheds, and went home to a cellar, an infested slum, or a flimsy shack with few cooking facilities and no water. Their diet was "a small bit of bacon cut up with the potatoes; lower still [on the poverty scale] even this disappears, and there remain only bread, cheese, porridge, and potatoes, until on the lowest round of the ladder, among the Irish, potatoes form the sole food." [24] They suffered one pregnancy after another, miscarriages, stillbirths, and the recurring pain of seeing their children die during the first years of life, or survive to be sent, at the age of five or six, to work a 12-hour day in the mines or a 16-hour day in the spinning mills.

Exhaustion and malnutrition were the killers. When Francis Place, a Neo-Malthusian devotee of contraception, issued a handbill in 1823 addressed to "the Married of Both Sexes," he mentioned pelvic malformation in the woman—a cause of serious difficulties in childbirth—as an important reason for using it. There are no statistics to show how common this problem was in Place's day, but deformity of the pelvis is frequently caused by rickets in childhood, and although the medical profession failed to recognize it until the middle of the century, rickets, a vitamin-D deficiency disease, was already the scourge of the manufacturing towns. By 1870, as many as one-third of the poor children of such cities as London and Manchester were suffering from visible symptoms of rickets; modern diagnostic techniques would have shown a far higher proportion.[25]

The women of the laboring classes suffered far more than men from the results of unregulated sex, for as long as *coitus interrup-*

tus and the condom (still a cumbersome and inconvenient device) remained the two most widely used means of contraception, wives were largely at the mercy of their husbands. There was little they could do to protect themselves other than resort to dangerous pills and potions, or abortions painfully and hazardously self-induced by inserting a knitting needle, a wire, or even a knife into the uterus to provoke the damage that would cause it to reject the embryo and placenta.

In this kind of situation, the motives of the people who tried to disseminate contraceptive advice were irrelevant. What was important was that men like Francis Place, politically motivated though they may have been, did their best to inform women about methods which, though far from new, were easy, reasonably effective, and controllable by the women themselves. Returning to the ancient Hebrews, Place suggested the sponge. "A piece of soft sponge about the size of a small ball attached to a very narrow ribbon, and slightly moistened (when convenient) is introduced previous to sexual intercourse, and is afterwards withdrawn, and thus by an easy, simple, cleanly and not indelicate method, no ways injurious to health, not only may much unhappiness and many miseries be prevented, but benefits to an incalculable amount be conferred on society." [26] Thirty years later, another influential writer, Dr. George Drysdale, whose *Elements of Social Science* ran into 26 editions between 1854 and 1887, recommended that the sponge be supplemented by a douche with tepid water after intercourse, which would certainly improve its efficacy.

But Drysdale's last editions were already out of date in terms of current technology, even if the changes that had begun to come about in the 1870s were at first to benefit only the upper and middle classes.

The perceptible decline in the birth rate which began in the 1880s in Britain and much of Europe was attributable to no single factor. Although historians often suggest that it occurred because the middle classes at last decided to choose an improved standard of living in preference to a large family, it would be truer to substitute the words "were able to" for "decided to." For the first time, condoms had become available that were sensually acceptable and relatively unobtrusive. But just as important was the fact that a considerable number of Victorian husbands began to feel compelled to use them, not so much for contraceptive as for prophylactic purposes. The long controversy over the Contagious Diseases Acts (see pages 366–67) had the salutary effect of reminding every man who ever visited a prostitute that he ran the risk of infecting his wife, and since wives, however privately, feared infection and at the same time saw a prospect of release from regular childbearing, they may have made only a token protest. If that. As historians of costume have pointed out, it can hardly be regarded as coincidence that respectable women first began in the 1880s to wear attractive nightdresses instead of the "markedly unappealing" ones of former times.[27] Freed from at least some of the fears that had helped to contaminate sex for them, they began to compete with prostitutes for their husbands' continuing attentions.

The condom had never been precisely cheap to buy or easy to make.* It did not fit very well, and had to be put on carefully and with both hands. But the discovery of vulcanization in 1843-44 led to the manufacture of a crepe rubber type that was an improvement in all ways, and by the 1870s it was being used with increasing frequency. An air of impregnable respectability was lent to it by packaging that featured full-color portraits of Queen Victoria and Mr. Gladstone.[29] Fifty years later, liquid latex and automation led to a considerable drop in price; there are no statistics for British or German manufacturers, but in America in the mid-1930s sales approached 317 million a year.[30]

Even more of an advance, but slower to come into general use because it required individual fitting, was the device for women that came to be known as the Mensinga diaphragm. In 1838, a German pioneer, Friedrich Adolph Wilde, proposed a refinement of an idea then current in rural areas of Europe and known in one form or another from the days of the early Egyptians, that of a plug or cap designed to block the cervical opening between the vagina and the uterus. But where crocodile dung, wads of linen, or pads of compressed leaves were the materials that had formerly been used, Wilde suggested taking a wax impression of the cervical opening and the ring of muscle surrounding it, and then molding from the wax a rubber shield that would fit snugly and could

---

* One mid-nineteenth-century recipe said, "Take the caecum of the sheep; soak it first in water, turn it on both sides, then repeat the operation in a weak ley [solution] of soda, which must be changed every four or five hours, for five or six successive times; then remove the mucous membrane with the nail; sulphur, wash in clean water, and then in soap and water; rinse, inflate and dry. Next cut it to the required length, and attach a piece of ribbon to the open end. Used to prevent infection or pregnancy."[28]

be kept in position all the time, except during menstruation. This, in fact, was an idea that ultimately developed into the modern cervical cap, but it does not seem to have been taken up at the time. Instead, it was the diaphragm developed in the 1870s by the German doctor Mensinga that gained swift popularity, notably in Holland and Britain, in the following decade, and subsequently in other countries. It remained rare in the United States until the 1920s. The diaphragm is a paper-thin sheet of rubber with a stiffened circular rim, fitted longitudinally into the vagina, one end stretching right to the back, and the other lodging under the pubic bone at the front. It covered a much wider area of the upper vaginal wall than the cervical cap, and so did not require precise individual fitting.

One problem about the dissemination of information on new devices such as these was that no one was entirely sure whether it was legal since there were gray areas in the laws of most countries. An important test case was brought in Britain in 1877, however, over whether birth control information came into the legal category of "obscene literature." The book in question was a fairly full American account of contraceptive practices—Dr. Charles Knowlton's *The Fruits of Philosophy; or, the private companion of young married people* (New York 1832)—which had been circulating unobtrusively in Britain for years before it became the focus of attention. The Solicitor-General described it in court as "a dirty, filthy book," whose object was "to enable persons to have sexual intercourse, and not to have that which in the order of Providence is the result of sexual intercourse," [31] and the jury dutifully found it "depraved." But the end result of the case, in which the defendants were condemned but soon released on a technicality, was that the authorities became wary of taking action on birth control literature for some time afterward. The subject moved a step nearer to becoming respectable, and Annie Besant, one of the defendants, founded the Malthusian League, a militant body of advocates for free discussion of birth control and wide dissemination of literature concerning it.

This, from the point of view of Europe's Neo-Malthusians, was becoming more urgent than ever. For despite all the poverty and starvation of the Industrial Revolution, in most countries there had been a slow but noticeable decline in the infant mortality rate. In the mid-eighteenth century, a baby born in one of England's larger towns had only one chance in three of living until its first birthday; by 1900 it had only one chance in four of dying before it.[32] To parents and population theorists alike, contraception was becoming a necessary substitute for infant mortality.

In America, as in France, parents had already taken the matter quietly into their own hands. In 1800, the fertility rate for white women had been 7.04. In other words, the average woman bore seven children in her lifetime—of whom only five, on average, survived. By 1880, the fertility rate had dropped to 4.24, and by 1900 to 3.56. It had been a long, slow decline, rather than a sharp one, and the theorists of the early twentieth century unanimously proclaimed that it had been deliberate, and that birth control practices had been at the root of it. But they were engaged in the "race suicide" debate that prompted Theodore Roosevelt to condemn the tendency toward smaller families as "decadent," and to blame women who avoided having children as "criminal against the race . . . the object of contemptuous abhorrence by healthy people." [33] In view of the Augustinian piety of the nineteenth-century American woman, it seems likely that abstention may have been as commonly used as "artificial" methods.

To begin with, there was no shortage of information on contraception. Robert Dale Owen's tract on *Moral Physiology; or, a brief and plain treatise on the population question* had appeared in 1831, and it was followed by a number of other works, including Knowlton's *Fruits of Philosophy*, which strongly advocated douching immediately after intercourse, and even more strongly recommended the syringe, which Knowlton claimed to have invented, and which certainly made douching more efficient; it was still in common use a hundred years later.

More colorful, though in the long run less influential, was John Humphrey Noyes, founder of the Oneida Community, one of the few successful radical communes of the many that came and went in the middle of the century. Noyes propounded "complex marriage"—which was not polygamy but omnigamy, a system whereby, subject to personal preference, any man and any woman in the community were at liberty to come together or separate at will— and a system of eugenics called "stirpiculture," which was designed to improve the stock by means of controlled reproduction. Birth limitation, practiced when the seniors of the community had not given permission to beget children, was achieved by means of *Karezza*—a new name for the *coitus obstructus* that had been used by both Chinese and Indians centuries before (see pages 171–72). The idea that it might be possible to avoid ejaculation by this means seems first to have occurred to Noyes in 1844, though he did not commit it to print until 1866, in the pamphlet *Male Continence*.[34] He believed that it was an entirely original idea and, in the sense that he had not himself heard of it before, this may well have been true. His arguments in favor of it were that it satisfied men's and women's sexual needs, avoided the excessive and "oppressive" procreation that was almost universal at the time, and yet did not require the use of "unnatural, unhealthy and indecent" condoms, sponges, and lotions, which were, "of course, destructive to love." [35] Although the method was not 100 percent effective as a contraceptive, it appears to have produced none of the side effects predicted by its critics. Noyes' son, Theodore, reported after 22 years that nervous diseases in the Oneida Community were far below the average in the country, and the death rate was almost unnaturally low for the time.[36]

Birth control, unfortunately, was about to become a public issue, partly thanks to the activities of Anthony Comstock, an official of the New York Society for the Suppression of Vice. Obscenity laws, in America, were not a matter for central jurisdiction but for individual states and municipalities. There was one way, however, in which Congress could influence the situation, and in 1873, relentlessly lobbied by Comstock, it passed a law prohibiting the mailing across state frontiers of obscene material; birth control information and devices were specifically defined as "obscene." Comstock himself subsequently became a special agent of the Post Office Department and claimed toward the end of his life that he had "convicted persons enough to fill a passenger train of sixty-one coaches, sixty coaches containing sixty passengers each, and the sixty-first almost full. I have destroyed 160 tons of obscene literature." [37]

The Comstock law was by no means as effective as Comstock and his followers made it appear. In states with a liberal attitude toward birth control, the situation remained virtually unchanged even if exports suffered. In the more straitlaced districts, however, it discouraged the underground circulation of information and materials and—everywhere—succeeded in making the whole subject appear faintly disreputable. And it proved a serious hindrance when, at the beginning of the twentieth century, a public movement in favor of nationwide family planning began to develop.

This movement, though it emerged later than in Europe, had a very similar purpose. The Neo-Malthusians had feared that their world would be reduced to starvation by the uncontrolled expansion of the laboring classes. It was a fear that had abated somewhat as the nineteenth century progressed, partly because substantial supplies of basic foodstuffs had become available for import, and partly because so many surplus millions of the European population had been exported to Australia, Canada, New Zealand, southern Africa, and, above all, America. But it was precisely this influx of immigrants into the United States in the last decades of the nineteenth century and the first of the twentieth that set Americans worrying about *their* population problem. Many—perhaps the majority—of these newcomers were uneducated, often Catholic by faith, and inclined to reproduce at a high rate. It was not the food supply that they threatened, but the traditional dominance of White Anglo-Saxon Protestants. When the WASPs began to advocate immigration restriction, or family limitation for immigrants, or both, they were as clearly elitist as the Neo-Malthusians of England had appeared to be almost a century before. Suffragists, it may be remarked, were more than a little ambivalent about birth control. It was not simply that their ostentatious morality forbade them to advocate what seemed an invitation to immorality; they were more concerned not to weaken their argument that votes for women was the natural way to offset the votes of immigrants.

The inevitable result of these developments was that birth control became, as it had already become in Europe, not a liberal-humanitarian solution for clearcut social problems, but a factor in class warfare—and one that took eugenics, "improvement of the stock," as its watchword. Ironically, the two women whose names became famous in the Western world for their pioneer work in spreading knowledge of birth control, who became admired as radicals intent on giving women, at last, control over their own destinies, were both committed elitists. "More children from the fit," wrote the American Margaret Sanger in 1919, "less from the unfit—that is the chief issue of birth control." [38] And Marie

Stopes, in England, given the opportunity, would have adopted Hitlerian methods for sterilization of those who failed to match up to the required mental and physical standards.

Arrogant though the birth control movement was, and hindered as it was by officialdom and by the persisting Victorian taboo on discussing anything to do with sex, it made erratic but continuing headway. Marie Stopes and Margaret Sanger opened clinics, wrote book after book with titles like *Married Love* and *Happiness in Marriage*, exchanged acrimonious letters with critics, appeared on platform after platform. Their clinical experience was interesting. Most of the women who attended for the first time had already used some form of contraception; discouragingly, follow-up studies in America showed that two years later fewer than half the patients were still using the method recommended by the clinic, the rest presumably having reverted to the systems that were more familiar to them. Of these the douche appears to have been most common, although a proportion of women used the sponge; in 1934 it was estimated that those who used it, even without medical advice, had a 50 per cent success rate. The clinics themselves advocated diaphragms and cervical caps, douches, sometimes the sponge, and sometimes olive oil alone.[39]

In America by 1930 there were 55 clinics in 23 cities in 12 states, while in England the Ministry of Health conceded that local health departments might be permitted to advise on birth control in cases where further pregnancy would be detrimental to health. The year 1937 saw the state of Carolina offer birth control services through its public health program, and other southern states soon followed; their motives were by no means irreproachable, but this was probably unimportant to black women who needed advice.

The old attitudes persisted for a surprisingly long time. Years after the eugenicists had retired from the fray, when birth control had returned—it might have been thought—to the realm of physical and economic common sense, the House of Commons witnessed an exchange between the Minister of Health and an Opposition questioner. "Is it not a ridiculous position," asked the questioner, "that even where family planning clinics are held in local authority premises, it is forbidden to advertise them or publicize them in any way?" The Minister saw nothing ridiculous in it and had no intention of urging local health authorities to tell anyone other than doctors that such family planning clinics even existed.[40] This was in 1962—a year after the Pill was first marketed in Britain.

It had been confirmed as early as the 1930s that injections of natural estrogen, progesterone, or the male hormone testosterone, would successfully prevent the release of eggs from woman's ovaries into the Fallopian tubes, where fertilization could take place, but it was not until 1955 that a progesterone-only Pill could be tested (in Puerto Rico), and another five years passed before the combined estrogen-progesterone Pill was settled on for general prescription. It proved to be just what women had been waiting for. Though there were often to be physical side effects, these were relatively minor; it was the social side effects that were to be major. Especially since the 1960s also produced two alternatives to the Pill that were, psychologically, equally free from intimations of traditional morality.

The IUD or intra-uterine device was extensively developed in the 1960s, usually taking the form of a small piece of flexible plastic (or sometimes copper) twisted into one of a variety of shapes, such as a coil or a loop, and anchored in place by an extension that curved round the cervix into the vagina. Like any other foreign body in the womb, this prevents conception (so the medical profession believes) by affecting the womb lining in such a way that the fertilized egg cannot implant itself. The IUD, like the Pill, proved to have side effects,* but it offered a satisfactory alternative to many women who did not respond well to the Pill or were lax about taking it. Once in position, the IUD can remain for two years or more.

The second alternative to the Pill was designed for men, not women. This was vasectomy, a minor operation that involves cutting and tying off the two tubes that carry sperm from the testicles

---

* Including some that could scarcely have been foreseen. In Sweden in 1974 a paternity suit was filed against Uri Geller, who had publicly demonstrated his ability to bend such things as spoons by power of thought. The girl involved did not claim that Geller had fathered her child, but that his magical powers had so altered her contraceptive loop that it became inoperative.[41]

to the penis. It had been used in India for some time, but the West only began to overcome its suspicions of something that appeared unnecessarily drastic when it was made clear that it did not affect virility and could, indeed, be reversed if the operation had been properly performed in the first place.

By 1970, the Western world at least appeared to have accepted contraception as a personal matter.* But the Western world could afford to, after almost a century of declining birth rates and increasing food supplies that appeared to prove conclusively that Malthus had been wrong. Almost at once, however, came the Great Population Scare, when ecologists, disappointed by the results of the Green Revolution, which had been expected to transform agricultural production in the Third World, began to express the gloomiest forebodings about the future. If the world population doubled between 1971 and 2007, as was generally forecast, there seemed little possibility of avoiding the most severe food shortages.

Third World countries not only took note but tried to take action. Mildly, in the case of the predominantly Catholic Philippines, where President Marcos, in 1976, issued a decree forbidding either Church or civil functionaries to officiate at a marriage where the couple had not attended a course on family planning. Ruthlessly, in the case of India, where after a preliminary skirmish with the problem during which vasectomy patients were given a transistor radio as a good-conduct prize, state administrations turned their attention to more forceful measures. In Maharashtra in 1976 it was even proposed that parents with more than two children who refused sterilization should be jailed for two years, and rural districts that could show the most sterilizations in the course of a year were promised priority status for irrigation facilities and drinking water supplies. In some areas during the run-up to the elections of 1977, villagers were afraid to appear in public places— or even, sometimes, to go home to sleep—in case they were picked up by sterilization teams. The government proudly reported that in 1976 seven million vasectomies had been carried out.[42] But the

---

* Though not abortion which, regarded by feminists as a necessary back-up to contraception, attracted from certain sections of the public an opposition that, in the later 1970s, took on a Biblical virulence. The demand to make it freely available met with much the same kind of legal resistance as the birth controllers had encountered a few decades earlier.

people of India were not impressed. Mrs. Gandhi's Congress Party suffered a crushing defeat at the polls. Since then, the birth control campaign has maintained a low profile, quietly promoting vasectomies and IUDs (Indian peasant women cannot be relied upon to take the Pill) and hoping that perseverance will succeed where coercion failed.

The special psychology of the developing countries is being taken very much into account by biochemists, although the improved contraceptives on which they are working seem likely to be just as beneficial to the West. There is the "tricycle" Pill, which reduces the frequency of menstruation (still considered unclean in many parts of the world) to four times a year. There are injections that have a six-months' contraceptive effect; although these are not yet regarded as safe by America and most European countries, they have been in large-scale use in Thailand for more than ten years. The future holds special vaccines, effective for two or three years, and a hormone capsule that, implanted in the arm or buttock, will function for the same length of time. There is even promise of a contraceptive taking the form of a nasal spray, particularly useful in countries where the common cold is *not* common. Vaginal pessaries with which women can safely self-induce abortions have been intensively tested. And the day of the male Pill is approaching.[43] There is little likelihood that any of these will turn out to be the one, ideal, risk-free, foolproof contraceptive, but they hold out hope to people for whom current methods have proved unsatisfactory.

THE FEMINIST REVOLUTION

Politics and the Pill between them helped to give the feminism of the late 1960s a unique character. Those of its spokeswomen who attracted most publicity in the Western world were combative, vocal, and frequently silly, but there was enough truth in what they said to attract support from even the most lukewarm liberals. The extremist wing of the movement, resentful idealists, aimed to sweep away all the social attitudes that had developed out of 5,000 years of male supremacy, but the more practical reformists saw the struggle for equality with men as, by and large, a legal one, and assumed that when laws were liberalized other problems would gradually disappear. By 1975, International Women's Year, they had won very nearly all their demands—except, in America, the absolute confirmation of their *right* to them as expressed in the proposed Equal Rights Amendment to the Constitution:

1. Equality of rights under the law shall not be denied or abridged by the United States or by any State on account of sex.

2. The Congress shall have the power to enforce, by appropriate legislation, the provisions of this article.

3. This amendment shall take effect two years after the date of ratification.

Even if custom often lagged behind the law, and the developing countries far behind the West, the feminists of 1975 had accomplished as much in seven years as their suffragist predecessors had accomplished in 70. It was not because they were clever, or more deserving, or more determined, but because they started out from a far more advantageous position, and above all because they lived in a world of television, radio, and mass circulation newspapers.

By 1979, all the jobs that Senator George H. Williams of Oregon had thought, in 1866, that women could never do, were being done by women. There were women soldiers and sailors, farmers and engineers, bankers and lawyers. There were women truck drivers, too, and brain surgeons, and jumbo jet pilots. In Britain, a woman was even elected head of government, while 51 of the

The nineteenth-century marriage bed

1,107 members of the House of Lords (nominated) were women, and 19 of the 635 elected members of the House of Commons. But in America, home of the feminist movement, only one of the 100 members of the Senate was a woman, and only 16 of the 435 members of the House of Representatives.

The immediate reason for women's higher political success rate in Britain, where the feminist movement was noticeably less dynamic than in America, was that they were still elected—though with the assistance of a stronger feminine awareness on the part of women voters—more on their merits as individuals than as "women with a capital W." In America, women who contemplated entering public life often had to contend with an antifeminist backlash more powerful than the feminist impetus itself.

Even so, considering the overall extent of the feminist achievement, the number of women running for public office—quite apart from those elected to it—was relatively low. Did this, perhaps, echo the neolithic situation of so long ago, when men did the talking and women got on with the work? Or was it, as geneticists continued to proclaim, a demonstration that men were still biologically programmed to the attainment of dominant, rule-making status?

Or was it a combination of both factors?

Epilogue

The people of medieval Europe had 12 generations during which to adjust to the idea that women were worthy of respect, the Victorians three generations to accept that they were worthy of the vote. The modern world has had to adapt to almost complete legal and sexual equality in less than a decade. Predictably, the results have been chaotic, and the psychological penalty is now having to be paid.

Because the first and most revolutionary aspect of woman's liberation was her new sense of sexual independence, humanity's 5,000-year-old instincts sustained a sudden and severe shock. Although much of the frenetic sexual activity that appeared to ensue was an illusion fostered not only by the fact that people began talking and writing about the subject with unheard-of frankness, but that they seemed to talk and write about nothing else, the effects were far-reaching and not always beneficial.

Man, for example, began to lose his nerve. Reeling under the combined assault of sex educators, pollsters, feminists, and sexologists—all of whom stressed that it was up to him to ensure his partner's sexual satisfaction—he began to go into retreat. Casual sex lost much of its appeal, and researchers in the early 1970s discovered that he was having intercourse less frequently, resorting more often to masturbation, and developing a taste for pornography, which by the middle of the decade reached plague proportions. Some of it amounted to no more than erotic titillation, but the hardcore movies were designed—cheaply, nastily, and sadistically—to feed man's deep (though usually suppressed) resentment over his own inadequacy vis-à-vis the popular image of the liberated woman. Surprisingly, and despite the Gay Liberation movement, homosexuals seem not to have become more numerous, only more visible. But the overall male response to the sex revolution did not do much for woman's own opinion of sex. Some withdrew into lesbianism, others into work, and the majority into blockbuster novels where masterful, passionate heroes could be relied on to bring a woman unerringly to ecstasy.

The tradition of marriage and family seemed to have no valid place in the feminist picture. As Cornell political sociologist Andrew Hacker remarked in 1970, "The trouble [is] ... that the institution we call marriage can't hold two full human beings—it was only designed for one and a half." [1] But, as St. Paul recognized so long ago, few people are equipped to lead a wholly independent life, and although in the West the official marriage rate dropped, an increasing number of couples began to live together in partnerships that were marriage in everything but legal documentation, characterized by the fidelity, dependence, and possessiveness so often apparent in conventional newlyweds.

All these uncertainties were compounded by the social and political situation. History shows that periods of excessive emphasis on sex very often coincide with spells not of affluence, as is sometimes argued, but of widespread social purposelessness. It was in the "golden ages" of most countries—imperial Rome, Gupta India, T'ang China, Louis XIV's France, and late Victorian England—when there appeared to be no more worlds to conquer, no more battles to be fought, that sex became of disproportionate importance. Ascetic observers have always deplored it as an indication of moral turpitude, depravity, and corruption, when the problem is usually one of occupational imbalance. Most people are aware that sex is not everything—but they sometimes act as if it is. And in the late twentieth century this situation has been exacerbated by the fact that it has developed, for the first time in history, in an era of mass communcations. It has become a matter not of minority, but of majority concern.

A swift result of the 1970s sexual revolution was moral confusion. When *Time* magazine conducted a survey toward the end of 1977, it found that 61 percent of the people interviewed were finding it "harder and harder to know what's right and what's wrong these days." In the 35 to 49 age group, 72 percent thought it was "morally wrong" for teenagers to have sexual relations; among the over-fifties the figure rose to 80 percent. Forty-two percent of those questioned believed women should be virgins at marriage, and 34 percent that men should be, too.. (There was an apparent conflict here between theory and practice, since another survey, a year earlier, had indicated that at least 55 percent of unmarried women and 85 percent of men had had intercourse by the age of 19.) Forty-seven percent still considered homosexuality "morally wrong," 43 percent did not, and 10 percent were unsure. Yet although 74 percent wanted the government to crack down on pornography in movies, book, and nightclubs, 70 percent subscribed to the statement that "there should be no laws, federal or state, regulating sexual practice." Men on the whole tended to be more liberal than women, Catholics more permissive than Protestants.[2]

And Americans and British, on the whole, were rather more confused than the peoples of other countries. In France in 1972, for example, only 30 percent of husbands and 10 percent of wives admitted to infidelity; in 54 percent of cases, *coitus interruptus* remained the favored means of contraception. In half of Switzerland, "living together" is still a crime. In Russia in 1977, sex continued to be a matter for bedtime and darkness, and the Byzantine tradition of female inferiority persisted, in bed, despite the revolutionary declaration of feminine equality in politics; wife-beating was common, the rear-entry position customary, and 45 percent of women never achieved orgasm. In China, Confucian prudery and the doctrinaire emphasis on duty and responsibility combined to smother both sex education and sex talk. In Iran in 1979, women entertainers were banned from public view, women lawyers banned from public office, and three brothel madams were shot for contributing to "corruption on earth." [3] The questioning and the resultant confusion are still to come in most of the world.

In the same year as the *Time* survey, a group of Catholic theologians came out with one of the most surprising documents in the history of the Church. Ignoring the Vatican's uncompromising 1976 condemnation of all sexual relations outside marriage as a defiance of God's "absolute and immutable" law, it argued that extramarital relationships, if they were truly "creative" and "integrative," were morally acceptable. It said that persons who had been widowed or divorced could not be expected to live as though they were "nonsexual beings"; that stable friendships for homosexuals could be preferable to sexual abstinence; that sterilization could be considered a legitimate form of birth control. It was concerned about masturbation only where there was "serious psychological maladjustment"; considered zoophilia pathological only if a person preferred such relations even when "heterosexual outlets are available"; and viewed most pornography as "neuter or amoral" to the majority of adults, and so not generally dangerous. Finally, it said that sex, whatever its form, might be considered moral if it was "self-liberating, other-enriching, honest, faithful, socially responsible, life-serving and joyous." [4]

The spirit of pre-Christian sex, still hovering somewhere up in the stratosphere, must have responded with a slightly sour smile.

By the beginning of recorded history, authoritarian societies had already discovered that by disciplining sexual relationships it was possible to exercise a control over the family that contributed usefully to the stability of the state. Governments, like tax men, are uneasy without an identifiable pattern. Even so, they interfered in sexual matters insofar as they related to areas of public concern—legitimacy, inheritance, and population control. This was as true in China and India as in the ancient Near East. Beyond legalities, the only morality of sex was the morality of human relationships.

"Right" and "wrong" as absolute values did not exist either in China or India until a relatively late stage of historical development, when they became necessary elements in social discipline. But both the Hebrews and the Romans of republican times took an unconditional attitude toward right and wrong that were naturally absorbed into the teachings of the Christian church. Here, there were to be no concessions. Love was for God; sex, with its burden of sin, for marriage. Christianity was a state of being, and every thought, deed, and emotion had to measure up to the philosophical yardstick hewn out of human preconception and prejudice by the early Fathers and their medieval successors. Not even the most private areas of the mind (or body) were to be exempt from supervision. The measure of the Church's success lies in today's continuing doubts about "what's right and what's wrong" where sex and sexuality are at issue. And because religious and secular law were for centuries so closely intertwined, the "morality of sex"—a purposeful myth that has been productive of more guilt and misery than any other aspect of human or divine law—has remained an important factor in social control.

The view that sexual relationships should be publicly assessed according to different criteria from other human relationships is now beginning to fade, less as a result of the sex revolution, perhaps, than as part of a generalized and growing resistance (in the Western world, at least) to a situation where computer espionage and invasion of privacy have reached unacceptable levels, and there seems a real danger that human beings will be reduced to ciphers. The restatement of individual identity includes a restatement of sexual identity, but whether society will come around, in the forseeable future, to the rebel theologians' view that most aspects of sex can be considered "moral" if they are "self-liberating, other-enriching, honest, faithful, socially responsible, life-serving and joyous"—in other words, good for those involved and bad for no one—remains debatable. Society has always felt the need, right from the beginning of recorded history, to exercise a degree of control over general sexual conduct. But if the sexual revolution of the 1970s has the ultimate effect of taking the more intimate aspects of sex out of the public domain and back into the private, then even a decade (and more) of psychological crises may prove to have been worthwhile.

Bibliography

This is by no means a full bibliography, which would run to several volumes; merely a representative selection covering, as far as possible, most aspects of the subject and most levels of scholarship. As well as individual studies, I have included a few general histories that are more directly valuable than their titles might suggest, and a number of surveys less illuminating for the facts they contain than the climates of opinion they reflect. To avoid repetition, primary sources have been confined almost entirely to the *Notes* (see pages 449-65). It should not be assumed that, because a particular work has been omitted, I am not acquainted with it; nor that all the works listed are of equal value. Sex brings out the eccentric in authors as in most other people. Where the *Notes* refer to an edition other than the first, the date of the quoted edition is given at the end of the entry in the bibliography. "Pb" means paperback.

Ackroyd, Peter. *Dressing Up. Transvestism and Drag: The History of an Obsession.* London, 1978.

Acton, William. *Prostitution, Considered in its Moral, Social & Sanitary Aspects.* London, 1857.

Ahlstrom, Sydney E. *A Religious History of the American People.* New Haven and London, 1972.

al-Masry, Y. *Le drame sexuel de la femme dans l'Orient arabe.* Paris, 1962.

American Anthropologist. Most years see one or two articles on aspects of sex, fertility, or family custom among tribal peoples.

[Ancillon]. *Eunuchism displayed, describing all the Different Sorts of Eunuchs . . . with Several Observations on Modern Eunuchs, written by a Person of Honour.* London, 1718, trs. from the French edn. of 1707.

Andersen, Jørgen. *The Witch on the Wall. Medieval Erotic Sculpture in the British Isles.* London, 1977.

Andreas Capellanus. *De amore,* trs. as *The Art of Courtly Love* by John Jay Parry. New York, 1941.

Annales, economies, sociétés, civilisations. This journal frequently carries studies of historical interest on sex- or family-related subjects.

Archer, W. G. *The Hill of Flutes. Life, Love and Poetry in Tribal India: A Portrait of the Santals.* London, 1975.

Ardener, S. "Sexual Insult and Female Militancy," *Man,* 1973, pp. 422-65.

Ariès, Philippe. *Centuries of Childhood.* London and New York, 1962.

Ashbee, *see* Fraxi.

Athenaeus. *The Deipnosophists,* trs. Charles Burton Gulik. Cambridge, Mass. and London, 1927.

Atkins, John. *Sex in Literature.* London, 3 vols., 1970-78.

Augustine of Hippo, Saint. *Works,* in J. P. Migne *Patrologia Latina,* vols. 32-47 (1845-49). English trs. by M. Dods, 15 vols., 1872-80.

Avicenna [Ḥusain Ibn 'Abd Allāh, called Ibn Sīnā]. "A Treatise on Love [Risāla fi-'l-'Ishq] by Ibn Sina," trs. Emil L. Fackenheim, *Medieval Studies* VII, 1945, pp. 208-28.

Bailey, Derrick Sherwin (1). *Homosexuality and the Western Christian Tradition.* London, 1955.

Bailey, Derrick Sherwin (2). *The Man-Woman Relation in Christian Thought.* London, 1959.

Balsdon, J. P. V. D. (1). *Life and Leisure in Ancient Rome.* London, 1969.

Balsdon, J. P. V. D. (2). *Roman Women. Their History and Habits.* London, 1974. Westport, Ct., 1975.

Banks, Joseph Ambrose. *Prosperity and Parenthood: A Study of Family Planning among the Victorian Middle Classes.* London, 1954.

Barber, Richard. *The Knight and Chivalry.* London, 1970. Totowa, New Jersey, 1975.

Baron, Salo Wittmayer, *A Social and Religious History of the Jews.* 2nd edn. New York, 1967.

Bary, William Theodore de (ed.). *The Buddhist Tradition in India, China and Japan.* New York, 1969.

Basham, A. L. *The Wonder that was India.* London, 1954.

Bataille, G. *L'érotisme.* Paris, 1957.

Batto, Bernard Frank. *Studies on Women at Mari.* Baltimore, 1975.

Bayet, Jean. *Croyances et rites dans la Rome antique.* Paris, 1971.

Beard, Mary R. *Women as Force in History: A Study in Tradition and Realities.* New York, 1946.

Beauvoir, Simone de. *The Second Sex*. London, 1953. New York, 1974. Harmondsworth Pb, 1972.

Becker, Paul. *Das Bild der Madonna*. Salzburg, 1965.

Bennett, H. S. *Life on the English Manor. A Study of Peasant Conditions 1150-1400*. Cambridge, 1937.

Berg, Barbara J. *The Remembered Gate: Origins of American Feminism. The Woman and the City 1800-1860*. New York, 1978.

Bergues, Hélène, and others. *La prévention des naissances dans la famille*. Paris, 1960.

Besterman, Theodore. *Men against Women: A Study of Sexual Relations*. London, 1934.

Bettelheim, Bruno. *Symbolic Wounds: Puberty Rites and the Envious Male*. London, 1955.

Beurdeley, M. (ed.). *The Clouds and the Rain: The Art of Love in China*. London, 1969.

Beyer, Stephan. *The Cult of Tārā: Magic and Ritual in Tibet*. Berkeley, 1973.

Bezzola, Reto R. (1). "Guillaume IX et les origines de l'amour courtois," *Romania* LXVI, 1940, pp. 145-237.

Bezzola, Reto R. (2). *Les origines et la formation de la littérature courtoise en Occident (500-1200)*. 3 vols., Paris, 1944-63.

Bharati, Agehananda. *The Tantric Tradition*. London, 1965.

Birch, Cyril (ed.). *Anthology of Chinese Literature*. New York, 1965. Pb Harmondsworth, 1967.

Blachère, R. "Les principaux thèmes de la poésie érotique au siècle des Umayyades de Damas," *Annales de l'Institut d'études orientales* V, 1939-41.

Blake, Nelson Manfred. *The Road to Reno: A History of Divorce in the United States*. New York, 1962.

Blassingame, J. W. *The Slave Community: Plantation Life in the Antebellum South*. New York, 1973.

Bloch, Iwan [E. Dühren]. *A History of English Sexual Morals*. London, 1936. (Previously published in English, 1934, as *Sex Life in England*; and again in 1938 as *Sexual Life in England, Past and Present*.)

Blofeld, John. *The Tantric Mysticism of Tibet*. London and New York, 1970. Pb New York, 1970.

Boak, A. E. R. *Manpower Shortage and the Fall of the Roman Empire*. Ann Arbor, 1955.

Boase, Roger. *The Origin and Meaning of Courtly Love: A Critical Study of European Scholarship*. Manchester, 1977.

Bogin, Meg. *The Women Troubadours*. London and New York, 1976.

Bomli, W. *La femme dans l'Espagne du Siècle d'Or*. The Hague, 1950.

Borneman, Ernest. *Lexicon der Liebe*. Munich, 2 vols., 1970.

Boserup, Esther. *Woman's Role in Economic Development*. London, 1970.

Boulay, F. R. H. Du. *An Age of Ambition: English Society in the Late Middle Ages*. London, 1970.

Bousquet, G.-H. *La morale de l'Islam et son éthique sexuelle*. Paris, 1953.

Bowie, Theodore, and Christenson, Cornelia V. (eds.). *Studies in Erotic Art*. London and New York, 1970.

Boxer, C. R. *Mary and Misogyny: Women in Iberian Expansion Overseas 1415–1815. Some Facts, Figures, and Personalities*. London, 1975.

Brandon, S. G. F. (ed.) *A Dictionary of Comparative Religion*. London and New York, 1970.

Brantôme, Le Seigneur de [Pierre de Bourdeille]. *Vies des Dames Galantes*. 1659. Paris, 1922.

Braudel, Fernand. *Capitalism and Material Life 1400–1800*. London and New York, 1973.

Bréhier, Louis. "La femme dans la famille à Byzance," *Annuaire de l'Institut de philologie et d'histoire orientales et slaves*, 1949, pp. 105–8.

Brend, William A. *Sacrifice to Attis. A Study of Sex and Civilisation*. London, 1936.

Brendel, O. J. "The Scope and Temperament of Erotic Art in the Greco-Roman World," in Bowie and Christenson, see above.

Briffault, Robert. *The Mothers. A Study in the Origins of Sentiments and Institutions*. 3 vols., London and New York, 1927.

Brinton, Crane. *History of Western Morals*. New York, 1959.

Brown, Dee. *The Gentle Tamers: Women of the Old West*. London, 1973. New York, 1974.

Browne, W. F. *The Importance of Women in Anglo-Saxon Times*. London, 1919.

Brownlee, W. Elliot and Mary M. *Women in the American Economy. A Documentary History, 1675 to 1929*. New Haven and London Pb, 1976.

Brunt, P. A. *Italian Manpower 225 BC–AD 14*. Oxford, 1971.

Bullough, Vern L., Legg, Dorr W., and Elcano, B. W. *An Annotated Bibliography of Homosexuality*. New York, 1975. London, 2 vols., 1976.

Burton, Sir Richard. *The Book of the Thousand Nights and a Night*. Benares, 10 vols. with further 6 vols. of "Supplemental Nights," 1885.

Cairncross, John. *After Polygamy was made a Sin. The Social History of Christian Polygamy*. London, 1974.

Cartwright, Frederick F. and Biddiss, Michael D. *Disease and History*. London and New York, 1972.

Castiglione, Baldesar. *The Book of the Courtier*, trs. George Bull. Harmondsworth Pb 1967. New York Pb, 1976.

Catt, Carrie Chapman, and Shuler, Nettie Rogers. *Women Suffrage and Politics*. New York, 1923.

Chand, Khazan. *Indian Sexology*. New Delhi, 1972.

Charrières, G. *La signification des répresentations érotiques dans les arts sauvages et préhistoriques.* Paris, 1970.

Chesney, Kellow. *The Victorian Underworld.* London, 1970 and New York, Pb, 1972. Harmondsworth Pb 1972.

Cirlot, J. E. *A Dictionary of Symbols.* London and New York, 1962.

Clark, Colin. *Population Growth and Land Use.* London, 1967.

Cockshut, A. O. J. *Man and Woman: Love and the Novel from 1740 to 1940.* London, 1977.

Cole, F. J. *Early Theories of Sexual Generation.* Oxford, 1930.

Cole, W. G. *Sex in Christianity and Psychoanalysis.* London, 1956.

Comfort, Alex (ed.). *The Joy of Sex: A Gourmet Guide to Lovemaking.* New York and London, 1972.

Conrad, Susan P. *Perish the Thought: Intellectual Women in Romantic America 1830-1860.* New York, 1976.

Coon, Carleton S. *The History of Man: From the First Human to Primitive Culture and Beyond.* New York, 1954, London, 1955. Pb, Harmondsworth, 1967.

Cordier, Henri. *Bibliotheca Sinica. Dictionnaire Bibliographique des Ouvrages relatifs à l'Empire chinois.* 2nd edn. Paris, 1904-8. Suppl., 1922-4. For continuation see Yuan T'ung-li.

Coulson, John (ed.). *The Saints: A Concise Biographical Dictionary.* New York, 1958. Pb, New York, n.d.

Craig, Alec. *Suppressed Books: A History of the Conception of Literary Obscenity.* Cleveland, 1963.

Crawley, A. E. (1). *Studies of Savages and Sex.* London, 1929.

Crawley, A. E. (2). *Dress, Drinks and Drums: Further Studies of Savages and Sex.* London, 1931.

Cruse, Amy. *The Victorians and Their Reading.* Boston, 1935.

Cunnington, C. Willett and Phillis. *The History of Underclothes.* London, 1951.

Daly, Mary. *The Church and the Second Sex.* Boston, 1968.

D'Arch Smith, Timothy. *Love in Earnest.* London, 1970.

Darlington, C. D. (1). *Genetics and Man.* London and New York, 1964.

Darlington, C. D. (2). *The Evolution of Man and Society.* London, 1969. New York, 1973.

Daube, David. *Civil Disobedience in Antiquity.* Edinburgh and Chicago, 1973.

Davidson, H. R. Ellis. *Gods and Myths of Northern Europe.* Harmondsworth Pb, 1964.

Davin, Delia. *Woman-Work: Women and the Party in Revolutionary China.* Oxford, 1976.

Davis, Katherine Bement. *Factors in the Sex Life of Twenty-Two Hundred Women.* New York, 1929.

Degler, Carl N. "What Ought to Be and What Was: Women's Sexuality in the Nineteenth Century," *American Historical Review,* Winter 1974, pp. 1467-90.

Delaney, Janice, Lupton, Mary Jane, and Toth, Emily. *The Curse. A Cultural History of Menstruation.* New York, 1977.

DeMause, Lloyd (ed.). *The History of Childhood.* New York and London, 1974.

Denevan, William N. *The Native Population of the Americas in 1492.* Madison, Wisc., 1976.

D'Enjoy, Paul. "Le Baiser en Europe et en Chine," *Bulletin Société d'Anthropologie,* 1897, pp. 181-5.

Desai, Devangana. *Erotic sculpture of India.* New Delhi, 1976.

Devereux, G. "Institutionalised homosexuality of the Mohave Indians," *Human Biology* 9, 1937, pp. 498-527.

Diaz del Castillo, Bernal. *The Conquest of New Spain.* Harmondsworth Pb, 1963. Magnolia, Mass. 1977.

Dickinson, R. L. *Human Sex Anatomy.* 2nd edn. London and Baltimore, 1949.

Dickinson, R. L. and Beam, Lura. *A Thousand Marriages.* London, 1932.

Diehl, Charles. *Figures byzantines.* 5th edn. 2 vols., Paris, 1912.

Dingwall, E. J. (1). *Male infibulation.* London, 1925.

Dingwall, E. J. (2). *The Girdle of Chastity: A Medico-Legal Study.* London, 1931.

Dover, K. J. *Greek Homosexuality.* London, 1978.

Droit, Roger-Pol, and Gallien, Antoine. *La Réalité Sexuelle.* Paris, 1974.

Dronke, Peter. *Mediaeval Latin and the Rise of the European Love Lyric.* 2 vols., Oxford, 1965-6. New York, 1969.

Duby, Georges. *Rural Economy and Country Life in the Medieval West.* London and Columbia, S. C., 1968.

Dudden, F. Homes. *The Life and Times of Saint Ambrose.* Oxford, 1935.

Duffy, J. "Masturbation and Clitoridectomy," *Journal of the American Medical Association* 186, 1963, pp. 246-8.

Early Christian Writings. The Apostolic Fathers, trs. Maxwell Staniforth. Harmondsworth Pb, 1968. New York, Pb, 1975.

Eden, Mary, and Carrington, Richard. *The Philosophy of the Bed.* London, 1961.

Eliade, Mircea. *Rites and Symbols of Initiation.* New York Pb, 1965.

Ellis, A. and Abarbanel, A. (eds.). *The Encyclopaedia of Sexual Behavior.* New York, 1961.

Ellis, Havelock. *Psychology of Sex: A Manual for Students.* London, 1933. Buchanan, New York, Pb, 1972.

Epstein, Louis M. (1). *Marriage Laws in the Bible and the Talmud.* Cambridge, Mass., 1942.

Epstein, Louis M. (2). *Sex Laws and Customs in Judaism.* Cambridge, Mass., 1948. New York, 1968.

Ernst, Morris L., and Seagle, William. *To the Pure ... A Study of Obscenity and the Censor.* London, 1929.

Evans, Richard J. *The Feminists: Women's Emancipation Movements in Europe, America and Australasia, 1840-1920.* London, 1977.

Farrell, Warren. *The Liberated Man: Beyond Masculinity, Freeing Men and Their Relationships with Women.* New York, 1974.

Feldman, David M. *Birth Control in Jewish Law.* New York, 1968.

Ferrante, Joan M. *Women as Image in Medieval Literature: From the Twelfth Century to Dante.* New York, 1975.

Feucht, O. E. and others. *Sex and the Church—a Sociological, Historical and Theological Investigation of Sex Attitudes.* St. Louis, Mo., 1961.

Field, James A. *Essays on Population and Other Papers.* Chicago, 1931.

Finch, B. E. and Green, H. *Contraception through the ages.* London and Springfield, Ill., 1963.

Flacelière, Robert. *Love in Ancient Greece.* London, 1962.

Flexner, Eleanor. *Century of Struggle: The Woman's Rights Movement in the United States.* Cambridge, Mass., 1959.

Forbes, Thomas Rogers. *The Midwife and the Witch.* New Haven, 1966.

Ford, Clellan S. and Beach, Frank A., *Patterns of Sexual Behavior.* New York, 1951, London, 1952.

Forel, Oscar. *L'accord des sexes.* Paris, 1953.

Forster, Robert, and Ranum, Orest (eds.) (1). *Biology of Man in History. Selections from the* Annales etc. Baltimore and London, 1975.

Forster Robert, and Ranum, Orest (eds.) (2). *Family and Society. Selections from the* Annales etc. Baltimore and London, 1976.

Foxon, David. *Libertine Literature in England 1660-1745.* London, 1964.

Frankfort, H. and H. A., Wilson, John A., Jacobsen, Thorkild, and Irwin, William A. *The Intellectual Adventure of Ancient Man. An essay on speculative thought in the ancient Near East.* Chicago, 1946.

Fraxi, Pisanus [Henry S. Ashbee]. *Index Librorum Prohibitorum.* London, 1877. Ed. P. Fryer, 1970, as *Forbidden Books of the Victorians.*

Frazer, Sir James George. *The Golden Bough: A Study in Magic and Religion.* 13 vols., London and New York, 1911-15. London abridged edn., 1 vol., 1922. New York, abridged, 1978.

Friedan, Betty. *The Feminine Mystique.* New York, 1963.

Fryer, Peter. *The Birth Controllers.* London, 1965.

Fuchs, E. *Illustrierte Sittengeschichte vom Mittelalter bis zu Gegenwart.* Munich, 3 vols., 1909-12.

Galot, Jean. *L'Eglise et la Femme.* Paris, 1965.

Gay, Jules. *Bibliographie des ouvrages relatifs à l'amour, aux femmes, au mariage, etc.* 4th edn. Lille, 4 vols., 1894-1900.

Gibbs, Margaret. *The D.A.R.* [*Daughters of the American Revolution*]. New York, 1969.

Gibson, Ian. *The English Vice: Beating, Sex and Shame in Victorian England and after.* London, 1978.

Giffen, Lois Anita. *Theory of Profane Love Among the Arabs.* London, 1973.

Gilgamesh, The Epic of, trs. N. K. Sandars. New York, Pb, 1960. Harmondsworth Pb, 1970.

Glass, D. V. and Eversley, D. E. C. (eds.). *Population in History: Essays in Historical Demography.* London, 1965.

Glass, D. V. and Revelle, Roger (eds.). *Population and Social Change.* London, 1972.

Goodland, Roger, *A Bibliography of Sex Rites and Customs.* London and New York, 1931.

Gordon, Linda. *Woman's Body, Woman's Right. A Social History of Birth Control in America.* New York, 1976, Harmondsworth Pb, 1977.

Gordon, Michael (ed.). *The American Family in Social-Historical Perspective.* New York, 1973.

Graves, Robert. *The Greek Myths.* Harmondsworth Pb, 2 vols., 1955. New York, 1959.

Gray, James H. *Red Lights on the Prairies.* Toronto, 1971.

Grigson, Geoffrey. *The Goddess of Love.* London, 1976. New York, 1977.

Grimal, Pierre (ed.). *Histoire mondiale de la femme.* Paris, 4 vols. 1965-7.

Grimes, Alan P. *The Puritan Ethic and Woman Suffrage.* New York, 1967.

Guerra, Francisco. *The Pre-Columbian Mind. A study into the aberrant nature of sexual drives, drugs affecting behavior, and the attitude towards life and death, with a survey of psychotherapy, in pre-Columbian America.* New York and London, 1971.

Guillaume, P. and Poussou, J. P. *La Démographie historique.* Paris, 1970.

Haböck, Franz. *Die Kastraten und ihre Gesangkunst.* Berlin-Leipzig, 1927.

Hafkin, Nancy J. and Bray, Edna G. (eds.) *Women in Africa. Studies in Social and Economic Change.* Stanford, 1977.

Hair, Paul (ed.). *Before the Bawdy Court.* London, 1972.

Halil Inalcik. *The Ottoman Empire. The Classical Age 1300-1600.* London, 1972.

Haller, John S., Jr. and Robin ᴍ. *The Physician and Sexuality in Victorian America.* Urbana, Ill., 1974.

Hamilton, G. V. T. *A Research in Marriage.* New York, 1929.

Hare, E. H. "Masturbational Insanity: the History of an Idea," *Journal of Mental Science* 108, 1962, pp. 1-25.

Harrison, Brian. *Separate Spheres: The Opposition to Women's Suffrage in Britain.* London, 1978.

Harrison, Fraser. *The Dark Angel: Aspects of Victorian Sexuality.* London, 1977.

Harrison, G. A. and Boyce, A. J. (eds.). *The Structure of Human Populations*. Oxford, 1972.

Harrison, Harry. *Great Balls of Fire: A History of Sex in Science Fiction Illustration*. London and New York, 1977.

Harvey, A. J. *Turkish Harems*. London, 1871.

Haskins, Charles Homer. *The Renaissance of the Twelfth Century*. Harvard, 1927.

Hayn, H. *Bibliotheca Germanorum Erotica et Curiosa*. Munich, 1912–29.

Hays, H. R. *The Dangerous Sex: The Myth of Feminine Evil*. New York, 1972.

Helleiner, K. F. "The Population of Europe from the Black Death to the Eve of the Vital Revolution," *Cambridge Economic History* IV, 1967.

Henry, G. W. *Sex Variants*. London, 1950.

Herodotus. *The Histories*, trs. Aubrey de Selincourt. Harmondsworth Pb, and New York, 1954.

Hess, Thomas B. and Nochlin, Linda. *Woman as Sex Object: Studies in Erotic Art 1730–1970*. New York, 1973.

Himes, Norman E. *Medical History of Contraception*. New York and London, 1936.

Hirschfeld, Magnus. *The Sexual History of the World War* (1914–18). New York, 1941.

Hite, Shere. *The Hite Report*. New York and London, 1976.

Hitti, Philip K. *Islam and the West. A Historical Cultural Survey*. Princeton, 1962.

Hopfner, T. *Das Sexualleben des Griechen und Römer*. Prague, 1938.

Hopkins, M. K. (1) "Contraception in the Roman Empire," *Comparative Studies in Society and History* 8, 1965–6, pp. 124–51.

Hopkins, M. K. (2) "A Textual Emendation in a Fragment of Musonius Rufus: a Note on Contraception," *Classical Quarterly* 10, 1965, pp. 72–4.

Howard, George Elliott. *A History of Matrimonial Institutions*. London and Chicago, 3 vols. 1904.

Huizinga, J. *The Waning of the Middle Ages. A Study of the Forms of Life, Thought, and Art in France and the Netherlands in the Fourteenth and Fifteenth Centuries*. London and New York, 1924. Harmondsworth Pb 1968.

Hunt, Morton. *Sexual Behavior in the 1970s*. New York, 1974.

James, E. O. *Marriage and Society*. London, 1952.

James, Edward T. with Janet Wilson James and Paul S. Boyer (eds.). *Notable American Women 1607–1950: A Biographical Dictionary*. Cambridge, Mass. and London, 1974.

Janeway, Elizabeth. *Man's World: Woman's Place*. New York, 1971. London, 1972.

Janus, Sam; Bess, Barbara; and Saltus, Carol. *A Sexual Profile of Men in Power.* Englewood Cliffs, New Jersey, 1977.

Jones, V. R. and Bevan. L. *Woman in Islam: A Manual with Special Reference to Conditions in India.* Lucknow, 1941.

Juvenal. *The Sixteen Satires,* trs. Peter Green. Harmondsworth Pb, 1967, and New York, 1967.

Kamasutra, see Vatsyayana.

Kapadia, K. M. *Marriage and Family in India.* Bombay, 1955.

Kardiner, A. *Sex and Morality.* London, 1955.

Karlen, Arno. *Sexuality and Homosexuality.* London, 1971.

Katz, Naomi, and Milton, Nancy. *Women of the Third World.* London, 1977.

Katzenellenbogen, A. *Allegories of the Virtues and Vices in Mediaeval Art.* New York, 1939.

Kennedy, David. *Birth Control in America: The Career of Margaret Sanger.* New Haven, 1970.

Kessler, Evelyn. *Women: An Anthropological View.* New York, 1976.

Kiefer, Otto. *Sexual Life in Ancient Rome.* London, 1934.

Kinsey, Alfred C. and others (1). *Sexual Behavior in the Human Male.* Philadelphia and London, 1948.

Kinsey, Alfred C. and others (2). *Sexual Behavior in the Human Female.* Philadelphia and London, 1953.

Kitchin, Shepherd Braithwaite. *A History of Divorce.* London, 1912.

Klaich, Dolores. *Woman plus Woman. Attitudes towards Lesbianism.* New York and London, 1975.

Kosambi, Damodar Dharmanand. *An Introduction to the study of Indian History.* Bombay, 1956.

Kosnik, Anthony. (ed.). *Human Sexuality: New Directions in American Catholic Thought,* New York, 1977.

Kraditor, Aileen S. *Ideas of the Woman Suffrage Movement, 1890–1920.* New York, 1965.

Krafft-Ebing, R. von. *Psychopathia Sexualis.* 1886, New York, 1965 and 1978 Pb.

Kramrisch, Stella. *The Art of India: Traditions of Indian Sculpture, Painting and Architecture.* London, 1954.

Kraus, Henry. *The Living Theatre of Medieval Art.* Bloomington, 1967.

Kronhausen, Phyllis and Eberhard (compilers). *Erotic Art: A Survey of Erotic Fact and Fancy in the Fine Arts.* New York, 1968.

Lacey, W. K. *The Family in Classical Greece.* London, 1968.

Larco Hoyle, Rafael. *Checan: Essay on Erotic Elements in Peruvian Art.* Geneva, 1965.

Laslett, Peter. *Family Life and Illicit Love in Earlier Generations.* Cambridge, 1977.

Laufer, B. "Sex Transformation and Hermaphrodites in Ancient China," *American Journal of Physical Anthropology* 3, 1920, p. 259.

Lea, Henry C. *History of Sacerdotal Celibacy in the Christian Church.* Philadelphia, 1867.

Leach, Edmund. "Virgin Birth," *Proceedings of the Royal Anthropological Institute of Great Britain and Ireland for 1966.* London, 1970.

Leake, Chauncey D. "Mood, behavior and drugs," *Science* 170, 1970, pp. 559–60.

Leakey, Richard E. and Lewin, Roger. *Origins.* London and New York, 1977.

Lederer, W. *The Fear of Women.* London and New York, 1968.

Legeza, Laszlo. *Tao Magic: The Secret Language of Diagrams and Calligraphy.* London, 1975.

Lehmann, Andrée. *Le Rôle de la Femme dans l'histoire de France au Moyen Age.* Paris, 1952.

Lejeal, Léon. "Rites phalliques, origine du théatre et des sacrifices humaines à Mexico," *Journal de la Société des Americanistes* 2, 1905, pp. 341–43.

Lewenhak, Sheila. *Women and Trade Unions.* London, 1977.

Lewinsohn, Richard. *A History of Sexual Customs.* London, 1958.

Lewis, Bernard. *Islam in History: Ideas, Men, and Events in the Middle East.* London, 1973.

Lewis, C. S. *The Allegory of Love.* Oxford, 1936.

Li-chi [Book of Rituals], trs. James Legge, in *Sacred Books of the East* vol. xxvii, ed. Friedrich Max-Müller. Oxford, 1885.

Licht, Hans [Paul Brandt]. *Sexual Life in Ancient Greece.* London, 1932.

Lietzmann, H. *The Era of the Church Fathers.* London, 1951.

Lifton, Robert Jay. *History and Human Survival. Essays on the young and old, survivors and the dead, peace and war, and on contemporary psychohistory.* New York, 1970.

Lindsay, Jack. *Men and Gods on the Roman Nile.* London, 1968.

Litchfield, R. Burr. "Demographic Characteristics of Florentine Patrician Families, 16th century to 19th century," *Journal of Economic History* 29, 1969, pp. 191–205.

Loewenberg, Bert James, and Bogin, Ruth (eds.) *Black Women in Nineteenth-Century American Life. Their Words, Their Thoughts, Their Feelings.* University Park, Pa., 1976.

Longworth, T. C. *The Devil a Monk Would Be: A Survey of Sex and Celibacy in Religion.* London, 1936.

Lorris, Guillaume de, and Meun, Jean de. *The Romance of the Rose,* trs. Charles Dahlberg. Princeton and London, 1971.

Lougee, Carolyn C. *Le Paradis des Femmes. Women, Salons, and Social Stratification in Seventeenth-Century France.* Princeton, 1976.

Lucie-Smith, Edward. *Eroticism in Western Art.* London, 1972.

Lucka, E. *Eros, the development of sex relations.* New York, 1915. (As *The Evolution of Love,* London, 1923).

Lybyer, A. H. *Government of the Ottoman Empire in the Time of Suleiman the Magnificent.* Cambridge, Mass., 1913.

McEvedy, Colin, and Jones, Richard. *Atlas of World Population History.* New York, 1974. London, 1978. Harmondsworth Pb, 1978.

Mace, D. R. *Hebrew Marriage.* London, 1953.

McNeill S. J., John J. *The Church and the Homosexual.* London and New York, 1976.

Madsen, William. "Anxiety and witchcraft in Mexican American acculturation," *Anthropological Quarterly* 39, 1966, pp. 110-27.

Mahl, Mary M. and Koon, Helene (eds.). *The Female Spectator. English Women Writers before 1800.* Bloomington, 1977.

[Maimonides]. *The Book of Women. The Code of Maimonides: Book Four,* trs. Isaac Klein. New Haven, 1972.

Malinowski, Bronislaw (1). *Sex and Repression in Savage Society.* London and New York, 1927.

Malinowski, Bronislaw (2). *The Sexual Life of Savages.* London, 1932.

Manchester, William. *The Glory and the Dream: A Narrative History of America 1932-1972.* Boston, 1974. London, 1975.

Marcus, Steven. *The Other Victorians.* New York and London, 1966.

Marcuse, Ludwig. *Obscene. The History of an Indignation.* London, 1965.

Marshack, Alexander. *The Roots of Civilisation. The Cognitive Beginnings of Man's First Art, Symbol and Notation.* New York and London, 1972.

Masters, R. E. L. *Eros and Evil: The Sexual Psychology of Witchcraft.* New York, 1962.

Masters, W. H. and Johnson, V. E. *Human Sexual Response.* New York, 1966.

May, Geoffrey. *Social Control of Sex Expression.* London, 1930.

Mead, Margaret. *Sex and Temperament in Three Primitive Societies.* London, 1935. New York, Pb, 1971.

Medieval Comic Tales, trs. Peter Rickard and others. Cambridge, 1974.

Ménagier de Paris, Le, ed. and trs. by Eileen Power as *The Goodman of Paris.* London, 1928.

Meyer, Johann Jakob. *Sexual Life in Ancient India: A Study in the Comparative History of Indian Culture.* 2 vols., London, 1930. (Based on the *Mahabharata* and the *Ramayana.*)

Millant, Richard. *Les Eunuques à travers les âges.* Paris, 1908 (as vol.xiii of the *Bibliothèque des perversions sexuelles*).

Miller, Casey, and Swift, Kate. *Words and Women: New Language in New Times.* New York and London, 1977.

Mitchell, Juliet, and Oakley, Ann (eds.) *The Rights and Wrongs of Women.* Harmondsworth Pb, 1976.

Moers, Ellen. *Literary Women.* New York, 1976. London, 1977.

Morewedge, Rosemarie Thee (ed.). *The Role of Woman in the Middle Ages.* Albany, 1975.

Morris, Ivan. *The World of the Shining Prince: Court Life in Ancient Japan.* London, 1964.

Müller-Lyer, Franz. *The Evolution of Modern Marriage: A Sociology of Sexual Relations.* London, 1930.

Muṣṭafā 'Alī's *Description of Cairo of 1599*, ed. and trs. Andreas Tietze. Vienna, 1975.

Needham, Joseph. *Science and Civilisation in China.* Cambridge, 1954 continuing. New York, 1956 continuing.

Nelli, R. *L'érotique des troubadours.* Toulouse, 1963.

[Nefzawi]. *The Perfumed Garden of the Shaykh Nefzawi*, trs. Sir Richard Burton. [1886]. London Pb, 1963. New York Pb, 1978.

Newman, F. X. (ed.). *The Meaning of Courtly Love.* Albany, 1968.

Noonan, John T., Jr. *Contraception. A History of Its Treatment by the Catholic Theologians and Canonists.* Cambridge, Mass., 1966.

Oakley, Ann. *Sex, Gender and Society.* London, 1972. New York, 1973.

O'Faolain, Julia, and Martines, Lauro. *Not in God's Image.* London and New York, 1973.

O'Malley, L. S. S. *Indian Caste Customs.* Cambridge, 1932.

Ostrogorsky, George. *History of the Byzantine State.* Oxford 1956 and Rutgers, N.J., 1969.

Ostwald, Hans. *Kultur- und Sittengeschichte Berlins.* Berlin, n.d.

[Ovid]. *The Art of Love. Ovid's Ars Amatoria with verse translation by B. P. Moore.* London, 1935.

Payen, Jean-Charles. *Les origines de la courtoisie dans la littérature française médiévale.* Paris, 2 parts, 1966-7.

Paz, Octavio. *The labyrinth of solitude: Life and thought in Mexico.* London, 1967.

Penzer, N. M. *The Ḥarēm, an account of the institution as it existed in the Palace of the Turkish Sultans with a history of the Grand Seraglio from its foundation to modern times.* London 1936.

Perella, Nicholas James. *The Kiss Sacred and Profane: An Interpretive History of Kiss Symbolism and Related Religio-Erotic Themes.* Berkeley and Los Angeles, 1969.

Perfumed Garden, see Nefzawi.

Pesle, O. *La Femme Musulmane dans le droit, la religion, et les moeurs.* Rabat, 1946.

Piaget, Jean. *The Child's Conception of Physical Causality.* New York, 1966.

Pinchbeck, Ivy, and Hewitt, Margaret. *Children in English Society.* London, 2 vols., 1970 and 1974.

Pliny the Elder. *Natural History*, trs. H. Rackham. London 1950.

Pomeroy, Sarah B. *Goddesses, Whores, Wives and Slaves: Women in Classical Antiquity.* London, 1975. New York, 1976.

Powell, Chilton Latham. *English Domestic Relations 1487-1653: A Study of Matrimony and Family Life in Theory and Practice as*

Revealed by the Literature, Law and History of the Period.
New York, 1917.

Praz, Mario. *The Romantic Agony.* London, 1933. New Edn. 1951. New
York, 1970.

Quéré-Jaulmes, F. *La Femme. Les grand textes des Pères de l'Eglise.*
Paris, 1968.

Rawson, Philip (1). *The Art of Tantra.* Greenwich, Conn. and London
Pb, 1973.

Rawson, Philip (2) and Legeza, Laszlo. *Tao: The Chinese philosophy of
time and change.* London Pb, 1973.

Reade, Brian (ed.). *Sexual Heretics: Male Homosexuality in English Literature from 1850 to 1900.* London, 1970.

Reade, Rolf S. [Alfred Rose]. *Registrum Librorum Eroticorum.* London,
2 vols., 1936.

Regnault, H. *La Condition juridique du bâtard au moyen âge.* Paris,
1923.

Reich, Wilhelm. *The Function of the Orgasm.* New York, 1961.

Riencourt, Amaury de. *Sex and Power in History.* New York, 1974.

Robinson, Paul. *The Modernization of Sex.* New York and London,
1976.

Rogers, Katherine M. *The Troublesome Helpmate: A History of Misogyny in Literature.* Seattle, 1966.

Rolleston, J. D. "The Folk-Lore of Venereal Diseases," *British Journal of
Venereal Diseases* XVIII, 1942, p. 5.

Rosaldo, Michelle Zimbalist, and Lamphere, Louise (eds.). *Woman,
Culture and Society.* Stanford, 1974.

Rosebury, Theodor. *Microbes and Morals. The Strange Story of Venereal Disease.* London, 1974. New York, 1976.

Rosen, Andrew. *Rise Up Women! The militant campaign of the
Women's Social and Political Union, 1903-14.* London, 1974.

Rossi, Alice S. *The Feminist Papers, from Adams to Beauvoir.* New
York, 1974.

Rossi, William R. *The Sex Life of the Foot and Shoe.* New York and
London, 1977.

Rostovtzeff, M. I. *Social and Economic History of the Roman Empire.*
Oxford, 2 vols., 1926.

Rougemont, Denis de. *Passion and Society.* London 1940. (As *Love in
the Western World,* New York 1940.)

Rowbotham, Sheila (1). *Women's Liberation and Revolution: A Bibliography Compiled by Sheila Rowbotham.* Bristol, 1972.

Rowbotham, Sheila (2). *Hidden from History. 300 Years of Women's
Oppression and the Fight Against It.* London Pb, 1973.

Rugoff, Milton. *Prudery and Passion. Sexuality in Victorian America.*
New York, 1971.

Runciman, Steven. *A History of the Crusades.* Cambridge, 3 vols., 1952.
Russell, J. Cox. *British Medieval Population.* Albuquerque, New Mexico, 1948.
Ryan, Michael. *Prostitution in London, with a Comparative View of that in Paris, New York etc.* London, 1839.
Rycroft, Charles. *A Critical Dictionary of Psychoanalysis.* London, 1968.

Saint, W. P. le. *Tertullian: Treatises on Marriage and Remarriage.* London, 1951.
Sanger, William W. *A History of Prostitution.* New York, 1859.
Schafer, E. H. "Ritual Exposure in Ancient China," *Harvard Journal of Asiatic Studies* 14, 1951, p. 130.
Schneir, Miriam (ed.). *Feminism: The Essential Historical Writings.* New York, 1972.
Schrank, Josef. *Die Prostitution in Wien in historischer, administrativer und hygienischer Beziehung.* Vienna, 2 vols. 1886.
[Sei Shōnagon]. *The Pillow Book of Sei Shōnagon,* trs. and ed. Ivan Morris. New York and Oxford, 1967.
Seltman, Charles. *Women in Antiquity.* London 1956.
Shêng Wu-shan. *Erotologie de la Chine: Tradition chinoise de l'Erotisme.* Paris, 1963 (as no. 11 of the *Bibliothèque Internationale de l'Erotologie*).
Shorter, Edward. *The Making of the Modern Family.* New York, 1975. London, 1976.
Shryock, Richard. *Medicine in America, Historical Essays.* Baltimore, 1966.
Sigerist, Henry E. *A History of Medicine: Primitive and Archaic Medicine.* New York 1951. New York Pb, 1967.
Simons, G. L. *A Place for Pleasure. The History of the Brothel.* Lewes, 1975.
Simons, H. J. *African Women.* Oxford, 1969.
Sinclair, Andrew. *The Better Half: The Emancipation of the American Woman.* New York, 1965.
Sion, Abraham A. *Prostitution and the Law.* London, 1978.
Slater, E. and Woodside, M. *Patterns of Marriage.* London, 1951.
Slater, Philip. *The Glory of Hera.* Boston, 1968.
Smith, Bradley. *The American Way of Sex: An Informal Illustrated History.* New York, 1978.
Smith, Daniel Scott. "Family Limitation, Sexual Control and Domestic Feminism in Victorian America," *Feminist Studies* 1 3-4, 1973.
Smith-Rosenberg, Carroll, and Rosenberg, Charles. "The Female Animal: Medical and Biological Views of Woman and Her Role in Nineteenth-Century America," *Journal of American History* 60:2, September 1973, pp. 332-56.
Solé, J. "Passion charnelle et société urbaine d'Ancien Régime," *Annales*

de la faculté des lettres et des sciences humaines de Nice. Nice, 1969.

Sonenschein, D. "Homosexuality as a subject of anthropological inquiry," *Anthropological Quarterly* 39, 1966, pp. 73–82.

Sourdel, D. and J. *La Civilisation de l'Islam Classique.* Paris, 1968.

Soustelle, Jacques. *Daily Life of the Aztecs on the Eve of the Spanish Conquest.* London, 1961. Harmondsworth Pb, 1968.

Spitz, R. A. "Authority and Masturbation," *Yearbook of Psychoanalysis* 9, 1953, pp. 113–45.

Stent, G. Carter. "Chinese Eunuchs," *Journal of the North China Branch of the Royal Asiatic Society,* New Series XI, 1877, pp. 143–84.

Stoddard, H. L. "Phallic Symbols in America," *American Antiquarian and Oriental Journal* 27, 1905, pp. 281–94.

Stoller, Robert. *Sex and Gender.* London and New York, 1968.

Stone, Lawrence. *The Family, Sex and Marriage in England 1500–1800.* Cambridge and New York, 1977.

Storr, Anthony. *Sexual Deviation.* Harmondsworth Pb, 1964.

Strauss und Torney, Lulu von. *Deutsches Frauenleben in der Zeit der Sachsenkaiser und Hohenstaufen.* Jena, 1927.

Suetonius. *The Twelve Caesars,* trs. Robert Graves. Harmondsworth Pb, and New York, 1957.

Swann, Nancy Lee. *Pan Chao: Foremost Woman Scholar of China.* New York, 1932.

Tacitus. *The Annals of Imperial Rome,* trs. Michael Grant. Harmondsworth Pb, 1956. New York, 1975.

Talbot, J. B. *Miseries of Prostitution.* London, 1844.

Tannahill, Reay (1). *Food in History.* New York and London, 1973.

Tannahill, Reay (2). *Flesh and Blood: A History of the Cannibal Complex.* New York and London, 1975.

Taylor, G. Rattray. *Sex in History.* London, 1953. New York, 1954.

Teal, Donn. *The Gay Militants.* New York, 1971.

Thompson, Roger. *Women in Stuart England and America. A comparative study.* London and Boston, 1974.

Thomson, Robert. *The Pelican History of Psychology.* Harmondsworth Pb, and New York, 1968.

Tripp, C. A. *The Homosexual Matrix.* New York and London, 1977.

Trudgill, Eric. *Madonnas and Magdalens: The Origins and Development of Victorian Sexual Attitudes.* London, 1976.

Tucci, Giuseppe. *The Theory and Practice of the Mandala, with Special Reference to the Modern Psychology of the Subconscious.* London, 1969.

Ucko, Peter J. "Penis sheaths: a comparative study," *Proceedings of the Royal Anthropological Institute of Great Britain and Ireland for 1969.* London, 1970.

Unwin, J. D. *Sex and Culture*. Oxford, 1934.
Upadhyaya, B. S. *Women in Rigveda*. Bombay, 1941.

Van de Velde, T. *Ideal Marriage: Its Physiology and Technique*. London, 1928. New York, 1965, rev. ed., Pb 1975.
Vanggaard, Thorkil. *Phallós: A Symbol and Its History in the Male World*. London and New York, 1972.
Van Gulik, Robert H. *Sexual Life in Ancient China. A preliminary survey of Chinese sex and society from ca. 1500 B.C. till 1644 A.D.* Leiden, 1961.
[Vatsyayana]. *The Kama Sutra of Vatsyayana*, trs. Sir Richard Burton and F. F. Arbuthnot. [1883]. London Pb, 1963. New York, 1964.
Veblen, Thorstein B. *The Theory of the Leisure Class*. 1899. Boston, 1973.
Vicinus, Martha (ed.). *A Widening Sphere: Changing Roles of Victorian Women*. Bloomington, 1977.

Walker, Benjamin. *Sex and the Supernatural*. London, 1970. New York, 1973.
Warner, Marina. *Alone of All Her Sex: The Myth and the Cult of the Virgin Mary*. London and New York 1976.
Washburn, Sherwood L. (ed.). *Social Life of Early Man*. Chicago, 1961, London, 1962.
Watkins, O. D. *Holy Matrimony*. London, 1895.
Weideger, Paula. *Menstruation and Menopause*. New York, 1976.
Weinberg, Martin S. (ed.). *Sex Research: Studies from the Kinsey Institute*. Oxford, 1976.
Weiner, Michael A. *Earth Medicine—Earth Foods: Plant Remedies, Drugs, and Natural Foods of the North American Indians*. New York and London, 1972.
West, D. J. *Homosexuality*. London, 1968. Minnesota, rev. ed., 1977.
Westermarck, E. *History of Human Marriage*. London, 1891.
Wiet, G. *La vie de plaisir à la Mecque et à Medine au 1er siècle de l'Islam*. Paris, 1959.
Williams, N. P. *The Ideas of the Fall and of Original Sin*. London, 1927.
Wilson, Edward O. *Sociobiology: The New Synthesis*. Cambridge, Mass., 1975.
Wilson, John Harold. *Court Satires of the Restoration*. Columbus, Ohio, 1976.
Witkowski, G. J. A. *L'art profane á l'Eglise*. Paris, 2 vols., 1908.
Witkowski, G. J. A. *Les licences de l'art chrétien*. Paris, 1920.
"Women in Antiquity" (essays by various authors), *Arethusa* 6:1, 1973, Buffalo, 1973.
Wood, Charles T. *The Age of Chivalry: Manners and Morals 1000-1450*. Cambridge, Mass., 1966. London, 1970.

Yuan T'ung-li. *China in Western Literature.* New Haven, 1958. A continuation of Cordier, see above.

Zimmer, Heinrich. *Myths and Symbols in Indian Art and Civilization.* New York, 1946.

Zoegger, J. *Le Lien du Mariage à l'époque merovingienne.* Paris, 1915.

Illustrations
and Sources

The author and publishers gratefully acknowledge the permission to reproduce granted by the galleries, collections, and photographers specified below.

[445]

with basket. *Museo Nazionale, Palermo. Photo: Mansell/Alinari.*

133 Ground plan of the Stabian Baths. After Sir Mortimer Wheeler, *Roman Art and Architecture* (1964).

140 St. Jerome, tempted. From the *Belles Heures de Jean de Berry*, f.186, Limbourg brothers, 1410–13. *Cloisters Collection, Metropolitan Museum of Art, New York.*

142 Adam and Eve expelled from Eden. Genesis scene from the Moutier-Grandval Bible, Tours, 834–43. *By permission of the British Library, London, MS Add. 10545 f.5v.*

146 Husband and wife, from a French manuscript of the *Roman de la Rose*, 1487–95. *Bodleian Library, Oxford, MS Douce 195 f.118.*

149 Tree of consanguinity. From a manuscript of Isidore of Seville's *Etymologiae*, Regensburg, c. 1150. *Bayerische Staatsbibliothek, Munich, Cod. lat. 13031 f.102v.*

154 The destruction of Sodom, from the Vienna Genesis Bible. *Bildarchiv der Osterreichisches Nationalbibliothek, Vienna, Cod. theol. griec. 31 f.9.*

167 "Misty landscape," attr. Mi Fei (1051–1107). Ink on silk. *Freer Gallery of Art, Washington, D.C.*

176 "Hovering butterflies" position, represented in a porcelain group of the mid-eighteenth century. *Gulbenkian Museum of Oriental Art, University of Durham.*

177 "Autumn days" position, on a *famille verte* porcelain cup of the K'ang-hsi period (1662–1722). *Gulbenkian Museum of Oriental Art, University of Durham.*

188 Confucian separation rules. From the Chinese scroll "Admonitions of the Imperial Instructress," attr. to Ku K'aichih (c. 344–c. 406). *By courtesy of the Trustees of the British Museum, London.*

192 Brothel scene from the Ming blockprint *Lieh-nü-chuan*, in the collection of the late R. H. Van Gulik. *By permission of E. J. Brill, Leiden.*

194 Compression of the foot resulted in swollen ankles which, for aesthetic reasons, were covered by leggings; these in turn became erotic. The illustration is drawn after a picture in the erotic album *Shêng-p'êng-lai*, of about 1550.

205 Prince waylaying a milkmaid. Deccan painting (Hyderabad), early eighteenth century. *Foreign and Commonwealth Office, London; India Office Library, Johnson Collection, album 37 f.4.*

208 "Multiple congress." Indian painting, probably Rajasthani, early nineteenth century. *Private collection, present whereabouts unknown.*

209 Intricate sexual posture. From the same source as the previous illustration.

215 *Satī*, or suttee. From a mid-seventeenth-century manuscript of Muhammad Riza Naw'i, *Suz u Gudaz. Bibliothèque Nationale, Paris, MSS Suppl. persan 1572 f.17.*

219 Kandariya Mahadev temple, Khujarao. *Photo: Michael Edwardes.*

219 Figures from the above.

226 The *ćakras* of the subtle body, after a Kangra painting of c. 1820.

227 Mongol zoophilia. Indian painting, probably Rajasthani, early nineteenth century. *Private collection, present whereabouts unknown.*

236 Dancing girls from an eighth-century mural from Baghdad. *Staatliche Museen zu Berlin.*

240 Slave market, c. 1237, from the *Makamat* of al-Hariri. *Bibliothèque Nationale, Paris, MSS arabe 5847 f.105.*

241 The women's baths, from a manuscript of the *Zanān-nāma* by Fazil. *University Library of Istanbul.*

251 Bronze castration clamp, probably used in Cybele rites. Romano-British, second or third century A.D. Somewhat over eleven inches long, the clamp was originally hinged and closed with a screw nut. *By courtesy of the Trustees of the British Museum, London, 56.7-1.33*

260 Center panel of fifteenth-century tapestry "The Lady with the Unicorn." *Cluny Museum, Paris. Photo: Mansell Collection, London.*

262 "The month of May," by Pol de Limbourg, from the *Très Riches Heures du duc de Berry.* Early fifteenth century. *Musée Condé, Chantilly. Photo: Giraudon.*

263 Ladies wearing hennins. Detail of a miniature showing Pierre Lebaud offering his *Histoire de Bretagne* to Jean de Derval. Fifteenth century. *Bibliothèque Nationale, Paris, MSS fr. 8266 f.393v.*

269 Symbolic figures from a fresco by Ambrogio Lorenzetti in the Palazzo Pubblico, Siena. *Photo: Mansell/Anderson.*

270 Virgin and child, not yet humanized, in a Byzantine ivory of the late eleventh or twelfth century. *Victoria and Albert Museum, London, 702-1884.*

270 Central detail of the panel "Vierge de la Miséricorde" commissioned from Enguerrand Charenton and Pierre Vilate in 1452. *Musée Condé, Chantilly. Photo: Giraudon.*

270 Virgin and child. Anonymous French drawing in silverpoint heightened with white on gray paper, c. 1400. *Kupferstichkabinett des Kunstmuseums Basel, Inv.U.XVI.1*

275 Fifteenth-century domesticity. *By permission of the British Library, London, MS Royal 15 D.1 f.18.*

276 Woodcut, c. 1540, by Vogtherr, showing woman wearing chastity girdle.

280 Fifteenth-century bath house, from a French manuscript of Valerius Maximus. *Staedtisches Bibliothek, Leipzig. Photo: Mansell/Giraudon.*

281 "The baths at [?] Leuk," by Hans Bock the Elder. 1597. *Kunstmuseum Basel, Inv.87.*

281 Syphilis. Engraving by Philip Galle, published c. 1600, after an original by Stradanus (Jan van der Straet). *Wellcome Institute for the History of Medicine, London, by courtesy of the Wellcome Trustees.*

282, 283 "Aretino's postures" is a term sometimes used to describe a series of sonnets by Aretino, and sometimes the engravings by Giulio Romano (Raphael's favorite pupil) which the sonnets were written to accompany. This joint enterprise achieved considerable notoriety, and the Pope gave orders for the engravings and the printing plates to be destroyed. The two illustrations reproduced here (from Eduard Fuchs, vol. 1—see Bibliography) seem to be "after" (probably about two hundred years after) rather than "by" Romano. A thriving trade in reconstructions began soon after the originals were destroyed.

287 Details from six different suits of armor dating from 1510 to 1562. Reproduced from Eduard Fuchs (see bibliography) vol. 1, *Renaissance, Ergänzungsband* 1909.

297 Peruvian stirrup-spout vessel (Viru).

Courtesy of The Art Institute of Chicago, 52.2674.

305 Mexican wedding, c. 1550. *From the Codex Mendoza, fol.61, Bodleian Library, Oxford.*

309 Spanish-Filipino *mestizo,* or "mestingo." A copy, by the Chinese painter Tinqua in about 1855, of a watercolor original by the Filipino artist Tristiniano Asumpción. *Courtesy of the Peabody Museum of Salem, M 3870-43.*

314 Englishman in India, c. 1800. *Foreign and Commonwealth Office, London; India Office Library, Indian painting Company style Add. Or. 2.*

324 Kyoto, the pleasure quarter. Japanese screen of the second half of the seventeenth century. *Museum of Fine Arts, Boston, 06.286.*

332 "Who wears the pants?" Print by Israel van Meckenem. *Rijksmuseum, Amsterdam.*

337 "*Le vrai bonheur.*" Engraved by Simonet in 1782, after an original by I. M. Moreau le Jeune. *Photo: Giraudon.*

343 Electric alarm, four-pointed urethral ring, and toothed urethral ring, from J. L. Milton, *Pathology and treatment of spermatorrhea* (London, 1887), pp. 132, 127, and 129. *Wellcome Institute for the History of Medicine, London, by courtesy of the Wellcome Trustees.*

344 Line engraving of spermatozoa, figs. 1 and 7 being human and the others of rams. *From A. van Leeuwenhoek Opera Omni (1719).*

344 The human beings contained in spermatozoa, from N. Hartsoeker, *Essai de dioptrique* (1694).

359 Cora Pearl and La Païva. *Bibliothèque Nationale, Paris.*

360 "Contemporary prostitution" c. 1910. From Eduard Fuchs (see Bibliography) vol. 3 *Das bürgerliche Zeitalter, Ergänzungsband, 1912.*

364 "A Private Room at Petron's." Lithograph (1840) by Paul Gavarni.

373 Drawing by Felicien Rops (1833-98).

376 "*A La Souris.*" Lithograph (1897) by Henri de Toulouse-Lautrec.

379 "A Well Known Nuisance." Anonymous ink drawing, c. 1890. *Special Collection Division, Tulane University Library.*

383 The Gibson girl. *Century* magazine, July 1898.

385 Illustration from an English flagellation manual. Same source as above.
391 Gavarni cartoon. *Bibliothèque Nationale, Paris, Est. 49A 3058.* Daumier cartoon. *Bibliothèque Nationale, Paris, Est. B 7617.*
395 Mormon family group. Steel engraving, c. 1885. *Mansell Collection.*

403 Rudolf Valentino in *Son of the Sheik,* 1926. *British Film Institute, National Film Archive, V 3-2-139.*
420 Lithograph by Alloras, "*Un mariage d'in térêt.*" *Bibliothèque Nationale, Paris, Est. A 5698.*

ACKNOWLEDGMENTS

The author and publishers are grateful to the following for permission to quote extracts from copyright works:

N. V. Boekhandel en Drukkerij v/h E. J. Brill (Leiden), for translations from the Chinese published in *Sexual Life in Ancient China,* by R. H. van Gulik; Doubleday and Company, Inc. (copyright 1933) for lines from "archy says," from *archy's life of mehitabel* by Don Marquis; Oxford University Press for extracts from *Ghazālī's Book of Counsel for Kings,* translated by F. R. C. Bagley (copyright university); Penguin Books Ltd for extracts from *The Histories of Herodotus* (copyright the Estate of Aubrey de Selincourt 1954, and A. R. Burn 1972), *The Sixteen Satires* of Juvenal translated by Peter Green (copyright Peter Green 1967, 1974), and *The Letters of Abelard and Heloise* translated by Betty Radice (copyright Betty Radice 1974).

Notes on
text sources

Where an abbreviated reference is given below, full details of the work referred to will be found in the bibliography. Pb = paperback edition.

1. In the beginning

1. John Usher, or Ussher, archbishop of Armagh, was responsible for working out the year, while the day and hour were contributed by John Lightfoot, master and later vicechancellor of Catharine Hall, University of Cambridge.
2. Leakey and Lewin.
3. Tannahill (1).
4. Darlington (2), pp. 54–55.
5. Ford and Beach, pp. 22–24.
6. N. I. Berrill *Sex and the Nature of Things* (London 1954).
7. Coon p. 39.
8. See, among numerous other studies of the chimpanzee, J. Goodall in *Advances in the Study of Behavior*, ed. Lehrman, Hinde and Shaw (New York 1970); J. B. Lancaster in *American Anthropologist* 70 (1968); A. Kortlandt in *Progress in Primatology*, ed. Starck, Schneider and Kuhn (Stuttgart 1967); Albrecht and Dunnett *Chimpanzees in West Africa* (Munich 1971); Teleki *Predatory Behavior of Wild Chimpanzees* (Lewisburg, Pa. 1973); Sugiyama in *Comparative Ecology and Behavior of Primates*, ed. Michael and Crook (London and New York 1973).
9. Wilson, Edward O.
10. Edward S. Deevey, "The Human Population," in *Scientific American* CCIII (1960), pp. 194–204.
11. Donald Kolakowski and Robert Malina in *Nature* 251 (October 4, 1974).
12. Diane McGuinness in *Perception* 5 (October 1976).
13. Darlington (2) pp. 52–53 and (1) pp. 276 and 329.
14. C. Packer in *Nature* 255 (May 15, 1975).
15. Tanner and Zihlman in *Signs* I iii 1 (Spring 1976).
16. World Health Organisation re-

view by Dr. Mark Belsey, reported in *Sunday Times* (London) October 3, 1976.

17. Deevey, see note 10 above.
18. William T. Divale in *World Archaeology* 4 (October 1972).
19. Calvin Wells *Bones, Bodies and Disease. Evidence of disease and abnormality in early man* (London 1964), pp. 177, 179.
20. Sigerist p. 223.
21. Dr. C. Gopalan in the *Lancet,* November 18, 1972.
22. Dr. John Dobbing in *Archives of Disease in Childhood* (October 1973).
23. Frazer pp. 293–94; and Whitmarsh *The World's Rough Hand.*
24. Gladys Planas and Joseph Kuc in *Science* (November 29, 1968); H. de Laszlo and P. Henshaw in *Science* (July 1954); and V. J. Vogel *American Indian Medicine* (Norman 1970).
25. R. Benedict, "Rituals," in *Encyclopaedia of the Social Sciences* XIII.
26. W. J. Perry *The Growth of Civilisation* (London 1924), pb 1937 p. 28.
27. Grahame Clark and Stuart Piggott *Prehistoric Societies* (London 1965), pb 1970 p. 71; in Grimal I p. 47; Walter Torbrügge *Prehistoric European Art* (New York 1968), p. 15; Lewinsohn p. 5; cited Clark and Piggott p. 87; and Seltman p. 22.
28. Wells, see note 19 above, p. 34.

2. Man into master

1. Toben Monberg in *Man* 10 (1975); G. Roheim *Australian Totemism* (London 1925); B. Malinowski (2); Anna Meigs in *Ethnology* 15 4 (1977); and P. M. Kaberry *Aboriginal Women, Sacred and Profane* (Philadelphia 1939).
2. J. H. Hutton *Caste in India* (Cambridge 1946).
3. Report in the *Sunday Times* (London) October 2, 1977.
4. Tannahill (2) pp. 5–18.
5. Bettelheim pp. 104–27.
6. G. Roheim, "The Symbolism of Subincision," in *The American Imago* VI (1949); M. F. Ashley-Montagu, "Ritual Mutilation among Primitive Peoples," in *CIBA Symposia* VIII (1946).
7. G. Devereux, "The Psychology of Feminine Genital Bleeding," in *The International Journal of Psycho-Analysis* XXXI (1950).
8. See Weideger, and others.
9. Deevey, see note 10 chapter 1 above.
10. Frank Hole and Kent V. Flannery in *Proceedings of the Prehistoric Society* (February 1968).
11. James Mellaart *The Neolithic of the Near East* (London 1975), pp. 98 and 132.
12. *Ibid.* p. 99.
13. Excavations at Franchthi cave, southern Greece, reported in *The Times* (London) August 15, 1973; and Hole and Flannery, see note 10 above.
14. Mellaart, see note 11 above, p. 108.
15. For the materials of ancient religious belief, see S. H. Hooke *Middle Eastern Mythology* (Harmondsworth pb 1963); also Brandon, under various headings.

3. *The First civilizations*

1. Report in the *Sunday Times* (London) February 5, 1978.
2. Bottero, in Grimal I pp. 164-65.
3. W. B. Emery *Archaic Egypt* (Harmondsworth pb 1961), pp. 65-69; Vercoutter, in Grimal I pp. 124-26; and Boris de Rachewitz *An Introduction to Egyptian Art* (London 1960), 1966 edn. pp. 70-71.
4. Herodotus I 184; Bottero, in Grimal I pp. 245-47.
5. Wells, see note 19 chapter 1 above, pp. 63-64, 53.
6. For women's employment in Egypt, see Vercoutter; in Babylon, Bottero; and among the Hebrews, Bottero. All in Grimal I, pp. 151, 206-17, 243-44.
7. For adultery among the Israelites, see Bottero; in Egypt, Vercoutter; both in Grimal I pp. 238, 136-37. In Babylon, H. W. F. Saggs *Everyday Life in Babylonia and Assyria* (London and New York 1965), pp. 140-43. Divorce among Israelites, see Bottero; in Egypt, Vercoutter; in Babylon, Bottero; all in Grimal I pp. 242-43, 140-41, 199. Also Saggs p. 143.
8. Quoted in Baron II p. 223.
9. D. D. Luckenbill *Ancient Records of Assyria and Babylonia* (Chicago 1926-27), II p. 240.
10. Vercoutter and Bottero, in Grimal I pp. 86-87, 110, 190; Baron II p. 225; and Saggs, see note 7 above, p. 143.
11. Vercoutter, in Grimal I pp. 78-81, 109-13, 135, 144.
12. Bottero, in Grimal I p. 187; Baron II p. 219; Vercoutter, in Grimal I p. 136.
13. Sigerist pp. 302-3, 332-4; F. Reinhard, "Gynäkologie und Geburtshilfe der altägyptischen Papyri," in *Archiv für Geschichte der Medizin* 1916-17 (Leipzig).
14. Bottero, in Grimal I p. 181.
15. *Ibid*; and report in *Sunday Times* (London) November 25, 1973.
16. Sigerist p. 241; Bottero, in Grimal I p. 193; Berlin Papyrus, quoted in Himes. p. 65.
17. Wells, see note 19 chapter 1 above, p. 67.
18. Bottero, in Grimal I p. 170; Leviticus 15 21-23, 34.
19. Sigerist pp. 243-44.
20. *Observer* (London) July 22, 1979.
21. Bettelheim pp. 129-31.
22. Middle Assyrian Laws para. 8, in G. R. Driver and John C. Miles *The Assyrian Laws* (Oxford 1935).
23. *Ibid*. para. 21; Heinrich Zimmern *Hethitische Gesetze aus dem Staatsarchiv von Boghazköi* (Leipzig), pp. 17-18.
24. Middle Assyrian Laws para. 53, see note 22 above; Leviticus 20 2-5; Brandon p. 448.
25. Josephus, quoted in Baron II p. 219; Deuteronomy 24 5; Leviticus 20 13 and 15-16.
26. By, for example, Ibn al-Baitar in his *Treatise on Simples*.
27. Himes pp. 59-78; on levirate marriage, Epstein (1) pp. 77-144.
28. Raban Asher, cited in Epstein (1) p. 262.
29. P. Ghalioungi, "A Medical Study of Akhenaten," in *Annales du Service des Antiquités d'Egypte* (Cairo 1947); E.

Snorrason, "Cranial Deformation in the Reign of Akhnaton," in *Bulletin of the History of Medicine* (Baltimore 1946); and Wells, see note 19 chapter 1 above, p. 108.

30. Darlington (2) pp. 118-9.
31. Immanuel Velikovsky *Oedipus and Akhnaton* (London 1960).
32. Herodotus I 199, p. 92
33. W. G. Lambert *Babylonian Wisdom Literature* (London 1960), pp. 14ff.
34. Bottero, in Grimal I, p. 179.
35. Quoted in Saggs, see note 7 above, p. 152.
36. Herodotus II 64, p. 127
37. Vercoutter, in Grimal I, pp. 132, 137.
38. "Can the image of God be made to lose its maleness?," report in *The Times* (London), June 24, 1974.
39. 1 14-15 from the King James version; 2 10-12 from the Common Bible. The theory propounded by Raban Gordis that the *Song of Songs* was originally composed on the occasion of one of Solomon's marriages is not, in fact, generally accepted. The Synagogue and the Church both consider it an allegory of the "matrimonial alliance" between Jehovah and Israel (c.f. Baron I pp. 336-37).

4. Greece

1. Hesiod *Theogony* 190; Hermaphroditos, Flacelière p. 32; Priapus, Licht pp. 220-24; Heracles, Pausanias IX 27 6-9 and Theocritus *Idylls* XIII. See also Robert Graves.
2. Straton in *Anthologia Palatinus (The Greek Anthology)* XII 4.
3. H. D. F. Kitto *The Greeks* (Harmondsworth pb 1951), pp. 126-31, 247-48.
4. Plato *Symposium* 213 d.
5. *Ibid.* 217 a-219 e.
6. *Ibid.* 183 a.
7. Aristophanes *Birds* 137-42.
8. See, for example, Athenaeus XIII 605.
9. Pseudo-Aristotle *Problemata* IV 26, quoted in Dover p. 169.
10. Dover pp. 99-102.
11. Plutarch *Erotikos* 768 F; Thucydides *Historiae* VI 54-59; Aristotle *Constitution of Athens* 18; Plato *Symposium* 179 a, b.
12. Cited Licht p. 438.
13. Aeschines *Contra Timarchum* 12, 138, 13-15.
14. Flacelière pp. 196-97.
15. Xenophon *Symposium* 2.
16. Plutarch *Life of Solon* 21.
17. *Ibid. De inimicorum utilitate* 7.
18. Hieronymus of Cardia *Historia Memoranda* frag. 6.
19. Speech against Neaera, quoted in Kitto, *see* note 3 above, p. 227.
20. Hesiod *Theogony* 585-612, and *Works and Days* 405-6.
21. Xenophon *Oeconomicus* VII 10; and Solon, reported in Plutarch *Erotikos* 769 A.
22. "The Betrothed," in *Departmental Ditties and other verses* (London and Calcutta, 9th edn. 1897).
23. *De republica* II 10 1271.
24. Aristotle *Works* IV 583a; Marie C. Stopes, "Positive and negative control of conception in its various technical as-

pects," in *Journal of State Medicine* XXXIX (1931).
25. Slater (Philip), *passim*.
26. C. J. Fyller *The Nayars Today* (Cambridge 1977).
27. Plutarch *Life of Lycurgus* 15.
28. Herondas *The Two Friends*, in *Mimiambus* 6.
29. Plutarch, see note 27 above, 18.
30. Demosthenes (attr.) *In Neaeram* 122.
31. Athenaeus XIII 567.
32. Thargelia, in Flacelière p. 126; Thaïs and Aspasia, Licht pp. 344, 351-52.
33. Alciphron *Letters of Courtesans* I 40.
34. Herodotus II 134-35.
35. Antiphon *De veneficio* 14.
36. Athenaeus II 468.

5. *Rome*

1. Juvenal *Sixth Satire* 1-11, p. 127.
2. Livy 34 2-4. Scholars consider Livy's account of the Oppian law debate to be nearer faction than fact, but it seems to have been based on contemporary records.
3. Valerius Maximus *Memorabilia* IX 1 3.
4. C. G. F. Simkin *The Traditional Trade of Asia* (London and New York 1968) p. 45; figures adjusted to compensate for a surplus zero in Professor Simkin's calculations.
5. Seneca *De brevitate vitae*.
6. Aristophanes, in Pollux *Onomasticon* VII 95, frag. 320; Eubulus *Garland Sellers*, frag. 98, in T. Kock (ed.) *Comicorum Atticorum Fragmenta* (Leipzig 1880-88).
7. Alexis, quoted in Athenaeus

XIII 568; see also Licht pp. 84-5.
8. Lucian (attr.) *Amores* 39.
9. Cited Sigerist pp. 478, 247.
10. Fuller details of the Roman woman's day may be found in Balsdon (2), pp. 252-81; Carcopino pp. 183-90; and Kiefer pp. 15-66 and *passim*.
11. Suetonius *Augustus* 31.
12. Plutarch *Numa* 10.
13. Livy 39 9ff.
14. Josephus *Jewish Antiquities* 18 65-84.
15. Juvenal *Sixth Satire* 227-28.
16. Gellius *Noctes Atticae* I 6.
17. Seneca *Fragmenta* XIII 61.
18. Tannahill (2) *passim*.
19. Cassius Dio *Historia Romana* 54 16; L. Friedländer, cited Kiefer p. 61.
20. Balsdon (2) pp. 187-88.
21. Nicole Belmont, "Levana; or, How to Raise up Children," in Forster and Ranum (2) p. 1.
22. Ovid III 779-82.
23. Lucretius *On the Nature of Things* IV.
24. Dover pp. 100-1.
25. Pliny XXVIII 80, XXX 49, and XXVIII 77.
26. Dioscorides *De materia medica* II 188, IV 19.
27. *On medicine, in sixteen books or discourses* XVI 17.
28. Soranus *Gynaecology* I 19 61-3.
29. Himes pp. 187-88.
30. All figures are to some extent speculative (see Brunt pp. 131ff.) The infant mortality rate may be underestimated.
31. William H. McNeill *Plagues and People* (Oxford 1977).
32. Dr. Robert Yule, consultant pathologist, quoted in *The*

Times (London) March 15, 1978.

33. Speech at Third International Congress of Human Genetics, Chicago, reported in *Time*, September 23, 1966.

34. Report in *The Times* (London) April 7, 1978.

35. Research at Mount Sinai School of Medicine, New York, reported in *New England Journal of Medicine*, October 7, 1976; Drs. Frederick Lemere and James Smith of the Shadel Hospital for the Treatment of Alcoholism, Seattle, reported in the *Sunday Times* (London) June 17, 1973.

36. Lemere and Smith, *ibid.*

37. Seneca *Epistolae Morales* 86.

38. Research by Dr. Howard Gabriel of the Health Planning Council, Wichita, Kansas, reported in the *Sunday Times* (London) March 24, 1974.

39. Balsdon (1) p. 195.

40. *Annals* 2 73.

41. *Pro Marcello* 23.

42. Witold Kula, "The Seigneury and the Peasant Family in Eighteenth-Century Poland," in Forster and Ranum (2) pp. 195–96.

43. For a fuller summary of the Lex Julia and the Lex Papia Poppaea see Brunt pp. 558–66.

6. *The Christian Church*

1. *Epistles* 50 5.

2. Eusebius *Ecclesiastical History* IV 29 etc.

3. *Acts of John*, frag. (J 266); *Acts of Andrew*, Vatican MS frag. v. (J 352).

4. *Epistles* XXII 7, and *Confessions* VIII 7 17.

5. Augustine *c. duas epist. Pelag.* I 34 17.

6. *Ibid. De nupt. et concup.* II 8, 12–13, 22; *de civ. Dei* XIII 13, XIV 17; *de pecc. merit. et remiss.* II 36 22; *c. duas epist. Pelag.* I 31.

7. *Sunday Telegraph* July 9, 1978.

8. Bailey (2) p. 152.

9. Council of Seville 590, iii.

10. Quoted Pierre Riché, in Grimal II p. 53.

11. Tertullian *Ad uxorem* I 5; also John Chrysostom, Cyril of Alexandria, Gregory I, Athanasius, Lactantius, Jerome, and Ambrose *inter alia.*

12. John Chrysostom *Epist. ad Rom.* XXX 3; Methodius *Conviv.* IX 4; Clement of Alexandria *Stromateis* II 23.

13. Ulpian *Cod. Just., Dig.* L xvii 30.

14. Cited Bailey (2) pp. 133–34 fn.

15. Tertullian *Ad uxorem*; Augustine *De nupt. et concup.* I 14–15.

16. Reported in *Time*, February 7, 1977.

17. I Peter iii 4; I Cor. xi 9, 3, xiv 34; I Tim. ii 11–12, 14.

18. Quoted Coulson p. 394.

19. *De cult. fem.* II 2.

20. *Paidagōgos* I 4, and *Stromateis* IV 8.

21. J.-N. Biraben and Jacques le Goff, "The Plague in the Early Middle Ages," in Forster and Ranum (1) pp. 48–80; and McEvedy and Jones p. 21.

22. Cited Darlington (2) p. 300.

23. Tannahill (1) pp. 184–5, 190–4.

24. Burchard *Decretum* 19, quoted Noonan p. 160.

25. Jerome *De custodia virginitatis*, quoted Himes p. 93.
26. Cummean II penitential, in Bergues p. 209.
27. For further material on the penitentials, see Noonan *passim*; Jean-Louis Flandrin, "Contraception, Marriage, and Sexual Relations in the Christian West," in Forster and Ranum (1) pp. 23–47; and R. C. Mortimer *Western Canon Law* (London 1953) pp. 24ff.
28. *Judicia Greg. Pap.* III 21, quoted in Bailey (1) p. 106.
29. *Sunday Times* (London) April 11, 1976.
30. F. Brown, S. R. Driver, and C. A. Briggs *A Hebrew and English Lexicon of the Old Testament* (Oxford 1952).
31. *De Abrahamo* XXVI 134–36.
32. Justinian *Novella* 77 1–2.
33. Procopius *Anecdota* XI 36.
34. *Novella 141* preamble, and para. 1.
35. *Apostolical Tradition* of Hippolytus II 16 20; Council of Elvira 305–6, 71.
36. Rule of St. Benedict, 22; Council of Tours 567, 14; Council of Paris 1212, II 21, III 2.
37. Council of Toledo 693, 3; Lex Visigoth. III 5 7.
38. For a discussion of the Latin commentaries on these canons, see Bailey (1) pp. 86–89.
39. Canons of the Synod of Llanddewi-Brefi; *Poenitentiale Burgundense*; Theodore's Penitential.
40. The homosexual provisions of the penitentials are discussed at some length in Bailey (1) pp. 100–10.
41. *Liber Gomorrhianus* 7.
42. Diocese of Cambrai 1300–1310, cited Flandrin, see note 27 above, p. 30.
43. *Time* January 26, 1976, September 20, 1976, and June 5, 1978.
44. Benedicti, echoing St. Jerome, in *La Somme des Péchez* (Paris 1601).

7. China

1. Ko Hung (Pao-p'u-tzû) *Nei-p'ien*, chap. 6; *Yü-fang-pi-chüeh*, from *I-shin-pō* chap. 28, quoted in Van Gulik p. 138. The late Dr. Van Gulik's book on sexual life in China prior to the Manchu period is an invaluable source not only of information but ideas.
2. *I-ching* I 5.
3. *Kuan-yin-tzu*.
4. Chang Hêng *Ch'i-pien*.
5. *Tung-hsüan-tzû* XII.
6. *Sunday Times* (London) November 7, 1976.
7. *Yü-fang-chih-yao*, in *I-shin-pō* 28 XVIII.
8. *Yang-shêng-yao-chi*, in *I-shin-pō* 28 XIX.
9. *Yü-fang-pi-chüeh*, in *I-shin-pō* 28 XIX.
10. Sun Szû-mo *Ch'ien-chin-yao-fang*, trs. in Van Gulik pp. 195–6.
11. See note 9 above, 28 II.
12. *Ibid.* XXIII.
13. See note 5 above, XIII.
14. *Ch'an-ching*, in *I-shin-pō* 28 XXI.
15. See note 10 above, p. 196.
16. See note 5 above, III, V–VII, IV, X.
17. *Ibid.* IX.
18. Quoted Van Gulik p. 83.
19. Issue of November 20, 1950.
20. Hsü Ying-ch'iu *Yü-chih-t'ang-*

t'an-hui, cited Van Gulik p. 160.

21. See Licht pp. 364ff. and 513ff. for Greek aphrodisiacs and other sexual magic.
22. See note 5 above, XVI.
23. Personal communication.
24. Quoted Michael Edwardes *Ralph Fitch. Elizabethan in the Indies* (London 1972) pp. 123–4; and Francesco Carletti *My Voyage around the World* [1594–1606], New York 1964 edn. pp. 181–3.
25. Quoted Van Gulik p. 261.
26. Confucius *Analects* XVII 25.
27. Quoted Van Gulik p. 60.
28. Lady Pan Chao *Nü-chieh (Women's Precepts)* IV–V.
29. Fu Hsüan *Yü-t'ai-hsin-yung.*
30. Quoted Van Gulik pp. 86–7.
31. *Li-chi,* section *Nei-tsê* I 12.
32. Cited Bailey (2) p. 73.
33. Cited Van Gulik p. 68.
34. *Pao-p'u-tzû* 25.
35. Nai-tê-wêng *Tu-ch'êng-chi-shêng.*
36. René Grousset *The Rise and Splendour of the Chinese Empire* (London 1952) pp. 171 and 236.
37. Quoted Van Gulik p. 269.
38. See Van Gulik pp. 246–50 for greater detail.

8. India

1. Needham I.
2. Recipes possibly from Caraka (1st–2nd centuries A.D.), quoted Himes pp. 119–21.
3. McEvedy and Jones pp. 182–3.
4. *Laws of Manu* IX 94.
5. Plutarch, quoted Licht p. 33.
6. For example, *Rg Veda* X 18 8.
7. Pseudo-Maurikios *Taktika* XI 5; Boniface *Epist.* no. 73 745–

6; and al-Masoudi (ed. J. Marquart) XXIV.
8. Michael Edwardes *Indian Temples and Palaces* (London 1969) p. 108.
9. Blofeld pp. 198–9.
10. Om Prakash *Food and Drinks in Ancient India (from earliest times to c. 1200 A.D.)* (Delhi 1961) pp. 210, 222, 260.
11. Rawson (1) p. 98.
12. Bharati p. 292.

9. Islam

1. Michael Edwardes *East-West Passage; The Travel of Ideas, Arts and Inventions between Asia and the Western World* (London and New York 1971) pp. 50–65; Hitti pp. 64–78; Anthony Baines (ed.) *Musical Instruments through the Ages* (Harmondsworth pb 1961), 1969 edn. pp. 327–30.
2. José Grosdidier de Matons, in Grimal III p. 33.
3. Koran IV 3.
4. *Ghazālī's Book of Counsel for Kings (Naṣīḥat al-Mulūk),* trs. F. R. C. Bagley (Oxford 1964), II 7 pp. 164–5.
5. *Ibid.* p. 172.
6. C. Pellat, "Les esclaves chanteuses de Gāḥiz," in *Arabica* X 2 (June 1963), pp. 121–47.
7. Quoted C. Pellat *Le Milieu Basrien et la formation de Gāḥiz* (Paris 1953) p. 254.
8. Djamil *Aghâni* VII.
9. For Arab love literature in general, see Nada Tomiche in Grimal III pp. 98–113.
10. Van Gulik p. 189.
11. *Kamasutra* IV 2, and V 6.
12. Penzer p. 13.
13. Marco Polo *Travels,* trs.

Ronald Latham (Harmonds-
worth 1958), London 1968
edn. p. 101.
14. Hitti pp. 30–31.
15. For Avicenna see Himes pp.
141ff.
16. Stent pp. 174–5.
17. Nefzawi IX p. 196.
18. *Ibid.* VI pp. 141–2.
19. Xenophon *Cyropaedeia* VII
60–65.
20. Reports in the *Sunday Times*
(London) September 28, 1975,
and *British Journal of Psychiatry* September 1974.
21. Quoted Saggs p. 151.
22. Bottero, in Grimal I p. 192.
23. Herodotus VI 32.
24. Stent pp. 147–50, 167.
25. Herodotus VIII pp. 533–4.
26. Suetonius XII 7.
27. Michael Psellus *Fourteen Byzantine Rulers (Chrono-
graphia)* IV 12.
28. *Ibid.* V 42.
29. Basham p. 173.
30. Burton *Suppl. Nights* I pp. 71–
2.
31. *Sixth Satire* 365–77, p. 141.
32. Stent pp. 162–3.
33. See note 30 above, p. 71 fn.
34. Lucian *De Syria dea* 19ff.
35. Alfred G. Francis in *Transac-
tions of the Royal Society of
Medicine* (January 1926).
36. Stent p. 171.
37. See note 34 above.
38. Stent p. 172.
39. Letter to Jen An, trs. in Birch.
40. *Historia calamitum*, and letter
IV of Abelard to Heloise, in
*The Letters of Abelard and
Heloise*, trs. Betty Radice
(Harmondsworth 1974), pp. 75
and 147–8.
41. See note 30 above, p. 71.
42. Penzer p. 150.
43. Osbert Sitwell *Escape with
me!* (London 1939), pb edn.
1948 pp. 279–89.

10. *Europe, 1100–1550*

1. Guillaume de Machaut *Le
Livre du Voir-Dit*, quoted
Huizinga p. 118.
2. Georges Duby and Robert
Mandrou *A History of French
Civilisation* (London 1965) pp.
101–2.
3. Anon. *Itinerarium Peregrin-
orum et Gesta Regis Ricardi*
(English trs. London 1848);
repr. London 1958 (as *The
Third Crusade*) p. 29.
4. Boase pp. 118–21.
5. There is a useful summary of
the evidence in Boase pp. 62–
75.
6. Ibn Hazm, French trs. in *Le
Collier du Pigeon*, L. Bercher
(Algiers 1949), p. 253.
7. See, for example, Bezzola.
8. Djamil *Aghâni* VII 85.
9. Andreas Capellanus p. 122.
10. Yves Lefèvre in Grimal II pp.
95–7.
11. Cited Warner p. 131.
12. *Summa Theologica* I 92 3 *resp;*
1 *resp;* 1 *ad.* 2; III suppl. 66 5.
13. *Ibid.* II–II 154 12 *ad.* 4; 12 *resp;*
4; 5; and Bailey (2) p. 160 fn. 4.
14. Norman Cohn *Europe's Inner
Demons. An Enquiry inspired
by the Great Witch-hunt*
(London 1975) p. 235.
15. *Ibid.* pp. 235–6.
16. *Summa Theologica* I 51 3.
17. H. C. Erik Midelfort *Witch
Hunting in South-western Germany 1562–1684. The Social
and Intellectual Foundations*
(Stanford 1972, Oxford 1973),
p. 187.

18. See note 14 above, p. 248.
19. See note 17 above, pp. 89, 96–8, 137; and Guido Bader *Die Hexenprozesse in der Schweiz* (Affoltern a. A. 1945) pp. 219, 217.
20. *Ménagier de Paris*.
21. For a general summary, see Dingwall (2).
22. Dr. John G. Kennedy in *Man* 5 (1970) p. 175.
23. Anon. *A Relation . . . of the Island of England . . . about the year 1500*, in C. H. Williams *English Historical Documents 1485–1558* (1967), pp. 192–201.
24. *Paston Letters* I 58, in H.S. Bennett *The Pastons and their England* (Cambridge 1921); and Brantôme *Discours premier* p. 105.
25. Dr. Ken Russell in *Sunday Times* (London) February 6, 1977.
26. Augustine *De ordine* II 4 [12]; and Aquinas *Summa Theologica* II–II 10 11.
27. Warner pp. 225–31.
28. André Rochon in Grimal II pp. 293–5.
29. Wells, see note 19 chapter 1 above, pp. 100–5.
30. Jakob Burckhardt *The Civilisation of the Renaissance in Italy* (London 1878) II pp. 146–7.
31. Lorenzo Valla, quoted André Rochon in Grimal II p. 219.
32. Brantôme *Discours premier* p. 110.
33. *Ibid*. p. 112.
34. Pedro Simon *Conquistas de Tierra Firme* (1627) III 1 p. 156, and 23 p. 219.
35. *Avisos 1654–1668* (Madrid 1892–4), July 1659.

36. Quoted Guerra p. 227.
37. Quoted Ernest Hatch Wilkins *A History of Italian Literature* (London 1954) p. 94.
38. *De remediis utriusque fortunae (Physic against Fortune)*.
39. Castiglione III p. 255.

11. *Imperial enterprises*

1. "Pudd'nhead Wilson's New Calendar," in *Following the Equator* (1897), II p. 33.
2. Tannahill (2) pp. 92–8.
3. Francisco de Vitoria *Obras*, ed. P. Teofilo Urdanoz (Madrid 1960), p. 660.
4. Papal bulls *Sublimis Deus* and *Veritas ipsa* of June 9, 1537; and Vitoria (see note 3, above), p. 1050 Fourth Conclusion.
5. *Historia de las Indias* (Mexico 1951), II p. 518.
6. Garcilasso de la Vega ("The Inca") *Comentarios Reales de los Incas* (1609), II 13 fol. 40.
7. Quoted in Guerra pp. 51, 52, 85–86, 99, 106, 125, 131.
8. Cited Guerra p. 272.
9. Juan de Torquemada *Ia-IIIa Parte de los veynte y un libros rituales y Monarchia Indiana con el origen y guerras de la Indias Occidentales* (Seville 1615), II xii 8, 11.
10. Gonzalo Fernandez de Oviedo *La Historia general de las Indias* (Seville 1535), fol. 49.
11. *Ibid*. fol. 50.
12. Anglerius [Pietro Martire d'Anghiera] *Opera . . . Oceani decas* [1511–16], trs. as *The Decades of the Newe Worlde or West India . . . Englysshe by Richard Eden* (1555), I, Decade 3, pp. 89–90.

13. Diaz del Castillo, pp. 225, 222–23.

14. Jerónimo de Mendieta *Historia eclesiástica Indiana* [1596] (Mexico 1870), II xxix pp. 137–38; and Bartolomé de las Casas *Apologética historia de las Indias* (Madrid 1909), ccxv p. 563.

15. Fernando de Alva Ixtlilxochitl *Obras historicas,* ed. Alfredo Chavero (Mexico 1891–92), I p. 324.

16. Anonymous Jesuit [? Blás Valera] "Relación de las costumbres antiguas de los naturales del Pirú," in *Biblioteca de autores epañoles* (Madrid 1968), vol. 209 p. 179.

17. Pedro Cieza de Léon *The Incas* [1553], trs. Harriet de Onís, ed. Victor W. von Hagen (Norman 1959), 101.

18. Garcilasso de la Vega, see note 6 above, III xiii fol. 71 (68).

19. Cited Guerra p. 271.

20. Cieza de León, see note 17 above, 49 and 52.

21. Coon p. 370.

22. Pedro Gutierrez de Santa Clara, "Quinquenarios; o Historia de las guerras civiles del Perú" [c. 1580], in *Biblioteca de autores españoles* (Madrid 1963), vol. 166 p. 259.

23. Gonzalo Fernandez de Oviedo *Oviedo de la Natural hystoria de las Indias* (Toledo 1526), fol. 44v.

24. Oviedo, see note 10 above, fol. 48.

25. Rafael Larco Hoyle *Checan;* and Guerra pp. 256–58.

26. Guerra p. 257.

27. Alonso de Molina *Confesionario mayor, en langua Mexicana y Castellana* (Mexico 1565), fol. 35.

28. Angel Serra *Manual de administrar los Santos Sacramentos a los españoles y naturales de esta provincia de Michoacan* [1697] (Mexico 1731), fols. 112–20.

29. Lima, Concilio Provincial *Tercero Cathecismo y exposición de la Doctrina Christiana, por Sermones* (Lima 1585), fols. 150–54.

30. Guerra pp. 242–43.

31. Anonymous Jesuit, see note 16 above, p. 178.

32. *Ibid.* p. 180; and Felipe Huaman Poma de Ayala *Nueva coronica y buen gobierno* (Paris 1936), p. 190.

33. Alonso de la Peña y Montenegro *Itinerario para Parachos de Indios* (Lyon 1678), I x 8 p. 183.

34. Agustin de Zárate *Historia del descubrimiento y conquista del Peru* [1555], trs. J. M. Cohen as *The Discovery and Conquest of Peru* (Harmondsworth pb 1968), p. 51.

35. Anonymous Jesuit, see note 16 above, p. 163; and Gutierrez de Santa Clara, see note 22 above, p. 215.

36. Dr. Woodrow Borah, reported in *The New York Times,* February 19, 1977.

37. Simoni, in Grimal III p. 514.

38. For example Soustelle, p. 187.

39. Simoni, in Grimal III p. 556.

40. Bernardino de Sahagún *Historia general de las cosas de Nueva España* [c. 1565] (Mexico 1938), III x 15 pp. 47–48.

41. Francisco López de Gómara *Historia general de las Indias* (Saragossa 1552), fol. 111.

42. *Codex Magliabecchi* (c. 1565), ed. Zelia Nuttall (Berkeley, Cal. 1903), Fol. 64/76 v.
43. Pedro de Castañeda [1565], "The narrative of the expedition of Coronado," ed. F. W. Hodge, in *Spanish explorers in the Southern United States* (New York 1953), p. 344.
44. Darlington (2) p. 588.
45. C. R. Boxer *The Portuguese Seaborne Empire 1415-1825* (London 1969), pb 1973 p. 82.
46. *Ibid.* pp. 307-8.
47. *Ibid.* pp. 104-5.
48. *Ibid.* pp. 52, 220, and 307.
49. William Sleeman *Journey through the Kingdom of Oude in 1849-50* (1858), II pp. 59-60.
50. Michael Edwardes *British India 1772-1947. A survey of the nature and effects of alien rule* (London 1967), pp. 100-3.
51. Kapadia p. 115.
52. Edwardes, see note 50 above, pp. 253-7.
53. Fernando Henriques *Children of Caliban. Miscegenation* (London 1974).
54. Quoted in C. R. Boxer *South China in the Sixteenth Century* (Hakluyt Society 1953), p. 149.
55. *China in the Sixteenth Century, the Journals of Matthew Ricci*, trs. Louis J. Gallagher SJ (New York 1953), p. 95.
56. Paul Hair *Before the Bawdy Court* (London 1972).
57. Van Gulik pp. 270-90.
58. *Ibid.* p. 330.

12. *Europe and America 1550-1800*

1. Quoted in Daniel Neal *The History of the Puritans* (London 1822), I p. 478.
2. Jean Chesneaux (ed.) *Popular Movements and Secret Societies in China 1840-1950* (Stanford, Cal. 1972), pp. 154, 66; and Sheila Rowbotham *Women, Resistance, and Revolution* (London 1973).
3. *Letters of Spiritual Counsel*, ed. and trs. T. G. Tappert (London 1955), letter to Wolfgang Reissenbusch, p. 274.
4. Jeremy Taylor *Ductor Dubitantium* I v 8 par. 17, in *Works* (London 10 v. 1847-56), IX pp. 246-7.
5. Jeremy Taylor *Holy Living* ii 3, in *ibid.* III pp. 62-4.
6. John Davenant *Exposition of the Epistle to the Colossians*, trs. J. Allport (London 1832), II pp. 40ff.
7. Luther, see note 3 above, letters to Jerome Weller pp. 292 and 204.
8. Quoted in Charles Angoff *A Literary History of the American People* (New York 1935), p. 132.
9. John Winthrop *The History of New England from 1630 to 1649* (Boston 1853), II p. 73.
10. Ahlstrom p. 4.
11. Peter Laslett (ed.) *Household and Family in Past Time* (Cambridge 1972).
12. Lawrence Stone, see biblio.
13. Glass, in Glass and Eversley p. 16.
14. Peter Laslett *Family Life*, see biblio; and Jacques Depauw, "Illicit Sexual Activity and Society in Eighteenth-Century Nantes," in Forster and Ranum (2) pp. 145-91.
15. Hajnal, in Glass and Eversley pp. 101-43.
16. Quoted in de Beauvoir p. 139.
17. See Depauw, note 14 above.

18. Himes pp. 188–200.
19. *Bulletin de la Société de Médecine* XIX (Paris 1925).
20. *Clarissa* II, letter vii.
21. *Ibid.* V, letter xxxviii.
22. *Monsieur Nicolas* v^e epoque.
23. *Juliette* (1796) in 1797 edn. *La Nouvelle Justine, ou les malheurs de la vertu, suivie de l'histoire de Juliette, sa soeur, ou les prosperites du vice,* II p. 127.
24. Tannahill (2) pp. 10–14.
25. Aristotle *De gen. animal.* I 18; Galen *De fac. nat.* I 6; and Clement *Paidagōgos* II 10.
26. Nefzawi VII p. 160.
27. G. Morris Carstairs *The Twice-Born. A Study of a Community of High-Caste Hindus* (London 1957), pp. 83–4.
28. Masters and Johnson, see biblio.
29. I. de Valverde *Historia de la composicion del cuerpo humano* (Rome 1556), III xv fol. 68.
30. Darlington (1) pp. 31–44, 66.

13. *The nineteenth century*

1. Martineau *Society in America* (1839), New York 1962 edn. p. 291.
2. Quoted in John W. Dodds *The Age of Paradox. A Biography of England 1841–1851* (London 1953), p. 72.
3. *Ibid.* pp. 56–7, and 481; and John Burnett *Useful Toil. Autobiographies of working people from the 1820s to the 1920s* (London 1974), pb Harmondsworth 1977, pp. 135–8.
4. Graves *Woman in America* (New York 1842) pp. 27–8;

Ellis, quoted in Dodds, see note 2 above, p. 71 and 72.
5. Cooper *Notions of the Americans* (Philadelphia 1828), I p. 105; A. Dowling *Reports of Cases Argued and Determined in the Queen's Bench Practice Courts* (London 1841) VIII pp. 630ff.
6. Ruth E. Finley *The Lady of Godey's: Sarah Josepha Hale* (Philadelphia 1931), pp. 102–5.
7. Sanger pp. 488–9.
8. Burnett, see note 3 above, p. 27; and Lee Holcombe *Victorian Ladies at Work* (Newton Abbot 1973).
9. Brownlee p. 175; Burnett, see note 3 above, p. 38; and Nicole Bothorel and Marie-Françoise Laurent in Grimal IV p. 117.
10. Alice B. Stockham M.D. *Tokology* (Chicago 1894), pp. 150–60. (Tokology was a regimen based on avoiding animal foods and encouraging continence.)
11. Burnett, see note 3 above, p. 153.
12. Leopold Deslandes *Manhood: the Causes of Its Premature Decline with Directions for Perfect Restoration* (Boston 1843).
13. Cited in S. C. Burchell *Imperial Masquerade. The Paris of Napoleon III* (New York, 1971), pp. 112, 104.
14. Ryan, see biblio.
15. Schrank I p. 242.
16. Cited in Rugoff, p. 252.
17. Dr. George H. Napheys *The Transmission of Life* (1869), pp. 113–4; and William Hepworth Dixon *New America* (Philadelphia 1867), pp. 267–8.

18. U.S. Commissioner of Labor, Fourth Annual Report, 1888, *Working Women in Large Cities* (Washington D.C., Government Printing Office, 1889), pp. 13–76.

19. Quoted in Burchell, see note 13 above, pp. 77–79.

20. *Untrodden Fields of Anthropology* (Paris 1898), I pp. 129–30.

21. Ostwald 2nd edn. p. 618.

22. Matthew Hale Smith *Sunshine and Shadow in New York* (Hartford Conn. 1868), p. 371.

23. *Time*, November 7, 1977; and *Sunday Times* (London) May 26, 1974.

24. Acton pp. 142–3.

25. Burchell, see note 13 above, p. 112; Lewinsohn p. 349; and Andrew Smith, in William Trufant Foster *The Social Emergency* (Boston 1914), p. 33.

26. Chesney pp. 423–33.

27. Edith Houghton Hooker, "The Case against Prophylaxis," in *Journal of Social Hygiene* (April 1919), pp. 163–84.

28. T. A. Storey *The Work of the U.S. Interdepartmental Social Hygiene Board* (New York 1920), p. 6.

29. Willi Frischauer, in *Sunday Times* (London) Colour Supplement, April 30, 1972, p. 46, "The Brothel Brigade."

30. A. Blaschke, "Verbreitung der Geschlechtskrankheiten," in *Vortragsbericht, Medizinische Reform* (1910, 4 and 5).

31. *Red Banner* (Poland), reported in *Sunday Times* (London) December 12, 1976.

32. *Epic of Gilgamesh* p. 66; and Achille Luchaire *Social France at the time of Philip Augustus* (1912), New York and London repr. n.d. but c. 1950, p. 403.

33. Iwai Hirosato, "The Buddhist Priest and the Ceremony of Attaining Womanhood during the Yüan Dynasty," in *Memoirs* of the Research Department of the Tōyō Bunko (Tokyo 1935); and Kiefer, p. 20.

34. Plutarch *Lycurgus* 15; Ephorus of Cyme *History of the Greeks*; Festus, quoted in Licht p. 19; Kapadia p. 189; Ford and Beach p. 184; Athens case reported in *The Times* (London) January 21, 1978.

35. Van Gulik p. 182.

36. Jean Renvoise *Web of Violence* (London 1978); and Ernest Bornemann *Die Umwelt des Kindes im Spiegel seiner "verbotenen" Lieder, Reime, Verse und Ratsel. Studien zur Befreiung des Kindes II,* (1975).

37. Preface to *Woman's Work and Woman's Culture* (1869); *Time*, November 28, 1977.

38. Timothy D'Arch Smith *Love in Earnest* (London 1970).

39. Lloyd Morris *Incredible New York* (New York 1951), pp. 216–9.

40. Quoted in Robert Baldick *Dinner at Magny's* (London 1971), pb Harmondsworth 1973, p. 106.

41. *Ibid.*

42. Cited in Burchell, see note 13 above, p. 181.

43. Maximilian Harden, "Fürst Eulenburg," in *Prozesse, Köpfe, Dritter Teil* (Berlin 1913), pp. 182–3.

44. 9 Geo. IV c. 31 pars. 15 and 18, quoted in Bailey (1) pp. 150-1.
45. Alan Harding *A Social History of English Law* (Harmondsworth 1966 pb original), p. 360.
46. 48 & 49 Vict. c. 69 par. 11, quoted Bailey (1) p. 152.
47. *Yokel's Preceptor; or more sprees in London etc.* (London n.d.), pp. 5ff.
48. *Pierre*, quoted in Rugoff p. 269.
49. W. T. Stead, in *Review of Reviews* (June 15, 1895).
50. "Under the Whip," in *Die Messalinen Wiens. Geschichten aus der guten Gesellschaft* (Leipzig 1873), pp. 126ff.
51. Matilda, in Matthew (Monk) Lewis *Ambrosio, or the Monk* (London 1795).
52. Report by Swedish Government Advisory Council on Equality Between Men and Women, February 1975.
53. Gautier *Mademoiselle de Maupin*, p. 240 approx., dependent on edition.
54. Swinburne, "Notes on Designs of the Old Masters in Florence," in *Fortnightly Review* (July 1868).
55. *Whippingham Papers*, in G. Lafourcade *La Jeunesse de Swinburne (1837-1867)* (Paris 1928), II p. 132.
56. *Masque of Queen Bersabe*. And for a general study of the "fatal woman" in nineteenth-century literature, see Praz pp. 187-286.
57. Taine *Histoire de la littérature anglaise* (1863), I p. 46.
58. Quoted Gibson, see biblio.
59. Bloch p. 340.
60. Fraxi pp. xl-xlvi.
61. Quoted in Baldick, see note 40 above, p. 104.

14. The great debate

1. Quoted Marion Mills Miller (ed.) *Great Debates in American History* (New York 1913), VIII pp. 26-27.
2. Johnny Faragher and Christien Stansell, "Women and Their Families on the Overland Trail, 1842-1867," *Feminist Studies* 2 (November 1975), pp. 151-62.
3. Quoted Kathryn Kish Sklar *Catharine Beecher: A Study in American Domesticity* (New Haven 1973), p. 211.
4. Quoted Philip Magnus *Gladstone. A Biography* (London 1954, New York 1964), p. 383.
5. Quoted Vineta Colby *The Singular Anomaly: Women Novelists of the Nineteenth Century* (New York 1970), p. 158; and Mrs. Humphry Ward *Delia Blanchflower* (London and New York 1914), p. 305.
6. Susan B. Anthony and Ida Husted Harper *The History of Woman Suffrage* (Rochester, N.Y. 1902), IV p. xxii.
7. Olive Schreiner *Woman and Labour* (London and New York 1911), p. 288.
8. See note 6 above, p. xxvi.
9. John Stuart Mill *Thoughts on Parliamentary Reform*. Pamphlet (London 1859).
10. Richard Hofstadter *Anti-Intellectualism in American Life* (New York 1963).
11. Quoted Sinclair, pp. 285-6.
12. Quoted Susan B. Anthony *History of Woman Suffrage*

(Rochester N.Y., 1887), III p. 736.
13. Grimes, pp. 65-7.
14. *New England Journal of Medicine* (January 15, 1976), p. 129.
15. Richard D. Poll, "A State is Born," *Utah Historical Quarterly* 32 (1964), p. 19.
16. Alexis Lichine *Encyclopedia of Wines and Spirits* (London and New York 1967), p. 459.
17. Grimes, pp. 114-5.
18. Susan B. Anthony, quoted in "Arguments of the Woman-Suffrage Delegates before the Committee on the Judiciary of the United States Senate, January 23, 1880," *Senate Miscellaneous Document no. 74*, 47th Congress, 1st Session, p. 26.
19. Ida Husted Harper, "Would Woman Suffrage Benefit the State, and Woman Herself?," *North American Review* 178 (1904), p. 373.
20. Kinsey reports, see biblio.
21. Quoted Peter d'A. Jones *The Consumer Society: A History of American Capitalism* (New York 1963), pb Harmondsworth 1967, p. 74.
22. Pierre Chaunu, "Malthusianisme démographique et malthusianisme économique," *Annales* 27 (January–February 1972); and André Burguière, "From Malthus to Max Weber: Belated Marriage and the Spirit of Enterprise," in Forster and Ranum (2), pp. 237-50.
23. *The Lancet* 1 (1869), p. 499.
24. Friedrich Engels *The Condition of the Working Class in England in 1844* (1845).
25. J. C. Drummond and Anne

Wilbraham *The Englishman's Food. A history of five centuries of English diet* (London 1939). Revised edn. 1957, pp. 379-82.
26. Himes, pp. 213-7.
27. Cunnington, p. 16.
28. *United States Practical Receipt Book*, p. 87.
29. John Camp *Magic, Myth and Medicine* (London 1974).
30. Himes, p. 201.
31. Quoted Alex Comfort *The Anxiety Makers. Some curious preoccupations of the medical profession* (London 1967), p. 164.
32. Jonas Hanway *Letters on the Importance of the Rising Generation* (1767); and *Report of the Interdepartmental Committee on Physical Deterioration, 1904*, quoted Drummond and Wilbraham, see note 26 above.
33. Theodore Roosevelt *Presidential Addresses and State Papers* (New York 1910), III pp. 282-91.
34. John Humphrey Noyes *Male Continence; or Self-Control in Sexual Intercourse. A Letter of Inquiry Answered.* Pamphlet (Oneida, N.Y. 1866).
35. *Oneida Circular* VIII (1870), p. 212.
36. *Medical Gazette*, October 22, 1870; and see Himes pp. 269-74.
37. Quoted Heywood Broun and Margaret Leech *Anthony Comstock: Roundsman of the Lord* (New York 1927), p. 15.
38. "Why Not Birth Control in America?," *Birth Control Review*, May 1919, pp. 10-11.
39. Marie E. Kopp *Birth Control*

in Practice: Analysis of Ten Thousand Case Histories of the Birth Control Clinical Research Bureau (New York 1934), p. 133.

40. Report in *The Guardian* (Manchester), May 15, 1962.

41. Report in *Sunday Times* (London), August 4, 1974.

42. Reports in *The Times* (London), February 24, 1976, and *Time*, March 14, 1977.

43. *British Medical Journal*, August 20, 1977; report in *Sunday Times* (London) January 18, 1976; Ford Foundation report *Reproduction and Human Welfare* (MIT Press 1977); reports in *The Times* (London), October 25, 1973, and Febru-

ary 20, 1976; *Nature*, December 8, 1977; and *The Lancet*, June 10, 1978.

Epilogue

1. Quoted *Time*, December 28, 1970.

2. *Ibid.* November 21, 1977.

3. *Report on the Sexual Behavior of the French* (1972); report in *Daily Telegraph* June 2, 1979; Mikhail Stern *La vie sexuelle en U.S.S.R.* (1979); report in *Sunday Telegraph* August 12, 1979; report in *Daily Telegraph* July 13, 1979.

4. *Human Sexuality*, etc., see biblio under Kosnik.

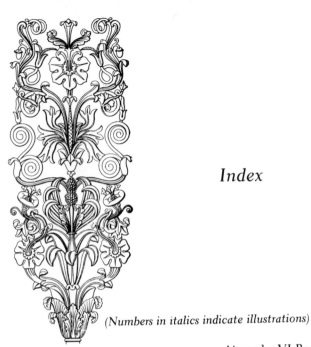

Index

(Numbers in italics indicate illustrations)